Trübner's Oriental Series

MODERN INDIA AND THE INDIANS

Trübner's Oriental Series

INDIA: HISTORY, ECONOMY AND SOCIETY
In 11 Volumes

I	Women in Ancient India	
	Clarisse Bader	
II	The Financial System of India	
	Gyan Chand	
III	A History of Civilisation in Ancient India Vol I	
	Romesh Chunder Dutt	
IV	A History of Civilisation in Ancient India Vol II	
	Romesh Chunder Dutt	
V	The Economic History of India Under Early British Rule	
	Romesh Chunder Dutt	
VI	The Economic History of India in the Victorian Age	
	Romesh Chunder Dutt	
VII	The Indian Empire	
	W W Hunter	
VIII	Modern India and the Indians	
	Monier Monier-Williams	
IX	Alberuni's India Vol I	
	Edward C Sachau	
X	Alberuni's India Vol II	
	Edward C Sachau	
XI	Racial Synthesis in Hindu Culture	
	S V Viswanatha	

MODERN INDIA AND THE INDIANS

MONIER MONIER-WILLIAMS

Routledge
Taylor & Francis Group
LONDON AND NEW YORK

First published in 1891 by
Routledge, Trench, Trübner & Co Ltd
2 Park Square, Milton Park, Abingdon, Oxfordshire OX14 4RN
711 Third Avenue, New York, NY 10017

First issued in paperback 2014

Routledge is an imprint of the Taylor and Francis Group, an informa business

© 1891 Monier Monier-Williams

All rights reserved. No part of this book may be reprinted or reproduced or utilized in any form or by any electronic, mechanical, or other means, now known or hereafter invented, including photocopying and recording, or in any information storage or retrieval system, without permission in writing from the publishers.

The publishers have made every effort to contact authors/copyright holders of the works reprinted in *Trübner's Oriental Series*.
This has not been possible in every case, however, and we would welcome correspondence from those individuals/companies we have been unable to trace.

These reprints are taken from original copies of each book. In many cases the condition of these originals is not perfect. The publisher has gone to great lengths to ensure the quality of these reprints, but wishes to point out that certain characteristics of the original copies will, of necessity, be apparent in reprints thereof.

British Library Cataloguing in Publication Data
A CIP catalogue record for this book
is available from the British Library

Modern India and the Indians
ISBN 0-415-24496-X
India: History, Economy and Society: 11 Volumes
ISBN 0-415-24288-6
Trübner's Oriental Series
ISBN 0-415-23188-4

ISBN 13: 978-1-138-86216-6 (pbk)
ISBN 13: 978-0-415-24496-1 (hbk)

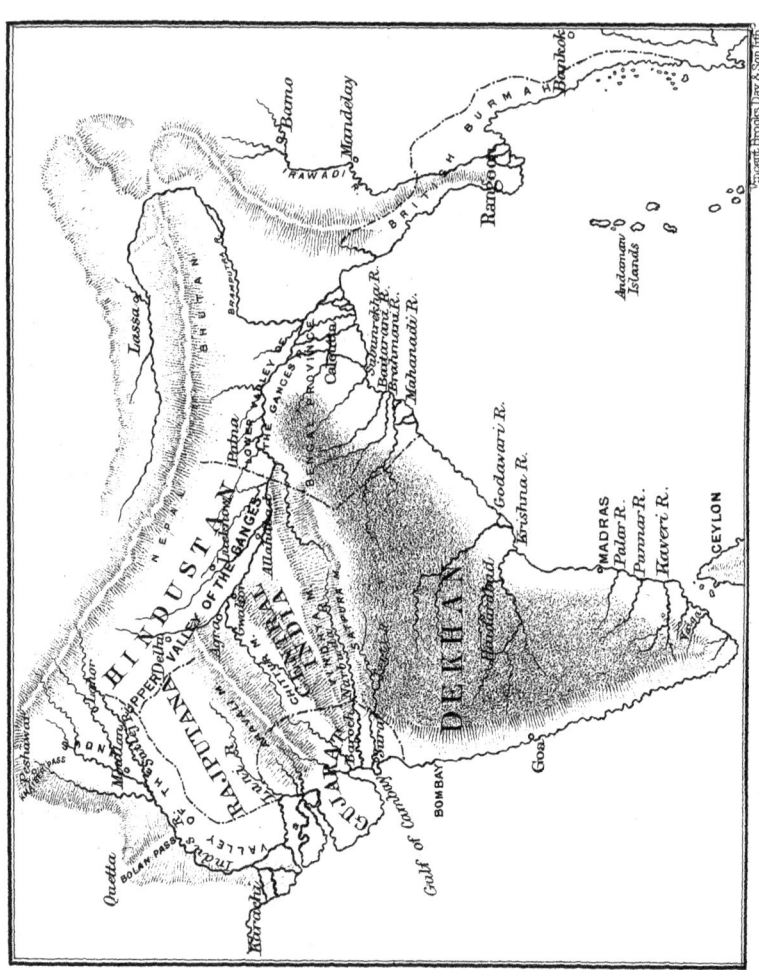

MAP OF INDIA.
TO ILLUSTRATE ITS PRINCIPAL PHYSICAL FEATURES AND GEOGRAPHICAL DIVISIONS

MODERN INDIA

AND

THE INDIANS

BEING A SERIES

OF IMPRESSIONS, NOTES, AND ESSAYS

BY

Sir MONIER MONIER-WILLIAMS, D.C.L.

HON. LL.D. OF THE UNIVERSITY OF CALCUTTA,
HON. MEMBER OF THE BOMBAY ASIATIC SOCIETY,
BODEN PROFESSOR OF SANSKRIT IN THE UNIVERSITY OF OXFORD

Fifth Edition

LONDON
ROUTLEDGE, TRENCH, TRÜBNER & CO., Lt^p.
1891

CONTENTS.

	PAGE
The Five Gates of India—Gibraltar, Malta, Port Said, Perim, and Aden	1
First Impressions	27
The Villages and Rural Population of India	39
Samādh, Sacrifice, Self-Immolation, and Self-Torture	64
The Towers of Silence, and the Pārsī Religion	80
Funeral Ceremonies and Offerings to Ancestors at Bombay, Benares, and Gayā	97
Indian Rosaries	108
Indian Famines	116
A Relief Camp	121
General Impressions and Notes after Travels in Northern India	125
General Impressions and Notes after Travels in Southern India	180
Indian and European Civilization in their relation to each other and in their effect on the Progress of Christianity	225
Indian Muhammadanism in its relation to Christianity, and the prospects of Missionary Enterprise towards it	238
The Three Religions of India compared with each other and with Christianity	246
Progress of our Indian Empire. Part I.	263
Progress of our Indian Empire. Part II.	301
Promotion of Goodwill and Sympathy between England and India	343

MODERN INDIA AND THE INDIANS.

THE FIVE GATES OF INDIA—GIBRALTAR, MALTA, PORT SAID, PERIM, AND ADEN.

THE good ship 'Venetia,' which took me to India on the occasion of my first expedition to the East, entered the Bay of Biscay on the 15th of October, 1875. Equinoctial gales had been raging for several days previously, and the Atlantic rollers, coming broadside on, soon discriminated between the passengers, instituting a process of natural selection, which resulted in the survival of those alone who were fittest to do justice to the diurnal bill of fare provided by the Peninsular and Oriental Company with a punctuality and regularity altogether weatherproof.

To be sure our decks were crowded with a motley assemblage of men, women, and children of all sorts and conditions; for example—a Duke and Prince of the Blood Royal, an Italian Countess, a general officer or two, some A. D. C.'s, several captains, one clergyman, numerous Indian civilians of various types, stations, and degrees, from judges of the High Court to the greenest of probationers just escaped out of the clutches of the Civil Service Examiners, sundry male oddities—long-bearded, short-bearded, and beardless, wived and wifeless—divers eccentric husbandless females of uncertain ages and vague antecedents, a few solitary wives on their way to join their husbands, one or two flirting bachelors, a bevy of pretty unmarried girls, a troop of young engineers from Cooper's

Hill, a batch of serious commercial men, an unpleasant pack of obstreperous children, and a residuum of unsortable nondescripts, not to speak of a heterogeneous crew of English sailors, Lascars, Negroes, and Chinamen. None of this miscellaneous collection of human beings made their presence felt so plainly as the children. Sea-sickness is a powerful leveller and merciless humiliator, but was powerless either to repress or depress the children. Their self-assertion was only aggravated by the prostrate condition of their natural guardians. Indian nurses easily succumb, and are generally very attenuated and miserable in appearance; but the opposite extreme is occasionally exemplified. We had one Ayah on board, who was quite a curious specimen of abnormal portliness and unnatural hypertrophy. Another was a tall graceful woman attired in a long red robe, gold necklace, bracelets and bangles. Notwithstanding her ladylike mien, she was, of course, a woman of very low caste, probably a Mhār (or Dheḍ). She had some very peculiar blue cross lines tattooed on her forehead between the eyebrows, and a similar mark on one temple. Like all Indian women of her station, she had invested all her savings in ornaments, and carried them on her person.

Our fourth night at sea brought us opposite the mouth of the Tagus, and in sight of the Lisbon lights. At daybreak next day we were approaching Cape St. Vincent.

Life is made up of compensations. Our patient endurance of four miserable days was rewarded by a grand spectacle. Noble cliffs rose to a great height out of the sea, some glowing with red tints as if covered with heather, others frowning with black crags, and shelving suddenly into perpendicular precipices or scarps of dark granite, riddled with countless holes and caverns by the sheer force of the Atlantic. Here and there isolated needle-like rocks, and others of fantastic shapes, separated from the cliffs by seething channels, stood out from the mainland, or seemed to thrust themselves forward as if to court the first dash of the waves which covered their sides with sheets of foam. In the distance were lofty mountains, whose gilded summits appeared loftier through the morning mist which still clung to them. Cape St. Vincent has a lighthouse and telegraph station. We hoisted our signals, and our approach was instantly notified at Gibraltar.

At night we were in the Straits (anciently called the Straits of Hercules), with the Bay of Tangier on our right. Tangier is a sea-port of Morocco, and is now the property of the Moors under the Emperor of Morocco; the capital of the province, Fez, being about a hundred miles inland.

In four days and a half, or 108 hours from the moment of our passing the Needles, we were close to Gibraltar. The night was dark and squally, and great caution was needed. I was kept awake by the intermittent throes and gasps of our engine, which seemed to struggle for breath like a moribund monster dying hard. Very early in the morning its fitful throbbings suddenly ceased, and the silence of death followed.

The first sight of the Bay is grand beyond all expectation. It bends round in a long curve or elongated semicircle, surrounded in the distance by ranges of high hills, the towering rock of Gibraltar—said to be nearly three miles long, and 1400 feet high—overhanging the whole of one side and forming a promontory running north and south, joined to the continent of Spain by a narrow isthmus of land called the neutral ground. The latter is washed on both sides by the Mediterranean. At the furthest extremity of the promontory is Europa Point, with a lighthouse. The town of Gibraltar, resting on a long line of batteries, climbs about one-third of the western side of the rock. Rising conspicuously above the houses is a fine ruined keep—once a strong castle when the place was possessed by the Moors, and still scarred and scored with the marks of subsequent sieges.

Nearly opposite, on the shore of the bay, is the Spanish

town of Algeciras. Further inland, on a hill near the bottom of the bay, is San Roque. At both towns bull-fights are popular amusements, and not despised by some of our own people, who resort to them from Gibraltar to relieve the monotony of their cramped and cage-like existence.

The rock of Gibraltar was first known to the Phœnicians under the name of Calpe. After them the Carthaginians, Romans, and Visigoths successfully gained a footing there. It did not rank as a fortress till A.D. 711, when it was fortified by a Saracen army under Tārik (or, according to some, Tārif), a Moorish conqueror, from whom it was called Jibal Tārik, or Tārik's mountain (in Arabic *Jabalu't tārik*). In 1309 Ferdinand IV took the fortress after it had belonged to the Moors for 598 years, but it was retaken by them in 1462, and held by them altogether for 726 years. We took it from Spain in 1704, and to us it has belonged, notwithstanding three attempts on the part of the Spaniards to recover it, for about 175 years. On a hill, at the lower end of the bay, is a stone cairn called the 'Queen of Spain's chair,' because a Spanish queen is said to have seated herself there during one of the sieges, and declared she would not rise from it till she had seen the English flag hauled down. This is such a hackneyed guide-book story that one is almost ashamed to repeat it.

Opposite Europa Point, on the coast of Barbary in Africa, is Ceuta—a town close under a rocky hill (Mount Abyla) which forms a pendant to the rock of Gibraltar, and represents the second pillar of Hercules. Near it is a much higher, grander, black-looking, craggy, precipitous hill, known as the Ape's Hill, which also claims, and with more apparent justice, to represent the other pillar. From this mountain at some primeval period came the tailless apes which to this day linger on the rock of Gibraltar like wild aborigines, hopelessly struggling to hold their own against civilized settlers. Eighteen apes are still left, and every one of them is known and held inviolable. To kill or even injure any one of them would be an unpardonable offence. Ceuta belongs to Spain, and is used by the government as a penal settlement. It is a most unpleasant place of residence, convicts being allowed to roam about loose. They cannot escape by land, as, once out of the town, they would certainly be killed by the Moors, between whom and the Spaniards inveterate enmity subsists. I believe some eccentric person, or persons, once started the idea that it would be well for England to restore Gibraltar to Spain and take Ceuta in exchange.

On landing at Gibraltar we lost no time in making our way to Europa Point, passing the Alameda—a name given to a kind of public square, or esplanade, planted with trees, which is an institution in all Spanish towns, and treated as consecrated ground by the inhabitants. The drive led up a hill over the lower slope of the rock, which on the town side is much less steep than towards the Spanish frontier. The vegetation is quite tropical. Prickly pears, cactuses, and pepper trees appeared to be growing luxuriantly, and aloes were as plentiful as blackberry bushes. Europa Point commands an unequalled view of the Straits, the coast of Africa, and Gibraltar Bay. The rock itself from this point reminded us of the Bastei in the district called Saxon Switzerland, near Dresden.

Returning to the town under a royal salute which announced the landing of H. R. H. the Duke of Connaught, we found it no easy matter to thread our way through the long principal street—crowded as it was with a motley multitude of Moors from Fez, Arabs, Negroes, Jews, Scorpions (or natives of Gibraltar familiarly so called), Spanish peasants, muleteers, English soldiers and sailors. The neutral ground on the northern side, opposite the Spanish lines, affords a striking view of the celebrated galleries which perforate the rock—here most precipitous. We could see the muzzles of monster guns protruding through innumerable port-holes. This, of course, would be the direction of an attack in case of a war with Spain. The wonderful construction of the galleries themselves, which we afterwards visited, is too well known to need description.

As we steamed out of the Bay the eastern side of the rock, which is much wilder and more craggy in appearance than the town side, showed itself to great advantage. Here a steamer passed us, crowded with Hājjīs, or pilgrims from Mecca, bound for Tangier. They were all dressed alike in coarse grey garments, with cowls on their heads, and were packed closely together like sheep in a pen. It is alleged that they never leave the deck, lie down, or change their clothes from the moment they quit Mecca till they reach home. Next, the grand range of the Sierra Nevada, with its sharp serrated outline, came into view on our left. I believe its principal mountain is little short of 12,000 feet high. About noon on the sixth day after leaving England, we passed Cape Tenez on the coast of Africa.

At sunset the whole western sky was on fire, while the serrated line of the African mountains seemed to be cut out of the glowing heavens, as if with a sharp knife, and painted jet black. When night fell we were opposite the Bay of Algiers, and could distinguish the lights of the town. Thence to Malta little of interest marked the ship's course. We passed Zembra, a fine rocky island (occasionally resorted to for coal) on one side of the Bay of Tunis, and about twelve miles west of Cape Bon. The latter is a noble headland on the African coast, with a lighthouse more than half-way down its precipitous sides. Pantelleria, the ancient Cossyra, came in sight—a grand volcanic island eight or ten miles long and thirty in circumference, said to be remarkable for a lake of unfathomable depth at the top of its highest mountain, and two caverns, one intensely hot and the other intensely cold, and hot springs in other parts. The town consists of a long line of staring white houses, with a large church and detached villas dotted at intervals over the slopes. I believe the island now belongs to Italy, and, until recently, was used as a convict settlement.

On the eighth day after leaving England we passed Gozo,

an island twelve miles long (called Gaulos by the Greeks), lying to the north-west of Malta and close to it, being only separated from the main island by a narrow channel, in the centre of which lies a much smaller island, called Comino. Soon afterwards we anchored in the quarantine harbour of Malta.

Early in the morning we took one of the boats that crowded round our vessel (in form rather like Venetian gondolas) and landed at Valetta, the principal town of Malta, built in 1566 by La Valette, the grandmaster of the Order of St. John of Jerusalem, to which Order the Emperor Charles V of Germany made over the whole island in 1530. The town is regularly built on an elevated promontory just behind the fortress of St. Elmo, which, with a lighthouse, occupies its extreme point.

On one side of the promontory is the quarantine harbour for merchant ships and steamers. On the other is the great harbour for ships of war, commanded at its entrance by the fortress of Ricasoli, and indented with numerous inlets or creeks, each forming a small separate harbour, and the whole capable of being swept by the fortress of St. Angelo, bristling with guns on a promontory in the middle. In fact, the entire line of coast on the northern side of the island is hollowed out into creeks by the force of the Mediterranean currents. It is a kind of Connemara on a small scale. One considerable inlet, forming quite a harbour, is called St. Paul's Bay, because, according to tradition, the ship which contained St. Paul and his fellow-prisoners was cast on shore here.

On landing we found it impossible to shake off a swarm of importunate natives, either vendors of the produce of the island or would-be guides, who followed us about like tiresome flies intent on settling on us. We visited the cathedral of St. John, where the knights are buried under a beautiful Mosaic floor; the governor's palace, where there is some celebrated tapestry and a fine armoury, interesting from a well-arranged collection of the armour of the Knights of St. John; and the gardens of San Antonio, five miles in the interior.

The houses of Malta are all of white stone, with flat roofs. Their architecture has a half Italian, half Oriental character. The streets are built on each side of the rocky promontory in parallel lines, so as to join at right angles a long central main street, which forms a sort of backbone along the summit of the ridge. One or two are ascended by picturesque tiers of steps. The whole island appears to be one vast rock and stone quarry. Instead of hedges, lines of white walls intersect the interior in every direction, one rising above the other like terraces, with square look-out towers at intervals. Here and there the dull monotony of the stone terraces is relieved by tufts of dark foliage, dotted about promiscuously in every direction. These represent the tops of well-grown trees, which rear their heads above the walls, as if to bear witness to the fertility of the soil in the gardens underneath. It is difficult, indeed, to understand how any garden can be productive when nothing but rock is visible around. The explanation, I believe, is that rich soil is transported in small vessels from Sicily, and kept together by the walls. The Maltese are very industrious. Their commercial instincts are certainly developed by their brief and fitful intercourse with their Anglo-Indian visitors, and notably exhibited in the sums asked for the products of their small island. Swarms of petty traders, not content with pestering every passenger who lands for a few hours, hover about the decks of the steamers offering lace and coral ornaments at four times their value. The knowing purchaser waits till the steamer is just starting, and then bids a fourth of the first price asked. I saw a black lace shawl reduced in this way from £4 10s. to £1.

The population multiplies so rapidly that the island is quite inadequate to support its inhabitants. Numbers emigrate and spread themselves over the Mediterranean. No less than 10,000 Maltese are said to be settled in

Tunis. Their own peculiar vernacular tongue is a corrupt form of Arabic largely intermixed with Italian words. No one who has seen the position of the noble harbours on the north coast of the island, can have any doubt that so long as we possess India and remain the greatest maritime power of the world, Malta must be held and its garrisons maintained by us in full efficiency *coûte qu'il coûte*. Protected by the guns of St. Elmo and Ricasoli, Tigne and St. Angelo, almost any number of our men-of-war and merchant vessels might find a safe anchorage. Strong northeasterly gales are the only winds that can affect them.

After leaving Malta we saw no land till we approached Port Said. The whole stretch of sea is, I believe, 900 miles long. Here would lie the danger to our commerce in case of any great naval power commanding the Black Sea and the coast of Syria. On Sunday the ship's company was mustered on deck before prayer-time. First, on the port side, appeared a line of twenty-two stewards and waiters, extending from the centre of the ship, every one in characteristic uniform. Next, on the same side, came eight or ten black, thick-lipped African negroes, commonly called Sīdīs or Sīdī boys, from the neighbourhood of Zanzibar. They were dressed in snow-white garments quite out of keeping with their occupation, which consists in shovelling the coal into the furnaces, and contrasting curiously with their glossy coal-black countenances and dark thick woolly hair. They are a happy smiling race, always in exuberant spirits, though exposed to roasting heat, drinking nothing but water and nourished by a vegetable diet. They may be seen sleeping as soundly on the iron gratings of the engine-room as on a bed of down. Then came the Āg-wālās—men employed about the engine and fires. These were described to me as Konkanī Musalmāns. from the neighbourhood of Bombay. They were also dressed in peculiar white costumes—picturesque and immaculately clean. This formed the line on the port side. At the stern were the English officers of the ship, and nearest the stern, on the starboard side, a few English quartermasters or superior English sailors. After them came the long line of Laskars (or, as they call themselves, Khalāsīs, 'free,' vulgarly Klasees), marvellously transfigured in appearance, and quite belying their own identity, in spotless dresses, embroidered turbans, and scarves.

The word Laskar is derived from the Persian *lashkar*, an army. The name is somewhat sarcastically applied to a crew of Indian sailors who, in their ordinary work-day aspect, have nothing whatever about them suggestive of military smartness or effectiveness. To the uninitiated passenger these Laskars appear a very miserable squad, and no one can look at them without conjuring up fearful pictures of disaster to the ship in the event of cyclones and other possible emergencies. Yet the captain declared that, though comparatively inefficient in a cold climate, they do better than English sailors under a hot sun; that they are more tractable and docile, and, what is more important, that they never get drunk. They are, of course, Musalmāns; for Hindūs even of the lowest caste have an unconquerable religious antipathy to voyages on the 'black water[1].' In fact, the lower the caste in India the more tenacious are its members of caste-purity, and the more pride does each man take in protecting himself from what he believes to be contamination. Nothing is more essential to the preservation of caste purity than unpolluted water, and nowhere is it so difficult to keep water ceremonially pure as on ship-board. As to the Musalmān Laskars, the best of them come from Kathiwar (more correctly written Kāṭhi-āwāḍ, the abode of the Kāthi tribes) and the neighbourhood of the Portuguese settlement of Daman. Their wages are, of course, less than those of English sailors, but if the Company save in this way, a *per contra* outlay is incurred, because more men are re-

---

[1] In Hindūstānī, *Kālā pānī*. This phrase is now commonly substituted for the more proper expression *Khārā pānī*, 'salt water.'

quired to counterbalance the want of muscular power in each individual.

I asked the captain about their food, and whether they would eat meat. 'Yes,' he said, 'we sometimes, while in harbour, give them a sheep, which they kill in their own way. On the voyage they generally eat dried fish, rice, and dāl, and are not very particular about it. Though they are Muhammadans, they will even sometimes eat pork if we have nothing else to give them. They ask no inconvenient questions, but tie the forbidden animal—slaughtered, however, according to the most orthodox rules of Islām—on to the end of a line, and drag it after the ship for an hour or so; after which one of their number hauls it in, calling out with great solemnity as if he were using a formula of consecration, *Jāo sū'ar idhar āo machchī,* "go away, pig; come hither, fish."'

The regiment of Laskars was headed in the muster by the Sarang—a title corrupted from *Sarhang,* the Persian word for a general, and humorously applied to the native boatswain, who, in his turban glittering with gold embroidery, and attended by his two Tindals, or boatswain's mates, would assuredly have been mistaken for an Indian prince if he could have been transplanted into the middle of a London crowd.

Conspicuous among the Asiatics was one Chinaman—the ship's carpenter—in a broad straw hat. The whole company would have well illustrated a lecture on the ethnology of the world. At any rate, they formed a singularly picturesque and interesting line of 132 specimens of the human species, methodically arranged for inspection round the quarter-deck of the ship. The mixed crowd of passengers—some lolling lazily and apathetically in the central space, others standing up to gaze with languid curiosity or serene self-complacency on the miscellaneous assortment of their fellow-creatures, ranged round them like animals in a zoological show—offered quite as curious an exhibition of diversified humanity in their own way, while the captain and first officer walked round with an air of calm professional assurance, casting critical glances of appreciation or depreciation at each member of the ship's company, and receiving respectful salutes in return. Then at a given signal the Sarang sounded his whistle, the whole circle of unbelievers melted away in an instant, leaving the crowd of believing Christians in the centre to settle down for Divine Service.

We reached Port Said at 6 A.M. on the 12th day after leaving England. The first sight of Egypt excites no emotions of any kind. The town of Port Said—called after the late Viceroy—is a collection of mushroom buildings which have sprung into existence since the commencement of the Suez Canal. It is now lighted with gas.

Nor is the entrance to the Canal at all imposing. The adjacent coast for miles is apparently below the sea-level, making the approach to the harbour almost impossible except by daylight; but a lofty lighthouse, which was cleverly constructed by erecting wooden moulds one above the other and filling them with concrete, stands on a pier on the right, and gives out a flashing electric light visible at an immense distance. There are also two long breakwaters, one lower than the other, constructed of huge blocks of concrete, running far into the sea on either side of the harbour, which effectually prevent the sand from drifting inside and choking the mouth of the Canal.

We entered very cautiously at dawn of day, and moored our ship to two buoys. Two British ironclads—the 'Invincible' and 'Pallas'—were already in the harbour, and another fine steamer, the 'City of Venice,' was waiting to make the passage after us, while the 'Serapis' had recently passed on ahead. In half an hour we had paid the dues, which I believe amounted in our case to about £1500, and had entered the Canal, the entrance being merely a continuation of the harbour, without lock-gates of any kind. Here, on the right, there is a narrow strip of land covered with sheds, owned by the British nation.

I was informed that when the works commenced, this land was offered to our Government for £800, and was declined. It is said to have been recently purchased by us for £26,000. This story will not appear incredible to any one old enough to remember the view Lord Palmerston took of the French engineer's great project.

Although the course of the Canal for the first thirty miles is as straight as an arrow, every mile of it abounds with interesting objects. The first thing noticed is an immense lagoon stretching for miles beyond the right bank, while on the left lies a trackless desert of sand, with here and there patches of what appears to be water, but is really nothing but the mirage produced by heated vapour. Then there are the natives on the bank in their picturesque costumes, the sturdy, half-naked Arabs at work in the water, the strings of camels with their burdens, the feluccas in the lagoon with their lateen sails, the myriads of water-fowl, and in the horizon long lines of flamingoes extending literally for miles, and standing motionless, like regiments of soldiers in white uniforms. But the one absorbing sight of all is the Canal itself. Such expressions as 'One of the wonders of the age,' 'a triumph of engineering skill,' give an inadequate idea of the magnitude of the work. It must be seen to be estimated at its right value.

Captain Methven, the commodore of the Peninsular and Oriental fleet, who watched the progress of the Canal from its commencement, and was one of the first of our fellow-countrymen to predict its success, favoured me with many interesting particulars which may be relied upon for accuracy. The lower platform at the base of the central channel is almost everywhere fully 70 ft. wide, and as the sides shelve off at an angle, there is generally a width of about 100 ft. at the surface of the water, the extreme depth of which is 27 ft., with a margin of 10 ft. or 12 ft. of shallow water on each side. The rule first made was that no ship drawing more than 26 ft. should be allowed to pass through. The ships in which I made the passage only drew about 22 ft. of water, and now it is found that any vessel drawing more than 25 ft. is likely to come to grief. Two large steamers (the 'Hibernia' and 'Seine'), laden with submarine cable, had just accomplished the passage. One of them, however, drawing 24 ft. 7 in., scraped her keel all through the Canal, and was obliged to steam at full speed to bring her through. The only difference in the level of the sea at the Mediterranean and Red Sea extremities is caused by the difference in the tides, the variation at the Mediterranean end being 18 in. in Spring tides, and that at the Red Sea end about 7 ft. or 8 ft. The effect of this difference is to cause a current at both extremities, and of course a tolerably strong flow from the Red Sea towards the great bitter lakes, situated near the centre of the Canal.

Every six miles there is a station-house (called by the French *gare*) and siding with signal-posts, fitted with black balls, by means of which the traffic is worked on the block system. As a rule, no ship is allowed to take less than one hour in steaming from one station to the next.

Two ships advancing towards each other in opposite directions are never allowed to meet while in motion. One is compelled to draw off to a siding while the other passes. This happened to us at a station called Kantárá, where we were made to shunt, while the 'Diomed,' a Liverpool steamer, passed us. Here a road—once the great highway between Egypt and Palestine, and still a high road between Cairo and Syria—leads over the Canal by a kind of flying bridge. A large caravan from Jerusalem, with hundreds of camels and a motley crowd of way-worn travellers—men, women, and children—were waiting to pass over close to our siding. It was a strange and interesting sight, which made us think of the going down of the Children of Israel into Egypt. Thence we glided on without interruption, but with the disagreeable accompaniment of an Egyptian plague of flies, passing on

THE SUEZ CANAL. 15

the right a statue of Lieutenant Waghorn, the pioneer and first organizer of the overland route in 1835.

At considerable intervals steam dredging-machines—four or five of which are now sufficient to keep the bed clear—were seen in active work. One was of monster proportions, and appeared to be ingeniously constructed for raising the sand from the bottom and delivering it on an inclined plane over the bank. The desert is occasionally dotted with patches of a kind of scrubby bush, the only merit of which is that it serves to relieve the intense glare, and to furnish food for camels. Here and there high banks of sand hid everything from our view. At 4 in the afternoon (having left Port Said at 7 in the morning) we emerged into the first bitter lake, called Lake Timsah, and steamed at increased speed close to the new town of Ismailia, named after the present Khedive. Here there is an oasis of green vegetation, and a principal station of the railway between Suez and Alexandria. De Lesseps himself has a house here. There is also a palace built by the Khedive for the sole purpose of receiving the Empress Eugénie, the Emperor of Austria, and other royal personages (but no representative from England) during the festivities at the opening of the Canal in November, 1870 [1].

On we steamed through the lake, and thence through a cutting to the second or great bitter lake, where we anchored for the night soon after sunset. These two remarkable lakes had nearly dry beds before the making of the canal. That happened to them which is now going on in the Dead Sea. The water had evaporated, and left a deposit of seven or eight feet of solid salt. The French engineers foresaw that this circumstance might be turned to account for the deepening of the central channel. When

---

[1] The Canal was first opened for traffic in 1869, and from 1870 to 1876 the net tonnage passing through it rose from 436,609 tons to 2,096,772 tons (the gross tonnage to 3,072,107); the receipts from £200,000 in 1870 to about £1,200,000 in 1875. Of the traffic 75 per cent. was British.

the waters of the Red Sea were allowed to flow in, the layer of salt was dissolved and nearly eight feet of depth gained. The climate in the neighbouring districts is likely to be advantageously affected by the re-creation of these lakes. We had evidence next morning of an accession of humidity which may one day turn barren ground into fruitful fields. When we attempted to move on soon after daybreak, a thick mist enveloped us, and kept us stationary for more than an hour. Meanwhile, our ship's stern stuck in the sand, but with a little wriggling worked itself off. Then we glided out of the great lake through a deep cutting, which extended for some miles. At one o'clock the same afternoon we had entered the Gulf of Suez, and were steaming rapidly towards one of its spacious open docks and quays (constructed at an immense cost and loss under exaggerated ideas of the future commercial importance of a port, converted by M. de Lesseps' great work into a mere place of call) almost before we became aware that we had emerged from the Canal. We had accomplished the whole distance of 100 miles in about fifteen hours. I was surprised to learn on good authority that the total cost from first to last of the miracle of engineering skill which had transported our huge ship from one sea to the other so easily and pleasantly, was only eighteen millions sterling. Those who are competent to pronounce an opinion on the result achieved by the outlay consider that it was cheaply done for that sum. About two millions of the amount was freely given by the late Khedive in money and labour.

The compulsory labour system was first tried, but soon given up. Cholera broke out, and English public opinion was brought to bear on the matter. Then it was that the genius of M. de Lesseps organized a system of paid labour, the extraordinary success of which in a country like Egypt could never have been predicted. All honour to the indomitable will and scientific ability of one man, who, fighting his way through apparently insuperable obstacles,—

physical, social, and political,—carried out one of the greatest projects of this wonder-working century.

But in appreciating to the full his energy and intellect, let us not withhold an equal tribute to the amazing tact and administrative capacity which enabled one man to train a whole army of ignorant and illiterate labourers, and inspire them with something of his own ardent, energetic, and enthusiastic spirit. Every individual, to the smallest donkey-boy, employed on the Canal seemed to take a pride and pleasure in doing his allotted task well, and contributing something towards the desired end. No great work has ever before been effected in Egypt with so much goodwill, cheerfulness, and activity, and with so small a sacrifice of human life. This will appear more remarkable when it is borne in mind that nearly a hundred steam dredging-machines were in constant operation, for the effective working of which a large number of men and boys with interdependent duties was indispensable.

And yet, after all, notwithstanding one's admiration of this great monument of scientific and administrative genius, it is singular that the chief impression it leaves on one's mind is that of incompleteness. The simple truth I believe to be that before the Canal can be pronounced really finished the width of the central channel must be doubled, and the banks from one end to the other lined with stone. If, when the success of the project was assured, and before the costly plant had been sold and the trained labourers dispersed, the principal European Powers had agreed to act in concert, each contributing its quota of a few millions, a really complete result might have been achieved, the capital expended might have been blotted out, and a Canal of the right dimensions presented to the commerce of the world. Now, the whole plant will have to be reconstructed, new workmen and labourers trained, and the entire process reorganized at a vast cost. Nevertheless, English enterprise and capital can do all that is needed, and will have to do it in the end.

So surely as Russia is setting her face steadfastly towards Constantinople must England concentrate her attention on Port Said, the Suez Canal, and the coast of Syria. The day may be coming—and perhaps must come very soon—when no corner of Europe will be allowed to suffer any longer from the 'impotence' of Turkish rule. What then is to happen to Egypt? England's duty will be plain. We shall have to take the Khedive in hand ourselves, and peremptorily insist on his governing his own country well, righteously, and economically[1]. To this end we must help him, not with money, but with men.

We have a whole band of Indian civilians—men like Sir George Campbell, Mr. Seton-Karr, and Mr. Cust—who have served their time in India and yet have plenty of energy left, which they are ready to devote to the welfare of their fellow-creatures. Let them consent to aid the Khedive, and simply do in Egypt the work they have done in India as commissioners, collectors, judges, magistrates, members of council, and lieutenant-governors. The Province adjacent to the Indus, commonly called Sinde, has been significantly styled 'Young Egypt.' Old Egypt and 'Young Egypt' have certainly much community of character and many points of resemblance. Those who have made 'Young Egypt' prosperous under a strong, righteous, and energetic administration, are quite competent to raise old Egypt out of the depths of misgovernment into which she is fast sinking, and convert her from a poverty-stricken into a rich and thriving country. I submit that this would be a satisfactory solution of the Eastern Question, so far, at least, as England is concerned.

Soon after our arrival at Suez, a party of us took a Felucca, or native boat, with three men, and sailed up the creek to the town of Suez, three miles distant. The behaviour of our boatmen interested me not a little. It

[1] Let this be read in the light of present events (July, 1879). It was written in the winter of 1876.

happened to be the concluding day of the fast of Ramazān (the ninth month of the Muhammadan year), and whether on this account, or because it was the stated hour of prayer, one of the men washed his face in sea-water, and then prostrated himself with his face towards Mecca in the bow of the boat. Soon afterwards we knocked our keel against some rocks and then scraped along a sand-bank, the tide running out very rapidly. Upon this two of the boatmen —very fine-looking fellows, half-naked, with well-developed muscular limbs—started up, seized two long poles, rushed towards the bow of the little vessel, applied the end of the poles to their shoulders, and running with naked feet along the upper edge of the boat's side, while they pushed the poles towards the stern, urged each other to increased exertions in the strongest guttural Arabic, till they had driven us in this manner over rocks and shoals for more than a mile, against a strong contrary wind, to the quay opposite the Suez hotel.

Their behaviour afforded a parallel to the practice of a certain good Christian, of whom it is recorded that he prayed always as if all results depended on God, but put forth all his energies as if success depended wholly on himself. It reminded one also of a story told of Muhammad. Travelling on a certain occasion through the desert, he refused to follow the example of his travelling companion, who, on arriving at the evening resting-place, turned his camel loose and then prayed fervently that God would keep the beast from straying; but, on the contrary, first took a good deal of trouble to tether his camel, and then prayed to God to prevent the animal from breaking loose.

We walked about Suez for an hour. Donkey-boys mobbed us at every corner, puffing the merits of their donkeys with much originality, if not in the most refined English. 'Dis de Claimant, Sar,' 'Try de Claimant, Sar,' 'Dis Sir Roger, Sar,' 'Dis very superior donkey, Sar,' 'Dis Kenealy, Sar,' 'Dis make loud bray, Sar.'

The town is a collection of flat-roofed ramshackle old

houses, most of them in an advanced stage of decay, with crooked narrow irregular streets in which dirt, dust, and bad smells wait upon each other in close companionship. Many of the ruined buildings looked as if they might have once sheltered the children of Israel, who are supposed to have crossed the Red Sea somewhere in the neighbourhood. Our interest in everything triumphed over our disgust, though it was difficult to say which was the strongest feeling when we entered the Bazaar, where, in addition to dirt, every hole and corner harboured vast accumulations of cobwebs, left undisturbed for years as a standing menace, I suppose, to swarms of irrepressible flies which settled in millions on the eatables exposed for sale on the open counters. The narrow lanes were thronged with a mixed multitude of turbaned men and veiled women; some respectably dressed and moderately clean, threading their way through the crowd with calm Oriental dignity; others ragged and filthy, jostling each other, and vociferating in genuine Suez vernacular.

On the morning of the fourteenth day we commenced our course down the Gulf of Suez. The line of hills overhanging Suez, called *Attāka*, looked grand, red and glowing, and stood out in striking contrast to the marvellous green and blue of the sea. Soon the rugged and majestic pile of mountains of the Sinaitic Peninsula, of which Mount Sinai forms a part, opened out upon our left. This peninsula divides the Red Sea into two narrow gulfs— one, that of Suez down which we were steaming, and the navigation of which is extremely intricate, the other, that of Akāba which is not quite so long, and is seldom navigated at all.

Towards evening we came in sight of the lofty range of Mount Aghrib, on the coast of Africa, in Egyptian territory. The highest mountain of the range is alleged to be 10,000 feet high. I certainly never before supposed that Egypt possessed anything much higher than a pyramid.

The time consumed in steaming down the Red Sea to

the Straits of Bābel Mandeb was five days. The coast is insufficiently lighted, and the sea unpleasantly full of coral reefs, sunken rocks, and small volcanic islands, but the P. and O. ships thread their way through all obstructions with as much precision as a well-driven hansom passes through Fleet Street. We had a steam punka in our sleeping cabin, besides the usual punkas in the saloon, but had nevertheless, to sleep on deck when the thermometer rose to ninety.

One evening we escaped a tremendous sandstorm, which, coming from the deserts of Africa eighty miles off, gathered over our heads in a densely black, ominous cloud. Happily the wind against which we were steaming carried the storm behind us, and we saw it descend in a dark column towards the northern horizon. Had the cloud burst over our heads we should have been half-blinded as well as smothered with sand, and the whole vessel so enveloped that a dense fog would have been less dangerous. The only showers in the Red Sea are showers of sand.

On the fourth day we passed the twelve rocky volcanic islands called the Twelve Apostles. In some of them coal-black scoria and ashes, looking as if quite recently ejected from crater-like cavities, were intermixed with bright red and yellow rocks and shone brilliantly in the fiery sunlight.

At dawn on the fifth day we were opposite Mocha on the Arabian coast, and had to take soundings. Rugged dark lines of mountains, some with sugar-loaf points, some with serrated edges, one behind the other, intensely arid and sterile in appearance, lined the coast. One long line of craggy hills presented the exact appearance of an old worn-out saw lying with its edge turned upwards. The opposite coast of Abyssinia was now drawing towards us. It is fringed with dark barren mountains resembling those on the Arabian coast, and in the distance was a lofty range, with one high peak, said to be somewhere in Abyssinia. The heat was intense, and the draught of air through the narrow channel, as the coast on each side began to close in upon us, made it penetrate more searchingly.

The small island of Perim was on our right as we steamed through the Straits of Bābel Mandeb (Arabic *bābu'l mandib*, 'gate of tears.'

The land opposite Perim juts out into a long narrow promontory covered with rugged, rocky hills. Under the principal rock on its barren and burning shore the French have built a large square house. They had once a settlement here, and I believe intended converting the promontory into an island by digging a canal across. Had they accomplished their object, their next engineering operation would have been a fort to balance ours at Perim, but the excitable and bellicose Arab tribes forcibly resisted the attempt to slice off a portion of their territory, and the French have now deserted the place. The staring house still remains, apparently in good repair, glittering in the glaring sunlight. Not a human being was to be seen about, but one or two deserted Arab fishing-boats were anchored near the shore.

Every person who passes Perim is sure to be asked whether he has heard the story of the stratagem by which we took possession of the island. I believe the anecdote rests on a basis of fact. But whether it does so or not, here is an epitome of it:—A French captain was sent in a man-of-war about five-and-twenty years ago to take possession of the island, and touched at Aden. Of course the English Commandant was too polite not to ask him to dine, and too hospitable not to ply him with good wine till he had drunk enough to exemply the old proverb *in vino veritas* and let out the secret of his expedition. Instantly the English Commandant, without leaving the dinner-table, gave private orders for despatching a gunboat with six sappers and miners, and one engineer officer, who landed on the island, planted the British flag on the heights, and next day were ready to receive the French captain and welcome him to British soil.

PERIM AND BĀBEL MANDEB.

Certainly the island is in an important position, at the very gate of the Red Sea, but its utter sterility, without a tree or even a blade of grass or bush to temper the glare of burning suns and cloudless skies, makes it even more entitled to be called an Eden than Aden itself—of course I mean on the *lucus a non lucendo* principle. It is simply a bare rock, about four or five miles in circumference, rising to an elevation of two or three hundred feet. The channel which separates it from the opposite point of Bābel Mandeb, and through which we sailed, is only one mile wide; but a channel of nearly eleven miles in width on the other side divides it from the African coast, and on that side the island possesses a small but deep harbour. We have built a lighthouse and insignificant fort on the highest point of the rock, and huts near it for a detachment of Sepoys with one or two Europeans. Since the erection of the lighthouse ships generally take the narrow channel.

We steamed through the channel against a strong heated blast of wind which blows constantly through the straits as through a funnel. In five days after quitting Suez dock we were well out of the Red Sea, and not sorry to see Perim receding from our sight, and our vessel making rapid way eastwards through the Indian Ocean in the direction of Aden, ninety miles distant When night fell, the lightship at the entrance of Aden harbour began to be visible.

By ten o'clock at night we were safely moored to two buoys near the lights of the town. The dark outline of the great rock of Aden loomed mysteriously in the weird light; lamps of various colours gleamed on the shore; native boats with vociferent Arabs crowded round our ship; half-naked men with dusky skins swarmed over the front of the vessel. It can easily be imagined that a place where rain only falls about once in two or three years must be pleasanter by night than by day. Yet, on the occasion of my second voyage, when we reached Aden by daylight, I greatly enjoyed a visit to the wonderful tanks three or four miles distant, dug out of the solid rock to catch the precious rain-water which occasionally makes up for lost time by pouring down in a deluge. The surrounding scenery is unequalled in ruggedness and sterility by anything I have ever seen. In fact, the whole place may be compared to a congeries of gigantic cinders or heaps of colossal coke. Yet it has many most striking and almost sublime features. It is certainly the Gibraltar of the Red Sea. The principal rock is even higher and grander than that of Gibraltar. It stands on a promontory in the same way, and is joined to the mainland by a narrow isthmus.

Among the institutions of the place are the diving boys —small Somali negroes imported from the opposite coast of Africa—who gather round the ship in their toy canoes, each little curly-headed urchin paddling his own tiny coracle with wonderful dexterity. Their knowledge of English is restricted to the one sentence ' I dive, Sare, I dive,' which they all vociferate with great animation, till on the first sight of a silver coin thrown from the ship, the whole troop suddenly disappear feet uppermost in the water, leaving canoes and paddles to take care of themselves, and heedless of the presence of formidable sharks which usually follow in the wake of steamers, seeking whom or what they may devour. The smallest coin never escapes the lynx-sight of these amphibious imp-like little urchins. The fortunate finder scrambles into his own canoe, first holding up his prize in triumph, then stuffing it into the hollow of his cheek for safety, and then baling out the water with which his little cockle-shell is half-swamped, while he joins more energetically than ever in the general chorus of ' I dive, Sare, I dive,' which is kept up with spirit as long as any passenger shows himself on deck.

We left Aden on the morning of the twentieth day of our voyage. The endless serrated line of the hills on the Arabian coast continued in sight for some time. Indeed the whole interior of Arabia—so far as I was able to observe it during my voyages—seems to be shut in by a barrier of ranges of dark rugged sterile mountains, one behind the other—some rising to considerable elevations—which completely enclose it and serve as an effectual bar to the curiosity and cupidity of intruders. At Aden we had an addition of some interesting first-class passengers—a Khoja, or Bombay merchant of a particular class, who has a house of business in Zanzibar, returning to India with his wife and family. He was a stout stalwart man, with a handsome countenance. I believe some of the ancestors of the *Khojas* (a name corrupted from Khwāja, 'noble') centuries ago were pirates inhabiting the coast of Kutch. They gradually became rich, turned Muslims, and gave up disreputable practices. But, although now Muhammadans and followers of a certain Āghā Khān, they retain much of their Hindū character and often their Hindū names. Our fellow-passenger told me that the trade of Zanzibar is rapidly increasing and the place becoming very prosperous. The language spoken there is Swaheli (a kind of lingua franca of Eastern Africa), which the Khoja speaks as well as his native tongue Kutchī, and to which he adds Gujarātī, Hindūstānī, and a little English. He was accompanied by a Pathān or Afghān from Peshawar returning home from the Hajj or pilgrimage to Mecca, which every true Musalmān endeavours to perform once in his life, the other four religious duties enjoined by Muhammad being prayer five times a day, fasting for a month every year, almsgiving, and repeating the creed daily. We took in at the same time a number of Baniyahs or Hindū traders, who stationed themselves on the forecastle, and were to be seen there every evening dead-asleep, rolled up like their own bales of goods in white winding-sheets.

The run from Aden to Bombay was accomplished on calm seas and under bright skies in six days and a half. The serenity of the Indian Ocean is rarely disturbed by high winds after the termination of the monsoon.

The morning of one day was spent in visiting the mail room and post-office. The three mail agents have to work ten hours a day from the time they leave Suez, sorting

about 46,000 letters and 35,000 newspapers, and distributing them in about 250 bags, ready for dispersion all over India immediately on the arrival of the ship at Bombay. The following is a specimen of the directions which occasionally tax the ingenuity of the sorters (copied literatim)—
> J. Faden
> Sapper
> Engear
> Bromeday.

This letter had been sent to three Bromleys in different parts of England before it was suspected that Engear meant India, and Bromeday, Bombay.

At daybreak on the twenty-seventh day after our departure from Southampton, the high land of the Ghāts, near Bombay, was visible about fifty miles distant. When the sun rose it disappeared in the haze. A few hours later we entered Bombay harbour, passing the 'Serapis' and several fine men-of-war lying at anchor. The advent of the Prince of Wales had preceded ours by about two days.

FIRST IMPRESSIONS.

BOMBAY, NOVEMBER 10, 1875.

WE need not quote a Western poet[1] in support of the trite truism that impressions on the mind, to be deep, must be made by scenes actually witnessed.

There is an Eastern saying that the distance between the ear and the eye is very small, but the difference between hearing and seeing is very great.

Much information can be gained about India from books and newspapers, and much by asking questions of old Indians who have spent their lives in the country, but, after all, India must be seen to be understood.

The instant I set foot on the landing-place at Bombay, I became absorbed in the interest of every object that met my sight—the magnificent harbour with its beautiful islands, secluded creeks, and grand background of hills; the picturesque native boats gliding hither and thither; the array of ships from every quarter of the globe riding at anchor—every feature in the surrounding landscape, every rock and stone under my feet, every animal and plant around me on the shore, every man, woman, and child in the motley throng passing and repassing on the quay, from the Bhīstī, or water-carrier, who laid the dust by means of a skin slung on his back, to the boy who importuned me for Bakhshīsh to exhibit a fight between

---

[1] 'Segnius irritant animos demissa per aurem
Quam quæ sunt oculis subjecta fidelibus.'

a snake held in his hand and a mongoose concealed in a basket.

Though I was born in India, and had lived as a child in India, and had been educated for India, and had read, thought, spoken, and dreamt about India all my life, I had entered a new world.

On the esplanade, in front of the chief public buildings of Bombay, an extraordinary spectacle presented itself. An immense concourse of people was collected, waiting for the Prince of Wales, who was expected at the Secretariat to hold his first levée—no dingy crowd of Londoners hustling each other in a foggy, smoky atmosphere, but at least a hundred thousand turbaned Asiatics, in bright coloured dresses of every hue, moving sedately about in orderly groups under a glittering sky. The whole plain seemed to glow and flash with kaleidoscopic combinations of dazzling variegated colours. Rows of well-appointed carriages belonging to rich Bombay merchants, some containing Pārsī ladies and children in gorgeous costumes, with coachmen in brilliant liveries, lined the esplanade. Gem-bespangled Rājas, Mahārājas, and Nawābs dashed by in four-horsed equipages, with troops of outriders before and behind.

One part of the spacious plain was set apart for 12,000 children, from various schools—Hindū, Pārsī, Muhammadan, Roman Catholic, and Protestant—collected from Bombay and the neighbourhood. The fact that it was possible to bring together from a limited area so vast an assemblage of children, male and female, all under education in an Eastern country, was in itself full of significance and interest. They were seated in rows, one behind the other, grouped according to the communities to which they severally belonged, a passage being left in the centre for the Prince. Every child was provided with a printed hymn, or poetical address to the Prince in Gujarātī, to be sung by the whole assemblage at the moment of his appearance among them.

I was told that the children were mostly from the middle ranks of the inhabitants of Bombay. Certainly it was difficult to believe in the poverty of their parents, dressed as they were, boys and girls, in rich silks, satins, brocades, and velvets of all colours, from bright red and yellow to simple white, with gold-embroidered caps and jewels of great value on their feet and arms, necks and ears.

It is no uncommon thing for parents to deck their children on festive occasions with ornaments worth hundreds of pounds. Their appearance and bearing suggested an idea that Asiatics think more of beauty of dress than beauty of form, Europeans more of beauty of form than of beauty of dress.

That same evening I left Bombay and travelled northwards through Gujarāt by the Bombay and Baroda railway. At the very first station out of Bombay, the anthill-like density of India's teeming masses made itself apparent. At least a thousand natives were collected, waiting for the train, some bound for Bombay to see the Prince of Wales, others on their way home after having witnessed the great Tamāshā. The vast crowd vociferated and swayed to and fro in an alarming manner. The sound was like the roaring of a mighty ocean. We began to think that a second mutiny was imminent, that our carriage would be stormed, and ourselves perhaps shot down on the spot.

Our fears were allayed on learning that the lower classes of Hindūs are in the habit of talking and shouting to each other at the top of their voices, in perfect good humour, whenever they are congregated in crowds [1]. Notwithstanding their apparent excitement, noisy demonstrativeness, and overpowering numbers, they made no attempt (as English excursionists would have done) to force their way into the first or second-class compartments, but sub-

---

[1] Sleeman remarks ('Rambles,' p. 77) that the stentorian voices of the natives are probably due to their meeting and discussing subjects connected with their own interests in the open air under trees.

mitted quite patiently and resignedly to be penned like sheep in third-class carriages, some of which had an upper story. It was evident that no caste-prejudices interfered with their making full use of our railways. As the morning dawned on us in our northward course, sensations of real cold made us forget we were in India, till, looking out, we were reminded of our locality by unmistakeable signs, and notably by certain ominous streaks of cloud in the horizon, which turned out to be flights of millions of locusts. When they are seen approaching, the natives assemble in crowds, fire guns, and make hideous noises to prevent their settling on their crops. After passing Surat, Broach, and Baroda, I alighted at the Mehmoodabad station, and began my Indian experiences in the Collector of Kaira's camp.

A brief description of my first day's adventures may give an idea of the kind of life led by Anglo-Indians when camping out in the country during an Indian winter.

My only room was of course a tent. It had four doors and no windows, and a fifth door leading into a kind of canvas lean-to or small annex, fitted up with a large bath. Happily no one need trouble himself with a portable bath in India, because this indispensable convenience is found everywhere. The tent had a lining of brown and yellow chintz, and for a carpet a stout blue and white cotton cloth laid on flax straw. All the doors had two coverings or rather flaps, one of the same material as the tent, the other a kind of wire screen, called a chick, to let in air, and keep out as far as possible inquisitive intruders—not men and women, but huge bees, wasps, grasshoppers, squirrels, snakes, and all manner of winged and creeping things innumerable. For furniture there were two or three chairs, a dressing-table, and a good iron bedstead with hard mattresses, woollen pillows, and musquito curtains, well tucked in all round. Let the reader, then, imagine me comfortably ensconced, after my month's voyages and travels, within my four canvas walls, and looking forward with pleasant anticipations to an undisturbed sleep in a veritable bed—my first since leaving England.

I go through every needful purificatory rite in my strange lavatory, and emerge refreshed from my tent door to peep at the scene outside and take my bearings. I find that we are in a large field or common, on one side of the Mehmoodabad station. The camp consists of about a dozen tents all under large spreading trees, with which the whole park-like country round is beautifully wooded. Most of the trees are new to me—the Mango, the Banian, the Pīpal, the Tamarind, the Nīm, and the Japanese Acacia with its lovely yellow flowers. No tent is ever pitched under a Tamarind. It is supposed, I believe, to exhale too much carbonic acid during the night-time. The Mango and Nīm are the tent-pitcher's favourite trees. Under one Mango there is a large pavilion-like erection for the Collector and his wife. Then there is another double tent, which serves as a dining-room and drawing-room, of ample dimensions, fitted up with carpets, tables, bookcases, easy chairs, sewing machine, and harmonium. Two or three others for visitors like myself; another for the baby and its Ayahs; another for the Portuguese butler, and of course a capacious tent with annexes, which together serve for the collector's Kutchery (properly written *Kacherī* or *Kachahrī*), magisterial court and other offices.

On one side under the dense foliage of a Banian is a circular canvas erection without any roof. This is the kitchen, where excellent dinners are cooked by means of two bricks and a hole in the ground. A little removed from the tents is the stable, an open space quite unprotected, except by foliage, where four Arab horses and two ponies are tethered by their heels, each attended by its man. Near them stand carriages, carts, and a curious vehicle called a Tonga (*Tāngā*), usually drawn by two ponies. It has two seats back to back, suspended on two wheels, and is covered by an awning. Not far off an all-but nude Bhistī, dark as a negro, is seen plying his occupation. He supplies the camp with water, by means of two water-skins slung over the back of a bullock. Ranging about the field in promiscuous places are other bullocks, buffaloes, goats, sheep, geese, ducks, and fowls. The bullocks are for the carts, the buffaloes and goats for producing milk and butter. The other creatures come in usefully as raw material, out of which the excellent dinners before alluded to are supplied. A sheep in these country places only costs, I am told, about four rupees, or eight shillings. It is, however, a melancholy reflection that infliction of death is essential to the maintenance of an Englishman's life. For life is everywhere exuberant around me, and every living thing seems to enjoy itself, as if it were certain of being unmolested. Natives never willingly destroy life. They cannot enter into an Englishman's desire for venting his high spirits on a fine day by killing game of some kind. 'Live and let live' is their rule of conduct towards the inferior creation.

I walk about admiring every living creature, particularly the birds—the Hoopoo with its lovely crest hopping about near me, the doves very like those at home, the bright parrots, the jays, the woodpeckers. Then little grey and brown streaked squirrels are playing all around me. They jump about with wonderful agility, peer in at the tent doors, and try to secure little bits of cotton for their nests. The sounds are not always melodious. I hear a screeching note above my head. It comes from a kind of grey and red Toucan seated trustfully on a branch, and quite undisturbed by my presence. Then another discordant cry, and a rush—a number of natives are driving away a troop of big, grey mischievous monkeys, some with little baby-monkeys clinging to them. They soon repel the invaders, but only by shouting in rather harsh vernacular 'the monkey-people, the monkey-people!' To shoot a monkey would be nothing short of sacrilege. I venture to follow the retreating intruders, but am

CAMP LIFE. 33

arrested by hedges of prickly pear. Then I fall into ecstasies over the creepers, many of them of gigantic size, which twine themselves everywhere, covering hedges, bushes, and trees with their brilliant red, orange, and white flowers.

I must not omit to mention that dotted about the field are mounted and unmounted sepoys, with here and there a belted government servant (called a Paṭṭi-wālā, or Paṭṭa-wālā, because distinguished by a belt)—all within call—all ready to answer instantaneously to the Sāhib's summons, and eager to execute his behests. As to the big Collector Sāhib himself, in the eyes of the people of his district he is every inch a king. He speaks like one, acts like one, and really has the power of one. He says to one man 'come,' and he cometh, and to another 'go,' and he goeth. His title of Collector gives a very inadequate idea of his real duties and authority; unless it be taken to mean that in him all the administrative functions of the district are collected and comprehended. He not only collects the revenue, but has high judicial powers, and the whole welfare of a small territory is committed to him. He superintends police, civil engineering, road-making, rural economy, municipal government, sanitation, education, every conceivable matter.

But if every Collector is a small king, every Englishman in India is regarded as a petty prince. Obsequious natives watch his movements, and hang upon his words. I try to stroll about, but as I circle leisurely round the compound, attendant satellites hover about my path. I am evidently expected to develope wants of some kind or other in the course of my ramble. I ransack my store of correct Hindūstānī just imported from Europe for the most polite way of requesting to be left alone; but I feel as helpless as a child, and as shy as a new boy at school. Disconcerted and humiliated, I long for a little temporary obscurity, and hastily hide my head within the walls of my tent. But my tenacious followers are not to be shaken

D

off so easily. I am conscious of being vigilantly watched through my barrier of canvas. By way of experiment I utter the magical formula *Qui hai?* (*Ko-ī hai?*), and a dusky form seems to rise out of the ground as if by magic. There he stands in an attitude of abject reverence and attention, waiting for me to issue my commands either in the best Gujarātī or purest Hindūstānī. But I do not rise to the occasion. I am not sure whether to be exhilarated by the opportunity of bringing my knowledge of Indian languages into play, or depressed by an uncomfortable consciousness of blank inability to deliver myself of any well-turned and highly idiomatic sentence expressive of a simple desire to know the dinner-hour. Just at this juncture I hear a commanding voice call out in the distance 'Khānā lāo.' This is the Collector's brief and business-like order for dinner. I repair with relief to the drawing-room and dining-room. The Collector and his wife, beaming with hospitality, make me sit down at a well-appointed dinner-table. I have a French *menu* placed before me. I eat a dinner cooked with Parisiàn skill, I drink wine fit for an emperor, and am waited on by a stately butler and half-a-dozen stately waiters in imposing costumes, who move about with noiseless tread behind my chair, and anticipate every eccentricity of my appetite. I am evidently on enchanted ground, and can only think of Aladdin in the Arabian Nights.

Dinner over, we sit out in the open air. The moon is shining with a lustre unknown in northern latitudes. We recline on lounging chairs round a blazing wood fire, not sorry to wrap ourselves up in our warm plaids. I retire early to my tent and compose myself for the luxurious slumber I had anticipated. But I am too excited to sleep immediately. With difficulty I gain the border-land between consciousness and unconsciousness. What is that sound, half snort, half snuffle, close to my head? I start, and sit up. Can it be the Brāhmanī bull I saw just before dinner roaming about at large in full enjoyment of a kind of sacred independence? Cautiously and guardedly I open my musquito curtains, intending to seize the nearest weapon of defence. Clink, clink! Clank, clank! Thank goodness, that must be the guard parading close to my tent; and sure enough there are sounds of a rush, and a chase, and a genuine bull's bellow, which gradually diminish and fade away in the distance.

Again I compose myself, but as night advances begin to be painfully aware that a number of other strange sounds are intensifying outside and inside my tent — croaks, squeaks, grunts, chirps, hums, buzzes, whizzes, whistles, rustles, flutters, scuffles, scampers, and nibbles. Harmless sounds proceeding from harmless creatures! I reason with myself. A toad is attracted by the water in my bathroom, a rat has scented out my travelling biscuits, musquitoes and moths are trying to work their way through my curtains, a vampire bat is hanging from the roof of my tent, crickets and grasshoppers are making themselves at home on my floor. 'Quite usual, of course,' I say to myself, 'in these hot climates, and quite to be expected!' Ah, but that hissing sound! Do not cobras hiss? The hissing subsides, and is succeeded by a melancholy moan. Is that the hooting of an owl? No! the moan has changed to a prolonged yell, increasing in an alarming manner. Yell is taken up by yell, howl by howl. Awful sounds come from all directions. Surely a number of peasants are being murdered in the adjoining fields. I am bound to get up and rush to the rescue. No, no, I remember. I saw a few jackals slinking about the camp in the evening.

Once more I try to compose myself, disgusted with my silly sensitiveness. Shriek, shriek, and a thundering roar! The midnight luggage-train is passing with a screaming whistle fifty yards from my head. At last I drop off exhausted into a troubled slumber. I dream of bulls, snakes, tigers, and railway collisions. A sound of many voices mingles with my perturbed visions. Crowds of natives are collecting for the six o'clock train two hours before sunrise. They talk, chatter, jabber, shout, and laugh to beguile the tedium of waiting, At five minutes to six the station bell rings violently, and my servant appears with my *choṭa hāzirī*, or little breakfast. I start up, dress quickly, remembering that I am expected to drink a cup of hot tea, and go out like a veteran Anglo-Indian, to 'eat the air' (*hawā khānā*), before the sun is well up.

I conform to the spirit of the trite precept *Si Romae fueris, Romano vivito more;* but the Collector and his wife are out before me, and are seen mounting their horses and starting off to scour the country in every direction for an hour or so. I find the morning breeze bite keenly, and am glad to walk briskly up and down the camp. I amuse myself by watching the gradual gathering of natives around the Kutchery—two or three policemen with a prisoner, a cheerful-looking man in a red turban and white garments carrying a paper or petition of some kind; several emaciated half-naked villagers bowed down to the dust with the weight of their poverty and grievances; a decrepit old man attended by a decrepit old woman; underlings who come to deliver reports or receive instructions; other persons who come to be advised, encouraged, scolded or praised, and others who appear to have nothing to do, and to do it very successfully. Every one has an air of quiet resignation, and nearly all squat on the ground, awaiting the Collector Sāhib's return with imperturbable patience. All these cases are disposed of by the Collector in person after our eight o'clock breakfast.

At eleven the post comes in; that is, a running messenger, nearly naked, brings in a pile of letters on his head from the neighbouring town. The Collector is immersed in a sea of papers until our next meal. Meanwhile a visitor from a neighbouring station makes his appearance riding on a camel, and is received in the drawing-room tent by the Collector's wife. Then a deputation of Brāhmans is seen approaching. They have come to greet me on my arrival; some of them are Pandits. A mat is spread for them in a vacant tent. They enter without shoes, make respectful salaams, and squat round me in a semicircle. I thoughtlessly shake hands with the chief Pandit, a dignified venerable old gentleman, forgetful that the touch of a Mleccha (English barbarian) will entail upon him laborious purificatory ceremonies on his return to his own house. We then exchange compliments in Sanskṛit, and I ask them many questions, and propound difficulties for discussion. Their fluency in talking Sanskṛit surprises me, and certainly surpasses mine. We English scholars treat Sanskṛit as a dead language, but here in India I am expected to speak it as if it were my mother-tongue. Once or twice I find myself floundering disastrously, but the polite Pandits help me out of my difficulties. Two hours pass away like lightning, the only drawback to general harmony being that all the Pandits try to speak at once. I find that no one thinks of terminating the visit. Native visitors never venture to depart till the Sāhib says plainly 'you may go.' I begin to think of the most polite Sanskṛit formula for breaking up my conclave, when I am saved from all awkwardness by a call to tiffin.

In the afternoon the sun acquires canicular power, the thermometer rises to eighty-two, and the temperature is about as trying as that of the hottest day of an English summer. Under the combined influence of tiffin, heat, exhilaration, humiliation, and general excitement, I am compelled to doze away an hour or two, till it is time to walk with the Collector to a neighbouring Bāolī, or old underground well (called in Gujarātī *Wau*), now unused and falling into ruins, but well worth a visit. It is more like a small subterranean tank than a well, and the descent to it is by a long flight of stone steps, surrounded by cool stone chambers built of solid masonry, and supported by handsome pillars. In Eastern countries, benevolent men who have become rich and wish to benefit their fellow-creatures before they die, construct wells and tanks, much as we build hospitals in Europe. I return with the Collector to his camp as the sun sets.

So much for my first day's experiences, which are so vivid that I may be pardoned for having recounted them in the present tense.

THE VILLAGES AND RURAL POPULATION OF INDIA.

ONE of my first acts after my day's rest in the Collector of Kaira's camp was to visit a neighbouring village called Khātraj.

The organization of Indian villages—meaning by a village not merely a collection of houses, but a rural commune or territorial division of cultivable land—is a highly interesting and instructive study both in its connexion with the early history of the Āryan races, and in its bearing on the present condition of rural society not only in India but in Europe. In no part of the world have the collection of communities which together make up the aggregate of a country's population been left so much to self-government as in India. Its village system is based on the purest form of Home-rule, which had its origin in the simple patriarchal constitution of society, when the family of brothers—joint owners of the family land—lived together and cultivated the soil, as co-partners under a paternal head.

Every Indian village is a collection of such families united in intimate corporate relations. And as each family is held together by a close interdependence of interests under a common father, so the members of each village community are united in close association under a presiding head-man, or chief of some kind. It must be borne in mind that the actual tillers of the ground in an Indian village constitute at least three-fourths of the population.

In Gujarāt these cultivators are called Kumbī (Sanskrit Kuṭumbī). The remaining inhabitants consist of various useful functionaries, artisans and mechanics, to be presently described—men of distinct castes and employments who are indispensable to the maintenance of every society, and minister to its wants in diverse ways.

Of course the detail of rural organization is not uniform in every part of India, nor does the system of self-government prevail with equal force everywhere. But in every village there is a close intertwining of communal relations, so that the separate existence and independence of any individual of the community is barely recognized.

The Sanskrit name for a village commune is Grāma. It is clear from Manu's law-book that a regular system of village-administration prevailed in some parts of India many centuries before Christ. There was first a supreme village-lord or governor who was called Grāmādhipati and who governed 1000 villages, subject to the king's suzerainty. Under him were the lords of 100 villages constituting a district now called a Parganah, and under these again were the chiefs of each separate village-community. Some similar gradation of administrative authority probably existed long before the time of Manu's code. But the interconnexion between the village system and the state, the nature of the links which have united the higher with the lower power, and the amount of control which the one has exercised over the other, have varied with each change in the Supreme Authority. What has remained unchanged has been the simple self-contained village corporation. This has survived all changes, all political, religious, and physical convulsions—all wars, massacres, pestilences, and famines—in a word, all the external and internal disturbing forces that have swept over and agitated the country for more than three thousand years.

At present, under British rule, the village-overseers, or head-men, have different names in different places, according to their various functions or powers. For example,

VILLAGE-SYSTEM. LAND-TENURE. 41

they are variously called Paṭel, Maṇḍal, Deśāī (=Deśādhi or Deśādhipati), Deśmukh (=Deśa-mukha), Mahā-jana, Lambardār, and Mukaddam. The two last names are more generally used in the Northern parts of India, Lambardār being a mongrel term made up of the English word 'number' corrupted into 'lambar,' and the Persian word 'dār,' a holder. In some Northern districts a large village will frequently consist of five or six rural communities, each under a distinct Lambardār, to whom a separate lease (*paṭa*) of a portion of land, with a number inscribed on the written document, is assigned. Sometimes a village is occupied conjointly by Hindūs and Muhammadans, who live very amicably and contentedly side by side. In such cases each religious community has its own Lambardār, who is its own special nominee and representative.

But the tenure under which the land is held by Indian cultivators and landowners varies throughout India in a very perplexing manner. In some villages the Ryots or immediate tillers of the soil, who constitute the mass of the population, are held to be the only hereditary proprietors. The land is parcelled out among them, and the tax assessed periodically by our own government-officers, all the cultivable ground thus divided being liable to further subdivision by the Hindū and Muhammadan law of inheritance, which gives an equal share to each son. Sometimes each cultivator holds his own share as a distinct estate, and is himself responsible for the payment of the government demand. Sometimes all the cultivators hold their lands as a common estate, dividing the profits as co-partners, and nominating their own head-man, or accepting one nominated by the Government, to whom the duty of collecting and paying the State assessment is committed.

In other villages the immediate cultivators are neither singly nor conjointly proprietors, but hold their lands on lease under one or more hereditary proprietors (sometimes called Pāṭi-dārs) to whom the whole collective area of the village territory, or some portion of it, is supposed to belong, and who are responsible to Government for the first charge on the produce, estimated at a certain value and always paid in silver. Again, in some parts of India the large proprietors of land are called Zamīndārs, or landholders. Such men not unfrequently have an hereditary right of property over areas larger than English counties, and in Bengal, Behār, and Orissa the perpetual settlement of 1793 converted them into actual proprietors who enjoy their estates in absolute ownership, on the sole condition of punctual payment of a fixed sum to the Government exchequer.

It is clear from these differences of tenure that the headmen of the village are not always employed as agents for the collection of the State assessment. Nor have they necessarily any connexion with Government at all. Yet every head-man must be a man of weight and influence among his own people. Indeed, he is elected by the community on account of some supposed superior qualifications, and is generally allowed independent jurisdiction in his own sphere. Frequently he has considerable powers committed to him. For example, he may arrange the village police, enforce sanitation, settle questions of ploughing and sowing, decide disputes among cultivators, provide for the entertainment of travellers. His remuneration consists of a certain proportion of the produce, or a fixed assignment of cultivable land rent free[1].

It must be noted that he is required to act in concert with the village council, or Panchāyat, of which he is the president. In India every village and every town has its Panchāyat, whose functions resemble in a manner those of European municipal boards. In fact the Panchāyat is a most ancient Indian institution, though differently constituted in different places. It must have consisted originally of five (*pancha*) members, but is nowhere now restricted to that number. Seven or eight members are now not

[1] In some parts of India he is allowed an acre in every twenty under cultivation.

uncommon. In Manu's time (at least 500 years B.C.) two councils are mentioned, one of four members and the other of eleven[1].

Every caste, every trade, every separate association has its own peculiar and special Panchāyat. At one time even native regiments elected their own officers, and small states their own rulers by means of Panchāyats. Everything was managed and settled in this manner. A common proverb is current throughout India that 'the voice of God is in the five' (*Panch men Parameśvara*). Happily for India, and for our own tenure of the country, our policy has always been to preserve existing native institutions as far as possible intact. We encourage the people to settle their own disputes among themselves in their own way. We make a point of upholding the action of native Panchāyats, though we do not, of course, give legal validity to all their decisions.

With regard to the other functionaries of the village, there are at least twelve different kinds of village officials under the head-man, each paid by the cultivators in kind according to the value of the services he renders to the community, and each belonging to a separate caste, determined by the nature of his employment.

1. First comes the Paṭwārī, or village accountant and registrar, who is a kind of Government land-steward, keeping the Jama-bandī or account of the lands, produce, rents and assessments of his village. He sometimes acts as Majmūdār (otherwise Majumdār, corrupted into Mujumdār) or State Record-keeper, and in some parts of Western India is called Talāti. This functionary comes next to the head-man in importance and influence, having often independent authority, irrespective of his office as a Government agent. He usually receives about half the emoluments of the head-man.

[1] See 'Manu,' xii. 110: 'Any matter of law settled by a council consisting of ten law-abiding men under one head, or by three such men under one head, should not be violated.'

2. Then secondly there is the village chaplain, or domestic priest (called in Sanskrit Purohita, and in Gujarātī Gor for Guru)—who performs all religious ceremonies for the villagers, the impure castes only excepted. He is supported by fixed allotments of grain, and by special presents of food at caste dinners, or by gifts of money on occasions of births, weddings, and other family solemnities. He often combines supplementary functions of a kindred nature. For example, he may be astrologer, almanac-maker, and schoolmaster. Furthermore he and his wife are generally the village match-makers, arranging all the marriages of the community with careful attention to caste-usages.

3. Next comes the Nāī, or barber (Sanskrit Nāpit, Arabic Hajjām, sometimes vulgarly called Wārand or Wāland, and in Gujarāt, Ghaenjo or Ghaeja)—who, with his kit of primitive razors and implements of the rudest description, does all the work expected of him admirably. No man in India thinks of shaving himself. Hence the barber is an important member of the community. His duties are not confined to shaving. He cuts nails, shampoos the limbs, and often acts as village doctor[1]. In some parts of India he helps to arrange marriages.

4. Fourth on the list may be placed the Kumbhār, or potter (Sanskrit Kumbha-kāra)—who by means of a wheel (*chakra*) of the simplest construction, makes all the earthenware pots and platters of the villagers with a skill truly surprising. He generally uses a donkey to fetch his materials, and from his cleverness in moulding clay into any shape, is facetiously called Prajāpati, 'the creator.'

5. Fifth must be mentioned the Sūtār, or carpenter (Sanskrit Sūtra-dhāra)—who also with the roughest tools does the village carpentering admirably. He ought perhaps to have been named earlier, as he ranks high in the social scale, and in proof of his superior pretensions even claims the privilege of wearing the sacred thread like a Brāhman.

---

[1] His wife is often the village midwife.

6. Then in close company with the carpenter will always be found the Lohār, or blacksmith (Sanskṛit Loha-kāra). These two useful workmen together make and mend all the village tools and agricultural implements.

7. Next comes the Dhobī, or washerman—an important personage, for no family ever thinks of saving money by washing at home. This operation can only be performed by a man of the right caste.

8. Eighth in the list may be placed the Bhīsti (properly Bihishtī), or water-carrier—sometimes called Pakhāli. He generally carries water in two leather-skins suspended over the back of a bullock, or in one skin suspended over his own back.

9. Next ought to be reckoned the Darzī (often corrupted into Darjī) or tailor—sometimes called Sūī from his use of the Sūchi or needle, and in the Dekkan Sipī or Simpī. He is not so important a person as in Europe, for the simple reason that an ordinary Indian's clothes need very little stitching. Still such sewing as may be required is always done by the tailor and his wife, never by the women of the family.

10. The tenth personage in the catalogue is the Mochī, or shoemaker—who repairs the shoes of the community, and makes the leather-work required in yoking the bullocks. Many of the villagers are content to remain shoeless, but the cultivators require good thick soles, frequently made of rhinoceros-hide brought from Zanzibar.

11. Last but one, but not nearly least in importance, comes the Chaukidār, or watchman (in Gujarāt called Rakhewād, or Paharī). Of these functionaries there are usually four, and in larger rural communes even fifteen or twenty. Though very poor, their trustworthiness when in charge of treasure or valuables of any kind is remarkable. In some places the watchman is also a Government official, who receives as his pay five acres of rent-free land. In Orissa, according to Dr. Hunter, he is generally allowed by the villagers to select the largest sheaf of corn in every field.

12. Under the twelfth head must be placed the impure castes who do all the dirty work of the village:—for example the Chamār, or tanner (Sanskrit Charma-kāra), who prepares and hands over to the shoemaker all the hides and skins of the sheep, oxen and other animals that die in the commune; the Dheḍ or Dher; and the Bhangī[1]. These last two personages are the village menials. Their work is absolutely necessary to the comfort if not to the very health and life of its population. They are not only sweepers and scavengers; they do other menial work, and are often trusted with the important duty of carrying letters. The Bhangī also shows the road to travellers, carrying a bamboo walking-stick with which he removes thorns and briars from the path. Both Dhers and Bhangīs are gross feeders. They devour the flesh of cows, buffaloes, and all animals that die a natural death in the village. They also drink spirituous liquor, but rarely become intoxicated. In some parts of Western India the low caste sweeper population are called Mhārs. In other parts of India the name Dom is common.

The various officials enumerated under the above twelve divisions along with the head-man, form the ordinary complement of servants and handicraftsmen needed for the maintenance of even the smallest rural communities. They are all paid by receiving portions of the grain or other produce in different proportions, according to the character and extent of their services.

Larger villages add other distinct functionaries, such as the *Guru*, or schoolmaster; the *Joshī*, or astrologer (Sanskrit *Jyotishī*), who names the lucky days for sowing, ploughing, marriages, journeys, &c., draws out horoscopes and almanacs, and tells fortunes—a most important personage, for nine-tenths of the people of India are slaves to astrological superstition; the *Vaid*, or village apothecary and doctor (Sanskrit *Vaidya*); the *Telī*, or oilman (Sanskrit *Tailī;* in

[1] The proper occupation of the Bhangī is said to be that of breaking (Sanskrit *bhanj*, to break) reeds to make baskets.

some places called *Ghanchī*); the *Kasārī*, otherwise *Kaserā*, or brazier; the *Kolī*, or weaver; the *Rangārī*, or dyer; the *Halwāī*, or confectioner. Then in some villages there is the *Gāpurgārī*, or hailstorm-charmer, who charms away hailstorms from the crops, and other varieties of charmers, such as the tiger-charmer, the snake-charmer, and above all the demon-charmer, who exorcises devils and other evil spirits.

In connexion with the subject of charmers, I extract a passage slightly abridged from Adam's educational report on the district of Nattore in Bengal, adding a few explanatory words of my own here and there.

In Bengal, he says, there is 'a class of pretenders, still lower than the village doctors, who go under the general name of conjurers or charmers. The largest division of this class are the snake-conjurers; their number in the single police division of Nattore being no less than 722. There are few villages without one, and in some villages there are as many as ten. These take nothing for the performance of their rites, or the cures they pretend to have effected. All is gratuitous, but they have substantial advantages which enable them to be thus liberal. When the inhabitants of a village, hitherto without a conjurer, think that they can afford to have one, they invite a professor of the art from a neighbouring village, where there happens to be one to spare, and give him a piece of land, and various privileges and immunities. He possesses great influence over the inhabitants. If a quarrel takes place, his interference will quell it sooner than that of any one else; and when he requires the aid of his neighbours in cultivating his plot of ground or in reaping its produce, it is always more readily given to him than to others.

The art is not hereditary in a family or peculiar to any caste. One charmer I met with was a boatman, another a Chaukidār, a third a weaver. Whoever learns the charm (perhaps consisting of some text from the Atharva-veda or from a Tantra) may practice it, but those are believed to practice it most successfully, who are 'to the manner born'; that is, who have been born under a favorable conjunction of planets. Every conjurer seems to have a separate charm, for I have found no two the same. No charmer objects to repeat his charm. He will even consent to do so for the mere gratification of a stranger's curiosity, and will allow it to be taken down in writing. Neither do such conjurers appear to have any mutual jealousy, each readily allowing the virtue of other incantations than his own.

Sometimes the pretended curer of snake-bites by charms professes also to possess the power of expelling demons, and, in other cases the expeller of demons disclaims being a snake-conjurer. Demon-conjurers are not numerous in Nattore; and tiger-conjurers who profess to charm away tigers or cure their bites, although scarcely heard of in that division, are numerous in those parts of the district where there is much jungle infested by wild beasts.

Distinct from these three kinds of conjurers, and called by a different name is a class of gifted (Sanskrit *guṇī*) persons who are believed to possess the power of preventing the fall of hail on the village crops. For this purpose when there is a prospect of a hailstorm, one of them goes out into the fields belonging to the village with a trident and a buffalo's horn. The trident is fixed in the ground, and the 'gifted' charmer makes a wide circle around it, running naked, blowing the horn, and pronouncing incantations. It is the firm belief of the villagers that their crops are by this means protected from hail-storms. Both men and women practice this business. There are about a dozen in Nattore, and they are provided for in the same way as the conjurers.

Some of these details may appear unimportant, but they help to give an insight into the character of the humble classes who constitute the great mass of the people, and whose happiness and improvement are identical with the prosperity of the country. And although they exhibit

IMPURE CASTES.   49

proofs of a most imbecile superstition, yet it is a superstition which has its origin in a childish ignorance of the common laws of nature, not in vice or depravity. Such superstitions are neither Hindū nor Muhammadan, being equally repudiated by the educated portions of both classes of religionists. They are probably antecedent to both systems of faith, and have been handed down from time immemorial.'

I must not omit to mention that one indispensable person in all the larger villages is the Baniya or shopkeeper and trader, who is also a money-lender and a kind of petty banker. In Gujarāt he is often a Mārwārī. This personage makes advances to the villagers and binds his helpless debtors by stringent penalties. At least half the village is generally in bondage to him, and not unfrequently a great part of the land passes into his possession.

With regard to the impure castes already alluded to as constituting one element of all village communes, it should be noted that although regarded by the Brāhmans as impure, their usefulness is not the less recognised. Their services are, in fact, felt to be indispensable, and the treatment they receive accords with the urgency rather than with the character of their duties. No greater mistake could be made than to suppose that the condition of the low-caste people of India is one either of serfdom or slavery. Neither the Dher nor the Bhangī are outcastes. Albeit their occupation is of a mean kind they take a pride in doing it well and patiently. They are consequently not only well treated by others but they themselves have the same feelings of self-respect and caste-respect as the other classes of society. Nay, they are often stricter in the observance of their caste rules than men of the higher classes. The Dher is a degree higher in the scale than the Bhangī, and is not a little proud of this superiority. He will on no account eat with the Bhangī, and they never intermarry. The Dhers place great faith in the Kalki—a future incarnation of Vishṇu—who is to appear on a

E

white horse with a flaming sword to take vengeance on unrighteous men, establish justice throughout the world, and restore the low castes to their proper position. Kalki, they say, is to marry a Dher woman, and the Dhers are then to take the place of the Brāhmans.

And I may here remark that the Hindūism of the present day is by no means a system that exists for the Brāhmans alone. It is no rigid unbending system of hard and fast lines. On the contrary it possesses great elasticity, and delights in compromises and compensations. If strict in some points it is lax in others; if it gives power to one caste it gives power of a different kind, or at least some compensating advantage to another.

The Bhangī, a man of the lowest caste in Gujarāt, may be despised by a few arrogant Brāhmans of the type described in Manu's Law-book. His touch, shadow, and very look may be avoided; yet the Bhangī has his hour of triumph, if not of revenge. The Brāhman is omnipotent during the day; his blessing makes rich, and his curse withers; but the moment the sun goes down, and darkness sets in, the Brāhman becomes powerless for good or evil. The tables are then turned, and the power of the Bhangī of Gujarāt begins. This is, curiously enough, displayed in some supposed command over the fords of rivers. No Gujarāt Brāhman of the strictly orthodox school will cross a ford after sunset, until he has asked permission of a Bhangī.

With regard to the general character of the rural population of Western India, I may state that an experienced military officer, for some time Surveyor-General of the Bombay Presidency, recorded, about fifty years ago, the impressions he formed in the course of a minute survey of the country[1]. At that time the villagers of every caste were found by him and his assistants to be 'simple

[1] See Lieut.-Colonel Monier Williams' 'Memoir of the Zilla of Broach,' p. 108. In quoting my father's authority, I may mention that his experience of India extended over twenty-four years of unbroken active service.

CHARACTER OF THE VILLAGERS.

and temperate' in their habits, 'quiet and peaceful' in disposition, 'obedient and faithful' in the fulfilment of duty. It was believed that they 'had the advantage of Europeans of the same class, not only in propriety of manners, but in the practice of moral virtues.' They had 'no conspicuous vices.' The affection and tenderness of parents was returned by the 'habitual dutifulness of their children.' Hospitality towards strangers 'was carefully observed.' Everywhere throughout the country 'there was charity without ostentation.' No beggars were to be seen 'except those who were religious mendicants by profession.' Though there was no poor law, 'the indigent and diseased were always provided for by the internal village arrangements.' There was everywhere such mutual confidence that 'no written documents in transactions involving money payments were required.' The cultivators paid their rents and took no receipts. Money and valuables were deposited 'without any other security than the accounts of the parties.' On a particular occasion at an immense religious fair on the banks of the Narbadā, two hundred thousand people were collected, yet there was 'no rioting, no quarrelling, no drunkenness nor disorder of any kind.' All were intent on their religious duties. The officers employed on the survey had 'no other guard but the village watchmen,' yet no robbery was committed, nor was the smallest article ever pilfered from the tents.

I cannot think that much change has passed over the people since this favourable impression made by their behaviour and general character fifty years ago. It is true that they now often appear in a very different light to their rulers. In our courts of justice they are constantly guilty of gross deception. But it seems doubtful whether Europeans would be very different in their attitude towards state officials under similar circumstances. Here in England a large number of people see no impropriety in evading the taxes, breaking the laws, and deceiving the police. In point of fact we are apt to judge the natives of India by the character they present to their foreign rulers, rather than by that they bear towards each other in their own homes. The same men who in our courts of law have no idea of the duty of truth will in their own Panchāyats settle disputes with erfect fairness.

As to the little village of Khātraj, which I have already mentioned as visited by me soon after my arrival in India, I found its inhabitants living in a collection of little better than mud huts and sheds, whose dilapidated walls looked as if they would revert to their primitive alluvium under the first heavy downpour of rain. All Indian agricultural labour depends on the ox, and much of the food of the peasantry comes from cows and buffaloes in the shape of milk and butter. Hence in Khātraj yards for cattle are interspersed everywhere with the mud tenements of the inhabitants. Men, women, children, cows, oxen, and buffaloes are huddled together in intimate communion and fellowship, amid dirt, dust, and strong smells of asafœtida and turmeric.

One curious feature in this village, as in most of the others I afterwards visited, was, that the walls of the dwellings were daubed with nasty-looking circular cakes, which looked like confections of mud and clay mixed with pieces of chopped straw. At first I was tempted to suppose that the children of the peasantry were addicted to the mischievous amusement of pelting the sides of their houses with dirt pies, which no one took the trouble to remove. But I found on inquiry that the whole fuel of the village is annually prepared and stowed away, by first kneading the excretions of the cattle into cakes, and then plastering them on the walls, where they are left to bake in the hot sun. It certainly strikes one as remarkable, and much to be regretted, that what ought to be devoted to the nourishment of the soil should be diverted from its proper use, and made to serve as an aliment for fire.

VILLAGE OF KHĀTRAJ.   53

Let no one, however, imagine that all was dirt, dilapidation, confusion, and disorder in this typical little village of Khātraj. On the contrary, I found an organized society subsisting harmoniously and in comfort on the produce of the village lands.

The plan of the village is very simple. It has one main irregular street crossed by two or three side alleys. Near the centre is an open space, on one side of which is a very primitive town-hall, consisting of a square plot of ground not bigger than the area of a small room, slightly elevated and protected above by a rough roof, supported by rude columns. The structure, though unimposing, obeys the usual law of adaptation found to prevail everywhere throughout the habitable globe. The thick roof is completely sun-proof, and the four open sides admit, as they ought to do, all the winds of heaven. Here, on all needful occasions, the village Panchāyat sits in dignified and comfortable coolness, if not in state and ceremony, the head-man of course presiding. In some smaller villages a cleared space under a large tree is the only meeting-place, and its foliage the only shelter from sun and rain. On the other side of the open space is another small raised platform of rough masonry, on which grow the Pīpal tree and Tulsī plant, the latter being held sacred as the favourite shrub of the god Vishṇu. There is a space all round for reverent circumambulation, as performed every day by the women of the community.

Furthermore, no village in India is without its temple or temples, though they are of a very rude kind. At Khātraj there are two shrines—one to Śiva (with his son Gaṇeśa, 'lord of demons') in his character of Father of all beings, the other to the local Mātā or Mother (otherwise called *Ambā*) of the village, generally identified by the Brāhmans with some form of Śiva's consort. But it must be observed that the village goddess (devī) has a special character and special name in every district and almost every village. In Khātraj she is called Khoḍiyār, or

'Mischief,' because she is supposed, when in an amiable mood, to shield from harm. She will, however, equally cause harm, when her temper is ruffled by the slightest omission of any formula in the daily process of conciliating her favour. Though euphemistically styled 'Mother,' she has little of a maternal character about her. She not unfrequently sends diseases. If cholera or small-pox break out in the village, the Mother is offended and must be appeased with additional offerings. She is sometimes represented by a rudely carved image, sometimes by a simple recumbent unworked stone.

I soon discovered that the women of India are, like the women in other parts of the world, more regular in the performance of religious exercises than the men. But they are also far more bigoted, intolerant, and superstitious. In most places they confine their religion to a diligent worship of the Tulsī plant. At Khātraj, on the occasion of my visit, a woman was performing circumambulation (*pradakshiṇa*[1]) round this sacred little shrub 108 times, her simple object being to secure long life for her husband, and a large family of sons for herself. The right shoulder must always be kept towards the object circumambulated, probably with the idea of following the sun's course.

The men are, however, by no means deficient in the practice of religious duties. On the contrary, religion of some kind enters largely into their everyday life. Nay, it may even be said that religious ideas and aspirations—religious hopes and fears—are interwoven with the whole texture of their mental constitution. A clergyman, who has resided nearly all his life in India, once remarked to me that he had seen many a poor Indian villager whose childlike trust in his god, and in the efficacy of his religious observances—whose simplicity of character and practical application of the principles of his creed, put us Christians to shame.

[1] Pradakshiṇa was in all likelihood originally connected with Sun-worship.

I asked one of the Khātraj Brāhmans to give me a specimen of his handwriting, or to write any sentence he liked best in the Sanskrit language. Thereupon he wrote as follows: *Brahmānandam parama-sukhadam kevalam jnāna-mūrtim ekam nityam vimalam aćalam sarva-dhī-sākshi-bhūtam namāmi*, that is (freely translated): 'I bow down before the One God, who is the only existing Being—who is all joy and the giver of all joy,—who is all knowledge—who is eternal, stainless, unchangeable, present as a witness in all consciences.' Another Brāhman, when asked to write his autograph, instead of his own name immediately wrote '*Bhagavate namah*'—'Reverence to God.' Another complied with a similar request for his autograph by writing the sacred monosyllable 'Om'—supposed to contain three letters symbolical of the three persons in the Hindū Triad of gods.

So much for rural life in India.

My next excursion was to the neighbouring towns of Mehmoodabad and Kaira. The name of the first (properly written Mahmūd-ābād, the city of Mahmūd) is an indication that it was founded by a Musalmān ruler. The latter is a mere corruption of the Sanskrit kheḍa, or kheṭa, a town.

More thoroughly Eastern towns could scarcely have been selected for a first introduction to Indian civic life. They are both small in area—especially Mehmoodabad—but densely populated. In the one case about fifteen thousand people, and in the other twenty thousand are packed together in spaces, which in England would not contain half that number.

Of course self-government prevails in the native towns as well as in the rural communes. The native head of a township, corresponding to the head-man of a village, is called in some parts of India Nagar-sheth or Nagar-seth (from the Sanskrit Nagara-sreshthin). He has always a Panch or council under him, which in some parts of Western India is called, I believe, Mājan (for Mahā-jana).

Our Government is laudably endeavouring to establish municipal institutions on European principles everywhere throughout India, but even a town like Kaira is as yet not advanced enough to bear any form of self-government different from that which it has possessed from time immemorial.

Unhappily dirt and disease follow inevitably on overcrowding, and reassert themselves after every effort on the part of the proper authorities to keep them down. Hence both Mehmoodabad and Kaira are redolent with those peculiarly Eastern odours that arise from the absence of all drainage, and the abundant use of asafœtida, and other pungent vegetable products.

It is well known that the site of Eastern cities has been constantly shifted by despotic rulers, sometimes out of mere caprice, sometimes for the simple reason that each potentate has been ambitious of founding a city of his own. But a traveller has only to walk through a town like Kaira to understand that the expedient of removing whole populations from one place to another has often been a matter of sheer necessity. It is frequently the only method of escaping the diseases engendered by malaria exhaling from a soil loaded with the noxious accumulations of centuries.

Neither Mehmoodabad nor Kaira have a single European habitation, with the exception of the Collector's official residence at the latter, occupied by him for three or four months every year. They are simply enlarged and improved editions of the village of Khātraj.

Most of the narrow streets of the smaller town are mere lines of thatched-roofed mud cottages, often however ornamented with wooden projections, the wood of which, under the chemical action of the sun's rays, becomes of a deep brown colour—not unlike that of some Indian complexions—and is often beautifully carved by village artists whose only tools are a hammer, a few rude chisels or rusty nails.

Kaira—the larger and the more important town of the two—is encircled by an old wall, and is still more remarkable for its beautiful wood carvings. It has also many loftier and better residences built of sun-baked bricks, some of which, notwithstanding, look as if they would tumble into ruins on very slight provocation. Here and there the walls of the houses have staring bright paintings representing animals—generally elephants or monkeys, or the grotesque figures of gods, heroes, and men, and not unfrequently well-known characters in the national epics, drawn with about as much artistic skill as might be expected from a European village sign-board painter.

The streets are constructed with some regularity, but are broken up at intervals by cattle-sheds. Not a pane of glass is to be seen in any part of the town. In the bazaars or streets of shops, all the houses have open recesses for shops—without the faintest approach to a glass-window—under projecting wooden eaves covered with cocoa-nut leaves or bamboos. In these recesses all kinds of curious indigenous commodities—notably strange sweetmeats and odd compounds of coarse sugar—are exposed for sale by their half-naked owners. Here, too, artisans of an amusingly archaic type ply their occupations almost in the open air, while just as in villages, beasts and birds mix everywhere sociably, and on the best possible terms, with the inhabitants. Here and there sacred bulls are seen roaming at large about the streets, and insinuating themselves into any open door that takes their fancy. Happening to pass through the streets in the morning, I found nearly all the male population cleaning their teeth outside the doors of their houses.

What struck me most forcibly was the number of temples, small shrines, and sacred trees. In every English town—not excepting our ancient city of Oxford [1]—there is a public-house at every corner. Now, if for every public-house were substituted a temple or sacred object of some kind, an idea might be formed of the proportion

---

[1] I am told that in Oxford we have one public-house to every 98 persons.

such objects bear to the other buildings of an ordinary native town. Of course many of these shrines are structures of a rough and ready character—often merely niches in walls containing perhaps nothing but a shapeless stone-symbol or grotesque idol smeared with vermilion. Often there is no idol at all but a mere daub of red paint on a wall or old tree. But they are all consecrated places notwithstanding, and the offerings of worshippers are always to be found near them.

At the very entrance to the town of Kaira there is a large temple dedicated to the great hero Rāma's monkey-ally Hanumān. It consists of an extensive enclosure surrounded by a Dharma-śālā or kind of cloister for the temporary accommodation of travellers. A rude image of the Ape-god smeared with vermilion—the sacred colour common to this god and Gaṇeśa—and surrounded with offerings of oil[1], occupies a central position under the principal shrine in the centre of the enclosure, while the image of the god Rāma, Hanumān's master, is placed quite subordinately on one side.

Between the two is a Dīpa-mālā or stone column for holding lamps arranged in circles, and lighted up on festival-days. Here also in the same enclosure is an image of Gaṇeśa and the Lingam, or symbol of Śiva, and a shrine to Sītalā, the goddess of small-pox, sometimes identified with Kālī or Durgā, Śiva's wife.

If any one inquires into the meaning of this miscellaneous medley of gods collected together in one locality, he is sure to be told that they all represent different manifestations of one and the same Supreme Being.

In the centre of the town, as at Khātraj, there is a quadrangular stone platform, on which are planted the Pīpal tree and the Tulsī shrub—the former sacred to Brahmā the Creator, the latter to Vishṇu the Preserver—with a space all round for reverential circumambulation.

---

[1] These, I was told, were the remains of 80 mānds of offerings of oil presented to the idol of Hanumān at a recent festival in his honour.

In a neighbouring street is a temple containing an image of Vishṇu as Vithobā. This is the form in which he is worshipped at Pandharpur in the Dekhan. The figure of the god is upright. It is quite black, and in a standing attitude with the arms akimbo. I saw that an offering of flowers and food had been recently presented. Incense was burning and two or three lamps were lighted before the image.

The priest of the shrine was very obliging and ready to answer all my questions, though he declined at first to accede to my request that the door might be opened, giving as his reason that the god was in the act of taking his midday repast, and ought not to be disturbed.

I visited another small shrine erected to the honour of a Sādhu or holy man, whose name I understood to be Parināma and who has no large number of followers. There was no image, but only an empty seat or throne (gādi). I was asked to take my shoes off before entering the sacred enclosure. In all Asiatic countries a man must uncover his feet, instead of his head, if he wishes to show respect.

Passing other temples of less importance I emerged on an open piece of ground, where was a small public garden and a building used as a public library well stocked with standard English works. A sacred bull was reposing here close to a picturesque well. Here also was a small shrine erected over the ashes of a Satī, a faithful wife, who had burnt herself on this very spot with the corpse of her husband many years before. It contained nothing but a flat circular stone on which were her supposed footprints. Such shrines are revered as sacred by all sects and parties and are scattered over the whole of India, bearing witness to the former prevalence of a monstrous superstition, now happily abolished [1].

[1] It must not be supposed, however, that the practice was ever universal. Only an infinitesimally small proportion of the wives of India ever became Satīs, and whenever a widow had children, her children saved her.

And what of the twenty thousand inhabitants? The streets are alive with men, women, and children, and the dark recesses of the ground-floor shops are veritable hives. As I walked along I was followed by crowds of curious but respectful observers. They behaved with the utmost decorum, and, if they occasionally pressed upon me a little too closely, were all kept in check by two sepoys.

By far the majority of the natives in Indian towns, even in times of plenty and prosperity, look half-fed and attenuated, and the old people quite emaciated. Here and there one is startled by the opposite extreme of abnormal obesity. A really fat Brāhman is a very comical and by no means uncommon spectacle. In fact excessive leanness and its opposite may be studied physiologically to great advantage in India. Very few men are oppressed by a superfluity of clothing, while the children, up to six or seven years of age, run about as they came into the world, without a single encumbrance, except perhaps a necklace and a few bangles.

The picturesque costumes of the better clothed—especially as shown in the graceful folds of their long loose robes, and the variegated colours of their turbans—the glossy skins of nearly nude youthful figures, and their movements and attitudes in walking or standing, would have thrown a true artist into ecstacies of delight and admiration.

As for the women, those that one sees in public are very seldom good-looking in any part of India; but nothing can equal the grace and charm of their attitudes and bearing when they go down in troops to the wells, carrying earthenware jars, or copper lotas for water on their heads. Their method of carrying their little children astride on their hips is not equally picturesque.

Their dress, happily for their husbands, is very simple, for no such thing as fashion exists in India. Indeed it may safely be affirmed that there has been no change in the character of an Indian woman's apparel for 3000 years.

Their whole costume consists of two articles—a simple bodice fitting close to the chest, and one long cloth wound gracefully round the person, and often brought over the head. In the case of women of the higher classes, who are rarely seen in public except in the Marātha country, this long robe, which is called a sārī, is at least ten yards long and often of very costly material. Nevertheless what the husband gains by the simplicity of his wife's taste in the matter of her two garments, is more than counterbalanced by her penchant for expensive jewelry.

And here I may observe that notwithstanding the apparent poverty of the common people of India, they are rarely poor to the point of discomfort. Thanks to the climate they have few wants, and are very thrifty. However small the weekly earnings, a little money is sure to be saved, and that little is never wasted on strong drinks. Instead, however, of being laid by as it ought to be, in the Post-office Savings Bank, it is generally invested in jewelry for the adornment of the women and children of the family. Certainly, after looking at Indian females, whether old or young—their arms, legs, fingers, and toes covered with bangles and rings, generally made of silver and not seldom of gold—it is difficult to believe in the poverty, much less in the alleged bankruptcy of India. Scarcely a woman of the poorest families is without a nose-ring in one nostril, and many of the better classes have also necklaces and earrings. Sometimes the nasal organ is decorated with a small circlet of five or six pearls set in gold, with an emerald in the centre. I once saw a woman who lived in a mud cottage, and earned 20 rupees a month as nurse. She had a double row of chased gold beads round her neck. Her nose-ring had six fine pearls, but she had not yet saved enough money for the central emerald, which is sure to be procured and duly inserted a few years hence.

Again when I was at Ahmedabad, I was invited into the house of a man who has a large family, and who has been earning about £100 a year as a Government servant for many years. He took me into a private room, opened a deal box in the corner and displayed the jewels worn by his wife and children on festive occasions. I believe I am under the mark when I say that they might have been sold in England for at least £1500.

So also one has only to go to a railway station when a local train comes in to see an almost incredible amount of jewelry in the third class carriages. Men and women are packed like sheep, the sexes being kept separate, but scarcely a woman, except the very poorest, is without a nose-ring in one nostril, or an earring in one ear, or gold or silver ornaments of some kind.

Again we were one day taken by the Collector of Kaira's wife to a girls' school. My companions were ladies who inspected it closely. They informed me that 35 girls were assembled in the class-room awaiting their arrival with six women superintendants. All the girls, however poor, wore ornaments of some sort or other, and two or three tiny children of three or four years of age, though wholly unencumbered with clothing, were literally bowed down by the weight of thick bracelets, necklaces, and ankle-rings. A few, only of the poorest, had necklaces and ornaments made of straw. The teachers, too, were profusely decorated, only one poor widow in sombre attire, and undecorated by a single ornament, stood aloof as if apologizing for being present in the room, or indeed for being present in the world at all.

The children sang a song in melancholy tones, moving round and clapping their hands. Some read and answered questions in Gujarātī. Others showed their needlework and coarse embroidery.

As to the boys' schools in towns like Mehmoodabad and Kaira, they are often conducted by native schoolmasters in the open air. We passed one consisting of about forty children. The boys were repeating or rather screaming out the multiplication table up to a hundred times a hundred with wonderful energy, and kept time together with such accuracy, that their combined voices made a piercing roar. I found that most of the bigger boys could read books in the Gujarātī character with ease and fluency.

Of course the teaching of girls, whenever any teaching is given at all either at school or at home, cannot be carried on beyond the age of eleven. At that age they all begin domestic duties in their husband's homes. Most of the evils, religious, moral, and physical, under which India is still suffering, are due to early marriages and the ignorance of its female population. In 1872–73 British India had only 5700 girls receiving public education.

SAMĀDH, SACRIFICE, SELF-IMMOLATION, AND SELF-TORTURE.

KAIRA DISTRICTS, 1876.

A REMARKABLE attempt at achieving a kind of canonization or saintship, by the accomplishment of an apparent Samādh, occurred in the district of Kaira in Gujarāt, presided over by Mr. Frederick Sheppard, the energetic Collector in whose camp I stayed on my first arrival in India. A brief account of the circumstances attending the discovery and interruption of the attempt may be acceptable to an increasing class of readers who take an interest in the various phases and peculiarities of Indian religious life. I propose, therefore, to introduce the narrative by a few remarks about sacrifice, immolation, and self-torture, all of which were once common in India.

In what may be called the Brāhmanical period, which succeeded the Vedic period of Hindūism, human sacrifice must have prevailed among the Brāhmanical races. This is sufficiently evident from the story of Śunaḥśepha in the Aitareya-brāhmaṇa. It is even believed by many that the sects called Śāktas (or Tāntrikas) formerly ate portions of the flesh and drank the blood of the victims sacrificed at their secret orgies. Among the wild Hill tribes and primitive races of India, the chief idea of religion has been the necessity of appeasing the malice of malignant beings by oblations of blood, and on occasions of great emergency by the outpouring of human blood. Their gods thirsted for blood and preferred that of men, while that of children was an irresistible delicacy certain to put them in the best of humours.

Very little more than thirty years has elapsed since the suppression of human sacrifices among the Kandhs (often written Kondhs or Khonds), an aboriginal tribe of Orissa. Their terrible Earth-god was supposed to send famines and pestilences unless propitiated by blood. According to Dr. Hunter (Statistics of Bengal, xix. 235) 'the victims were of either sex, and generally of tender age. The detestable office of providing them formed a hereditary privilege of the Pāns, one of the alien low castes attached to the Kandh villages. Procurers of this class yearly sallied forth into the plains, and bought up a herd of promising boys and girls from the poorer Hindūs. Sometimes they kidnapped their prey; and each Kandh district kept a stock of victims in reserve, " to meet sudden demands for atonement." Brāhmans and Kandhs were the only races whose purity exempted them from sacrifice, and a rule came down from remote antiquity that the victim *must be bought with a price.*

'After a village had purchased a victim, it treated him with much kindness, regarding him as a consecrated being, eagerly welcomed at every threshold. If a child, he enjoyed perfect liberty; but if an adult, the chief of the village kept him in his own house, and fed him well, but fettered him so that he could not escape[1]. When the time of atonement had come, the Kandhs spent two days in feasting and riot; on the third they offered up the victim, shouting as the first blood fell to the ground, " We bought you with a price; no sin rests with us." '

Our Government, by Act XXI of 1845, entirely suppressed these horrible sacrifices, and established a special agency for enforcing obedience to the order for their abolition. Human sacrifices were offered in the city of Saugor during the whole of the Marātha Government

[1] A similar practice of feeding, fattening, and petting consecrated human victims prevailed, I believe, in Mexico.

up to the year 1800, when they were put a stop to by the local native Governor, a very humane man.

'I once heard,' writes Colonel Sleeman, 'a very learned Brāhman priest say that he thought the decline of the Governor's family arose from this *innovation*. "There is," said he, "no sin in not offering human sacrifices to the gods where none have ever been offered; but where the gods have been accustomed to them, they are very naturally annoyed when the rite is abolished, and visit the place and people with all kinds of calamities."'

Human sacrifices, however, were probably rare among the purely Āryan races, while the sacrifice of animals became universal. The first idea of sacrifice of any kind—whether of grain, fruits, or animals—seems to have been that of supplying the deities with nourishment. Gods and men all feasted together. Then succeeded the notion of the need of vicarious suffering, or life for life, blood for blood. Some deities were believed to thirst for human blood, and the blood of animals was substituted for that of men. One of the effects of Buddhism was to cause a rapid diminution of animal sacrifice. It is now rarely seen, except at the altars of the fierce goddess of destruction (Kālī), or of forms and near relations of Kālī (such as the *Grāma-devatās*, 'village deities,' and *Mātās*, 'village mothers,') and at the altars of the tutelary deity Ayenār, and at devil-shrines in the South. I myself saw very few animals sacrificed even to the bloody goddesses, though I took pains to visit them on the proper days.

Other forms of immolation were once common in India. The Thugs (properly written *Ṭhags*) maintained that they sacrificed their victims to the goddess Kālī.

Now that Thuggism has been suppressed by us, a good deal of datura-poisoning is practised by the same class of people. Not long ago, an old man and his son were poisoned by a gang of these poisoners for the sake of a new blanket which the old man had purchased and imprudently hung on a tree near his hut. The gang appeared to be travellers, and effected their object by making friends with him, cooking their dinner near him, and giving him a portion previously poisoned for his own use.

The killing of female infants once prevailed extensively in the Panjāb and Rājputāna, owing to the difficulty of providing daughters with suitable husbands and the immense expenses entailed by nuptial festivities. Through our instrumentality the practice has now been discontinued, or if rare cases of female infanticide occur, they are perpetrated with great secrecy.

Again, in former days, self-immolation was common. Many fanatical pilgrims, while labouring under violent excitement amounting to religious frenzy, immolated themselves at the festivals of the God Śiva (the proper god of destruction), and even at the great car-festivals (*rathayātrā*) of the god Vishṇu, voluntarily throwing themselves under the enormous wheels not only of the car of Jagan-nāth (Kṛishṇa or Vishṇu, as 'lord and preserver of the world'), at Purī in Orissa, but of other similar idol-cars also.

I found such cars attached to every large Vishṇu pagoda in the South of India. They are supposed to typify the moving active world over which the god presides, and the friezes of grotesque sculptures, one under the other, with which they are covered, exhibit the world's good and bad, pure and impure characters in disgustingly incongruous juxtaposition. Some of them are so large and heavy that they require to be supported on sixteen wheels, and on a particular day, once a year, they are drawn through the streets by thousands of people. Every now and then persons are crushed under the wheels; for a rather unexpected consequence of our civilisation has been to increase religious gatherings among the natives by creating facilities of communication, and the best government cannot always prevent accidents.

Indeed, if the Orissa devotees are true to their own creed, 'accidental death' ought to be the formal verdict in every case of seeming suicide at Purī. For nothing, in fact, is more abhorrent to the principles of all Vishṇu-worship than the infliction of any kind of death on the most insignificant animal, and to die by one's own hand is a form of destruction to be shrunk from by a true Vaishṇava with the most intense religious horror.

The Jagan-nāth festival, writes Dr. W. W. Hunter, in the 19th volume of his Statistical Account of Bengal (p. 59)[1], 'takes place according as the Hindū months fall, in June or July, and for weeks beforehand pilgrims come trooping into Purī by thousands every day. The whole district is in a ferment. The great car is forty-five feet in height. This vast structure is supported on sixteen wheels of seven feet diameter, and is thirty-five feet square. The brother and sister of Jagan-nāth have separate cars a few feet smaller. When the sacred images are at length brought forth and placed upon their chariots, thousands fall on their knees and bow their foreheads in the dust. The vast multitude shouts with one throat, and, surging backwards and forwards, drags the wheeled edifices down the broad street towards the country-house of the world's lord (Jagan-nāth). Music strikes up before and behind, drums beat, cymbals clash, the priests harangue from the cars, or shout a sort of fescennine medley, enlivened with broad allusions and coarse gestures, which are received with roars of laughter from the crowd. And so the dense mass struggles forward by convulsive jerks, tugging and sweating, shouting and jumping, singing and praying. The distance from the temple to the country-house is less than a mile; but the wheels sink deep into the sand, and the journey takes several days. After hours of severe toil and wild excitement in the July tropical sun, a reaction necessarily follows. The zeal of the pilgrims flags before the garden-house is reached; and the cars, deserted

---

[1] In twenty volumes, just published by Messrs. Trübner and Co.

by the devotees, are dragged along by the professional pullers with deep-drawn grunts and groans. These men, 4200 in number, are peasants from the neighbouring Fiscal Divisions, who generally manage to live at free quarters in Purī during the festival.

'Once arrived at the country-house, the enthusiasm subsides. The pilgrims drop exhausted upon the burning sand of the sacred street, or block up the lanes with their prostrate bodies. When they have slept off their excitement, they rise refreshed and ready for another of the strong religious stimulants of the season. The world's lord is left to get back to his temple as best he can; and in the quaint words of a writer half a century ago, but for the professional car-pullers, the god "would infallibly stick" at his country-house.

'In a closely-packed eager throng of a hundred thousand men and women, many of them unaccustomed to exposure or hard labour, and all of them tugging and straining to the utmost under the blazing tropical sun, deaths must occasionally occur. There have, doubtless, been instances of pilgrims throwing themselves under the wheels in a frenzy of religious excitement; but such instances have always been rare, and are now unknown. At one time several unhappy people were killed or injured every year, but they were almost invariably cases of accidental trampling. The few suicides that did occur were, for the most part, cases of diseased and miserable objects, who took this means to put themselves out of pain. The official returns now place this beyond doubt. Nothing, indeed, could be more opposed to the spirit of Vishṇu-worship than self-immolation. Accidental death within the temple renders the whole place unclean. The ritual suddenly stops, and the polluted offerings are hurried away from the sight of the offended god. According to Ćaitanya, the apostle of Jagan-nāth, the destruction of the least of God's creatures is a sin against the Creator. Self-immolation he would have regarded with horror.'

Self-immolation, in other ways, was once extensively prevalent. Arrian, it is well known, describes how, in the time of Alexander the Great, a man named Kalanos —one of a sect of Indian wise men who went naked— burned himself upon a pile. This description is like that of the self-cremation of the ascetic Śarabhanga in Rāmāyaṇa, iii. 9. Cicero alludes to it in a celebrated passage : ' Est profecto quiddam etiam in barbaris gentibus praesentiens atque divinans : siquidem ad mortem proficiscens Calanus Indus, cum adscenderet in rogum ardentem; O praeclarum discessum, inquit, e vitâ.' (De Divin. i. 23.)

There are some sand-hills in the Sātpura range dedicated to Mahādeva—supposed, as Mahākāla, to preside over destruction. From a rock on these hills many youths have precipitated themselves, because their mothers, being childless, have dedicated their first-born sons to the god.

According to Col. Sleeman, ' when a woman is without children, she makes votive offerings to all the gods who can, she thinks, assist her ; and promises of still greater offerings in case they should grant what she wants. Smaller promises being found of no avail, she at last promises her first-born, if a male, to the god of destruction, Mahādeva (Siva). If she gets a son, she conceals from him her vow till he has attained the age of puberty ; she then communicates it to him, and enjoins him to fulfil it. He believes it to be his paramount duty to obey his mother's call ; and from that moment considers himself as devoted to the god. Without breathing to any living soul a syllable of what she has told him, he puts on the habit of a pilgrim or religious mendicant, visits all the celebrated temples dedicated to this god in different parts of India ; and at the annual fair on the Mahādeva hills, throws himself from a perpendicular height of four or five hundred feet, and is dashed to pieces on the rocks below. If the youth does not feel himself quite prepared for the sacrifice on the first visit, he spends another year in pilgrimages, and returns to fulfil his mother's vow at the next fair. Some have, I believe, been known to postpone the sacrifice to a third fair; but the interval is always spent in painful pilgrimages to the celebrated temples of the god [1].'

This mode of suicide is called Bhṛigu-pāta, 'throwing one's-self from a precipice.' It was once equally common at the rock of Girnār, in Kāthiāwār, and has only recently been prohibited.

We have made great efforts to put a stop to these horrors by doing away with the fair. On one occasion our efforts were assisted by the cholera, which broke out among the multitude. This visitation was considered by the people as an intimation on the part of the god that they ought to have been more attentive to the wishes of the *white men*. It is noteworthy that Mahādeva is the only Hindū god represented of a fair colour—probably from his connection with the Snowy Mountains.

With regard to the immolation of the faithful wife, commonly called Sutee (= Sanskṛit *Satī*) who followed her husband in death, and burned herself on his funeral pile, everywhere in India I saw, scattered about in various places, monuments erected over the ashes of Satīs, and everywhere such monuments (often enshrining the supposed footprints of the faithful wife) are still regarded with the greatest veneration by the people.

Sometimes the poor women in their horror of burning have submitted to the alternative of being buried alive with their husbands. The practice of Satī was for a long period thought to be so intimately connected with the religious belief of the Hindūs, that our Government did not venture to put a stop to it. It was known to be enjoined in certain comparatively modern Indian codes, and for some time it was not discovered that the fanatical Brāhmans, to obtain the requisite authority for insisting on the continual observance of the rite, had permitted the

---

[1] Sleeman's 'Rambles and Recollections,' p. 133.

fraudulent substitution of the words *agneh*, 'of fire,' for *agre*, 'first,' at the end of the Ṛig-veda text (X. 18. 7), thus translatable : 'without tears, without sorrow, bedecked with jewels, let the wives go up to the altar *first.*'

Our Government prohibited the burning of any widow except under strict regulations, and except with her own full consent; but, in consequence of our half-sanction, the number of widows actually returned as burnt in Bengal rose in one year to 839, while in other years the average was 500. In Lord Amherst's time the seven European functionaries in charge of the seven newly-acquired districts, one and all declared against the abolition of widow-burning, and such great authorities as Colebrooke and H. H. Wilson were against interference. Yet under Lord William Bentinck's administration a law was passed in 1829 (Reg. XVII) which suppressed the practice with entire success, and without difficulty or disturbance of any kind, notwithstanding all the bigotry, fanaticism, and prejudice brought to bear in opposition to the measure.

We have also prevented the burying alive of lepers, and others afflicted with incurable diseases, which was once universally prevalent in the Panjāb, and common in some other parts of India.

Of course leprosy in India, as in other Eastern countries, is a kind of living death. Lepers are excluded from society, and can find no employment. They often gave themselves up of their own accord to be buried alive, the motive simply being a desire to be released from physical suffering.

This burying one's self alive is called performing Samādh (= Sanskṛit *Samādhi*). The word properly means intense concentration of the thoughts on some holy object, or a temporary suspension of all connexion between soul and body by religious abstraction.

The tomb of a Sannyāsī, or holy Brāhman, who has given up all worldly connexions and abandoned caste-obligations, is also called a Samādh (=*Samādhi*). A holy man of this kind is never burnt, but buried; and his entombed body is supposed to lie for centuries in the Samādh trance. Such tombs are often great places of pilgrimage, resorted to by thousands from all parts of India.

Colonel Sleeman (in his 'Rambles and Recollections,' p. 345) describes how he once knew a very respectable Hindū gentleman who came to the river Narbadā, attended by a large retinue, to perform a kind of water Samādh, in consequence of an incurable disease under which he laboured. After taking leave of his family, he entered a boat, which conveyed him to the deepest part of the river. He then loaded himself with sand, and, stepping into the water, disappeared.

Self-immolation by drowning was once very common at Benares. Bishop Heber describes how many scores of pilgrims from all parts of India came to Benares every year expressly to end their days and secure their salvation. They purchased two large pots, between which they tied themselves. Thus equipped they paddled into the stream, the empty pots supporting their weight. Then they proceeded to fill the pots with the water which surrounded them, and in this manner sank into eternity. The British Government in the Bishop's time had not succeeded in suppressing the practice. Indeed, when a man has travelled several hundred miles to drown himself, it is never very likely that a police-officer will be able to prevent him.

I now come to the remarkable fact that two attempts at Samādh have occurred in the Collector of Kaira's district quite recently. A certain devotee announced his intention of adopting this extraordinary method of securing perfect abstraction and beatitude, and was actually buried alive in the neighbourhood of a village. His friends were detected by the villagers in pouring milk down a hollow bamboo, which had been arranged to supply the buried man with air and food. The bamboo was removed, and the interred man was found dead when his friends opened the grave shortly afterwards.

The other attempt is still more recent, and I here give Mr. Sheppard's own account of it almost in his own words: 'As I was shooting near my camp one evening, a mounted orderly came up with the news that a Bhāt had performed Samādh that afternoon in a neighbouring village, and that there was much consequent excitement there. Not having a horse with me, I directed the orderly to ride off to the village (picking up my police escort as he passed through my camp), to dig up the buried man, and to take into custody any persons who might endeavour to oppose the execution of my orders.

'On returning to my camp, I ordered the apprehension of all those who had assisted in the Samādh; and soon afterwards received a report that the man had been actually buried in a vault in his own house, but had been taken out alive. He was, however, very weak, and died the following morning. It was then reported to me that the limbs, though cold, had not stiffened; and the people, ready as of old to be deceived, and always inclined to attribute the smallest departure from the ordinary course of events to supernatural agency, declared that the Bhāt was not dead, but lying in the Samādh trance. There was, however, no pulse; and as it was clear that, even if the supposition of the villagers was correct, medical treatment would be desirable, I sent the body in a cart to the nearest dispensary, distant some six or seven miles, and in due time received a certificate of death from the hospital assistant in charge of that institution, together with a report of a post-mortem examination of the body, which showed that death had resulted from heart-disease.

'Meanwhile I visited the village and ascertained the following facts:—

'The deceased was a man in fairly comfortable circumstances, and with some religious pretensions. It was well known that he aspired to a still higher reputation for sanctity, and that with this view he had for several months been contemplating Samādh. The proper date for this rite had been finally settled after many solemn ceremonies, and the due observance of fasting, prayer, and charity.

'On the afternoon fixed for the Samādh he assembled the villagers, and told them that it had been imparted to him in a vision that the Deity required him to pass six weeks in religious abstraction, and that he felt compelled to obey the Divine command, and to remain in the vault prepared for him during that period. He then produced and worshipped a small earthen vessel containing the sacred Tulsī plant, and afterwards carefully planted therein twenty grains of barley, telling the villagers to watch for their growth, as it had been revealed to him that the grains represented his life. If, at the end of the six weeks, the grains had sprouted, the villagers were to understand that the Bhāt was still alive. He was then to be removed from the vault, and worshipped as a saint. If, on the other hand, germination had not taken place, they were to understand that the Bhāt was dead also, and the vault was in that case to be permanently bricked up, and the Tulsī planted over the grave.

'After giving these directions, the devotee recited some Mantras and entered the vault, bidding farewell to the world, and declaring his belief that his life would be miraculously preserved. The vault was then roofed over with boards, and plastered thickly with mud. About two hours after this event, he was removed from the vault by the police under my orders, and placed in the verandah, the house itself being locked up.

'After ascertaining the above particulars, I caused the house to be opened, and then discovered that a gross attempt at imposture had been practised. The grave was about three feet deep, being a hole dug in the floor of the inner room of the house. The wall of the room formed one side of the vault. The roof over the latter was a clumsy structure, and had been partly demolished to allow of the removal of the devotee. As usual in India, the only light admitted to the room was through the door, and the unsubstantial nature of the roof was not likely to attract the attention of the villagers. But I satisfied myself that the occupant of the vault might, with great ease, have demolished the covering which was supposed to shut him off from the world.

'The vault itself was of course dark. I entered it in order to ascertain how much space had been allotted to the occupant. I found therein the rosary of the deceased, and the chaplet of flowers which he had worn before his self-immolation. There was sufficient room for me to sit in tolerable comfort. On one side of the vault I felt a small wooden plank apparently let into the wall, and on obtaining a light I found that a trap-door about a foot square had been ingeniously contrived to communicate with the other room of the house. The trap-door was so hung as to open inwards towards the vault, at the pleasure of the inmate. On going into the outer room, into which communication had thus been opened, I found that a row of the large earthen jars, which Horace would have called *amphoræ*, and which are used in India to store grain, had been arranged against the wall. The trap-door into the vault was effectually concealed by them, and the supply of air, food, and water to the impostor within thus cleverly provided for. The arrangement was neatly contrived, and was not likely to have attracted suspicion. Had the Bhāt been a strong man, and in good health, he might, without any danger to life, and with only a minimum of discomfort, have emerged triumphantly after his six weeks' Samādh, and have earned a wide reputation. But the excitement and fasting were too much for him.'

As to the practice of self-torture this cannot be entirely prevented by our Government, but is rapidly dying out. Formerly it was possible for devotees,—with the object

SAMĀDH. SELF-TORTURE.

of exciting admiration or extorting alms, or under the delusion that their self-torture was an act of religious merit,—to swing in the air attached to a lofty pole by means of a rope and hook passed through the muscles of the back. Such self-inflicted mutilation is now prohibited.

Yet, even in the present day, to acquire a reputation for sanctity, or to receive homage and offerings from the multitude, or under the idea of accumulating a store of merit, all sorts of bodily sufferings, penances, and austerities, even to virtual suicide, are undergone—the latter being sometimes actually perpetrated out of mere revenge, as its consequences are supposed to fall on the enemy whose action has driven the deceased to self-immolation.

Three Brāhmans in a native State, who had their daughters forced from them by Muhammadans beyond the reach of justice, complained to the governor of the province; but finding no redress, they all swallowed poison and died at the door of his tent.

The practice of sitting in Dharnā was once common, but was made punishable by Reg. VII. 1820. It was thus performed:—A person who wished to compel payment of a debt due to him, sat at the door of a debtor's house and observed a strict fast. If he died from want of food, the consequences of his death were supposed to fall on the debtor, and if the person sitting was a Brāhman, the terrible guilt of Brahmanicide was believed to be incurred.

I saw a man not long since at Allahabad, who has sat in one position for fifty years on a stone pedestal exposed to sun, wind, and rain. He never moves except once a day, when his attendants lead him to the Ganges. He is an object of worship to thousands, and even high-caste Brāhmans pay him homage.

I saw two Ūrdhva-bāhus—one at Gayā and the other at Benares—that is, devotees who hold their arms with clenched fists above their heads for years, until they become shrivelled and the finger-nails penetrate through the back of the hands.

Another man was prostrating himself and measuring every inch of the ground with his body round the hill of Govardhan when I passed. He probably intended continuing the painful process till he had completed a circuit of twenty miles one hundred and eight times.

In most of the cases I have described, the laudable humanity of our Government in endeavouring to preserve human life has given rise to fresh evils and difficulties.

In the first place, population is increasing upon us in a degree which threatens to become wholly unmanageable. Then widows never marry again; not even if their boy-husbands die, leaving them widows at the age of six. A woman is supposed to be sacramentally united to one husband, and belongs to him for ever. Every town, every village, almost every house, is full of widows who are debarred from all amusements, and, if childless, converted into household drudges. They often lead bad lives. Their life, like that of the lepers, is a kind of living death, and they would often cheerfully give themselves up to be burned alive if the law would let them. The spirit of Satī still survives.

Only the other day in Nepāl, where our supremacy is barely recognized, the widows of Sir Jung Bahādur became Satīs, and burned themselves with their husband.

Then, again, the increase in the number of girls who cannot find suitable husbands is now causing much embarrassment in some districts. Even the lepers, whose lives we preserve, involve us in peculiar difficulties. These unfortunate creatures often roam about the country, exacting food from the people by threatening to touch their children. Here and there we have built leper-villages— rows of cottages under trees devoted to their use; and we make the towns contribute from local funds to support them, while charity ekes out the miserable pittance they receive.

Yet notwithstanding all the fresh evils which our philanthropic efforts have introduced into the country, no one will, I think, dispute my assertion when I maintain that the suppression of Samādhs, human sacrifices, self-immolations, and self-tortures are among the greatest blessings which India has hitherto received from her English rulers.

THE TOWERS OF SILENCE, AND THE PĀRSĪ RELIGION.

THE Pārsīs are descendants of the ancient Persians who were expelled from Persia by the Muhammadan conquerors, and who first settled at Sūrat between eleven and twelve hundred years ago. According to the last census they do not number more than 70,000 souls, of whom about 50,000 are found in the city of Bombay, the remaining 20,000 in different parts of India, but chiefly in Gujarāt and the Bombay Presidency. Though a mere drop in the ocean of 241 million inhabitants, they form a most important and influential body of men, emulating Europeans in energy and enterprize, rivalling them in opulence, and imitating them in many of their habits. Their vernacular language is Gujarātī, but nearly every adult speaks English with fluency, and English is now taught in all their schools. Their Benevolent Institution for the education of at least 1,000 boys and girls is in a noble building, and is a model of good management. Their religion, as delivered in its original purity by their prophet Zoroaster, and as propounded in the Zand-Avastā, is monotheistic, or, perhaps, rather pantheistic, in spite of its philosophical dualism, and in spite of the apparent worship of fire and the elements, regarded as visible representations of the Deity. Its morality is summed up in three precepts of two words each—'good thoughts,' 'good words,' 'good deeds;' of which the Pārsī is constantly reminded by the triple coil of his white cotton girdle. In its origin the Pārsī system is closely allied to that of the Hindū Āryans—as repre-

THE TOWERS OF SILENCE. 81

sented in the Veda—and has much in common with the more recent Brāhmanism. Neither religion can make proselytes.

A man must be born a Brāhman or Pārsī; no power can convert him into either one or the other. One notable peculiarity, however, distinguishes Pārsīism. Nothing similar to its funeral rites prevails among other nations; though the practice of exposing bodies on the tops of rocks is said to prevail among the Buddhists of Bhotan.

And truly among the interesting contrasts which everywhere meet the eye of an observant European traveller, when he first arrives at Bombay, may especially be noted the different methods adopted by the adherents of different creeds for the disposal of their dead.

There in Bombay one may see, within a short distance of each other, the Christian cemetery, the Muhammadan graveyard, the Hindū burning-ground, and the Pārsī Dakhmas, or Towers of Silence. These latter are erected in a garden, on the highest point of Malabar Hill—a beautiful rising ground on the north side of Back Bay, noted for the bungalows and compounds of the European and wealthier inhabitants of Bombay scattered in every direction over its surface.

The garden is approached by a well-constructed private road, all access to which, except to Pārsīs, is barred by strong iron gates. I obtained leave to visit the Towers on two different occasions, and thanks to the omnipotent Sir Jamsetjee, no obstacles impeded my advance. Each time I made my appearance before the massive gates they flew open before me as if by magic. I drove rapidly through a park-like enclosure, and found the courteous Secretary of the Pārsī Panchāyat, Mr. Nasarwānjee Byramjee, awaiting my arrival at the entrance to the garden. On the occasion of my first visit he took me at once to the highest point in the consecrated ground, and we stood together on the terrace of the largest of the three *Sāgrīs*, or Houses of Prayer, which overlook the five Towers of

Silence. These Sāgrīs are indispensable adjuncts to all Pārsī burial-towers in large towns such as Bombay, Surat, and Poona, but are not found attached to them in less important localities. They are not only places of prayer, they are sanctuaries for the sacred fire, which, when once kindled and consecrated by solemn ceremonial, is fed day and night with incense and fragrant sandal by a priest appointed for the purpose, and never extinguished. It is noteworthy that the wall of the Bombay Sāgrī has an aperture or apertures, so arranged that the light streaming from the sacred fire, or from a consecrated oil-lamp, kept burning throughout the night, may pass through similar apertures in the parapets of the towers, and fall on the bodies lying in the interior. The view we enjoyed when standing near the principal Sāgrī can scarcely be surpassed by any in the world. Beneath us lay the city of Bombay, partially hidden by cocoanut groves, with its beautiful bay and harbour glittering in the brilliant December light. Beyond stretched the magnificent ranges of the ghauts, while immediately around us extended a garden, such as can only be seen in tropical countries. No English nobleman's garden could be better kept, and no pen could do justice to the glories of its flowering shrubs, cypresses, and palms. It seemed the very ideal, not only of a place of sacred silence, but of peaceful rest.

But what are those five circular structures which appear at intervals rising mysteriously out of the foliage? They are masses of solid masonry, massive enough to last for centuries, built of the hardest black granite, and covered with white chunam, the purity and smoothness of which are disfigured by patches of black fungus-like incrustations. Towers they scarcely deserve to be called; for the height of each is quite out of proportion to its diameter. The largest of the five may be described as an upright cylindrical stone structure, in shape and solidity not unlike a gigantic millstone, about fourteen feet high and ninety feet in diameter, resting on the ground in the midst of the garden. It is built of solid granite, except in the centre, where a well, ten feet deep and about fifteen across, leads down to an excavation under the masonry, containing four drains at right angles to each other, terminated by holes filled with sand, or in some cases, with charcoal. Round the upper and outer edge of this circular structure, and completely hiding its upper surface from view, is a high stone parapet. This is constructed so as to seem to form one piece with the solid stone-work, and being, like it, covered with chunam, gives the whole erection, when viewed from the outside, the appearance of a low Tower. Clearly, one great object aimed at by the Pārsīs in the construction of these strange depositories of their dead is solidity. We saw two or three enormous massive stones lying on the ground, which had been rejected by the builders simply because they contained almost invisible veins of quartz, through which it was possible that impure particles might find their way, and be carried, in the course of centuries, by percolating moisture, into the soil. Earth, water, and fire are, according to Zoroaster, sacred symbols of the wisdom, goodness, and omnipotence of the Deity, and ought never, under any circumstances, to be defiled. Especially ought every effort to be made to protect Mother Earth from the pollution which would result if putrifying corpses were allowed to accumulate in the ground (*Vandidād* iii. 27). Hence the disciples of Zoroaster spare neither trouble nor expense in erecting solid and impenetrable stone platforms fourteen feet thick for the reception of their dead. The cost of erection is greatly increased by the circumstance that the Towers ought always to be placed on high hills, or in the highest situations available (*Vand.* vi. 93). I was informed by the Secretary that the largest of the five Towers was constructed at an outlay of three lakhs (300,000) of rupees.

The oldest and smallest of the five was built 200 years ago, when the Pārsīs first settled in Bombay, and is now only used by the Modi family, whose forefathers built it; and here the bones of many kindred generations are commingled. The next oldest was erected in 1756, and the other three during the succeeding century. A sixth Tower stands quite apart from the others. It is square in shape, and only used for persons who have suffered death for heinous crimes. The bones of convicted criminals are never allowed to mingle with those of the rest of the community.

But the strangest feature in these strange, unsightly structures, so incongruously intermixed with graceful cypresses and palms, exquisite shrubs, and gorgeous flowers, remains to be described. Though wholly destitute of ornament, and even of the simplest moulding, the parapet of each Tower possesses an extraordinary coping, which instantly attracts and fascinates the gaze. It is a coping formed, not of dead stone, but of living vultures. These birds, on the occasion of my visit, had settled themselves side by side in perfect order, and in a complete circle around the parapets of the Towers, with their heads pointed inwards, and so lazily did they sit there and so motionless was their whole mien that, except for their colour, they might have been carved out of the stone-work.

And now as to the interior of the Towers, the upper surface of the massive granite column is divided into compartments by narrow grooved ridges of stone, radiating like the spokes of a wheel from the central well. These stone ridges form the sides of seventy-two shallow open receptacles or coffins, arranged in three concentric rings, the last of the three encircling the central well[1]. The

---

[1] I hear from Mr. Cursetjee Rustamjee Cāma (who is a great authority on all points connected with his own religion) that all the Dakhmas have not seventy-two receptacles. Smaller towers have fewer receptacles. The number is not a fixed one, but depends on the needs of the place where a Dakhma is erected.

ridges are grooved—that is, they have narrow channels running down their whole length, which channels are connected by side ducts with the open coffins, so as to convey all moisture to the central well, and into the lower drains. The number three is emblematical of Zoroaster's three moral precepts, 'Good thoughts, good words, and good deeds' (*Vand.* v. 67), and the seventy-two open stone receptacles represent the seventy-two chapters of his Yaśna, a portion of the Zand-Avastā.

Each concentric circle of open stone coffins has a pathway surrounding it, the object of which is to make each receptacle accessible to the corpse-bearers. Hence there are three concentric circular pathways, the outermost of which is immediately below the parapet, and these three pathways are crossed by another conducting from the solitary door which admits the corpse-bearers from the exterior, and which must face the east, to catch the rays of the rising sun. In the outermost circle of stone coffins, which stands for 'good deeds,' are placed the bodies of males; in the middle, symbolizing 'good words,' those of females; in the inner and smallest circle, nearest the well, representing 'good thoughts,' those of children. Each tower is consecrated with solemn religious ceremonies, and after its consecration no one, except the corpse-bearers—not even a high-priest—is allowed to enter, or to approach within thirty feet of the immediate precincts.

The first funeral I witnessed was that of a child. While I was engaged in conversation with the Secretary outside the Fire-temple, a sudden stir among the vultures made us raise our heads. At least a hundred birds, collected round one of the Towers, began to shew symptoms of excitement, while others swooped down from neighbouring trees. The cause of this sudden abandonment of their previous apathy soon revealed itself. A funeral procession was seen to be approaching. However distant the house of a deceased person, and whether he be young or old, rich or poor, high or low in rank, his body is always carried to the Towers by the official corpse-bearers, the mourners walking behind. The corpse-bearers are properly divided into two classes, named Nasa-sālārs and Khāndhiās. The former alone are privileged to enter the Towers, but they are assisted in carrying the bier by the Khāndhiās, and they carry the dead bodies of little children without the aid of the Khāndhiās. As these Nasa-sālārs are supposed to contract impurity in the discharge of their duty, they are obliged to submit to certain social disadvantages. For instance, they are generally expected to eat apart from the rest of the community at social gatherings[1]. They enjoy, however, a compensating advantage in being highly paid for the work they have to do.

Before they removed the body of the child from the house where its relatives were assembled, funeral prayers were recited, and the corpse was exposed to the gaze of the sacred dog, to be afterwards described.

Then the body, swathed in a white sheet, was placed on a curved metal trough[2], open at both ends, and the corpse-bearers, dressed in pure white garments, proceeded with it towards the Towers. They were followed by the mourners at a distance of at least 30 feet, in pairs, also dressed in white, and each couple joined by holding a white handkerchief between them. When the two corpse-bearers reached the path leading by a steep incline to the door of the Tower, the mourners, about eight in number, turned back and entered one of the prayer houses. 'There,' said the Secretary, 'they repeat certain Gāthās, and pray that the spirit of the deceased may be safely transported on the fourth day after death to its final resting-place.'

The Tower selected for the child's burial was one in

[1] My authority here is Mr. N. J. Ratnāgar, who contributed some valuable remarks on this subject to the January number of the 'Indian Antiquary' for this year.

[2] This form of bier is only used in the case of young children. See the description of the second funeral witnessed by me.

which other members of the same family had before been laid. The two bearers speedily unlocked the door, reverently conveyed the body of the child into the interior, and, unseen by any one, laid it uncovered in one of the open stone receptacles nearest the central well. In two minutes they re-appeared with the empty bier and white cloth. But scarcely had they closed the door when a dozen vultures swooped down upon the body, and were rapidly followed by flights of others. In five minutes more we saw the satiated birds fly back and lazily settle down again upon the parapet. They had left nothing behind but a skeleton. Meanwhile the bearers were seen to enter a building shaped like a huge barrel. There, as the Secretary informed me, they changed their clothes and washed themselves. Shortly afterwards we saw them come out and deposit their cast-off funeral garments on a stone receptacle near at hand. Not a thread leaves the garden, lest it should carry defilement into the city. Fresh garments were supplied at each funeral. In a fortnight, or at most four weeks, the same bearers return, and with gloved hands and implements resembling tongs, place the dry skeleton in the central well. There the bones find their last resting-place, and there the dust of whole generations of Pārsīs commingling is left undisturbed for centuries.

The revolting sight of the gorged vultures made me turn my back on the Towers with ill-concealed abhorrence. I asked the Secretary how it was possible to become reconciled to such a usage. His reply was nearly in the following words:—'Our Prophet Zoroaster, who lived 6,000 years ago, taught us to regard the elements as symbols of the Deity. Earth, fire, water, he said, ought never, under any circumstances, to be defiled by contact with putrefying flesh. Naked, he said, we came into the world, and naked we ought to leave it. But the decaying particles of our bodies should be dissipated as rapidly as possible, and in such a way that neither Mother Earth nor the beings she supports should be contaminated in the slightest degree. In fact, our Prophet was the greatest of health officers, and following his sanitary laws, we build our Towers on the tops of the hills, above all human habitations. We spare no expense in constructing them of the hardest materials, and we expose our putrescent bodies in open stone receptacles, resting on 14 feet of solid granite, not necessarily to be consumed by vultures, but to be dissipated in the speediest manner, and without the smallest possibility of polluting the earth, or contaminating a single living being dwelling thereon. God, indeed, sends the vultures, and, as a matter of fact, these birds do their appointed work much more expeditiously than millions of insects would do, if we committed our bodies to the ground. In a sanitary point of view nothing can be more perfect than our plan. Even the rain water which washes our skeletons is conducted by channels into purifying charcoal. Here in these five Towers rest the bones of all the Pārsīs that have lived in Bombay for the last 200 years. We form a united body in life, and we are united in death. Even our leader, Sir Jamsetjee, likes to feel that when he dies he will be reduced to perfect equality with the poorest and humblest of the Pārsī community.'

When the Secretary had finished his defence of the Towers of Silence, I could not help thinking that however much such a system may shock our European feelings and ideas, yet our own method of interment, if regarded from a Pārsī point of view, may possibly be equally revolting to Pārsī sensibilities.

The exposure of the decaying body to the assaults of innumerable worms may have no terrors for us, because our survivors do not see the assailants ; but let it be borne in mind that neither are the Pārsī survivors permitted to look at the swoop of the heaven-sent birds. Why, then, should we be surprised if they prefer the more rapid to the more lingering operation ? and which of the two

THE TOWERS OF SILENCE. 89

systems, they may reasonably ask, is more defensible on sanitary grounds?

On the occasion of my second visit to the Towers I was permitted to witness the funeral of a Mobed, or one of the second order of priests, whose flowing white costumes (supposed to be emblematical of purity) are everywhere conspicuous in the Bombay streets. I may here mention parenthetically that I believe the word Mobed is merely a corruption of a Zand word equivalent to Sanskrit *Magapati*, 'chief of the Magians.' Dastūr, the name of the high-priest, is a modern Persian word, the best equivalent for which would perhaps be 'chief ruler.' According to some the name Herbad (or Erwad)[1], is applied as a generic term to the whole sacerdotal order. In the Zand-Avastā the entire priestly class are called Athravan (in Pāzand Athornan). In the present day the rest of the community —all laymen in fact, who are not Herbads—are generally styled Behadīn, or Behdīn, that is, 'followers of the best religion.' They have also the name Ostā.

I reached the garden surrounding the Towers about half an hour before sunset. At that time the funeral procession was already winding up the hill. The deceased man had died early in the morning, and a rule of the Pārsī religion requires that no corpse shall be exposed on the platform of the Towers, to be consumed by birds of prey, unless the rays of the sun can first fall on it. Foremost in the procession walked a man carrying a loaf or two of bread wrapped up in a cloth. Then came the bier, which was flat and made of iron bars[2], having the body of the de-

[1] Mr. Cāma informs me that Herbad means simply a religious teacher. Another name for a Herbad is Nāvar, meaning one who has performed the Nāvar ceremony. Originally it may have meant a new member of the ecclesiastical fraternity. Every son of a priest is a Herbad. But some Herbads instead of becoming Dastūrs or Mobeds adopt a secular profession, discarding the white turban for a dark one. In that case they generally abandon the name Herbad. In fact, priestly denominations have fallen into disrepute. The title Dastūr is applied ironically to every one with a white turban.

[2] In the case of a child it is a curved metal trough.

ceased stretched out upon it, covered only with a white sheet, and borne by four Khāndhiā bearers, accompanied by two Nasa-sālārs. After the bearers, at an interval of a few yards, followed a man leading a white dog, and behind him a long procession of at least a hundred priests in their robes of spotless white, besides relations of the deceased, also in white garments, walking in pairs, each couple following closely on the other, and each man connected with his fellow by a handkerchief held between them in token of sympathy and fellow-feeling. The procession advanced to a point about thirty yards distant from the portal of the largest Tower. There it stood still for a minute while the dog was brought towards the corpse, made to look at the features of the dead man, and then fed with bread.

Meanwhile all who followed the bier turned round, and walked back to the *Sāgrī*, or house of prayer erected near the entrance to the garden. There they chanted prayers while the corpse-bearers entered the Tower with the dead body, and exposed it naked in one of the receptacles on the stone platform. Their appointed task being then completed, they instantly quitted the Tower, and were seen to repair to a reservoir of water near at hand, where they went through the usual process of ablution, changing all their clothes, and depositing the cast-off garments in an open stone pit, almost hidden from view, on one side of the garden. And what happened in the Tower? Scarcely had the bearers closed the portal ere forty or fifty vultures, before seated motionless on the stone parapet, swooped down on their prey. In ten minutes they had finished their work. The body was reduced to a skeleton before the mourners in the *Sāgrī* had finished their prayers. There, in the open stone coffin, exposed to the dews of heaven, the bones rested for three or four weeks, till the Nasa-sālārs returned and reverently placed them in the central well, where the skeletons of the dead, whether of high or low degree, are left to turn into dust together.

THE TOWERS OF SILENCE. 91

When I enquired about the meaning of the dog, I was told that, according to the teaching of Zoroaster, dogs as well as birds are regarded as sacred animals [1], and were formerly allowed to consume the dead bodies of Pārsīs. According to Mr. Khambātā ('Indian Antiquary,' July, 1878), the dog is of all animals the most dear to Pārsīs, on account of its undeviating faithfulness. Hence they keep up the practice of feeding a dog as a sacred obligation. In the present day a representative dog kept for the purpose accompanies the corpse, and is fed with bread as a substitute for the flesh of the dead body. Moreover, dogs are supposed to possess some mysterious power in preserving the spirits of men from the attacks of demons [2]. It is on this account that the corpse must be shewn to a dog, and if a proper dog cannot be found, any common dog taken out of the streets is brought, and the ceremony of exposing the dead body to its gaze, called Sag-dīd (from the Persian *sag*, and *dīdan*, to see), is performed some time after death. If this is not done, the soul of the deceased is liable to be assailed by evil spirits during the three days which intervene between death and judgment.

I should state here that in the belief of the Pārsīs the spirits of wicked persons are supposed to hover about in a restless state for the three days immediately succeeding death, in the neighbourhood of the Dakhmas, where also swarms of evil spirits congregate [3]. On the morning of the fourth day the soul is taken to judgment, which is passed on it by Mithra and the angels. It has then to pass a narrow bridge called *Chinvat-peretum,* 'the bridge where decision is pronounced.' The souls of the sinful,

[1] See *Vandidād* vii. 75, viii. 28; Bleeck's *Avesta,* Vol. I. pp. 104-109; Wilson's *Pārsī Religion,* pp. 325-328, 330.

[2] *Vandidād* (Bleeck) xiii. 25; Wilson's *Pārsī Religion,* pp. 49, 252.

[3] So at least says the Avastā, but according to Mr. Cāma the Pārsīs of the present day do not believe in the presence of evil spirits near the Dakhmas. He informs me that the Dakhmas of the Avastā were subterranean vaults and tombs, not towers.

being unable to pass this bridge, imagined to be sharp as a razor, fall into hell on endeavouring to cross over. The Zand-Avastā even gives the names of certain dogs believed to protect the souls of men from the assaults of evil demons before crossing the bridge. The *Vandidād* (viii. 41, 42), moreover, states that a particular devil called Naśus is frightened away by a yellow dog with four eyes, and that such a dog ought to be led along the road of a funeral procession three times.

On this account, as was explained to me by a learned Pārsī, the funeral dog is supposed to be four-eyed—that is to say, it is supposed to have two real eyes and two round spots like eyes, just above the actual eyes. I was told, too, that many yellowish-white dogs in India have this peculiarity, and that the Pārsīs try to procure such dogs, and keep them for their funeral processions. I observed nothing of the kind in the funeral dog on the occasion of the particular funeral I have here recorded. It seemed to me that the dog was a mere cur of a very ordinary type; but it struck me (before I knew that the same idea had occurred to German scholars) that the singular practice of leading a white dog at the head of the procession points to the common origin of the Pārsī and Hindū religions. For in the latter system the god of death, Yama, has two four-eyed brindled watchdogs, children of Saramā [1], who guard the road to his abode, and whose favour and protection against evil spirits are invoked every day by pious Hindūs when they perform the *kāka-bali*, or offering of rice to crows, dogs, and animals at the end of the *Vaiśvadeva* ceremony before the midday meal. The mantra recited is as follows :—*Dvau śvānau śyāma-śabalau Vaivasvata-kulodbhavau tebhyām piṇḍo*

---

[1] Saramā is the dog of Indra, and is represented in *Ṛig-veda* X. 14. 10 as the mother of Yama's dogs, called in the *Mahābhārata, Ādi-parvan* 671, Devā-śunī. In the *Ṛig-veda* this dog is said to have tracked and recovered the cows stolen by the Paṇis. Saramā is even said to be the authoress of part of the *Ṛig-veda*, X. 108.

mayā datto rakshetām pathi mām sadā, 'May the two dogs, dark and brindled, born in the family of Yama, protect me ever on the road! To them I present an offering of food.'

Having thus attempted to give some idea of the nature of a Pārsī funeral, and of the unique arrangements by which the Pārsīs endeavour to carry out the precepts of their prophet Zoroaster in the disposal of their dead, it will not be inappropriate if I add a brief account of Pārsī doctrines, and of the initiatory ceremonies performed on admission of young Pārsīs to the Zoroastrian religion, and on their incorporation as members of the Pārsī society.

I may first mention that according to the pure form of the Zoroastrian faith—as propounded by learned Pārsīs of the present day—Ormazd (sometimes written Hormazd, contracted from the full expression Ahura Mazda) is the name of the Supreme Being, to whom there is no equal, and who has no opponent. It is a mistake to suppose that Ormazd is opposed to a being called Ahriman, commonly regarded as the spirit of evil. The true doctrine is that Ormazd has created two forces in nature, not necessarily antagonistic, but simply alternating with each other—the one a force of creation, construction, and preservation; the other a force of decay, dissolution, and destruction. The first of these forces is named Spenta-mainyus, while the second or destructive power, is commonly called Ahriman, or Hariman, for Anhra-mainyus (or *Anhro-mainyus*=Sanskrit *Anho-manyu*). It is interesting to observe the analogy between the Hindū and Zoroastrian systems, Vishṇu and Rudra (Śiva) in the former being equivalent to Spenta-mainyus and Anhra-mainyus in the latter, while Brahma (neuter) corresponds to Ormazd. In later times the purity of the original doctrine became corrupted, and Ahriman was personified as a spirit of evil. In fact, all the evils in the world, whether moral or physical, are now attributed to Ahriman, while Ormazd is erroneously held to be the antagonistic principle of good.

In short, it is contended that the Pārsī religion, in spite of its apparent dualism, is properly pure Monotheism, and that the elements and all the phenomena of Nature are merely revered as creations of the one God, and as symbolical of His power.

There can be little doubt, however, that with the majority of Pārsīs the elements are regarded as simple manifestations, or rather as *developments* of the Deity, and that which is called Monotheism is really a kind of Pantheism very similar to that of Brāhmanism. The absence of all image-worship, however, is very refreshing after the hideous idolatry of the Hindū system.

So much for the Pārsī creed; and now for a few words as to the form of admission into the charmed circle of the Pārsī community.

It is a controverted point whether if any outsider wished to become a Pārsī it would be possible, even in theory, to entertain the question of his being admitted to membership by his making public confession of his faith in the Zoroastrian system. As a matter of fact no one is at present allowed to become a Pārsī unless he is born a Pārsī. No provision seems to exist for the reception of converts, and the only form of admission is for the children of Pārsīs, though occasionally the children of non-Pārsī mothers by Pārsī fathers are permitted to become members of that community. Nevertheless it is certain, from a particular form of prayer still used by Pārsī priests, that Zoroaster himself enjoined on his disciples the duty of making proselytes, and had in view a constant accession of fresh adherents, who were all to be received as converts, provided they were willing to go through certain prescribed ceremonies.

With regard to the children of Pārsī parents, every boy is admitted to membership as a disciple of the Zoroastrian religion some time between the age of seven and nine, but more usually at seven years of age, in the following manner. He is first taken to one of the fire-temples, and in a room outside the sanctuary made to undergo a kind of baptism,—that is to say, he is placed nearly naked on a stone seat, and water is poured over his head from a loṭā by a Mobed appointed to perform the rite. Next, the child is taken out into an open area, made to sit on another stone seat, and required to eat one or two leaves of the pomegranate tree—a tree held very sacred by the Pārsīs, and always planted in the precincts of their fire-temples for use in purificatory ceremonies (*Yaśna* viii. 4). After eating the leaves he is made to drink a small quantity of the water of a white bull [1]— also kept at fire-temples, and held in high estimation for its purifying properties. This completes the first portion of the ceremony. The concluding act is performed in an apartment of the fire-temple, and consists in investing the child with the sacred shirt or under-garment (called *sadara*), and sacred girdle (*kustī*). In the case of rich Pārsīs, several Mobeds, presided over by a Dastūr, are employed in celebrating this part of the rite, which is very like the Hindū *upanayana*, or induction into the condition of a twice-born man by means of the *yajñopavīta*. When parents are poor, two Mobeds may perform the ceremony, or even one may be sufficient, and a private room answers all the purposes of a fire-temple. The Mobeds sit on the ground, and the child is placed before them nearly naked. The sacred shirt is then put on, and the white woollen girdle fastened on around it, while the boy is made to repeat word by word the form of prayer which he is required to say ever afterwards, whenever the girdle is taken off or put on again (*Khurdah-Avastā* iv). The sacred shirt and girdle are the two most important outward signs and symbols of Pārsīism, and an impostor laying claim to the privileges of the Zoroastrian religion would be instantly detected by the absence of those signs,

---

[1] The Bull, whose urine is used, is called in Gujarātī *Varasīo*, and according to Mr. Khambātā must be entirely white. If a single hair of its body is not white, the bull is considered unfit for use at fire-temples.

or by his wrong use of them. But they are far more than outward signs,—they are supposed to serve as a kind of spiritual panoply. Unprotected by this armour, a man would be perpetually exposed to the assaults of evil spirits and demons, and even be liable to become a demon himself. The shirt is made of the finest white linen or cambric. It has a peculiar form at the neck, and has a little empty bag in front to show that the wearer holds the faith of Zoroaster, which is supposed to be entirely spiritual, and to have nothing material about it. The sacred shirt has also two stripes at the bottom, one on each side, and each of these stripes is separated into three, to represent the six divisions of each half-year.

It has also a heart, symbolical of true faith, embroidered in front. The *kustī*, or girdle, is made of seventy-two interwoven woollen threads, to denote the seventy-two chapters of the Yaśna, but has the appearance of a long flat cord of pure white wool, which is wound round the body in three coils. Each end of the girdle is divided into three, and these three ends again into two parts. Every Pārsī ought to take off this girdle and restore it to its proper position round the body at least five times a day. He has to hold it in a particular manner with both hands; and touching his forehead with it to repeat a prayer in Zand invoking the aid of Ormazd (*Ahura-Mazda*) for the destruction of all evil beings, evil doers —especially tyrannical rulers—and imploring pardon for evil thoughts, evil words, and evil deeds. The girdle must then be coiled round the body three times, and fastened with two particular knots (said to represent the sun and moon), which none but a Pārsī can tie in a proper manner. Every Pārsī boy is taught the whole process with great solemnity at his first initiation. When the ceremony is concluded the high-priest pronounces a benediction, and the young Pārsī is from that moment admitted to all the rights and privileges of perhaps one of the most flourishing and united communities in the world.

FUNERAL CEREMONIES AND OFFERINGS TO ANCESTORS AT BOMBAY, BENARES, AND GAYĀ.

WHEN I commenced my researches in India I was prepared to expect much perplexing variety in religious and social usages, but the actual reality far outdid my anticipations.

On one occasion, soon after my visit to the Pārsī Towers of Silence, I gained admission to the Hindū burning-ground on the shore of Back Bay at Bombay, and witnessed a curious funeral ceremony there. The body of a man about forty years of age had been burnt the day before. On the morning of my visit about twenty-four men, his relations, gathered round the ashes to perform his funeral rites and soothe his departed spirit supposed to be hovering near in a state of feverish excitement after the fiery process to which the body had just been subjected. They offered no objection to my standing close to them, nor even to my asking them questions. The ceremony commenced by one of their number examining the ashes, and carefully separating any portions of the bones that had not been calcined by the flames on the previous day. These he collected in his hands and carried outside the burning-ground, with the intention, I was told, of throwing them into the sea near at hand. This being done, the whole party gathered round the ashes of the pyre in a semicircle, and one of the twenty-four men sprinkled them with water. Then some cow-dung was carefully spread in the centre of the ashes so as to form a flat circular cake of rather more than a foot in diameter, around which a stream of cow's urine was poured from a metal vessel. Next, one of the men brought a plantain-leaf, and laid it on the circle of cow-dung so as to form a kind of dish or plate. Around the edge of the leaf were placed five round balls (*piṇḍas*) probably of rice-flour, rather smaller than cricket-balls, mixed with some brown substance. Sprigs of the Tulsī plant and fresh leaves of the betel, with a few flowers, were inserted in each ball, and a coloured cotton cord loosely suspended between them. Next, one of the relations covered the five piṇḍas with the red powder called gulāl. Then five flat wheaten cakes were placed on the plantain-leaf inside the circle of the five piṇḍas, and boiled rice was piled up on the cakes, surmounted by a small piece of ghī mixed with brown sugar.

The funeral ceremony being so far completed the deceased man's nephew, or sister's son, took an empty earthenware vase, filled it with water, and held it on his right shoulder. Starting from the north side he commenced circumambulating the five piṇḍas and the five wheaten cakes, with his left shoulder towards them, while one of the relatives with a sharp stone made a hole in the jar, whence the water spouted out in a stream as he walked round. On completing the first circuit and coming back to the north, a second incision was made with the same stone, whence a second stream poured out simultaneously with the first. At the end of the fifth round, when five streams of water had been made to spout out from five holes round the five piṇḍas, the earthenware vase was dashed to the ground on the north side, and the remaining water spilt over the ashes. Next, one of the relatives took a small metal vessel containing milk, and, with a betel-leaf for a ladle, sprinkled some drops over the rice piled on the wheaten cakes. After which, taking some water from a small lotā—or rather making another relative pour it into his hand—he first sprinkled it in a circle round the piṇḍas, and then over the cakes. Finally, bending down and raising his hands to his head, he performed a sort of pūjā to the piṇḍas, which were supposed to represent the deceased man and four other relations. This was repeated by all twenty-four men in turn. After the completion of the ceremony, the balls and cakes were left to be eaten by crows.

At Benares, honorific ceremonies and offerings in honour of departed ancestors, called Śrāddhas, are constantly performed near the Maṇi-karṇikā-kuṇḍ. This is a well, or small pool, of fetid water, not more than three feet deep, and perhaps not more than twenty feet long by ten broad, lying at a considerable depth below the surface of the ground, and declared in the Kāśī-Khaṇḍa of the Skanda-Purāṇa to have been originally created by Vishṇu from the perspiration which exuded from his body. Its highly sacred character in the eyes of the orthodox Hindū may therefore be easily understood. It is said to have been named Maṇi-karṇikā, because Mahādeva on beholding Vishṇu's well was so enraptured that his body thrilled with emotion, causing an earring to fall from his ear into the water. It is also called Mukti-kshetra, 'holy place of emancipation,' and Pūrna-śubhakara, 'cause of complete felicity.' This wonderful well is on a ghāt, by the side of the Ganges, and is resorted to by thousands of pilgrims, who may be seen all day long descending the flight of steps by which the shallow pool is surrounded on all four sides. Eagerly and with earnest faces they crowd into the water, immersing their whole bodies repeatedly, while Brāhmans superintend their ablutions, repeat and make them repeat Mantras, and receive handsome fees in return. In a niche upon the steps on the north side are the figures of Vishṇu and Śiva, to which the pilgrims, after bathing, do honour by bowing down and touching the stones underneath with their foreheads. The bathers, though manifestly much dirtier from contact with the foul water, go away under the full conviction that they are inwardly purified, and that all their sins, however heinous, have been washed away for time and for eternity.

There is another well of almost equal sanctity, named the Jnāna-vāpī, or 'pool of knowledge,' situated under a handsome colonnade in the interior of the city, between the mosque built by Aurangzīb on the site of the original Viśveśvara-nāth temple and the present Golden Temple. It is a real well of some depth and not a pool, but the water is so abominably offensive, from the offerings of flowers and rice continually thrown into it and left to putrefy, that I found it impossible to do more than take a hasty glance into the interior of the well, or even to remain in the neighbourhood long enough to note all the particulars of its surroundings. All the day long a Brāhman stands near this well and ladles out putrid water from a receptacle before him into the hands of pilgrims, who either lave their faces with the fetid liquid, or drink it with the greatest reverence. The supposed sanctity of this well is owing to the circumstance that the idol of Siva was thrown into it when the original temple of Viśveśvara-nāth was destroyed by the Musalmāns. Hence the pool is thought to be the habitation of Mahādeva himself, and the water to be permeated by his essence.

On the ghāṭ near the pool of Maṇi-karṇikā, on the day I visited it, a man was performing a Śrāddha for his mother, under the guidance of a nearly naked and decidedly stout Brāhman. The ceremony was the Daśama-śrāddha, performed on the tenth day after death. The officiating Brāhman began by forming a slightly elevated piece of ground with some sand lying near at hand. This was supposed to constitute a small vedi or altar. It was of an oblong form, but only about eight or ten inches long by four or five broad. Across this raised sand he laid three stalks of kuśa grass. Then taking a number of little earthenware platters or saucers, he arranged them round the vedi, putting tila or sesamum seed in one, rice in another, honey in a third, areca or betel-nut in a fourth, chandana or sandal in a fifth. Next, he took flour of barley 'yava) and kneaded it into one large piṇḍa, rather smaller than a cricket-ball, which he carefully deposited in the centre of the sand vedi, scattering over it jasmine flowers, khaskhas grass and wool, and placing on one side of it a betel-leaf with areca-nut and a single copper coin. Then having poured water from a loṭa into his hand, he sprinkled it over all the offerings, arranged in the manner I have described. Other similar operations followed:—Thus, for instance, an earthenware platter, containing a lighted wick, was placed near the offerings; ten other platters were filled with water, which was all poured over the piṇḍa; another small platter with a lighted wick was added to the first, then some milk was placed in another platter and poured over the piṇḍa, and then once more the piṇḍa was sprinkled with water. Finally the Brāhman joined his hands together and did pūjā to the piṇḍa. The whole rite did not last more than ten or fifteen minutes, and while it was proceeding, the man for whose mother it was performed continued to repeat Mantras and prayers under the direction of the officiating Brāhman, quite regardless of much loud talking and vociferation going on around him.

The ceremony was concluded by another ceremony called the 'feeding of a Brāhman'—that is to say, another Brāhman was brought and made to sit down near the oblations, while the man for whose mother the Śrāddha was celebrated fed him with flat cakes, ghī, sweetmeats, vegetables, and curds placed in a plate of palāśa leaves. I observed that these eatables were devoured with the greatest avidity by the man for whom they were prepared, as if he had been nursing his appetite with the intention of doing full justice to the feast.

I come now to the celebrated Śrāddha ceremonies performed in the neighbourhood of the well-known Vishṇu-pada temple at Gayā. The city of Gayā is most picturesquely situated on the river Phalgū about sixty miles south-west of Patna, near some isolated hills, or rather short ranges of hills rising abruptly out of the plain. The town itself crowns two low ridges, whose sides, covered with the houses of its narrow tortuous streets, slope down to an intervening hollow occupied by the temple and sacred tank dedicated to the Sun.

But the most sacred temple and the great centre of attraction for all Hindūs who wish to perform once in their lives a Gayā-śrāddha for their fore-fathers, is the Vishṇu-pada temple, situated on one of the ridges, and built of black stone, with a lofty dome and golden pinnacle. It contains the alleged footprint of Vishṇu in a large silver basin, under a silver canopy, inside an octagonal shrine. Piṇḍas and various kinds of offerings are placed by the pilgrims inside the basin round the footprint, and near it are open colonnades for the performance of the Śrāddhas. About six miles from the city is the well-known place of pilgrimage called Bodh-Gayā, celebrated for a monastery and numerous temples, but chiefly for the ancient tower-like structure said by the natives to be more than 2,200 years old, and originally a Buddhist monument. It has near it other alleged footprints of Vishṇu (probably once assigned to Buddha), under an open shrine. Behind the tower, on an elevated stone terrace reached by a long flight of steps, is the sacred Pīpal tree, under which, according to popular belief, the Buddha attained supreme knowledge. The tree must be many centuries old, but a succession of trees is secured by planting a new one inside the decaying stem of the old. In a chamber at the bottom of the tower-like Buddhist monument—now used as a temple—a substitute for the original figure of Buddha (carried off by the Burmese about a hundred years ago) has been placed, for the sake of the Buddhist pilgrims who come to repeat prayers and meditate under the tree; and in the same place a linga has been set up, to which the Hindūs do pūjā. When I visited the spot many persons were in the act of worshipping, and several members of the Burmese embassy, who had come to meet the Prince of Wales at Calcutta, were to be seen reverentially kneeling, praying, and meditating under the sacred tree.

ŚRĀDDHA CEREMONIES AT GAYĀ. 103

Before describing the Śrāddhas at Gayā, I may state that I asked several Pandits in different parts of India, to give me the reasons for attaching special efficacy to the celebration of religious rites for ancestors in that locality. The only reply I received was that in the Gayā-māhātmya and Gayā-śrāddha-paddhati it is declared that a powerful demon (*asura*), named Gaya, formerly resided there and tyrannized over the inhabitants. Vishnu took compassion on them, fought and killed the demon, and left a print of his foot (Vishnu-pada, vulgarly called Bishanpad) on the spot where the fight occurred, ordaining that it should be ever after called Gayā and should be consecrated to him, and that any Śrāddha performed there for fathers, forefathers, and relatives should be peculiarly efficacious in securing the immediate conveyance of their souls to his own heaven, Vaikuntha.

It is also stated in the Gayā-māhātmya that the great Rāma, hero of the Rāmāyana (himself an incarnation of Vishnu), and other heroes set the example of performing Śrāddhas to their fathers at Gayā. Brahmā is also said to have performed an Aśvamedha there, and to have consecrated the whole locality by this act. The plain truth probably is that as the Indo-Āryans proceeded southwards, the Brāhmans found it necessary to invent reasons for attaching sanctity and attracting pilgrims to other spots besides those already held sacred in the North-West.

It was on this account that the Māhātmyas of various places were gradually written and inserted in the Purānas Some of these additions, intended to exalt the importance of places like Gayā, are comparatively modern, and the Māhātmyas of one or two tīrthas, such as Pandharpur in the Dekhan, are said to have been added during the last fifty or a hundred years. I was even told that Pandharpur has become of late years a kind of rival to Gayā. Alleged footprints of Vishnu like those of Gayā are shown, and the Vithobā sects perform Śrāddhas there.

Models of the Gayā Vishnu-pada are made in brass and

in black stone, and sold for worship. Several were presented to me. They are often placed, like the Sālagrām stone, in the houses of the natives, for domestic pūjā.

With regard to the Śrāddha ceremonies generally, there seems to be much confusion of thought and obscurity, besides great inconsistency, in the accounts given by Pandits of the exact object and effect of their celebration. It may be well to explain that a distinction is made between Śrāddhas and funeral ceremonies (*antyeshṭi*). The latter are *amangala*, 'inauspicious,' while the former are *mangala*, 'auspicious.' To understand the reason for this, it should be borne in mind that when a man dies his *sthūla-śarīra* or 'gross body' is burned, but his soul quits it with the *linga-śarīra* or 'subtile body,' sometimes described as *angushṭha-mātra*, 'of the size of a thumb,' and remains hovering near. The deceased man, thus reduced to the condition of a simple individual soul invested with a subtile body, is called a preta, i.e. a departed spirit or ghost. He has no real body capable of enjoying or suffering anything, and is consequently in a restless, unsatisfactory and uncomfortable plight. Moreover, while in this condition he is held to be an impure being. Furthermore, if he dies away from his kindred, who alone can perform the funeral ceremonies, and who perhaps are unaware of his death, and unable therefore to perform them, he becomes a pisācha, or foul wandering ghost, disposed to take revenge for its misery upon all living creatures by a variety of malignant acts. I heard it remarked not long ago by a Pandit that ghosts are much less common in India now than formerly, and, on my enquiring the reason, was told that communication was now so rapid that few die without their deaths becoming known and without having funeral rites performed very soon afterwards. Besides, he added, it is now easy to reach Gayā by rail and by good carriage roads. The object, then, of the funeral rites, which are celebrated for ten days after death, is not only to soothe or give śānti by libations of consecrated water to the troubled spirit, but

ŚRĀDDHA CEREMONIES AT GAYĀ. 105

to furnish the preta with an intermediate body, between the *linga* or 'subtile' and the *sthūla* or 'gross' body—with a body, that is to say, which is capable of enjoying or suffering, and which is composed of gross particles though not of the same kind as those of the earthly gross body.

In this manner only can the preta obtain *gati*, or 'progress' onward through the temporary heaven or hell (regarded in the Hindū system as a kind of purgatory) to other births and ultimate emancipation. On the first day after death a piṇḍa or 'round ball' (generally of some kind of flour) is offered, on which the preta is supposed to feed, and which endows it with the rudiment or basis of the requisite body, whatever that basis may be. Next day another piṇḍa is offered, which gives it, perhaps, limbs, such as arms and legs. Then it receives hands, feet, &c. This goes on for ten days, and the offering of the piṇḍa on the tenth day gives the head. No sooner does the preta obtain a complete body than it becomes a pitṛi, when, instead of being regarded as impure, it is held to be a *deva*, or 'deity,' and practically worshipped as such in the Śrāddha ceremonies. Hence a Śrāddha is not a funeral ceremony, but a *worship of departed ancestors*; which worship, however, is something different from pūjā to a god. It is continued at stated periods with a view to accelerate the *gati*, or 'progress,' of the pitṛis either towards heaven—and so through the various stages of bliss, called Sālokya, Sāmīpya, and Sārūpya—or through future births to final union with the Supreme (*sāyujya*). The efficacy of Śrāddhas performed at Gayā is this, that wherever in this progress onwards departed relatives may have arrived, the Śrāddhas take them at once to Vaikuṇṭha or Vishṇu's heaven. The departed relatives especially entitled to benefit by the Śrāddha rites are as follow:—1. Father, grandfather, great-grandfather; 2. Mother, mother's father and grandfather; 3. Stepmother, if any; 4. Father's mother, grandmother, and great-grandmother; 5. Father's brothers;

6. Mother's brothers; 7. Father's sisters; 8. Mother's sisters; 9. Sisters and brothers; 10. Fathers-in-law.

An eleventh person is sometimes added, viz. the family spiritual teacher (*guru*).

Let no one suppose that the process of performing Śrāddhas at Gayā is either simple or rapid. To secure the complete efficacy of such rites, a whole round of them must be performed at about fifty distinct places in and around Gayā, besides at the most holy spot of all—the Vishṇu-pada temple—the time occupied in the process being at least eight days, and sometimes protracted to fifteen, while the money spent in fees to the officiating priests (who at Gayā are called Gaywāls = Gayā-pālas, regarded by some as an inferior order of Brāhmans) is never less than Rs. 40. But only the poorest are let off thus easily. The Mahārāja of Kaśmīr, who is a very strict Hindū, and performed Śrāddhas at Gayā the other day on his way to Calcutta, is reported to have distributed Rs. 15,000 to the Gaywāl Brāhmans.

With regard to the Śrāddhas I myself witnessed at Gayā, they were all performed in colonnades and open courts round the Vishṇu-pada temple. One example will suffice. The party celebrating the rite consisted of six men, who were of course relations, and one Gaywāl. The men sat on their heels in a line, with the officiating Gaywāl (sometimes called Paṇḍa) priest at their head. Twelve piṇḍas were formed of rice and milk, not much larger than the large marbles used by boys (called 'alleys'). They were placed with sprigs of the sacred Tulsī plant in small earthenware platters. Then on the top of the piṇḍas were scattered kuśa grass and flowers. I was told that the piṇḍas in the present case were typical of the bodies of the twelve ancestors for whom the Śrāddha was celebrated. The men had kuśa grass twisted round their fingers, in token of their hands being perfectly pure for the due performance of the rite. Next, water was poured into the palms of their hands, part of which they sprinkled on the ground, and part on the piṇḍas. One or two of the men then took threads off their clothes and laid them on the piṇḍas, which act is alleged to be emblematical of presenting the bodies of their departed ancestors with garments.

Meanwhile Mantras, or texts, were repeated, under the direction of the Gaywāl, and the hands were sometimes extended over the piṇḍas as if to invoke blessings. When all the Mantras were finished, and one or two added to pray for pardon if any minute point in the ritual had been omitted, the whole rite was concluded by the men putting their heads to the ground before the officiating Brahmān and touching his feet. Of course the number of piṇḍas varies with the number of ancestors for whom the Śrāddhas are celebrated, and the size of the balls and the materials of which they are composed differ according to the caste and the country of those who perform the rite. I saw one party in the act of forming fourteen or fifteen piṇḍas with oatmeal, which were of a much larger size than large marbles This party was said to have come from the Dekhan. Sometimes the piṇḍas were placed on betel-leaves with pieces of money (afterwards appropriated by the priests), and sometimes the water used was gradually taken out of little pots by dipping stalks of kuśa grass into the fluid, and sprinkling it over the balls. At the end of all the ceremonies the earthen platters employed were carried to a particular stone in the precincts of the temple and dashed to pieces there. No platter is allowed to be used a second time.

Amid this crash of broken crockery, the tedious round of rites, ceremonies, and vain repetitions, which, if they effect nothing else, certainly serve to enrich a goodly company of Brāhmans, is perhaps not inappropriately concluded.

INDIAN ROSARIES[1].

ROSARIES seem to be common in nearly all religious systems which attach more importance to the repetition, than to the spirituality, of prayers. It might be supposed, à priori, that to no one would a rosary be more useless and meaningless than to a Christian, who is taught when he prays to enter into his closet, to avoid vain repetitions, to pour out his heart before his Father in secret, and to cultivate spiritual intercessions 'which cannot be uttered.' Yet we know that in some Christian countries rosaries are regarded as indispensable aids to devotion. Palladius, who lived in the fourth century, tells of a certain abbot who used to repeat the Lord's prayer 300 times every day, and who secured a correct enumeration of the repetitions by dropping small pebbles into his lap.

The Kurān enjoins prayers five times a day, and good Muslims are very particular in going through prescribed forms morning, noon, and evening. It cannot, therefore, be matter of wonder that the use of rosaries (called *tasbīh*, 'praise,' and furnished with tassels called *shamsa*) is common among Indian Muhammadans. In all probability they were common among Hindūs and Buddhists long before the Christian era. Indeed, the Indian name for a rosary well expresses its meaning and use even in Roman Catholic countries. It is called in Sanskrit *japa-mālā*, 'muttering-chaplet' (and sometimes *smaraṇī*, 'remembrancer'), because

---

[1] This article and that on Samādh appeared first in the Athenæum.

by means of its beads the muttering of a definite number of prayers may be counted. But the pious Hindū not only computes his daily prayers as if they were so many rupees to be added to his capital stock in the bank of heaven, he sets himself to repeat the mere names of his favourite god, and will continue doing so for hours together.

When I was at Benares, I went early one morning to inspect the temple of the goddess Anna-pūrṇā. A devotee was seated at the door, with a rosary in his hand, muttering 'Rām, Rām, Rām' incessantly. When I had occasion to pass by a long time afterwards, I found him seated in precisely the same position, and engaged in precisely the same occupation, except that instead of repeating the god's name he prefixed to it that of his wife Sītā. I have no doubt that the whole day was divided between Rām and Sītā-ram, and an accurate account kept of the total number of repetitions.

In this respect Hindūism is behind the most corrupt forms of Christianity. It has been calculated that about ninety names and attributes are applied to Christ in the Bible. But no Romanist, however ignorant and superstitious, so far as I know, attaches any merit or efficacy to the repetition of the mere names of God.

Muhammadans reckon ninety-nine sacred names, or rather attributes, of the Deity. Some consider that the principal name, Allāh, must be counted separately. The tale is thus brought up to one hundred. I saw only ninety-nine names carved on Akbar's marble tomb near Agra, Akbar, 'the Great One,' being one of the ninety-nine. (See note at the end of this chapter.)

The voracious appetite of a Hindū in any matter connected with religious superstition far outdoes that of any other nation on earth. If one hundred titles of the Deity will satisfy the piety of an earnest-minded Muslim, nothing short of that number multiplied by ten will slake the devotional cravings of an ardent Hindū. The worshippers of Vishṇu adore him by 1,000 sacred names, and the votaries of Śiva by 1,008 names. The whole catalogue is given in the Mahā-bhārata and the Purāṇas.

Curiously enough among the names of Śiva occur Haya, 'a horse,' and Gardabha, 'an ass' (Mahā-bhārata XIII. 1149), which the Vedāntist has no difficulty in accepting as suitable titles of the One universal Being with whom the god Śiva and every existing thing in the universe is identified.

It is not unreasonable to conjecture that the original invention of rosaries is due to India. They were as much the offspring of necessity as was the invention of the Sūtras, or brief memorial rules for the correct performance of the complicated ritual. No other country in the world stands in such need of aids to religious exercises. Vaishnavas, Śaivas, Buddhists, Jains, and Muhammadans depend upon these contrivances for securing the accurate discharge of their daily round of interminable repetitions.

The rosary of a Vaishṇava is made of the wood of the Tulasī (vulgarly *Tulsī*), or holy basil, a shrub sacred to Vishṇu, and regarded as a metamorphosis of Rāma's pattern-wife Sītā. This rosary should consist of 108 smooth beads. That worn by Śaivas consists of thirty-two and sometimes sixty-four berries of the Rudrāksha tree (Elæocarpus). These seeds are as rough as the Tulsī beads are smooth, and are generally marked with five lines, the roughness symbolizing, I suspect, the austerities connected with the worship of Śiva, and the five lines standing for the five faces or five distinct aspects of the god.

The Musalmān *tasbīh* contains one hundred beads, which are generally made of date-stones, or of the sacred earth of Karbalā. They are used in repeating the hundred names of God or certain words of the Kurān, every decade of beads being separated by a tassel. Some Sunnīs are prohibited from employing rosaries, and count by means of the joints of their fingers.

It might be wearisome if I were to attempt a description

of the diverse uses to which different kinds of rosaries are applied in India.

I was told by a Gṛihastha, or layman of the Svāmi-Nārāyan sect of Vaishṇavas, that he was able by help of his *japa-mālā* to go on muttering Svāmi-Nārāyan, Svāmi-Nārāyan, Svāmi-Nārāyan one hundred and eight times with perfect precision at his morning and evening devotions, and that he attributed great efficacy to the act.

High-caste Brāhmans, on the other hand, merely use their rosaries to assist them in counting up their daily prayers, especially the well-known Gāyatrī from the Ṛigveda (*Tat savitur vareṇyam bhargo devasya dhīmahi dhiyo yo naḥ praćodayāt*), which is repeated five, ten, twenty-eight, or one hundred and eight times at the dawn and sunset Sandhyās. The very sound of this precious mantra (called Gāyatrī, from the metre in which it is composed), quite irrespectively of the sense (which may be rendered, 'Let us adore that excellent glory of the divine Vivifier: may he enlighten our understandings'), is a mine of inexhaustible spiritual wealth to those favoured beings whose second spiritual birth—conferred by investiture with the sacred thread—entitles them to repeat it. Manu (II. 77) declares that this sacred text was 'milked out' of the three Vedas and ordains that 'a Brāhman may attain beatitude by simple repetition of the Gāyatrī, whether he perform other rites or not,' and 'that having repeated the Gāyatrī three thousand times he is delivered from the greatest guilt.'

It is noticeable, moreover, that the proud Brāhman who claims to be the true owner of this valuable piece of religious property is careful to conceal his hand in a sort of bag called a Gomukhī while engaged in counting out his morning and evening store of accumulated Gāyatrīs. In fact, every Hindū is persuaded that jealous demons are ever on the watch to obstruct his religious exercises, and ever eager, like cunning thieves, to abstract a portion of their merit. This is the true secret of the universal homage paid throughout India to Gaṇeśa, lord of the demon-hosts. I have myself often seen Brāhmans seated on the margin of sacred streams, with their faces turned towards the east, and apparently intently occupied in gazing on vacancy. On a closer inspection, I found that their right hands were mysteriously concealed in a red bag. Prayers were being repeated and counted up by help of the *japa-mālā*, and the repeater, even if too proud to betray any fear of thievish demons, seemed at any rate to understand that the value of his prayers would be increased by his taking heed not 'to be seen of men.' We must not forget, too, that a Hindū is taught by many of his own sacred precepts that the merit of religious exercises is destroyed by ostentation.

Nothing, however, comes up to the Buddhist's idea of the efficacy of repeated prayers. His rosary, like that of the Vaishṇavas, consists of 108 beads, which in China are often arranged in two rings. I never met with any native who could explain the proper meaning of *om maṇi padme hūm*, 'hail to the jewel in the lotus!' although every Buddhist in Tibet believes that the oftener this six-syllabled formula is repeated by help of rosaries and prayer-wheels the greater merit will accrue to the repeater. According to some, the repetition of the six syllables exercises some sort of protective or preventive influence with reference to the six Gatis, or forms of transmigration. In China the repeated prayer is 'Omito Fat' or 'Omito Fo' (for *amita Buddha*, 'the infinite Buddha'), or 'Nama Amitābha, and in Japan, 'Namu Amida Butsu' (for *nama amita Buddhāya*, 'honour to the infinite Buddha').

It is not uncommon to meet Buddhists in the neighbourhood of Darjīling who, while they are talking to you, continue whirling their prayer-wheels, held in their right hands, and made to revolve like a child's toy. The wheel consists of a metal cylinder on which the form of prayer is engraved. It must be whirled, by means of a handle, in a particular direction (I think with the sun); if made to revolve the other way the number of its rotations will be set down to the debtor rather than the creditor side of the owner's account.

A friend of mine who had to hold a conversation with a pious Buddhist, intent on redeeming every instant of time for the repetition of prayers, came away from the interview under the impression that all Buddhists regard all Europeans as possessed with evil spirits. The Buddhist's diligent gyration of his wheel was mistaken by my friend for a form of exorcism.

It is said that the Buddhist monks of Ladakh have a still more economical arrangement, and one not unworthy of the attention of monks in other monasteries—when regarded, I mean, from the point of view of an ingenious contrivance for saving time and making the most of both worlds. An infinite number of prayers are repeated, and yet the whole time of the monastery is saved for making money by industrial occupations. Long strips of the usual Buddhist prayer are rolled round cylinders, and these cylinders are made to revolve, like the works of a clock, by means of heavy weights wound up every morning and evening. A single monk takes five minutes to set the entire spiritual machinery in motion, and then hastens to join his brothers at their mundane occupations; the whole body of monks feeling that the happiness and prosperity of the community are greatly promoted by the substitution of the precept 'laborare est orare,' for 'orare est laborare.'

It should be mentioned that in times of emergency or difficulty additional weights are attached to the cylinders, and an additional impetus thus given to the machinery, and, of course, increased force and cogency to the rotatory prayers.

My friend the Collector of Kaira, in whose camp I stayed for about a fortnight, had occasion one day to ascend a hill in his district much overgrown with trees. There to his surprise he came suddenly upon an old hermit, who had been living for a long time without his knowledge in the jungle at the summit. Mr. Sheppard found the ancient recluse in a hut near a rude temple, concealed from observation by the dense underwood. He was engaged in his evening religious exercises, and, wholly regardless of the presence of his European visitor, continued turning with both hands and with evident exertion a gigantic rosary. A huge wooden roller, suspended horizontally from the posts of the shed, supported a sort of chain composed of fifteen rough wooden balls, each as big as a child's head. As he kept turning this enormous rosary round and round, each ball passed into his hands, and whilst he held the several balls in his grasp he repeated, or rather chanted in a low tone, a short prayer to the god Rāma. All the wooden balls underwent this process of pious manipulation several times before he desisted. The muscular exertion and consequent fatigue must have been great, yet the entire operation was performed with an air of stoical impassiveness. Then the devotee went into another shed, where on another cross-beam, supported by posts, were strung some heavy logs of hard wood, each weighing about twenty pounds. Having grasped one of these with both hands, he dashed it forcibly against the side post, and then another log against the first. Probably the clashing noise thus produced was intended to give increased effectiveness to the recitation of his prayers.

Sleeman somewhere relates how he happened once to be staying in the neighbourhood of an Indian village, the inhabitants of which were divided into two religious parties—those who advocated a noisy musical worship, and those who attributed greater efficacy to a quiet religious ceremonial. The two parties lived together very amicably, agreeing to set apart certain hours of the day for an alternate use of the village temple. When the noisy faction had possession the din was terrific.

In short, almost every religious idea that the world has ever known has in India been stimulated to excessive growth, and every religious usage carried to preposterous extremes. Hence, if a Hindū temple has a choir of musicians, its excellence is estimated by the deafening discord it gives out at the morning and evening pūjā; and if a devotee uses a rosary its effectiveness is supposed to depend on the dimensions of its beads, which may vary from small seeds to heavy balls as big as a human skull.

Note.—The ninety-nine names or attributes of the Deity are called by the Muhammadans *ism-i'azīm,* 'The glorious names.' Some of these are as follow :—The Lord (Rabb), the King (Mālik), the Merciful (Rahmān), the Compassionate (Rahīm), the Holy (Kuddūs), the Creator (Khālik), the Saviour (Salām), the Excellent ('Azīz), the Omniscient ('Ālim), the Omnipotent (Jabbār), the Pardoner (Ghafūr), the Glorious (Majīd), the Beneficent (Karīm), the Wise (Hakīm), the Just ('Ādil), the Benign (Latīf), the One (Wāhid), the Eternal (Bākī), the Survivor (Wāris), the Last (Ākhir), the Guide (Hādī), the Director (Rashīd), the Patient (Sabūr).

INDIAN FAMINES.

In the course of my travels through some of the famine-districts of India I made notes of a few particulars which came under my observation? These notes I here give just as they were written down at the time.

The area of the scarcity and famine is immense, stretching, as it does, from the neighbourhood of Poona, not far from Bombay, to Tinnevelly, near the extreme south of the Madras Presidency. But it must not be supposed that the drought has been equally severe everywhere. Although in many places, where the usual rainfall is thirty-five or forty-five inches, only fifteen or twenty have fallen, yet other parts of the country have been more favoured. Moreover, all the belts of land reached by the grand system of irrigation, which stretches between the Godāvarī, Kistna, and Kāveri rivers—fertilizing the soil wherever it penetrates, and forcing even haters of the English rule to admit that no other Rāj has conferred such benefits on India—present a marvellous contrast to the vast tracts of arid waste which meet the eye of the traveller as he journeys by the Great Indian Peninsula, Madras, and South Indian Railways.

A sad feature in the spectacle is the condition of the cattle. As I travelled from one place to another, often diverging from the neighbourhood of the railway to less frequented outlying districts, I saw hundreds of lean, half-famished kine endeavouring to eke out a doomed existence on what could only in mockery be called herbage. When it is remembered that the cow is a principal source of sustenance to Hindūs of nearly all castes, and that no such animal as a cart-horse is to be found in India—all agricultural labour depending on the ox—some idea may be formed of the terrible calamity involved in a mortality among cattle. Even the cows and oxen that survive will be almost useless. Utterly enfeebled and emaciated, they will have little power left either to yield milk or to drag a plough through soil caked and indurated by months of unmitigated sunshine.

But the saddest feature of all is the condition of the human inhabitants of this great peninsula. I will simply recount what I know and testify of what I have seen with my own eyes in the Madras Presidency. Only a fortnight ago, I saw many thousands of poor famine-driven creatures from the villages round Madras collected on the shore and on the pier. They were crowding round the sacks of rice-grain, with which the sands for at least a mile were thickly covered and almost concealed from view, the grain-bags being often piled up in mounds to the height of fifteen or twenty feet. Yet no onslaught was made on the grain. A few men scattered about, armed with canes, were guarding the sacks for the merchants who owned them, and were sufficient to prevent any attempts at depredation though here and there I detected surreptitious efforts, not so much to make incisions, as to enlarge any happy defects apparent in the material which enclosed the coveted food. What generally happened was this:—Very few of the grain-bags were so well made as to make any leakage impossible, and sprinklings of rice were thus scattered about everywhere. The knowledge of this circumstance was the cause of the vast concourse of miserable, half-starved, emaciated creatures who had walked many miles to the spot. Men and women, old and young, even cripples, mothers with infants on their hips, and naked children—all more or less pitiable in their leanness and in their hard-set aspect of misery — were earnestly engaged in gleaning up every grain that escaped from the sacks on the pier and on the shore. Many were provided with coarse sieves, by means of which a few rice-grains were, with infinite pains, separated from bushels of sand. On the pier every crevice was searched, and every discoloured grain eagerly scraped up, mixed as it was with dirt, ejected betel-juice, and filth of all kinds. This is a brief and imperfect description of what I saw with my own eyes.

And now it will be asked, what measures are being taken to meet and mitigate the impending calamity? My answer is that, so far as I have observed, the Governments of Madras and Bombay are fully alive to their duty. They are organizing relief as speedily as possible. Before I left Madras, I saw thirty ships laden with grain at anchor in the roads. Large surf-boats were continually plying between the ships and the shore; heavily laden trucks were passing and repassing on the pier; and dozens of huge cranes, worked by countless coolies, were refilling the trucks as they returned empty. Thirty-five thousand human beings were daily being fed at Madras with cooked food or supplied with raw rice, but of these about two-thirds were taken in hand by benevolent rich natives. Kuddapah, Bellary, Kurnool, and other towns were also feeding a large number; some as many as 2,000 every day. As I left Madras the rail was blocked with trucks laden with grain. Indeed, all the districts near the railway are tolerably certain of being adequately relieved. But how is it to be conveyed to distant corners of the famine-stricken land? And, worse still, how is the 'water-famine' likely to ensue two or three months hence to be met? There is a large tank near here which usually contains fifteen feet of water, and is now nearly dry. Possibly partial showers of rain may yet fall in particular districts. At Trichinopoly, where I have recently been staying with the Collector Mr. Sewell, more than three inches of rain fell on Sunday and Monday last. This downpour will, I trust, check the cholera already gaining ground there. Here at Madura scarcely any rain fell, while the adjoining district was being drenched.

It is evident, indeed, that the most severe trial has yet to come, and a hard task lies before the Collectors and Deputy-Collectors everywhere. They must not intervene with aid before the proper time, and they must by no means intervene too late. They have to inquire when and where and how relief is to be given, and they ought to provide work for all who are relieved. Many Collectors are at work from morning to night in their offices deciding these difficult questions.

Surely, then, I may be allowed to close this imperfect account of the distressing scenes through which I have lately passed by adding a tribute to the energy and devotion of our fellow-countrymen—the rulers of this land—who are everywhere exerting themselves to the utmost in the present crisis. Numbers who had a right to furlough, or were looking forward to a holiday at Delhi, are remaining cheerfully at their posts.

Indeed, my second visit to India has impressed me more than ever with the desire shown by the Queen's officers in this country to govern India righteously and to make our rule a blessing to the people. Evidences of the benefits we have conferred, and are still daily conferring, meet one at every turn. But I crave permission to add a word or two of warning. In our anxiety to conciliate the natives, let us beware of alienating our own officers. Let the Central Governments balance the scales evenly between the two. Our hold of India depends mainly on the personal influence of the representatives of those Governments in the several districts, and the personal influence of these representatives depends mainly on the degree of support they receive from the central seats of authority. Every Commissioner and Collector is a little Viceroy in his own territory. He has vast responsibilities laid upon him, and he ought to be trusted by his superiors. It is right that the British public should be made aware that while the Queen is being proclaimed Empress at Delhi, and the loyalty of her Indian subjects is being evoked by the holding of Darbārs and the distribution of rewards to deserving natives in every Collectorate, much irritation of feeling is apparent among her European subjects. Over and over again I have heard able officers exclaim, 'I dare not act on my own responsibility in this emergency. Cholera may break out; symptoms of serious riots may show themselves; people may be dying of famine; instant action is needed, but I dare not trust to my own life-long knowledge and experience of India—I must telegraph for instructions.' There can be no doubt that the energy of the most successful administrator will be paralyzed if he is made to feel that a single blunder or an act of indiscretion will be visited by a formal reprimand, which is sure to find its way into every native newspaper and become the talk of all the bazaars throughout his district. I much fear that the benefits which have accrued to India from the trust reposed by the old East India Company in its officers are in danger of being sacrificed to the present mania for the centralization of authority.

A RELIEF CAMP.

In my previous notes on some of the famine districts, I expressed a doubt as to whether any organization for the relief of the sufferers, however complete, would be able to reach every corner of the immense area over which the drought and dearth extend. Now that I have travelled in various directions over a great part of the country from Bombay to Cape Comorin, and noted with my own eyes what is being done to spread a network of this organization over every separate district, so as to embrace the most remote places, I am bound to admit that my fears were unfounded. Indeed, it would be difficult to use exaggerated language in speaking of the zeal, ability, and devotion displayed by Indian civilians and other executive officials in the present emergency.

I have recently been staying with the energetic Collector of Salem (Mr. Longley), and early one morning I visited with him one of the Relief Camps now being constructed in the large district over the welfare of which he presides. The spot chosen for this Camp is an elevated piece of ground beautifully situated near a spring of excellent water, close under some chalk hills (supposed by the natives to be formed of the bones of the mythical bird Jaṭāyus, killed by Rāvaṇa when carrying off Sītā), and not far from the base of the Shervaroy Hills—the sanatarium of this part of India. On this ground nearly twenty long huts or sheds—each capable of accommodating forty persons—had already been constructed with bamboo poles, course cocoa-nut matting, and palmyra leaves. I was told that as only three months of the famine have passed, and at least four months have still to be provided for, it will be necessary to erect 100 similar huts in this one Camp, with accommodation for 4,000 or 5,000 people.

In fact, these Relief Camps may be described as temporary workhouses with wards for the old, feeble, and infirm, where the famine-driven inhabitants of outlying districts will take refuge, and where they will be comfortably housed, fed, and, if strong enough, made to work, till better times arrive.

In Mr. Longley's camp the two classes of workers and non-workers into which every camp-community will be divided were plainly distinguishable from each other. The former were engaged in making new huts, breaking stones for a road, clearing the environs of the Camp, and keeping the whole place clean; while the non-workers were sitting on the ground in three rows, exposed, by their own choice, to the heat of a tropical sun for the sake of the warmth which insufficient food made necessary to them. It was piteous to see the emaciated old men and shrivelled old women, many of them blind or crippled, whose existence is being prolonged for a few months by the minimum of nourishment they are now receiving at the hands of a paternal Government; but still more sad to look upon the unclothed skeletons of young men, boys, and little children with drawn features, shoulder bones standing out, legs like thin sticks, and ribs enclosing the feeble organs of their shrunk bodies, like bony cages, every bar of which was visible.

Yet I was told that the great difficulty in Indian famines is not so much the effective distribution of relief as the effective application of any proper method of detecting the vast number of undeserving applicants who ought not to be relieved at all. We were informed that about 300 applicants for food, without work, ought to have been present on the day of our visit, but that more than half had run off during the night, either because they disliked the confinement to which they had been subjected, or because they had heard of the intended visit of the Collector and other Sahibs, and were filled with vague suspicions and fears of being questioned too closely. Yet no one is admitted to the Camp without a ticket, which is supposed to be given to deserving objects only. Those who were seated on the ground in our presence had empty earthenware bowls before them, in each of which about a pound of good boiled rice was placed while we looked on. This, with another meal administered in the evening, is held to be sufficient to keep the body and soul of a non-worker together. The workers are, of course, better fed. It was curious to observe the cleverness with which some of the recipients of the dole of boiled rice quietly pressed down the eagerly accepted ration with their hands, hoping thereby to be served with a little more than the due allowance. Each recipient then made a hole with his hands in the centre of his mess, and waited patiently till the half-pint of pepper-water (*mulliga tanir*), to which every one was entitled, had been poured into the cavity. Finally, by means of the spoons, with which every man was naturally provided, and in a manner which those only can understand who have seen a low-caste native seated on his hams with head bent back, mouth expanded to its utmost limits, and all four fingers and thumb converted into a convenient scoop for introducing into the aperture as much rice as a human being is capable of swallowing at once, every grain was disposed of before our eyes—in most cases with the utmost avidity and apparent satisfaction.

It is intended, I understand, that caste prejudices shall be, as far as possible, respected. Those of the same caste will be grouped together in separate companies, and cooks of sufficiently high caste will be provided. But no genuine Brāhman is ever likely to enter a Relief Camp. He will rather starve than submit to the chances of pollution, which to him would be worse than death. Starving

Brāhmans, who in some parts of the country may be even more plentiful than starving Śūdras, will have to be cared for by their own richer caste-fellows. I am sorry to have to add to this brief narrative that pestilence is following closely in the track of famine. At Madras three Europeans have recently succumbed to attacks of cholera, and the number of fatal cases among the natives is increasing every day. In some country towns and villages I have visited I have been cautioned to beware of a bad type of the disease prevalent all around. Of course, I could go into further details, but what I have written will, at least, give an idea of how the seven or eight millions of pounds sterling[1] which the present famine is likely to cost will be spent.

[1] The actual cost turned out to be thirteen millions.

GENERAL IMPRESSIONS AND NOTES AFTER TRAVELS IN NORTHERN INDIA.

BOMBAY, MARCH 6, 1876.

THE 'Serapis' is now lying at anchor before our eyes in Bombay Harbour, reminding us that the Prince of Wales is on his road to this port, and that England will soon be preparing to welcome his return home. The interest excited by his tour has now culminated, and special correspondents are either bound homewards or addressing themselves to an effective winding up of their communications by a telling description of the closing scene. Even after the Prince's return his doings in India are certain to continue a fashionable theme of conversation during the London season of 1876, and the Session will assuredly be marked by a constant recurrence to Indian topics. Every Parliamentary orator will drag in, relevantly or irrelevantly, allusions to the expedition and its results for the benefit of his constituents. Newspapers, reviews, and periodicals will contain trenchant articles, bristling with point, epigram, and criticism, if they do not cut the knot of our Indian difficulties.

Meanwhile, I will endeavour to record, in plain language, a few particulars relative to our Indian possessions, which have impressed themselves on me most forcibly in the course of my tour in the Prince's track.

It must be confessed that the impressions of a flying traveller are not generally worth recording; but as circumstances have given me peculiar opportunities of observing the country, and mixing with the natives, after many years spent in studying their languages and literature, some value may possibly attach to my experiences, which I propose to recount under distinct heads, commencing with a few notes on the political divisions of India, ancient and modern.

Ancient Political Divisions.

India has no historical literature of its own. Hence there are only three means of arriving at any knowledge of its early history; 1. By sifting fact from fiction, sober narrative from poetical exaggeration in its early heroic poetry, especially in its two great poems, the Rāmāyana, and Mahā-bhārata; 2. By examining the inscriptions on rocks, pillars, and monuments, on copperplate grants of land, and coins scattered in various places from Kaśmīr to Kuttack; 3. By putting together all allusions to India, and observations on its condition to be found in the literature of other countries. The accounts written by two Chinese travellers—Fa-hian in the beginning of the fifth century of our era, and Hiouen Thsang in the beginning of the seventh—who made pilgrimages to all the early Buddhist shrines, have done good service in this latter way.

The very name India is partly derived from a foreign source. It is the European adaptation of the word Hindū, which was used by the Persians for their Āryan brethren, because the latter settled in the districts surrounding the streams of the Sindhu (pronounced by them *Hindhu*, and now called Indus). The Greeks, who probably gained their first conceptions of India from the Persians, changed the hard aspirate into a soft, and named the Hindūs Ἰνδοί (Herodotus IV 14, V. 3). After the Indo-

Āryans had spread themselves over the plains of the Ganges, the Persians called the whole of the region between the Panjāb and Benares Hindūstān, or 'abode of the Hindūs,' and this name is used in India at the present day, especially by the Musalmān population.

The classical names for India, however, as commonly employed in Sanskṛit literature and recognized by the whole Sanskṛitic race, are *Āryāvarta*, 'abode of the 'Āryas,' and *Bhārata-varsha,* 'the country of king Bharata' (a prince of the lunar dynasty, who must have ruled over a large extent of territory in ancient times). The former name is more particularly applicable to India above the Vindhya mountains.

After its occupation by the great Āryan race, India appears to have yielded itself up an easy prey to every invader. According to Herodotus (IV. 44), it was subjugated by Darius Hystaspes (called in Persian Dārā Gushtasp). This conquest, if conquest it deserves to be called, probably took place between 521 and 518 B.C., about the time of the rise of Buddhism, and must have been very partial. It was doubtless followed by a certain amount of traffic between Persia and India, and to this commercial intercourse may be due the introduction into India of many new ideas—religious and philosophical—and perhaps also of the Phœnician alphabet, with which that of some of the Aśoka edicts and inscriptions is thought to be connected (see p. 129, note 1).

The expedition of Alexander the Great (called by the Hindūs, Iskandar, or Sikandar) to the banks of the Indus, about 327 B.C., is a well-known and better authenticated fact. To this invasion is due the first trustworthy information obtained by Europeans concerning the north-westerly portion of India and the region of the five rivers, down which the Grecian troops were conducted in ships by Nearchus.

The first reliable date in Indian History is the era of Ćandra-gupta (= Sandrokottus)—the founder of the Maurya dynasty, who, after taking possession of Pāṭaliputra (Palibothra, Patna) and the kingdom of Magadha (Behār), extended his dominion over all Hindūstān, and presented a determined front towards Alexander's successor, Seleukos Nikator, the date of the commencement of whose reign was about 312 B.C. When the latter contemplated invading India from his kingdom of Bactria, so effectual was the resistance offered by Čandra-gupta that the Greek thought it politic to form an alliance with the Hindū king, and sent his own countryman Megasthenes as an ambassador to reside at his court[1].

To this circumstance we owe the earliest authentic account of Indian manners, customs, and usages by an intelligent observer who was not a native, and Megasthenes's narrative, preserved by Strabo, furnishes a basis on which a fair inference may be founded that Brāhmanism and Buddhism existed side by side in India on amicable terms in the fourth century B.C. There is even ground for believing that King Čandra-gupta himself was secretly a Buddhist, though in public he gave homage to the gods of the Brāhmans.

Čandra-gupta's reign is thought to have lasted from 315 to 291 B.C., and that of his son and successor Vindusāra from 291 to 263 B.C.

Aśoka (who called himself Priyadarśin) the grandson of Čandra-gupta, did for Buddhism what Constantine did for Christianity—gave an impetus to its progress by adopting it as his own creed. Buddhism, then, became the state religion, the national faith of the whole kingdom of Magadha, and therefore of a great portion of India. For gradually during this period most of the petty princes of India from Peshāwar and Kaśmīr to the river Kistna, and from Surat to Bengal and Orissa, if not actually brought under subjection to the kings of Magadha, were compelled to acknowledge their paramount authority. Aśoka's reign

[1] In the second century B.C. some of the Bactrian kings made conquests in India.

AŚOKA'S EDICTS. ROCK INSCRIPTIONS. 129

was remarkable for a great Buddhist council (the third since Buddha's time), held about 246 or 247 B.C., when the Tripiṭaka or three collections of writings in the Pāli language (brought from ancient Magadha, and a form of Māgadhī Prākrit, though different from Jain Māgadhī), containing all the teachings of Buddha—who is supposed to have never written anything himself—was finally settled.

Moreover, Aśoka's edicts in Pāli[1] inscribed on rocks and stone pillars (probably between 251 and 253 B.C.) furnish the first authentic records of Indian history. According to Mr. R. N. Cust[2], ten of the most important inscriptions are found on five rocks and five pillars, though numerous other monuments are scattered over the whole of Northern India, from the Indian Ocean on the west to the Bay of Bengal on the east, from the slopes of the Vindhya range on the south to the Khaiber Pass on the north.

The five most important rock inscriptions are those on (1) the Rock of Kapurda-garhi in British Afghānistān, forty miles east-north-east of Peshāwur; (2) the Rock of Khalsi, situated on the bank of the river Jumnā, just where it leaves the Himālaya mountains, fifteen miles west of the hill-station of Mussourie; (3) the Rock of Girnār, half a mile to the east of the city of Junagurh, in Kathiāwār; (4) the Rock of Dhauli in Kuttack (properly Katak), twenty miles north of Jagan-nāth; (5) the Rock of Jaugaḍha, in a large old fort eighteen miles west-north-west of Ganjam, in Madras.

The five most important pillars are: (1) the Pillar at

[1] These inscriptions are in two quite distinct kinds of writing. That at Kapurda-garhi—sometimes called Northern Aśoka or Ariano-Pāli—is clearly Semitic, and traceable to a Phœnician source, being written from right to left. That at Girnār is not so clearly so. It probably came through a Pahlavī channel, and gave rise to Deva-nāgarī. General Cunningham believes this character—sometimes called Southern Aśoka or Indo-Pāli—to have originated in India.

[2] See an interesting article in the 'Journal of the National Indian Association,' for June 1879.

Delhi, known as Firoz Shāh's Lāt; (2) another Pillar at Delhi, which was removed to Calcutta, but has recently been restored; (3) the Pillar at Allahabad, a single shaft without capital, of polished sandstone, thirty-five feet in height; (4) the Pillar at Lauriya, near Bettiah, in Bengal; (5) another Pillar at Lauriya.

The inscriptions on these monuments present us with the best and most interesting edicts of Aśoka. They prohibit the slaughter of animals either for food or for sacrifice, appoint missionaries for the propagation of Buddhistic doctrines in various countries, inculcate peace and mercy, charity and toleration, morality and self-denial, and what is still more remarkable, enjoin seasons of general national humiliation and confession of sin every five years.

Seven Buddhist kings of the Maurya dynasty, under whom the kingdom of Magadha continued to enjoy great prosperity (though probably not an equally extended dominion), reigned after Aśoka, until the year 195 B.C. They were succeeded by the Sanga Rājas, the chief of whom built the great Buddhist tope at Sanchī about 188 B.C., and by another line of Buddhist kings called Kanwa, who reigned till about 31 B.C. An Āndhra dynasty then acquired power in Magadha.

There were of course many rival principalities existing in India long before the rise of the kingdom of Magadha, some of which traced back the pedigrees of their kings to the ancient dynasties of the heroic period. No one kingdom ever acquired universal dominion, though occasionally a single prince, conspicuous for unusual energy and administrative power, compelled a large number of less able chieftains to submit to his suzerainty, in which case he was sometimes called a Mahārājādhirāja, and sometimes a Ćakravartī.

To fix the chronological order of the most ancient dynasties, is of course impossible. It will be sufficient to enumerate some of the most important (with occasional approximate dates) from the earliest times, merely pre-

ANCIENT KINGDOMS OF NORTHERN INDIA. 131

mising that two lines of monarchs were originally dominant in the north of India, one of which was called Solar, because fabled to have derived its origin from the god of the Sun, while the other, called Lunar, pretended to trace back its pedigree to the god of the Moon. Some of the modern Rājput princes claim to belong to one or other of these two lines.

I begin with an enumeration of the chief kingdoms in Northern India [1]:—

1. The ancient kingdom of Kośala, or Ayodhyā, the capital of which was Ayodhyā (now Ajūdhya) on the river Sarayu, or Saryu (now Gogra). Here reigned Daśaratha, of the solar race, and afterwards his son Rāma, the hero of the Rāmāyaṇa.

2. The ancient kingdom of Videha (modern Tirhut) of which the first capital was Mithilā, and afterwards Benares. Rāma's wife, Sītā, was the daughter of Janaka, king of this country.

3. The ancient kingdom of the city of Hastināpur, 57 miles north-east of the ancient Delhi (Indra-prastha). These were the capitals of the heroes of the Mahā-bhārata and kings of the Lunar line, some of whom appear to have dwelt at Pratishṭhāna (Allahabad).

4. The kingdom of Avanti or Oujein (Ujjayinī) in Mālwa, reigned over by the celebrated Vikramāditya, whose reign is the starting point of the Hindū Samvat era, 57 B.C. He is said to have driven out the Śakas or Scythian (Turanian) tribes from Western India, and established his dominion over almost the whole of Hindūstān. According to some, he was afterwards defeated by the very tribes he first conquered.

5. The kingdom of Magadha already described.

6. The ancient kingdom of Kanyā-kubja or Kanauj, in the neighbourhood of Oudh (Panćāla). It was intensely

---

[1] A good summary which I have here consulted, will be found in a 'History of India for Schools,' by Mr. E. Lethbridge.

Brāhmanical and always took part with the Brāhmans against the Buddhists. A dynasty called Gupta (supposed to be descended from the great Rāma) was established here in the second century of our era. This dynasty conquered the Sāh or Sinha[1] dynasty of Gujarāt about the middle of the third century, and founded a powerful kingdom and a second capital at Vallabhī in Kāthiāwār. It may be noted that a dynasty of Rājputs called Rāhtor subsequently ruled in Kanauj from about A.D. 470.

7. The Vallabhī Gupta dynasty, just named, which reigned over Gujarāt till about the middle of the 7th century, and extended its dominion into Hindūstān and the Dekhan. Its second king, Samudra-Gupta, is said to have conquered Ceylon. One of its monarchs, named Śilāditya, who reigned in the fifth century, was converted to the Jaina religion. Its last king, Toramāna, was expelled by an invasion of Persians. The Vallabhī dynasty then migrated to Mewār or Rājputāna (where it became the founder of the Rājput state of Mewār or Udaipur). It left behind a Rājput tribe named Chaura who became the rulers of Gujarāt, and transferred their capital from Vallabhī to Anhalwāra, now called Patan. They were superseded by the Salonkhyas, about A.D. 942.

8. The Rājput state of Mewār or Udaipur founded by the Vallabhī Guptas from Oudh, as described above.

9. The Chaura kingdom established at Anhalwāra (now Patan) as mentioned above.

10. The Delhi Rājput dynasty, of which the last king was Prithivī Rāja (the hero of Chand's poetry), who was first victorious over and finally conquered by Muhammad Ghori in 1175.

11. A Brāhmanical dynasty settled at Lahor, in the Punjāb, known by its coins, having a bull on one side and

---

[1] The Sāhs or Sinhas are thought to have been of Parthian origin, and to have worshipped the Sun. A list of nineteen monarchs of the dynasty has been deduced from its coins, which are marked by an image of the Sun. Their capital was Sehore, but their sway extended over nearly the whole of what is now the Bombay Presidency.

ANCIENT KINGDOMS OF SOUTHERN INDIA. 133

a horseman on the other. The last king was Bhīmapāl, whose predecessor Jaipāl was taken prisoner by Māhmūd of Ghaznī.

12. The kingdom of Gaur (Gauda) or Bengal. Not much is known of its earliest dynasties noticed in the Mahābhārata. The Pāl line of kings, who were Buddhists, reigned from the 9th to the 11th century of our era, and one of them was acknowledged as a Mahārājādhirāja. They were succeeded by the princes called Sena, one of whom (Ādiśvara) invited five pure Brāhmans to come from Kanauj to Bengal. These came, attended by men of the Kāyastha (writer) caste, and became the ancestors of the five classes of Brāhmans and Writers now found there. The capital of the Bengal dynasty was first Gaur and afterwards Nuddea.

The following are some of the ancient South Indian kingdoms:—

1. The Pāndya kingdom founded by a man named Pāndya who came from Ayodhyā. Its capital was Madura. It lasted from the fifth century B.C. till the eleventh century A.D.

2. The Chola kingdom, founded by Tayaman Nāle. Its capital was Kānchīpuram (Conjeveram). For a long period (between 350 B.C. and 214 A.D.) the Chola kingdom was united with the Pāndya, but again became independent. Then its capital was transferred to Tanjor. In the fourteenth century it was merged in the Marātha kingdom.

3. The Chera kingdom comprising Travankor, Malabar and Western Mysor. It existed from the first to the tenth century A.D.

4. The kingdom of Patan on the Godāvarī in the Dekhan, ruled over by the celebrated Śālivāhana, whose birth 77 or 78 after Christ is the beginning of the Śaka era. He himself was prince of the Śakas or Scythian (Turanian) races, who arrived in India before the Āryans, and were the great opponents of Vikramāditya.

5. The kingdom of a powerful tribe of Rājputs called Chālukya said to have come from Oudh and established at

a place called Kaliān in what is now the Western part of the Nizām's territory, in 250 A.D. Its power was greatest during the fourth and fifth centuries and then extended over the Pāndyas and Cholas in the south, and Āndhras in the east. It became extinct in 1182.

6. The Ballāla dynasty which succeeded the Cheras, and ruled at Dwāra Samudra in North Mysor. One of its Jaina kings was converted by the Vaishnava reformer Rāmānuja in 1133.

7. The great Āndhra kingdom in the eastern part of the Dekhan established at Warangal, to the east of Hyderābād.

8. The kingdom of Deogarh (now Daulatābād) ruled over by a Yādava dynasty. It was very powerful in the twelfth century, and conquered the kingdom of Kaliān.

9. The kingdom of Orissa ruled over by the Kesari dynasty from an early date till 1131 A.D., and again by the Gajapati line of princes established at Katak.

10. The Bahmanī dynasty which held sway for 150 years (from A.D. 1347 to 1526) over a great part of the Dekhan. It ultimately became divided into the five Muhammadan kingdoms next enumerated.

11. The five Muhammadan kingdoms of (1) Bījāpur, founded by Ādil Shāh, A.D. 1489; (2) Ahmad-nagar, founded by Malik Ahmad, A.D. 1487; (3) Golkondah, founded by Kutb-ul-Mulk, A.D. 1512; (4) Berār (whose capital was Ilichpur) founded by Fath-Allah, A.D. 1574; (5) Bīdar and Galbargah, founded by Barīd Shāh.

12. The Hindū kingdom of Vijaya-nagar (Bījā-nagar) which became a strong power in the Dekhan, and was nearly co-extensive with the Madras Presidency. It lasted till the time of Akbar in 1565, and at its fall a line of Hindū Rājas maintained its independence in Mysore against the Mahrattas, the Nizams of the Dekhan and Nawābs of the Carnatic until 1761, when an officer in the Rāja's army named Haidar usurped the government and became King of Mysore.

One of the princes of Vijaya-nagar was king Bukka, the patron of Sāyanāćārya, the Rig-veda commentator.

I may usefully add here a brief notice of the Muhammadan occupation of India.

Of course, many of the Hindū dynasties just enumerated were flourishing at the epoch when Muhammad, the Prophet of Islam, laid the foundation of a new empire in Arabia, soon after his flight to Medina in A.D. 622.

Muhammad's successors, after occupying Damascus for about one hundred years, fixed their capital at Baghdad in 750, and thence their power extended into Afghānistān. The Arabs, however, never gained more than a temporary footing in India. Under the Khalīf Wālid I, in 711, Muhammad Kāsim was sent at the head of an army into Sindh, which was then added for a time to the Khalīfate, but the Muslims were expelled in 750; and for two centuries and a half India was left unmolested by invaders from the west.

About the year 950, when the power of the Arabs began to decline in Asia, hardy tribes of Tartars, known by the name of Turks (not the Ottoman tribe which afterwards gained a footing in Europe, but hordes from the Altai mountains), were employed by the Khalīfs to infuse vigour into their effeminate armies.

These tribes became Muhammadans and gradually took the power into their own hands. In the province of Afghānistān, Sabaktagīn, once a mere Turkish slave, usurped the government. His son Mahmūd founded an empire at Ghaznī about the end of the tenth century. A zealous iconoclast and great warrior, he made his first of sixteen incursions into India in the year 1000. In one of his later inroads he devastated the shrine of Somnāth in Gujarāt and carried off the sandal-wood gates of the temple as a trophy to Ghaznī. He was the first of a long series of Afghān kings who maintained a dominion in India for 500 years. One of his successors was Muhammad Ghorī, who, after his assumption of the empire of Ghaznī, defeated and put to death Pṛithivī Rāja of Delhi, at the second battle of Thānesvar, and became the first Muhammadan conqueror of Delhi, and the real founder of the Musalmān power in India, 1193 A.D. Nevertheless, Kutb ud dīn, his lieutenant and successor (1206-1210), was perhaps the first real king of Delhi, as Muhammad Ghori returned home after the completion of his conquests.

During the thirteenth century the Mongol or Moghul hordes, under the celebrated Jangīz Khān, overthrew the Turkish or Tartar tribes; and in 1398 Tīmūr, uniting Tartars and Mongols into one army, made his well-known invasion of India. After desolating the country then ruled by the Afghān kings he retired, but the sixth in descent from him, Baber (*Bābar*), conquered Afghānistān, and thence invading India about 1526, founded the Moghul empire, which his grandson Akbar (son of Humāyūn) established on a firm basis in 1556. Previously to Akbar, however, and during the reign of Humāyūn an Afghān chief named Shīr Shāh Sūr, who had conquered Bengal, usurped, for a time, authority over Hindūstān. He was a wise and energetic ruler, and raised the empire to great prosperity.

The power of the Moghuls was at its height for a period of 150 years. It rapidly increased under Akbar, Jahāngīr, and Shāhjahān, until it culminated under Aurangzīb, began to decline under Shāh Ālam (Bahādur Shāh), Jahāndār Shāh, and Farrukh-Siyar; and under Muhammad Shāh, the fourth from Aurangzīb, took place the Persian invasion of Afghānistān and thence of India, undertaken by Nādir Shāh (A.D. 1738) to avenge on the Afghāns their inroads into Persia.

Hence, it appears that in all cases the Muhammadan invaders of India came through Afghānistān, and generally settled there before proceeding to conquer the Hindūs. For this reason, and from the proximity of Afghānistān, it has followed that the greater number of Muhammadan immigrants have been of Afghān blood.

As to the development of European influence and British rule in India, a brief account of this subject will be found in the first chapters on 'the progress of our Indian Empire' at the end of this volume.

Modern Political Divisions.

Let me note, for the benefit of those who have hitherto given little heed to the progress of our Eastern Empire, that the old tripartite separation of India into three Presidencies gives an inadequate, if not inaccurate, idea of its present political divisions.

The term Presidency is still conveniently retained for Bombay and Madras (whose governments correspond directly with the Secretary of State, and not through the Governor-General), but cannot now be suitably applied to the twelve divisions [1] more immediately under the Viceroy, and generally supplied with officers from the Bengal Civil Service.

[1] Mr. Trelawny Saunders in commenting on my *Times*' letter, June 14, 1877, enumerated these twelve divisions, and gave an official explanation of the present political divisions of India, part of which I here extract as useful and instructive, though his description of what he states ought still to be called the Bengal Presidency is likely to bewilder the general reader:
'Ever since the reduction of the lower Provinces of Bengal from being the chief Presidency to the position of a Lieutenant-Government, it has been the fashion in certain official quarters to deny the existence of the Bengal Presidency, and, indeed, of the Presidencies altogether. As, however, the officials of Madras and Bombay have not suffered any detraction from their rank as Presidencies, the fashion which prevails in Calcutta does not appear to have extended to Madras and Bombay; and thus the Professor allows that "the term may be conveniently retained" in their cases.

'But the Presidency of Bengal (or, technically, Fort William in Bengal), so far from having been abolished, has become so largely extended as to require that the local Government of the original Presidency should be delegated by the Governor-General of the extended Presidency to a Lieutenant-Governor, just as other parts of the Presidency have been. The honours of the Bengal Civil Service are now, therefore, no longer confined to the area under the Lieutenant-Governor of Bengal, but are disseminated throughout India, excepting Bombay and Madras. A reference to the "India List" will prove that, as a rule, it is Members of the Bengal Civil Service who are employed, not only in (1) the Lieutenant-Government of Bengal Proper, but also in (2) the North-Western Provinces (of Bengal) and Oudh, (3) the Punjab, (4) Rājputāna and Ajmir, (5) Central India, (6) the Central Provinces, (7) Hyderabad and Berar, (8) Mysore and Coorg, (9) Assam, (10) Manipur, a little state, east of Assam, on the frontier of Burmah, (11) British Burmah, (12) the Andaman and Nicobar

It would be better, I think, to speak of Modern British India as divided into eight Provinces, each under its own Government. These are:—1. Bengal (sometimes called the Lower Provinces, consisting of Bengal, Behār, and Orissa); 2. the North-West Provinces (so called from their position relatively to Bengal); 3. the Panjāb; 4. the Central Provinces; 5. British Burmah; 6. Assam; 7. Bombay; and 8. Madras.

Till quite recently the province of Oudh formed a ninth division under a separate Government, but is now attached to the North-West Provinces.

Then there are now nine principal native territories surrounded by, or contiguous to, these eight British Provinces; and of course protected and controlled by us through Residents and Political Agents, viz. 1. Rājputāna; 2. Central India (including the dominions of Sindia and Holkār); 3. the Bombay Marāṭha States (especially that of the Gaikwār of Baroda); 4. Hyderabad or the Nizām's territory; 5. Mysor; 6. Travankor; 7. Nepāl; 8. Kaśmīr; 9. Afghānistān.

The recent war has added Afghānistān to the list. We have had to settle the question whether that country should be Russianized or Anglicized [1].

Most of these nine native states are independent of us in regard to their internal affairs, but all acknowledge our

Islands. All these distinct governments, whether under Lieutenant-Governors, Commissioners, Superintendents, or Native Princes, with political agents as their advisers, are supplied with British officials of the Bengal Civil Service, and are subject to the superior control of the Governor-General in Council. The Presidencies of Madras and Bombay cover the remainder of India, and have their own distinct Civil Services (making in all fourteen great political divisions). The tripartite organization of India is also determined by this fact—that, although there are fourteen separate governments in India, including Madras and Bombay, the twelve divisions of the Bengal Presidency have no correspondence with the Secretary of State except through the Governor-General. Bombay and Madras, as separate Presidencies, retain that distinction.'

[1] In their speeches at the end of the present Session (August 14, 1879) Sir Stafford Northcote and Mr. E. Stanhope well pointed out what the war has achieved for us: viz. absolute control over the foreign relations of Afghānistān; the appointment of a British Resident (Major Cavagnari) at Kabul; a greatly improved frontier, both military and political, through the

supremacy. Hyderabad (where we have a Resident), though completely environed by British territory, is the largest and most powerful. It is the only great Muhammadan power that has survived the dissolution of the Moghul empire in India. It has an area of 100,000 square miles, and a population of eleven millions, and maintains an army of 50,000 men. No other native state approaches it either in area or population; Mārwār (Jodhpur) in Rājputāna, which is the next largest, having an area of only 36,000 square miles, and a population of less than two millions.

There are, however, five minor Muhammadan states, viz. Khairpur, bordering on Sindh; Bhāwalpur, contiguous to the Panjāb; Rāmpur in the North-West; Bhopāl (for Bhūpāl) in Central India; and Tonk in Rājputāna.

Of course some of the nine principal native territories include an immense number of separate states and principalities. For example, there are nineteen Rājputāna states, of which the three chief are (1) Jodhpur, or Mārwār, (2) Jaipur, and (3) Udaipur, or Mewār[1]. These (especially the last) are the most ancient sovereignties of India. Central India includes the state of Gwālior (with more than 33,000 square miles, a population of nearly three millions, and an army of more than 22,000 men), ruled by Sindia; and that of Indore (with little more than 8,000 square miles and half a million population, and, according to Colonel Malleson an army of 8,500 men), ruled by Holkār.

The Bombay Marāṭha states include (besides that of the Gaikwār of Baroda in Gujarāt) a large number of minor principalities in Kāthiāwār, and in the South, so that the grand total of native states and feudatories great and small. throughout India, is not far short of five hundred.

occupation of advanced strategical positions which give us the command of all the important Afghān stations and passes, as, for example, Quetta with the Bolan, Khuram, Sibi, Peshīn, Ali Masjid with the Khaiber; a commercial treaty with Afghānistān; and the opening out of an enormous trade with Central Asia; and lastly, the power of conciliating, humanizing, and civilizing the lawless mountain tribes.

[1] Or Maiwār, said to be a contraction of *Madhyawār*, central region.

Geographical and Physical Features.

It is no part of my plan to describe the physical geography of India. Let me merely direct attention to eight principal geographical divisions marked in the map which accompanies this volume thus:—

1. The lower valley or basin of the Ganges, including Bengal, Behār and Orissa; 2. the upper basin of the Ganges from Patna to the Sutlej, constituting Hindūstān proper, this being the only part of India properly called Hindūstān[1]; 3. the whole basin of the Indus, embracing the Panjāb and Sindh; 4. the Indian desert, including Rājputāna; 5. Gujarāt, forming with the peninsula of Kāthiāwār[2], or ancient Saurāshtra, a large extent of fertile country of a horse-shoe shape, whose area is about equal to that of Great Britain; 6. the triangular plateau of Central India, including Mālwa, and on the east Bandelkhand, and in its widest sense comprehending the whole region between the Āravali and Vindhya ranges; 7. the plateau of the Dekhan, or, more properly, Dakhin, that is to say, the South Country, including part of the southern Marātha country, the central provinces, the Nizām's territory and Mysor[3]; 8. the valley of the Brahma-putra, including Assām.

With a view to clearness, the physical boundaries are

[1] The whole of Northern and Central India from the Himālayas to the Vindhya range is sometimes called Hindūstān, to distinguish it from the Dekhan.

[2] Properly written Kāthiāwāḍ, and meaning the abode of a tribe called Kāthi.

[3] The whole triangular plateau south of the Vindhya mountains as far as Cape Comorin (Kumārin) is correctly called the Dekhan or South Country, but it would be more in conformity with modern usage to say that the river Kṛishna divides the south into two plateaux, the Northern of which is the Dekhan proper, while Mysor forms the Southern plateau. In fact, the map of India may be conveniently divided into three broad belts, viz. 1. the Northern belt called Hindūstān, extending from the Himālaya to the Vindhya range; 2. the upper Southern belt called the Dekhan, extending from the Vindhya range to the river Kistna; 3. the lower Southern belt called the Peninsula, extending from the Kistna to Cape Comorin.

GEOGRAPHICAL AND PHYSICAL FEATURES. 141

purposely exaggerated in the map, and with the same object the true hydrographical lines are not quite correctly drawn.

The first noticeable feature is the vast alluvial plain which bends round in an immense curve from the mouths of the Indus to the mouths of the Ganges. Then, observe how the gigantic Himālayas (the abode of snow[1]) curve round as if to form a stupendous ring-fence towards the two seas; next, how the less lofty Vindhya[2] and Sātpura[3] ranges, traversing the centre of the country, have acted as a line of separation to mark off Central and Northern India, and Hindūstān from the table-land of the Dekhan, or Southern India, and helped to preserve a certain degree of individuality in each region; thirdly, how the line of the Vindhya range and Sone river, taken in conjunction with the line of the Ganges valley, and that of the Chittūr range and Chambal river, form the three sides of a central triangular plateau embracing Mālwa and Bandelkhand[4], or the Central India native states; fourthly, how the Ārāvali[5] range, running parallel with the Chittūr hills, shuts off Central India,—or, speaking roughly, the country called Mālwa—from the desert of Rājputāna.

India, like China, Babylonia and Egypt, owes much of its early prosperity and civilization to its inexhaustible supply of living waters. Indeed the history of the world proves that rivers are a country's very life-blood. If we compare the condition of India in this respect with that of the peninsula of Arabia, which has not a single navigable stream, it will not surprise us that rivers, like every

---

[1] From Sanskrit *hima*, ice or snow, and *ālaya*, abode. Where they separate the Panjāb from Afghānistān, they have the name Sulaimān, and where they divide Sindh from Bilūchistān various local names, such as Halā, &c.

[2] *Vindhya* may be derived from the Sanskrit *bind*, for root *bid*, to divide.

[3] *Sātpura* is probably for *Sāt-puḍa* for *Sāt-puṭa*, seven folds, or sinuosities.

[4] *Mālwa*, or more properly Mālava = *Madhya-deśa*, the middle country: *Bandelkhand* = the country of the Bandela tribe.

[5] From Sanskrit *āra*, a point, and *āvali* a line.

other object in nature from which great benefits arise, are personified and worshipped by the Hindūs as actual divinities.

Almost all the rivers in India have significant Sanskṛit names. The Indus is properly in Sanskṛit *Sindhu*. It has a special interest of its own, because it gives its name to India, the first settlements of the Indo-Āryans having been on its banks. Like the Brahma-putra it has a course of about 1800 miles.

But the first in importance, though not in length—its course being only 1514 miles—is the Ganges, the 'great goer,' its name in Sanskṛit being *Gangā* (from the root *gam*, to go). It has numerous important tributaries, such as the Jumnā (Sanskṛit *Yamunā*), the Chambal, the Gandak (Sanskṛit *Gaṇdakī*) and the Sone (Sanskṛit *Śoṇa*).

Both the Indus and the Ganges, through taking opposite courses to the sea, have their sources, along with that of the Brahma-putra, at no great distance apart in the snows of the Himālayas; and, it may be noted, that the Ganges and Brahma-putra, flowing in the same direction, though on opposite sides of the vast mountain range, have deltas which run into each other and become intermixed in the plains around Calcutta.

Of the other principal rivers those which flow, like the Indus, into the Western or Arabian Sea, the Narbadā [1]— 800 miles long—is perhaps the next most sacred river after the Ganges. Hence its proper Sanskṛit name is *Narma-dā*, or 'bliss giver.' Almost every river, however, rivals the Ganges in being held by those who live near it to have more sanctifying power than any other river.

The Taptī, 400 miles long, on which Surat is situated, takes its name from a word *tapatī* [2], derived from the Sanskṛit root *tap*, 'to be warm.'

[1] Broach (which is probably a corruption of Bhṛigu-kacha) is on this river. Its other name is Revā. The territory of the Rāja of Rewah (Revā) surrounds the sources of this river.

[2] More properly *tapantī*, heating, hot, warm. Another name for it is

The Lunī[1], lying between it and the Indus, may be so called from its saline (*lavaṇa*) properties. The Sābharmatī[2] is said to be so named from Sanskrit Sābhramatī, but is more probably from Śvabhramatī, 'having holes,' (*Śvabhra* being 'the hole of an animal').

Then come those rivers which flow like the Ganges into the Eastern Sea, or Bay of Bengal, viz., the great Brahmaputra (meaning in Sanskrit 'Son of Brahmā') whose course is chiefly on the other side of the Himālayas; and the Mahā-nadī[3] (or 'great river'), 520 miles long. Then those which descend from the water-shed of the western ghāts, such as the Go-dāvarī[4] (meaning 'water-giver') with a long course of 898 miles; the Kistna (corrupted from Kṛishnā) 800, and the Kāverī[5], 472 miles long. There are three smaller rivers nearer to the mouths of the Ganges called the Subanrekha (for Sanskrit *Suvarṇa-rekha*, 'golden-streaked'), the Baitaraṇī[6], and the Brāhmaṇī (respectively 317, 345, and 410 miles long), and some other less important streams, such as the Punnār and the Vaiga, may be noted in the south.

Extensive irrigation works have been successfully carried out in connection with the Go-dāvarī, Kistna, and Kāverī rivers. These are due to the skill and energy of Sir Arthur Cotton, and are of incalculable benefit to the country in times of drought and famine. The three districts watered and irrigated by these rivers, especially the Delta of the Kāverī round Tanjore, instead of adding millions to the grand total of famine-stricken people during the recent

Payoshṇī, 'warm as milk.' Surat ought to be pronounced Sūrat; it is from the Persian word for beauty of form.

[1] Loṇī is probably for Lavaṇī, lavaṇa meaning salt.
[2] Ahmedabad is on this river.
[3] Mahī in Sanskrit means the earth. Baroda (a name said to be derived from *vaṭa*, the Indian fig-tree) is near this river.
[4] Godāvarī may also mean in Sanskrit cow-giver. It is held very sacred.
[5] The Kāverī is said by those who live near it to have a fourth more power of washing away sin than the Ganges. It is however called by some *Ardha-Gangā*, half the Ganges.
[6] For Vaitaraṇī, the name of a fabulous river in the infernal regions.

famine, poured millions of bushels of grain into the starving regions.

A study of the most prominent physical features of India makes it less difficult to comprehend how the Indo-Āryan settlers elaborated out of their own imaginations the singular, and to us ridiculous, system of geography recorded in their Purāṇas. Extending their immigrations first southwards and then towards the east and west, and surrounded on all sides either by the sea or by vast rivers, which in the rainy season spread themselves out like seas, they imagined India to be a flat circular continent, bounded on all sides by a ring-shaped ocean, to which they added six other ring-shaped continents[1], each surrounded by its own ring-shaped sea. Far off in the horizon the vast pile of the Himālayas towered upwards into the sky. Hence they believed the furthest ocean to be encircled by an impassable mountain wall, which formed the boundary and limit of the universe. Beyond this barrier neither land nor sea existed, and the light of the sun could not penetrate. All was blank space and total darkness.

And, in truth, this self-contained peninsula of India presents the students of physical geography, as well as every other student of nature and every admirer of scenery, with an epitome of the world. Where can be seen more wonderful contrasts, where such amazing variety? Monotonous plains, sandy deserts, noble rivers, fertile fields, immense districts wooded like English parks, forest, grove, and jungle, gentle undulation, hill and dale, rock, crag, precipice, snowy peak—everything is here. The one exception is lake scenery. India has nothing to offer like the picturesque lakes of Europe.

But the grand distinctive feature which impresses a traveller most is the sublime range which, stretching from

[1] The Indians were not so far wrong in their notion of seven continents, for America may fairly be reckoned as two continents, and a seventh continent is supposed to surround the South Pole.

the east towards the west, blends with other ranges northwards, and surrounds the whole upper part of India (as the Alps surround Europe) with a mighty natural rampart, shutting it out from the rest of the continent of Asia, and, indeed, from the rest of the world, except from the sea. It is true that constant incursions have taken place from the earliest times through the principal passes of Afghānistān (especially the Khaiber and Bolan), as well as along the course of the Brahma-putra; and the later Muhammadan invaders have had little difficulty in following the same route; but all these invasions occurred before the existence of steam-navies, ironclads, railroads, and telegraphs. A great aggressive power like Russia may, hereafter, give us trouble by stirring up disaffection among the people of Afghānistān, and the excitable tribes in the neighbourhood of the passes [1], but no power that cannot beat us at sea is ever likely to dispossess us of India.

My first view of the Himālayan range on a clear evening from a point about 150 miles distant was absolutely overpowering. Imagine the Jung Frau piled on Mont Blanc, and repeated in a succession of peaks, stretching apparently nearly half round the horizon in an unbroken line, far more extended than that of the Alps as seen from Berne, and a faint idea may be formed of the sublimity of the spectacle presented by this majestic pile of mountains, some of which tower to a height of nearly 30,000 feet above the plain.

In regard to climate, too, India, which is in other respects a complete world in itself, seems to include all the climates of all countries. Far from being 'deadly' (at least, from November till April), as I have heard it described, I believe the winter climate of Northern India to be more salubrious than that of England. Perpetual sunshine, balmy breezes, perfect dryness of air and soil, with lovely flowers and summer foliage constantly before the eyes, cannot fail to exhilarate the spirits and benefit

[1] This was written in 1876, and may be read in the light of recent events.

the health. Many invalids, who habitually resort to Italy to escape the damp and gloom of our English climate, would do well to devote a winter to India. The facilities now offered by the Suez Canal, and the beautiful weather prevalent in the Red Sea and Indian Ocean from November to April, make the passage itself not the least delightful part of the expedition; and if English tourists would oftener turn their steps towards our Eastern possessions, the present lamentable ignorance on Indian subjects, amounting in most cases to Cimmerian darkness, would be replaced by a better appreciation of the character of the country.

Would, too, that a few more students of astronomy could be induced to wend their way towards India! I inquired in vain for professional astronomers, and only came across one amateur during the course of my travels in Northern India. The sight he gave me of the planet Saturn through his well-appointed telescope at Allahabad, will remain indelibly impressed on my memory. How is it, then, that there are not more telescopic batteries directed against the heavens in an atmosphere unequalled for clearness, stillness, and all the conditions favourable to new conquests in the field of astronomical research?

Nor can I refrain from expressing my surprise that zoologists and botanists do not resort in larger numbers to India and revel in the rich fare—the endless variety spread out in every direction, and asking to be appreciated and enjoyed. For my own part, I would rather see them abound than sportsmen, of whom, indeed, there is no lack at all. It must be confessed that the omnipresent insects which most people execrate as the greatest pest incident to an Indian climate, are a little too demonstrative for the ordinary traveller and resident. Various appliances may temper extremes of heat and cold, but what can repress the irrepressible mosquito, or check the unpleasant exuberance of every form of insect life? 'If I could get £200 in England,' I have often heard irritated young civilians exclaim, 'I would give up my £800 a year in this country.' Certainly there are many drawbacks to a life in Eastern climates, and the insect nuisance is not the least of them. But one man's plague may be another man's prize. To an entomologist the study of Indian ants alone would be an inexhaustible subject of interest, while to the ordinary amateur what can be more attractive than the whole butterfly world of India. I well remember how, walking in a secluded lane, I was suddenly surrounded by a flight of at least a hundred gorgeous specimens of this form of insect life. How is it then that I looked in vain for entomologists and butterfly-collectors in my travels?

Races and Languages.

India, including the slopes of the Himālayas, presents us with examples of all the principal races of the world; for example, the Caucasian—Āryan in the Brāhmans and Rājputs, and Semitic in the Arabs[1]—the Mongolian, and even the Negro, some of the aboriginal hill tribes being manifestly either negroid or negrito. And all races are more or less blended. Yet Brāhmans, Rājputs, Jāts, Baniyas (in Sanskrit *Banijas = Vaiśyas*), Śūdras, and hill tribes differ as much *inter se* as Greeks, Italians, Saxons, Slaves, Celts, Finns, and Laps.

In point of fact, the insularity of India, caused by its vast natural barriers of mountain and ocean, enables us to understand how it has happened that when the whole country once became filled with Turanian and Āryan settlers, their manners, customs, domestic usages, religious ideas, and languages, have undergone less change through extraneous influences than they have in other parts of the world to which the same races have immigrated.

For there are really only three principal gateways through the mighty wall of the Himālayas, as roughly indicated in

---

[1] But it must be admitted that there is no great admixture of Arab blood.

the map. Two of these are by the passes of the North-west, and the third by the Brahma-putra valley on the East into Bengal.

Few invaders have entered India except through the long and difficult passages constituting these gateways. Both Turanians[1] and Āryans came one after the other through the two North-western passes, some through the Khaiber Pass into the Panjāb, some through the Bolan Pass into Sindh.

The Indo-Turanians, whose original home was probably somewhere in Northern Turkestān, were nomad races who passed into India at different times and were the first to occupy all the Northern and Central regions.

The Āryans, who were half nomad, half agricultural, came from the more southerly districts of Central Asia and Turkestān—probably from the Pamīr plateau and the region surrounding the sources of the Oxus. They, too, entered India by successive waves of immigration, but their incursions did not begin till some centuries later.

The more peaceful Āryan immigrants finding the Turanians already in possession of the country settled down with them on the soil, and in conjunction with them formed the great class of the Vaiśya or agricultural population[2].

Other incursions of the Āryan race followed, and those who were intellectually superior took advantage of that growth of religious ideas which generally accompanies political growth, and formed themselves into a body of religious teachers, afterwards called Brāhmans,—while the more warlike tribes (afterwards called Kshatriyas), advancing southwards, drove the more independent and less submissive of the Turanians towards the Southern Peninsula. There these Turanian races retained their own languages,

[1] This term is properly only applicable to the people of Turkestān, though it is sometimes loosely applied to the omnium-gatherum of all races not Āryan or Semitic.

[2] Even now the great mass of the Hindū population are agriculturists, but they are no longer called Vaiśyas or 'settlers on the soil' (from the root *viś*), this name being applied to traders. The pure Vaiśya caste no longer exists.

acquired an independent civilization, and were called by a distinct name — Drāvidians[1] — though they ultimately amalgamated to a great extent with the advancing Āryan immigrants and became Āryanized in religion, literary culture, and social usages.

The Drāvidians of the South were the Rākshasas, or powerful demons of Indian Epic poetry. The non-Āryan and non-Drāvidian races (consisting of the Kols, Santāls, Jūangs, &c., of Chotā Nāgpur, and neighbouring districts) are now usually called Kolarian. Some of them may be of Tibetan origin, while others are rude aborigines whose origin cannot be traced beyond their present locality, and who have a manifest affinity with Negritos and Australian savages. The Tibetan tribes probably entered India through the Eastern gateway long before either Indo-Āryans or Drāvidians. These non-Drāvidian and aboriginal tribes were the monkeys of Indian Epic poetry.

As to the Muhammadan invasions of India, they were really little more than further incursions of Tartar (Turkish) races who had become converted to Islām, and who overran Sindh, Gujarāt, and the Panjāb, after first settling in Afghānistān and fusing to a certain extent with the Afghāns.

The Pārsīs represent a remnant of the ancient Persians, who, when the Khalīfs conquered Persia in the 7th and 8th centuries, retained their own religion, settling first at Yazd in Persia, and afterwards, to escape persecution, emigrating to the Western coast of India.

It is clear, then, that India has been continually overrun by successive immigrants and invaders from time immemorial. And of these immigrants the best fitted by physical energy, character and habits to achieve ascendancy were the Āryan races. In point of fact, these races have continued dominant in moral and religious influence, though political power has long since passed out of their hands. They may

[1] Properly Drāviḍāh, from Drāviḍa, the name given to the extreme South or Tamil part of the Peninsula.

be called by the general name Indo-Āryans to distinguish them from the Āryans who spread themselves over Europe, and differences distinguish them as great as those which divide European Āryans.

Indeed, from their admixture with the Turanian and aboriginal races it is difficult to find pure Brāhmans[1], Kshatriyas[2], or Vaiśyas anywhere. A purely ethnical arrangement of the people of India is now practically impossible.

Reckoning, however, Āryans and non-Āryans, and taking difference of speech as marking and perpetuating separation of populations, though not as necessarily determining distinction of race, we are able to distinguish sixteen separate peoples in India, constituting what might almost be called sixteen separate nationalities.

First come eight divisions of the Indo-Āryans, all of whose languages are more or less Sanskṛitic in structure as well as in vocabulary.

1. *Hindī*, which we may calculate as spoken by about one hundred million persons in Hindūstān proper, including the High Hindī and the Muhammadan form of it called Hindūstānī, and the various dialects, called Braj, Kanaujī, Mewārī, Old Pūrbī, Awadhī, Bhojpurī, and Mārwārī, the last being particularly deserving of notice as spoken throughout Jodhpur, the most extensive of all the Rājput states.

2. *Bengālī*, spoken by about thirty-seven millions in Bengal, a little more than half of whom are Hindūs and the remainder Muhammadans.

3. *Marāṭhī*[3], spoken by about eleven or twelve millions chiefly Hindūs, throughout Mahārāshṭra or the Marātha country in the Dekhan, part of the province of Bombay

---

[1] The northern division of Brāhmans in Hindūstān claim to be of pure descent, especially the Kānyakubja and Sārasvata Brāhmans.

[2] The Rājputs of Rājputāna claim to be pure Kshatriyas.

[3] Mr. Beames considers that Maraṭhī has been formed by the Māgadhī and Śauraseni Prākrits quite as much as by the Mahārāshṭrī.

and the Central Provinces, including a dialect in the Konkan, known as Konkanī.

4. *Gujarātī*, spoken by about seven millions in Gujarāt, and regarded by some as a mere dialect of Hindī.

5. *Panjābī*, spoken by twelve or thirteen millions in the Panjāb, of whom one half are Muhammadans. It is really a mere dialect of Hindī.

6. *Kaśmīrī*, a sister language of Hindī, spoken (with Dogrī, a dialect of Panjābī) by nearly two millions in the kingdom of Kaśmīr. According to Dr. Bühler there are three varieties of Kaśmīrī. The Kaśmīrī Pandits are among the finest types of the Āryan race.

7. *Sindhī*, spoken by about two millions in Sindh, of whom one fifth only are Hindū, the remainder being Muhammadan. Dr. Trumpp has published a scientific grammar of this language.

8. *Oriya*, spoken by about eight millions, chiefly Hindūs, in Orissa.

Next, taking the non-Āryans, we have eight other race-differences, which we may also mark by the names of eight languages. In the first place, six Drāvidian races (numbering nearly forty-six million persons), as follow :—

1. *Tamil*, spoken by about fifteen millions throughout an extensive region, beginning with the northern portion of Ceylon, and extending from Cape Comorin northward along the South of Travankor, and what is called the Karnatic; that is, along the southern part of the Coromandel coast to about a hundred miles north of Madras [1].

2. *Malayālam*, almost a dialect of Tamil, spoken by nearly four millions in Travankor and along the southern portion of the Malabar coast.

3. *Telugu*, called from its softness the Italian of India, spoken by nearly sixteen millions throughout a region beginning from a line about a hundred miles north of Madras, and extending along the northern part of the

[1] Tamil has an imperfect alphabet, and makes use of a separate literary character (*grantha*) for writing Sanskrit.

Coromandel coast, or Northern Circars, and over part of the Nizām's territory.

4. *Kanarese*, spoken by rather more than nine millions in Mysore, in the southern portion of the Bombay Presidency, in Kanara, and part of the Malabar Coast.

There are also two semi-cultivated Drāvidian dialects scarcely deserving enumeration, viz :

5. *Tulu*, spoken in a small district of Kanara by about 300,000 persons, and

6. *Koorg* or *Kodāgu*, spoken by only 150,000 persons in the hill district to the west of Mysore.

Then comes the chief uncultivated Drāvidian language, viz :—

7. *Goṇḍ*[1], spoken by nearly two million persons, divided into clans, some of whom are almost savages, while others are comparatively civilized, inhabiting Goṇḍwana (for Goṇḍavana, the forest of the Goṇḍs) in the Central Provinces. The language of the Goṇḍ race has been lately systematized and expressed in Deva-nāgarī characters.

The other uncultivated Drāvidian dialects, viz :—Orāon, Rājmahal, Khoṇḍ, Toḍa and Koṭa, belong to insignificant tribes rather than to races.

Lastly come the wholly uncultivated and barbarous non-Āryan and non-Drāvidian dialects, called,—

8. *Kolarian*, belonging to wild tribes inhabiting the plateau of Choṭā Nāgpur and some adjacent hills[2], and numbering more than three millions. They speak about seven rude dialects, of which the best known are those of the Kols, the Jūangs (the most primitive tribe in all India), the Santāls, the Mundas, and the Hos.

In the above enumeration are not reckoned the languages

---

[1] Goṇḍ may be a corruption of *Govinda*, a cow-herd. These tribes straggle southwards into the Tamil country as far as the latitude of Madras. They have adopted many Tamil words.

[2] The Kols are found not only at Rānchī but also at Sumbhulpur, and in hills belonging to the Sātpura range, and even at Nāgpur, Elichpur, and still further south at Kālahandī. The Bhīls are probably Drāvidian.

which belong, so to speak, to the outer fringe of India proper, e.g. the Pashtu or Pakhtu of Afghānistān, the Nepālī or Nepālese of Nepāl, the Assamese of Assam, the Burmese of British Burmah, and the Sinhalese of Ceylon; besides an immense number of dialects spoken by tribes inhabiting the mountains of Nepāl, Bhūtān, and Assam (some of them coming under the Himālayan family, and many of them more or less connected with Tibetan), making about two hundred languages and dialects, cultivated and uncultivated, in the whole of India.

We see, therefore, that just as all the principal races of the world are represented in India, so also are all families of languages—Āryan, Semitic and Agglutinative (Turanian).

Perhaps the chief bond of union between the races is religion. All who believe in the Veda and the Brāhmanical system, whether they be Āryan or non-Āryan, may be called Hindūs, provided it be clearly understood that the term Hindū has no real ethnical significance. Similarly all who believe in the Kurān and the teaching of Muhammad may be called Muslims or Muhammadans, it being understood that they may have originally belonged to Hindū races.

Two languages also act as linguistic bonds—Sanskrit and Hindūstānī. Sanskrit is, as everyone knows, the ancient classical language of all India, and the elder sister of Latin and Greek. It is to the Hindūs what Arabic is to the Musalmāns. The one is the language of the Veda, the other of the Kurān. Wherever the Hindū religion prevails there Sanskrit is cultivated and venerated. It is a dead language like Latin, but is still spoken fluently by learned men throughout India as Latin once was throughout Europe. Moreover, though in one sense dead, in another it has the utmost vitality. It lives and breathes in the eight Āryan dialects already enumerated, which are merely spoken forms of it.

As to Hindūstānī, it is simply a modern modification of Hindī, serving as a lingua franca for the whole of India, like French in Europe. It is a highly composite language, and, like English, reflects the composite character of the people who speak it. In fact, Hindūstānī scarcely existed as a distinct language till the time of the Emperor Tīmūr—about the year 1400 of our era—when it was finally formed in his *Ūrdū*[1], or camp, by the blending of the Arabic and Persian of the conquering Muhammadans with the Sanskṛit and Hindī of the conquered Hindūs. Hence it has an Āryan stock, but has adopted a vast number of Semitic words, and is now taking English words largely from us. Few languages have a greater power of assimilating foreign vocables.

I have heard it asserted that English is likely to supplant Hindūstānī as a general lingua franca for the whole population of India. I see no signs whatever of this. On the contrary, English has scarcely made its way at all among the masses of the people. Nevertheless, the cultivation of the language of the ruling race is becoming increasingly common at all the principal towns. It is taught at all Government and Missionary Schools and Colleges, and even at all larger native schools. Everywhere I found it both cultivated and spoken fluently by most educated Indians—to the neglect, I am sorry to say, of their own vernacular languages. Not that English is often studied for its own sake, but rather, I fear, from purely interested motives, a knowledge of it being an indispensable qualification for Government situations.

Character of the People.

I have found no people in Europe more religious—none more patiently persevering in common duties, none more docile and amenable to authority, none more courteous or respectful towards age and learning, none more dutiful to parents, none more faithful in service. Superstition,

---

[1] This word, meaning camp, is of Turkish origin, and is often applied to the Hindūstānī language.

CHARACTER OF THE PEOPLE. RELIGIONS.

immorality, untruthfulness, pride, selfishness, avarice, all these and other faults and vices, of course, abound, but not more than they do in other countries unpenetrated by the spirit of true Christianity, and not more than will be found among those merely nominal Christians who, after all, constitute the real mass of the people in Europe.

While on this subject, let me notice a few leading particulars as to creeds and religious usages.

Religious Creeds.

Just as all races and families of languages are represented in India, so are the four principal religious creeds in the world—namely, Brāhmanism or Hindūism, Buddhism, Islām or Muhammadanism, and Christianity.

The term Brāhmanism should, in my opinion, be restricted to the purely pantheistic and not necessarily idolatrous system evolved by the Brāhmans out of the partly monotheistic, partly polytheistic, partly pantheistic religion expressed in the sacred works collectively termed *Veda*. This system was fully developed in a still later work following on the Veda, called the Vedānta philosophy, where it is designated by the term *Advaita*—Non-Dualism. Brāhmanism, in fact, is a mere assertion of the unity of all being. Nothing really exists, it affirms, but the one Universal Spirit (named Brahman, from the root *brih*, 'to spread and pervade'), and whatever appears to exist independently is identical with that Spirit.

But it has also other characteristics. It may be described as in one sense the most self-annihilating system in the world, for it asserts that there can be no real *self* (*ātman*) existing separately from the one self-existent Supreme Self—called *Paramātman*, as well as *Brahman*, and when by the act of that Self the individuated spirits of men are allowed for a time an apparent separate existence, the ultimate end and aim of such spirits should be to attain complete reunion with the one Eternal Self in entire self-annihilation. A Brāhman, who holds this doctrine, thinks the religion of the Christian, who is conscious of severance from God, and yearns for reunion with Him, and yet does not wish his own self-consciousness to be merged in God, a very selfish kind of creed, compared with his own. It is evident, however, that there may be more real selfishness in the self-annihilating creed. For whatever may be said about the bliss of complete union (*sāyujya*) with the Supreme Spirit, the true aim of Brāhmanism, pure and simple, is not so much extinction of self, as extinction of personal existence for the sake of release from the troubles of life, and from the consequences of activity.

The term Hindūism, on the other hand, may be used to express Brāhmanism after it had degenerated—to wit, that complicated system of polytheistic doctrines and caste-usages, which has gradually resulted out of the mixture of Brāhmanism, first with Buddhism and then with the non-Āryan creeds of Drāvidians and aborigines. This system rests on the whole series of Hindū sacred writings—the four Vedas with their Brāhmaṇas and Upanishads, the Sūtras, the laws of Manu, and Rāmāyaṇa and Mahā-bhārata, the eighteen Purāṇas and sixty-four Tantras. Hence, Hindūism is something very different from Brāhmanism, though the one is derived from the other. It encourages idolatry—that is to say, worship before the images and symbols of Vishṇu, the Preserver, and Rudra-Śiva, the Destroyer and Regenerator (the highest manifestations of Brahman) and other deities, as a help for weak-minded persons; and every enlightened Brāhman admits that the unthinking and ignorant, who are by far the majority, adore the idols themselves.

In fact, Hindūism is like a huge irregular structure which has had no single architect but a whole series, and has spread itself over an immense surface by continual additions and accretions. The gradual growth of its congeries of heterogeneous doctrines is exactly reflected in the enormous mass of its disjointed sacred writings which, beginning with the Ṛig-veda, about the time of the composition of the Pentateuch, extend over a period of 2500 years. It is perhaps the only religion in the world which has neither any name derived from any single founder, nor any distinct designation of any kind. We may call it Brāhmanism and Hindūism, but these are not names recognized by the natives themselves. Its present aspect is that of an ancient overgrown fabric, with no apparent unity of design—patched, pieced, restored and enlarged in all directions, inlaid with every variety of idea, and, although looking as if ready at any moment to fall into ruins, still extending itself so as to cover every hole and corner of available ground, still holding its own with great pertinacity, and still keeping its position securely, because supported by a hard foundation of Brāhmanism and caste. It is only, however, by the practice of a kind of universal toleration and receptivity—carried on through more than 2000 years—that Hindūism has maintained its ground and arrived at its present condition[1]. It has been asserted that Hindūism is unlike Buddhism in not being a missionary religion. Certainly Buddhism was once a proselyting system (though its missionary spirit is extinct), and it is very true that a Brāhman *nascitur non fit*, but it is equally true that Hindūism could not have extended itself over India if it had never exerted itself to make proselytes. In point of fact, it has first borne with and then accepted, and, so to speak, digested and assimilated something from all creeds. It has opened its doors to all comers—and is willing to do so still—on the two conditions of their admitting the spiritual su-

[1] Moor, in his 'Pantheon' (p. 402), tells us that a learned Pandit once observed to him that the English were a new people, and had only the record of one Avatāra, but the Hindūs were an ancient people, and had accounts of a great many, and that if the Purāṇas were examined, they would probably be found to record the incarnation of Christ.

premacy of the Brāhmans, and conforming to certain caste-rules about food, intermarriage, and professional pursuits. In this manner it has adopted much of the Fetishism of the aborigines of India; it has stooped to the practices of various primitive tribes, and has not scrupled to appropriate and naturalise the adoration of the fish, the boar, the serpent, rocks, stones, and trees; it has borrowed ideas from the various cults of the Drāvidian races; and it may even owe something to Christianity. Above all, it has assimilated nearly every doctrine of Buddhism except its atheism, its denial of the eternal existence of soul, and its levelling of caste-distinctions.

Buddhism originated in India about 500 B.C. It was a reformation of Brāhmanism introduced by a man named Gautama (afterwards called Buddha, 'the Enlightened') of the Śākya tribe, whose father was king of a district situated under the mountains of Nepāl.

It is noteworthy that the images of Buddha—which are probably, like the pictures of Christ, merely ideal—generally represent him with features and hair of an Egyptian or Ethiopian type, and with the curly hair of a Negro[1]. He is usually described as a Kshatriya, or man of the kingly and military class. According to some, it is not impossible that the tribe to which he belonged may have been of aboriginal extraction, or even Mongolian.

Buddhism was originally no new religion, but a mere modification or reconstruction of Brāhmanism, and even now has much in common with it. But the Buddha, in opposition to the Brāhmans, refused to admit that the doctrines of a supreme eternal Spirit, and of the eternity of the human soul were susceptible of proof, and repudiated the authority of the Veda, caste-distinctions, sacrifices, and sacrificing priests. His own doctrines were afterwards collected in the sacred writings called *Tri-piṭaka* or 'Triple-collection' (written in Pāli, the ancient lan-

[1] It is curious that the figures in the caves of Elephanta have also curly hair.

guage of the Magadha district closely allied to Sanskṛit). He maintained that the only deity was man himself, when brought to a condition of Buddha-hood or perfect wisdom, and he made *Nirvāṇa*, 'extinction of all being,' take the place of *Sāyujya*, 'identification with one sole Being of the Universe,' as the great end and object of all human effort. His doctrines soon spread to Ceylon, Burmah, and other countries, but pure Buddhism does not exist any longer anywhere. In India it first co-existed with Brāhmanism, then met with some persecution, and finally lapsed back into Brāhmanism about the ninth century of our era.

Jainism, the home of cold indifferentism, even more unworthy to be called a religion than Buddhism, is now the only representative of Buddhistic ideas in India proper. I believe that, according to the last census, the number of Buddhists under our rule in British Burmah amounts to about two millions and a half. The Jainas or Jains, in India proper, only number about 380,000, at least half of whom are in the Bombay Presidency. They congregate most thickly in the districts round Ahmedabad.

The Jainas maintain that their system originated earlier than Buddhism, and from an independent source. Recent researches tend to show that there is ground for this assertion. Jainism and Buddhism probably represent two parallel lines of philosophical inquiry. One thing is certain, that Jainism has much in common with Buddhism, however it may differ from Buddhism in various ways. Perhaps the chief point of difference is that the Jainas retain caste-distinctions, but this again may be a later innovation. They are divided into two sects—the Śvetāmbaras, 'clothed in white,' and the Dig-ambaras, 'sky-clothed'—of which the latter sect was probably the earliest. The doctrines of both sects rest on sacred books, called Āgamas (divided into Angas, Upāngas, &c.), many of which are common to both. They agree with the Buddhists in rejecting the Veda of the Brāhmans. Formerly the Dig-ambaras, who are now the least numerous, were forbidden to wear clothing, and even to the present day they are said to eat naked.

The principal point in the creed of Jainas (as of Buddhists) is the reverence paid to holy men who by long discipline have raised themselves to a kind of divine perfection. The Jina, or 'conquering saint,' who having conquered all worldly desires reveals true knowledge, is with Jainas what the Buddha or 'perfectly enlightened saint' is with Buddhists.

Great numbers of the Mārwārīs and Baniyas, or traders of Western India, who claim to be Vaiśyas, are Jains. If a Jain wishes to acquire religious merit, he either builds a new temple to hold an image of one or all of the twenty-four Jina saints, or a hospital for the care of worn-out animals. No one thinks of repairing the work of his predecessor, though it be that of his own father. At Pālitāna, in Kāthiāwār, there are hundreds of new temples by the side of decaying old ones.

Jainism, like Brāhmanism and Buddhism, lays great stress on the doctrine of transmigration, or repeated births. Hence Jainas carry their respect for animal life—even that of the most minute infusoria—to a preposterous extreme. Their only worship, like that of the Buddhist, is adoration of human perfection. Though they dissent from the Veda, they regard themselves as Hindūs.

I have already (p. 93) described the religion of the Pārsīs, or, as it is sometimes called, Zoroastrianism. It represents the religion of ancient Persia imported into India by a small body of Persian immigrants, when driven out of Persia by the Muhammadan invaders, and rests on certain sacred writings called the Zand-Avastā—attributed to the prophet Zoroaster about 500 B.C.—which have suffered more from the inroads of time than any of the other religious books of the world. I may here add that the religion of the ancient Persians had a common origin with that of the Hindūs, and that Pārsīism, like Brāhmanism, is based on a kind of Monotheistic Pantheism.

It has not, however, advanced beyond the stage of regarding Fire, Sun, Earth, and Sea as principal manifestations of the one Supreme Being, called by the Pārsīs Ormazd (the creator of the two forces of construction and destruction, Spentamainyus and Ahriman). It has never lapsed, like Brāhmanism, into gross and degrading idolatry.

The Pārsīs are certainly near relations of the Brāhmans, but they have kept themselves separate from the other races of India, and retained much of the natural vigour and energy of the Āryan character.

And now a few words on the subject of Hindū religious services and ritual. Of ancient Vedic sacrificial ceremonial and public religious worship very little is left. Nor is congregational worship performed in temples. The priests in charge of the idols decorate them and bathe them with sacred water on holy days, and do them homage (*pūjā*) with lights and a rude kind of music at stated periods, generally both morning and evening. Moreover, offerings of flowers, grain, fruits, &c., are presented to the idols of the most popular gods (practically to the priests) by lay worshippers, and *mantras* or texts are repeated with prostrations of the body. Common prayer, in our sense, there is none.

The religion of the mass of the people—much of which is probably aboriginal and pre-Āryan—resolves itself, I fear, into a mere matter of selfish superstition. It is principally displayed in endeavouring to avert the anger of evil demons and in doing homage to local divinities, supposed to guard their worshippers from the assaults of malignant beings, and believed to be specially present in rude idols, trees, rocks, stones, and shapeless symbols, often consecrated with daubs of red paint. In place of public worship, however, great attention is given to private religious usages and to the performance of domestic ceremonies at births, marriages, funerals, &c., conducted by Brāhman priests, who have nothing whatever to do with temples or with worship performed in temples. Moreover, homage to ancestors and to the spirits of deceased fathers, grandfathers, and great-grandfathers, enters largely into the religious rites of the Hindūs as into those of the Chinese.

All these observances vary with caste, and caste is now so divided and subdivided that even the Brāhmans are broken up into innumerable classes and tribes, one claiming superiority over the other. Some of these are little more than groups of families bound together by peculiar usages. In other cases, caste is only another name for an association of men united by common occupation in a kind of trade union, every such combination being cemented in the same way by the practice of distinctive religious observances. In fact, caste in India is an essential part of religion. It is no longer to the same extent as it once was, a bond of union among large bodies of men. Its action tends to split up the social fabric into numerous independent communities, and to prevent all national and patriotic combinations. In the present day the family-bond (*bhāī-band*) appears to be stronger than that of caste. Certainly both these ties operate far more powerfully in India than in Europe, because they are both intimately associated with religion. I fear, however, that other ties are proportionately weak, and that Indians, as a rule, have few sympathies and little disposition to co-operate with others beyond the circle of their own families, and none at all beyond the limits of their own immediate castes.

Indian Muhammadanism.

Turn we next to a brief consideration of Indian Muhammadanism. The position of Islām, with reference to the idolatry of India, is very similar to that once occupied by Judaism relatively to the idolatry of Egypt and Canaan, and very similar to its own original position relatively to the Sabeanism of Arabia. In fact, Islām may be regarded as an illegitimate child of Judaism born in Arabia in the seventh century. It was a protest against the Sabeanism, idolatry, and fetish stone-worship prevalent in that country, and a declaration of God's Unity made by Muhammad in supposed continuation of the original revelation transmitted by Abraham through Ishmael, rather than through Isaac[1].

Indeed at one time it seemed likely that the religious reform preached by Muhammad would develope into a sect of Christianity, and had not the corrupt Christian doctrines with which Muhammad came in contact prevented his perceiving that the statement of a Trinity in Unity is also the strongest assertion of a Unity in Trinity, we might have had another Eastern Church in Arabia answering to those founded in Egypt, Syria, Armenia, and Constantinople.

The name Muhammad is simply the passive participle of the Arabic verb *hamada*, 'to praise,' and no more admits of any variety of spelling than our word 'praised,' nor can I see why the numerous arbitrary violations of orthography to which the false prophet's name has given rise should be perpetuated any longer.

It should be noted that although Muhammad was a self-deluded enthusiast, he did not put himself forward as the founder of a new religion, and would have indignantly forbidden the use of such a term as Muhammadanism. According to his own views he was simply the latest of four prophets (the others being Moses, Elias, and Christ), who were all followers of Abraham, the true founder of the doctrine of Islām, and were all Muslims because all preached the Unity of God and submission to His will[2]. In this

[1] The Ka'ba, or small cube-shaped temple of Mecca, is supposed to have been built by Abraham (who is called by Muhammad the first Muslim) over the spot where he was about to sacrifice Ishmael. The sacredness of the small black stone imbedded in the eastern angle is probably the result of the fetish stone-worship once prevalent in Arabia. Abraham is supposed to have stood upon this stone when he built the Ka'ba.

[2] In the Kurān, the Old Testament and the Gospel are spoken of with the greatest reverence, as the word of God. Muhammad never threw any doubts on the inspiration of either; faith in them was enjoined on penalty of hell. But the Kurān was a later revelation, and therefore a higher authority.

respect he was like the other great religious leaders—
Zoroaster, Buddha, and Confucius.

In the end, however, the necessities of his position
obliged him to break away from both Jews and Christians,
with whom at first on his flight to Medina (A.D. 622) he
contemplated an alliance. Nor did his doctrine, like that
of Buddhism, win its way anywhere in the world by per-
suasiveness, except on its first propagation. It is true that
Muhammad at the commencement of his career fought his
way through the idolatry around him with no other
weapons but argument and persuasion, but when he had
collected sufficient adherents, the force of circumstances
compelled him to adopt a more summary method of conversion. His conversions were then made at the point
of the sword, Muhammad became a conqueror and a ruler,
and Islām became as much a State polity as a religion.

About forty-one millions of the inhabitants of India
are Muhammadans. Indeed, one of the unexpected facts
brought out by the last census was the vast increase of
Indian Muslims. Great numbers of them are the descendants of Hindūs converted to Islām by the Muhammadan
conquerors, and are much Hindūized in their habits and
ways. In some places the lower classes of Musalmāns do
homage to the Hindū goddess of smallpox, and take part in
the Holī festival. It is certain that numbers of low-caste
Hindūs formerly became Muhammadans with the sole object
of raising themselves in the social scale. For all Muslims
are theoretically equal, and since there is no equality, nor
even any real citizenship, in a Muhammadan State for those
who are not Muslims, it has often happened that whole
communities have adopted Islām merely to place themselves
within the pale of State protection, patronage, jurisdiction,
and authority.

Unhappily, however, the Indian Muslims do not imitate
the Hindūs in their toleration of each other's sectarian
divisions.

There are, as most people know, two principal sects of

Muslims, called Sunnīs and Shī'as. The Shī'as deny that the three immediate successors of the prophet—Abūbakr, Omar, and Othmān—were true Khalīfas. They declare that Alī, Muhammad's son-in-law, was his first rightful successor. The Turks and nearly all Indian Musalmāns, except those connected in any way with Persia, are Sunnīs. All Persians are Shī'as, and the animosity between the two divisions is even greater than between Roman Catholics and Protestants. I have heard it humorously said that, besides the Shī'as, there are seventy-two subordinate sects, each of which considers that the other seventy-one will assuredly go to hell.

I observed in my travels that the mass of Indian Muhammadans, who are ignorant and uneducated, have a tendency to deify either Muhammad himself, or his son-in-law Alī, or the innumerable Muhammadan saints (*Pīrs*), whose tombs are scattered everywhere throughout Hindūstān and the Dekhan. Many regard them as mediators.

Moreover, the Islām of India appears to have borrowed something not only from Hindūism but from Buddhism. I saw relics of Muhammad, including a hair from his head, preserved as sacred objects in Delhi and Lahor, and the impress of his foot is revered much as the Hindūs and Buddhists revere the footstep of Vishṇu and Buddha. When Islām thus lapses into too great exaltation of Muhammad, it may fairly be called Muhammadanism.

The attitude of a Muhammadan towards Christianity is far more hopelessly hostile than that of a Hindū, and it is generally believed that, although Indian Muslims in some parts of India are more active and intelligent than Hindūs, the teaching of the Kurān has a tendency to make them more intolerant, more sensual and inferior in moral tone. They are certainly more proud and bigoted, and are often left behind by the Hindūs for the simple reason that they refuse to avail themselves in the same way of the educational advantages we offer.

With regard to Christianity, I have no hesitation in

declaring my conviction that it has more points of contact with Hindūism (notwithstanding the hideous idolatry encouraged by that system) than with Buddhism, Jainism, or even Islām. For example—Hindūs are willing to confess themselves sinful. They acknowledge the necessity of sacrifice. They admit the need of supernatural revelation, and they have a doctrine of inspiration even higher than our own. Their sacred scriptures are not the work of one mind like the Kurān, but represent a process of gradual accretion and progressive expansion like the sixty-six books of our own Holy Bible. They are familiar with the ideas of a divine trinity, of incarnation, and of the need of a Saviour, however perverted these ideas may be. Their Gāyatrī, a prayer repeated morning and evening by every Brāhman throughout India, might with slight alteration be converted into a Christian prayer. They believe in the 'vanity' of all earthly concerns. They affirm that the Supreme Being is a Spirit, omnipotent and omnipresent, and their dogma that 'God is existence, thought, and bliss,' is only inferior to the Christian assertion that 'God is love.'

With regard to the progress of Christianity in India, I will only at present record my opinion that the best work done by the missionaries is in their schools. In some important places, such as Benares, the missionary schools are more popular than those of the Government, although the Bible is read and religious instruction given in the former, and not in the latter. Education is, indeed, causing a great upheaving of old creeds and superstitions throughout India, and the ancient fortress of Hindūism is in this way being gradually undermined. The educated classes look with contempt on idolatry.

In fact, the present condition of India seems very similar to that of the Roman Empire before the coming of Christ. A complete disintegration of ancient faiths is in progress in the upper strata of society.

Most of the ablest thinkers become pure Theists or Unitarians. In almost every large town there is a *Samāj*, or society of such men, whose creed would be well expressed by the first part of the first Article of the Church of England. They retain the name Brahma as applicable to the Supreme Being, but they regard him as a personal god, to be addressed by prayer as well as praise. No sooner, however, is a Samāj formed than, as is usual in India, it splits up into subdivisions, some founding their theism on the Veda, others partially appealing to it, and others rejecting it altogether. Even great leaders like Keshab Chandra Sen, of Calcutta, are unable to unite all Indian Theists into one body.

Christianity has made most progress among people of low caste and with some of the aboriginal tribes, and will probably gradually work its way upwards as it did on its first propagation by our Lord and His disciples. The religion of conquerors is never likely to be popular with either the higher or lower classes, if it offers no political or social advantages; and controversial discussion, though it may convince the head, will not touch the heart. It should always be borne in mind that, unlike the Muhammadans and Roman Catholics, we have abstained, as a conquering government, from enforcing our religion by government influence and authority. Hence conversions to Christianity bear no adequate proportion to the teeming millions of India (as indeed the Indian Bishops themselves allow in their circular of November 27th, 1873). Nor will conversions, in my opinion, be more common until our religion is presented to the Hindūs in a more Oriental form,—that is, in a form more like that which belonged to it on its first foundation at Jerusalem; and by more Orientalized missionaries,—that is, by men who will consent to live among the natives and become themselves half Indianized. It is even a question whether certain caste-customs might not be tolerated among Indian converts.

At any rate, an Indian ought not to be expected to have less caste-prejudices than a European. He ought to be allowed, as a convert to Christianity, to retain such of his caste-customs as may not be inconsistent with his submitting to the test of baptism, and meeting other converts on terms of perfect equality at the communion table.

Our Administration of the Country.

No one can travel in India and shut his eyes to the benefits conferred on its inhabitants by English rule. In fact, our subjugation of the country affords an exemplification of the now trite truth that the conquest of an inferior race by a superior, so far from being an evil, is one of the great appointed laws of the world's progress and amelioration.

We are sometimes accused of governing India in the interest of England and English commerce—of making India the *corpus vile* of political, social, and military experiments, of thinking more of what is called the maintenance of our prestige than of the welfare of the country. Yet the traveller has only to look around to see everywhere conspicuous monuments of the good intentions, integrity, and efficiency of our administration. I believe that in no part of the world is so much work done, and so well and conscientiously done, and with such a single regard to the discharge of duty, as by the Queen's servants in India. Even men of inferior energy and mental calibre, who, in England, would do little to benefit society, are, by the circumstances of their position in India, drawn out and developed into useful officers and able administrators.

And what are the results? The picture once presented to our view was that of a country devastated by intestine wars, oppressed by despotic rulers, depopulated by famine, and left to succumb unresistingly to the attacks of pestilence or to the destructive energy of physical forces. Instead of which, what do we now find? The same forces tamed and controlled, steam and electricity made to subserve the purposes of traffic and intercourse, good roads, canals, and waterworks constructed, rights of all kinds secured, justice impartially administered, education actively promoted, and everywhere a thriving, law-abiding, rapidly increasing population.

Yet our very anxiety to do all we can for India may sometimes lead to our doing too much. The extension of the telegraphic system has necessarily caused greater centralization of Government authority at Calcutta. But India is a collection of countries which differ so essentially, and require such varied treatment, that each would probably be better governed by carefully-chosen men of strong will and judgment, if more power of independent action were conceded to them.

And now, again, submarine telegraphy has led to further centralization, so that India is at present more governed from the central terminus of Queen, Lords, and Commons, than by those who are at the Indian end of the wires. Formerly the ignorance and apathy of Parliament were of little importance; now its interposition may often complicate our difficulties.

Moreover, the possibility of conveying a message backwards and forwards between the India Office and Calcutta in a few hours fosters a forgetfulness of the enormous distance dividing the Western from the Eastern Empire, and of the vast gulf separating the condition of England and of English society and habits of thought from those of India. Hence it is often supposed that Western ideas may be suddenly transfused into an Eastern mind, and English institutions abruptly transplanted to an Indian soil, when neither the one nor the other is prepared to receive them. It may certainly be questioned whether we are not prone to too much and too frequent legislation, and whether, in many places, we are not fifty, or even a hundred, years too early with some of our laws and regulations, with our civil courts and trials by jury, with our appeals to supreme tribunals, and our modern municipal institutions.

The Collector of a large district assured me that, as chairman of a municipal board in a large town, he could make native members vote in any way he chose to direct. Clearly that town is not advanced enough for the ratepayers to elect their own municipal authorities. Yet India has for centuries been accustomed to a form of municipal self-government in its village corporations. What is wanted is a wise and cautious progress, a zeal according to knowledge, a discreet adaptation of legislation to varying conditions of time and place.

Our Connection with the Native States.

Few persons are aware that the number of native States and Principalities still remaining in India exceeds 460. They cover an area of about 600,000 square miles and are inhabited by about 50 million persons. They are certainly instrumental in preserving the distinctive nationalities of the separate races of India which are apt to melt into each other or lose the sharpness of their definition under our rule. Some frontier countries, like Nepāl, merely acknowledge our supremacy; others pay us tribute, or provide military contingents. Some have powers of life and death, and most of them are obliged to refer capital cases to English Courts. Nearly all are allowed to adopt on failure of heirs, and their continual existence is thus secured. In fact, we are bound by treaty to maintain them, provided they govern well. Some think that in case of a rising in our own territories, the native States will increase our risks and weaken our position, instead of becoming havens of refuge and sources of strength. No doubt, in such a case, most of the Mahārājas would be individually eager to aid us, because they know that their own existence is bound up in ours. Few of them would survive the anarchy that would inevitably follow if we were cruel enough to leave India to govern itself. Hence they would strive to help us. But very few have sufficient personal authority and influence with their own people, and even with their own troops, to control their hostility to us. I fear that the people generally prefer maladministration and a limited amount of oppression under their own rulers to good government under ours.

I ought here, however, to remark that it is naturally considered rather surprising that we only employ an army of 190,000 men (65,000 Europeans and 125,000 Natives) for the government of the 190 millions of people under our own direct administration, while native states with a population of only fifty million are allowed by us to employ armed men to the amount of nearly 315,000.[1] Of these men the troops of the Nizām and of Sindia are the best disciplined; and in case of a mutiny among our own native army they would probably add very seriously to our difficulties instead of helping us out of them.

Granted that of the others some troops would be controlled by loyal chiefs and ministers, as the Nizām's soldiers formerly were. Granted, too, that a vast number would be simply contemptible either as allies or as opponents. Yet the expediency of permitting the native feudatory princes to organize and equip, at the expense of their impoverished people, unnecessarily large forces, is certainly a matter which has not yet awakened the attention it deserves.

The external and internal security of the native states is guaranteed by our administration; and all they need is an effective police force, the maintenance of which would not drain the resources of their territories as standing armies do.

I believe that the gross revenue of all the feudatory states subject to our rule is about sixteen millions, and that out of that amount a sum of only three quarters of a million sterling is annually contributed towards the Imperial administration which guarantees to them complete immunity from foreign invasion and from internal rebellion. Surely a portion of the money now wasted on needless armaments and senseless military show, might reasonably be compelled by us to flow into channels which would improve and

[1] Col. Malleson enumerates the fighting men of the native states thus: 241,063 foot soldiers, 64,172 cavalry, 9,320 trained artillerymen, 5,252 guns.

enrich the condition of the people. In this manner each particular state would be enabled to make an adequate return for the protection it receives, both indirectly and directly— indirectly by augmenting the general prosperity, directly by paying an equitable contribution to the Imperial Treasury.

At Calcutta, and other places in India, during the Prince's tour, I had unusual opportunities of becoming acquainted with the principal Mahārājas, and occasional interesting conversations with them and their Ministers. Some are enlightened men. Many have been brought up under our superintendence with great care. But I fear the truth about many of them is this. On coming of age they are allowed to manage their kingdoms, under the eye of our Residents and political Agents, who watch them without direct interference. At first they give great promise, but soon become surrounded by designing Ministers, who, to serve their own interests—which are better promoted by bad government than by good—encourage the young Rājas in a life of dissipation. Very few resist the evil influences of their surroundings for any length of time. By degrees they succumb and degenerate. In the end they fall into excesses and become debilitated in body and mind. Then their feeble sons, if they have any, generally die early, and an heir is adopted.

Happily, there are remarkable exceptions to this rule, and examples might be given of good native princes who devote themselves to the welfare of their territories.

As an illustration I may state that, when I was at Calcutta, I accepted the invitation of the Mahārāja of Kaśmīr to pay him a visit at Jammu. He is a son of Gulāb Singh, a Rājput chief who served under the Sikhs, and to whom we made over the Dogra district, of which Jammu is the capital, and Kaśmīr, of which Srinagar is the capital, for a stipulated sum of money after the first Panjāb war. The present Mahārāja is most desirous of pleasing us, and opens his kingdom to our travellers for eight months in the year, providing them with accommodation at his own ex-

NATIVE STATES. JAMMU.

pense. He himself prefers living in the town of Jammu (probably named from the Jambu tree common in the neighbourhood), because it commands the entrance to his territories, which altogether cover an area larger than England. The town most picturesquely crowns one of the undulations which, rising abruptly from the Panjāb plains, are succeeded by wave after wave of higher ranges till they terminate in the white crests of the Himālayas. From the King's palace a grand view of the Tavī Valley, shut in at the further end by snowy ranges, may be obtained. Another palace, very like a large railway station, was built the other day for the occupation of the Prince of Wales at an alleged expense of £60,000.

The Mahārāja, whose appearance is handsome and soldier-like, is unwearied in his royal duties. He rises early, is strict in his devotions, and temperate in his habits, and every morning for several hours may be seen in a room overlooking the courtyard of his palace, surrounded by able advisers, and diligently superintending the affairs of his kingdom. What chiefly deserves mention as distinguishing him from the generality of native Sovereigns is his encouragement of literature. He is the Augustus of Indian Princes. Not only has he established the best native schools I have seen in India for the teaching of Sanskrit, Arabic, Persian, and English, but he has also set up a press, with a type foundry, and keeps around him a large staff of Pandits and other learned men who are constantly engaged in translating the best European works into the dialects of the country. This dialect is a modification of Panjābi—called Dogra, as belonging to the Dwigarta district, between the Rāvī and the Chenāb. Translations have already been made of works on grammar, history, geography, mathematics, surveying, architecture, medicine, and several of the physical sciences. A dictionary has also been commenced in six languages. Moreover, a standard alphabet has been constructed with much skill by employing the Devanāgarī to improve the imperfect graphic system formerly current in the country. The King's zeal for learning was rather curiously exhibited for my benefit. He had a detachment of soldiers manœuvred before me that I might listen to the words of command, which were all in Sanskṛit. The spread of education and knowledge in the Mahārāja's dominion during the last ten years is most remarkable.

There are other examples of well-governed States, notably that of the Mahārāja of Travankor; but the description of one must here suffice.

Our Education of the People.

It is commonly alleged that if we go on educating on our present plan we shall soon lose India. No one will dispute that whatever the consequences may be our duty is to continue educating. Whether, however, our system is altogether wise, admits of question. I can certify that a vast work has been effected and is still proceeding. Everywhere there are schools—primary, intermediate, middle, and high—besides Colleges and Universities—and every year witnesses an increasing number of scholars and students. At Bombay I saw 12,000 children—all under education—assembled to greet the Prince of Wales. I also saw 1,263 candidates being examined for matriculation, and among them some young Princes. At Calcutta I saw even a greater number, and the standard of proficiency seemed higher than in England. Yet we have merely penetrated the outer fringe of society. Very little impression has yet been made on the masses of the people, and the chasm separating the educated from the uneducated is enormous. India cannot be said to possess a real middle-class, so that any middle education like that in England is impossible. Even in the case of those supposed to be under the higher form of education, I fear the work effected is rather information than education—rather informing the mind than forming the character and raising its tone.

This sort of education is, in some cases, better than nothing, but too often inflates young men with conceit, unhinges their faith in their own religion without giving them any other, leads them to despise the calling of their fathers, and to look upon knowledge as a mere stepping-stone to Government situations which they cannot all obtain. I heard it stated (possibly with some exaggeration) that not long ago there were 500 applications for a municipal post at Kurnoul, worth only Rs. 15 per month. Those who are unsuccessful in gaining appointments will not turn to manual labour, but remain discontented members of society and enemies of our Government, converting the little real education they have received into an instrument to injure us by talking treason and writing seditious articles in native journals. I believe the defects of our present system are beginning to be acknowledged. Many think we shall be wiser to educate the generality of natives in their professions and callings rather than above them—to make a good husbandman a better one, a good mechanic more skilful in his own craft—and only to give higher forms of education in exceptional cases.

With regard to female education, although its bearing on the moral and intellectual and even physical progress of India can scarcely be overrated, little impression, I fear, has yet been made on the mass of the population. Scattered efforts are prosecuted with much energy and some success, but too often show signs of languishing. The truth simply is that, before we can raise the women of India, we must first raise the men. We must do more than inform their minds—we must form their whole characters and cast them in a higher mould; and if we cannot convert them to the dogmas of Christianity, we must instil into them Christian ideas and ways of thinking. When we have thus elevated the men, we may safely leave the women to their keeping. The women will then be raised to the level of the men by the act of the men themselves without our interference. At present Hindū women are generally faithful wives and devoted mothers, and have great influence with their families, but they are grossly ignorant; and to their ignorance, bigotry, and subjection to the Brāhmans, the maintenance of superstition and idolatry, which would otherwise rapidly lose ground among the men, is, I suspect, mainly due.

Disposition and Attitude of the Natives towards us and our Rule.

In the first place, how are they disposed to us personally? I am sorry to say that my travels in India have revealed to me that between the ruler and the ruled in India there is a great gulf fixed, which, since the Mutiny, has widened and is becoming more and more difficult to be bridged over. The very arrangement of every large town bears witness to the truth of this statement, the European residences being collected in a quarter of their own quite distinct from the native town. Another significant fact is that on railways Europeans and natives are never seen together in the same carriages.

The causes which lead to this separation are mostly patent, but a remedy is not easily applied. First, there is what is called the race feeling, by which is meant the natural antipathy between races of different coloured skins —a feeling which, however manifestly unreasonable, is difficult to overcome. Then there is the caste feeling, which we have quite as strongly in our own way as Indians. With us, however, it is of a different kind. It is not part of our religion. In the case of the Hindūs the principal result of caste, in relation to us Europeans, is that although they may be of the same rank as ourselves they will not consent to eat with us, or to drink water touched by us or our servants. We, on the other hand, are accustomed to regard dining together as essential to social intercourse, and are apt to resent their declining to sit at meat with us, as if we were personally insulted.

But we ought to bear in mind that eating and drinking is, with a Hindū, bound up with his religion, or rather with its system of purificatory rites ; and that the killing of animals (especially oxen) for food is regarded as an impious act, so that the absence of Hindūs from our tables ought not to offend us more than their absence from our churches.

Then there is the feeling naturally springing up between governors and governed. A commanding tone of voice may often be necessary for the maintenance of authority, but I fear we rulers are sometimes unnecessarily imperious. We are naturally conscious of our superiority, but need our bearing towards those we are ruling make them feel their inferior position too keenly?

An advanced native, of independent character, once complained to me that most Englishmen appeared to him to walk about the world with an air as if God Almighty intended the whole universe to be English. He had probably been thrown with young civilians recently imported from England. Few others would think of lording it over their Indian brethren in any offensive manner. A reaction in this respect has set in all over India. I could enumerate many cases in which the mild Hindū is not a whit milder in manner than those who are set over him.

Then there are other feelings springing from early training, habits, and association. It is difficult for a European, who has never been in the East, to estimate the difference in ideas and ways of thinking arising from this source. Not only is there a different standard of taste as shown in dress, music, &c., but even to a certain extent of right and wrong. For instance, if a Hindū thinks it wrong to kill animals for food, much more does he object to destroying life of any kind for sport. Again, an Asiatic, whether Hindū or Musalmān, thinks it highly improper for women to mix familiarly with men who are not relations, much more to dance with them. Then there are differences in nearly every common custom. For example, a Hindū shows respect by covering his head when a European uncovers it. In a few cases assimilation of habits has been effected, but when this has occurred the Indian has become more Europeanized than the European has become Indianized. It would be foolish to expect these differences to cease. What is really to be regretted is the estrangement they produce.

And now, in the last place, what is the attitude of the natives of India towards our Government? The most intelligent are quite ready to admit that they enjoy greater benefits under our rule than they would under any other; and the wiser, who know that universal disorder would follow its cessation, even pray for its continuance; but the mass of unthinking people would rather be badly governed by their own chiefs than well governed by us. In the native states they will acquiesce in exactions which in our territories would be regarded as intolerable. Of course nothing will conciliate those who are determined to dislike us. But even the wiser, who value our rule, consider that they have certain grievances. Why—I have often been asked—are we treated as if in mental capacity and moral tone we were all inferior to Europeans? Why are we never allowed to rise to the highest executive appointments? Why are those of us who compete for the Civil Service forced to go to England for examination? Supposing we are not yet fit for representative government, why are we not allowed deliberative assemblies, like the Houses of Convocation in the English Church, that our opinions may be made known before fresh laws are enacted? Why cannot justice be administered more cheaply and directly, and with fewer delays? Why does the Government spend so much of the revenues on public works and give us no new serais and tanks? These are a few of the complaints I have heard.

Perhaps some of them are not real, and others are in course of redress. I believe our Government admits that when natives can show themselves mentally and morally fit for the highest administrative offices they must be allowed to fill them[1]. We are certainly doing our best to redress political grievances. Let us also endeavour to do more than we have hitherto done towards bridging over the social chasm that at present separates the two races and complicates the difficulties of our position in India. Our great English Universities may contribute something towards this important object, if they will make facilities for the reception of young Indians and for their intercourse with young Englishmen. I believe that the young men of England and India may learn useful lessons from each other, and yet preserve their separate nationalities. We must of course be conscious of our own superiority in religion, morality, and general culture; but let us give our Indian fellow-subjects credit for such excellencies as they possess, and condescend to admit that good may accrue from some interchange of ideas and mutual attrition between the two races. Assuredly a better feeling between them must result from consciousness of reciprocal benefits bestowed.

One thing at least is certain, that India is given to us to conciliate as well as to elevate, even if she offers us nothing to imitate. In my opinion the great problem that before all others presses for solution in relation to our Eastern Empire is, how can the rulers and the ruled be drawn closer together? How can more sympathy and cordial feeling be promoted between them?

[1] By 33 Vict. cap. 3, sec. 6, it is no longer necessary for Indians to come to England that they may be eligible for civil appointments. The local governments can nominate a certain proportion (one fifth of the number of Europeans) every year, and the number of civilians selected in England is then diminished in a corresponding degree. The native candidates selected in India are not allowed to be more than twenty-five years of age, except in cases of special ability, and they are obliged to serve on probation for two years. The great difficulty is the adjustment of salaries. How can those of Europeans, working as exiles from their country and homes in a hot climate not always suited to their constitutions, be estimated on the same scale as those of natives?

GENERAL IMPRESSIONS AND NOTES AFTER TRAVELS IN SOUTHERN INDIA.

SOUTHERN India may be regarded as embracing all India below the twenty-second parallel of latitude—that is to say, speaking roughly, all within the northern tropical line. It will, therefore, include that part of the Bombay Presidency south of the Narbadā, of which Bombay and Poona are the capitals; that portion of the Central Provinces, of which Nāgpur is the chief town; Orissa; the Nizām's territory, of which Hyderabad is the capital; Mysor, and the whole Madras Presidency, with Travankor as far as Cape Comorin. To these may be added the island of Ceylon, the south point of which is within six degrees of the Equator.

Climate of Southern India.

I described my experience of a winter in the Northern parts of India as delightful, and now a winter passed in the South has not changed my opinion as to the superiority of the Indian climate to our own for at least five months in the year. Indeed, I am satisfied that to those who can retire to the Hills for a time in the hot and rainy seasons, residence in India all the year round is attended with as little risk to health as residence in England.

But India is like a continent which offers every variety of sanitary condition, and it must not be forgotten that the whole of Southern India is within the Tropics. It has places which are correctly described as deadly in their effect on the health of Europeans, and in certain jungly districts, where there is no lack of moisture and the temperature is persistently high, rank deciduous vegetation generates fever as a matter of course. The rainfall on the western coast is the greatest, and with abundant tropical rain, and abundant tropical vegetation, comes inevitable malaria. It must be admitted, too, that so far as my experience has gone during the past winter, I found the climate of the whole of Southern India more trying to the health than that of the districts north of the Narbadā river and Vindhya hills. It is true that there is not the same intensity of summer heat in the South, and the temperature from one year's end to the other is more equable, but there are no intervals of bracing cold either in the winter or in the night time. I believe it may be proved by statistics that cholera is always more prevalent in the South than in the North. Certainly, in the beginning of 1877 a bad type of the disease prevailed in some of the districts through which I travelled, and I heard of many Europeans being attacked. Probably, however, the drought, famine, and badness of the water may have caused an exceptionally unhealthy season.

Physical Features of Southern India.

What strikes one most in travelling through any part of India is the vastness of the country. No sooner does one land in Bombay than one's whole ideas of distance have to be cast in a new mould. You are told that an old acquaintance is residing close to your hotel, and you find to your surprise that a visit to his house involves a drive of ten miles. The sense of vastness is not so overpowering in Southern India as in Northern, and yet the Nizām's territory alone embraces an area little less than that of the kingdom of Italy.

Perhaps the most remarkable physical feature of Southern India is the existence of an immense triangular plateau of table-land caused by the circumstance that the high ranges of hills on the western coast slope down gradually, but with numerous irregular depressions and isolated elevations, towards the eastern coast, where the plateau breaks up into lower ranges, leaving much level land between the heights and the sea. The two eastern and western coast ranges, which come to a point near Cape Comorin, are called Ghāts because they recede like steps (Sanskrit *Ghaṭṭa*) from the sea-shore; and the triangle of table-land formed by their junction with the two extremities of the Vindhya range which traverses the centre of India, is called the Deccan, from Prakrit *Dakkin*, for Sanskrit *Dakshin*, 'the south country.' The great Indian Peninsula Railway from Bombay to Jabalpore and Raichor conducts to this plateau by a wonderful piece of engineering skill up the Bhore Ghāt. Poona, the capital of our part of the Deccan, is nearly 2,000 feet above the sea; so is our military station of Secunderabad, close to Hyderabad, the capital of the Nizām's portion of the Deccan; and our station of Bangalor, in the Mysor country, is about 3,500 feet above the sea level. There is an extensive tract of ugly flat country round Madras, along the Coromandel coast and Northern Circars. But there is no lack of grand scenery on the Western Ghāts, especially towards their southern extremity, on the Nīlgiri, Animalli, Pulney, and Asambhu hills, some of which rise to an altitude of more than 8,000 feet. The ascent to Ootacamund is quite equal to the finest Swiss pass I ever saw. What it loses by the absence of snow is counterbalanced by the glories of its tropical vegetation. Moreover, all Europe cannot boast such waterfalls as the Gairsappa Falls, on the Malabar coast, and those of the River Kāverī in Mysor. The former even in the dry season present a perpendicular fall of a large mass of water 900 feet high. I have heard this called the third sight of India, the Himālayas coming first, and the Tāj at Agra second.

Madras.

As to the chief town of the Madras Presidency, a situation more unsuited to a great capital can hardly be conceived. Madras has no harbour and no navigable river, and the ships anchored in its roads are in constant danger of being driven ashore, as the 'Duke of Sutherland' was the other day. Its drainage—if any is possible where the ground is often below the sea level—is so bad that cholera is never absent. Indeed, so far as my experience goes, Madras is inferior to Bombay and Calcutta, not only in a sanitary point of view, but in nearly every other particular, except perhaps in the one point that more English is spoken by the native servants. Its inhabitants are now making a great effort to improve its trade, and the present Governor, who has a decided penchant for engineering, is developing his taste in the interest of the merchants by promoting the construction of an artificial harbour, the cost of which is to be defrayed out of the revenues of India. Untold sums of money are being thrown into the sea in the shape of huge blocks of concrete, each of them about 12 feet long by 10 feet in breadth and 8 feet in thickness, for the formation of a breakwater, which is to encircle the present pier with two projecting arms. But the difficulty of enclosing a sufficient area of water, and the perpetual drifting of sand along the coast, make the success of the undertaking highly problematical. Under any circumstances, Madras, though large enough to attract a trade of its own, will never overcome its own natural disadvantages of position, so as to compete with either Bombay or Calcutta, the former of which is destined to become the great commercial emporium and capital of all India (if not of all Asia), the wealth and importance of which will be vastly increased so soon as the Baroda Railway is connected with Ajmere, Agra, and the North-West. Calcutta, too, is likely to continue the political capital of India, both from the convenience of its situation on the Ganges, in the midst of a naturally peaceful and law-abiding population, and from the obstacles its position offers to an attack from the sea.

Animal and Plant Life in Southern India.

Perhaps the most striking point of difference between Northern and Southern India is due to the circumstance that the South possesses all the characteristics of the Tropics in the greater exuberance of all kinds of life and vegetation. To realize this exuberance fully one must go to the extreme South and Ceylon. There one may come across almost every animal, from a wild elephant to a fire-fly. There, as one strolls through a friend's compound or drives to a neighbouring railway station, one passes the choicest plants and trees of European hothouses growing luxuriantly in the open air. As to animals, they seem to dispute possession of the soil with man. They will assert with perfect impunity their right to a portion of the crops he rears and the food he eats, and will even effect a lodgment in the houses he builds as if they had a claim to be regarded as co-tenants. This is a good deal owing to the sacredness of animal life in India. Not only is there an absolute persuasion in the mind of a Hindū that some animals, such as cows, serpents, and monkeys, are more or less pervaded by divinity, but most Indians believe that there are eighty-four lakhs of species of animal life through which a man's own soul is liable to pass.

In fact, any noxious insect or loathsome reptile may be, according to the Hindū religion, an incarnation of some deceased relative or venerated ancestor. Hence, no man, woman, or child among the Hindūs thinks it right to kill animals of any kind. Hence, too, in India animals of all kinds appear to live on terms of the greatest confidence and intimacy with human beings. They cannot even learn to be afraid of their enemies the European immigrants. Musquitoes will settle affectionately and fearlessly on the hands of the most recent comer, leeches will insinuate themselves lovingly between the interstices of his lower garments, parrots will peer inquisitively from the eaves of his bedroom into the mysteries of his toilet, crows will carry off impudently anything portable that takes their fancy on his dressing-table, sparrows will hop about impertinently and take the bread off his table-cloth, bats will career triumphantly round his head as he reads by the light of his duplex lamp, monkeys will domesticate themselves jauntily on his roof, and at certain seasons snakes will domicile themselves unpleasantly in his cast-off garments, while a whole tribe of feathered creatures will build their nests confidingly under the trees of his garden before the very eyes of the village boys who play near his compound. I have heard it said in England that the tigers of India will soon be exterminated; yet I looked down from the heights near Ootacamund on a tract of country swarming with tigers and wild animals of all kinds. Such animals are on the increase in these and other similar localities, notwithstanding the active hostility of rifle-armed English sportsmen. The truth is that those Europeans who venture into such jungles to shoot down tigers are themselves struck down, like Lord Hastings, by jungle fever; and before we can induce the natives to wage a war of extermination against beasts of prey, we must disabuse them of the notion that men are sometimes converted into wild beasts, and that the spirit of a man killed by a tiger not unfrequently takes to riding about on the animal's head[1].

With regard to plant life, it must be borne in mind that in the creed of the Hindūs even plants may be permeated by divinity or possessed by the souls of departed relatives. No Hindū will cut down the divine Tulsī, or knowingly injure any other sacred plant. As to the holy Pīpal, it may indulge its taste for undermining walls and houses, and even palaces and temples, with perfect impunity. Happily, there is a limit to even the most pious Hindū's respect for plant life.

[1] See Sleeman's 'Rambles and Recollections,' p. 162.

Perhaps the most demonstrative and self-asserting and, at the same time, most useful of tropical trees is the palm. Palm trees are ubiquitous in Southern India, and yet the eye never wearies of their presence. One hundred and fifty different species may be seen in Ceylon, among which the most conspicuous are the cocoa-nut, the palmyra, the date, the sago, the slender areca, and the sturdy talipot—often crowned with its magnificent tuft of flowers, which it produces only once before its decay, at the end of about half a century. Avenues of palm trees overshadow the roads and even line the streets of towns. The next most characteristic tree of Southern India is the banyan. The sight of a fine banyan tree is almost worth a voyage from Southampton to Bombay, and it can only be seen in perfection in the South. One I saw in a friend's compound at Madura was 180 yards in circumference, and was a little forest in itself. Then there is the beautiful plantain, with its broad, smooth leaves, rivalling the palm in luxuriance and ubiquity. Then one must go to Southern India to understand how the lotus became the constant theme of Indian poets, as the symbol of everything lovely, sacred, and auspicious. Space indeed would fail if I were to tell of groves of mangoes and tamarinds, clumps of enormous bamboos, gigantic creepers in full blossom, tree ferns, oranges and citrons, hedges of flowering aloes, cactus, prickly pear, wild roses, and geraniums, or even if I were to descant at large on such useful plants as coffee, cinchona, tea, and tobacco.

With regard to these last I will merely say that our thriving colony of Ceylon is the true home of the coffee plant, and that I found coffee-planting there in a peculiarly flourishing condition. About £5 per cwt. was given in 1876 for coffee which formerly realised only £2 10s.[1] The

---

[1] According to a correspondent of the *Times*, 749,870 cwt. of coffee was shipped up to June 20, 1879, as compared with 529,807 cwt. for last year, and 770,679 for the year previous. It appears that there is now a certainty of ridding coffee plantations of that destructive pest—*Hemeleia vas-*

island owes much of its present prosperity to Sir William Gregory's energetic governorship. Coffee in great quantities is also grown on the Nīlgiris, the hill districts of Mysor, the Wynaad, Travankor, and the Asambhu hills. Cinchona (yielding quinine) is being cultivated with great success in Ceylon, Sikkim, and some hill stations of Southern India. As to tea, ever since the tea-plant was found to be indigenous in Assam and Kachār, its cultivation has gone on increasing so rapidly that it is likely to become one of the staple products of India, and will vie as an export with rice, opium, cotton, and jute. It is said that 357,000 chests were exported last year from Assam, Kachār, and Darjiling—the three chief tea districts—alone. Tea cultivation is also carried on in other hill stations of Northern and Southern India. I am told that a great future is in store for tobacco, and that it will take the place of opium as a source of revenue should the Chinese demand for the latter cease. All that is wanted is skill in its cultivation, and more delicate manipulation in the rolling of the leaves of the plant for the manufacture of cigars. Its success in British Burmah is remarkable. But enough of plants; let me turn to men.

Character of the People in Southern India.

If the most apathetic traveller is astonished by the nature of the climate, by the vastness of the country, by the diversity of the scenery, by the exuberance of animal and plant life in Southern India, much more is his wonder excited by the multiplicity of races which constitute its teeming population, by the variety of their costume, manners, social institutions, usages, religious creeds, and dialects. Biologists, ethnologists, archæologists, and philologists will find here (as in Northern India) a rich banquet set before them, from which they may always rise with an appetite for

tatrix—popularly known as leaf-disease, by means of a mixture of sulphur and lime recently invented by a certain Mr. Morris.

more. The inhabitants of Bombay, whose number exceeds that of any other city in the British Empire (except London and Calcutta), may be said to belong partly to Gujarāt, partly to the Konkan, and partly to the Marātha country. When we have ascended the Bhore Ghāt and are in that part of the Deccan of which Poona is the capital, we are fairly among the Marāthas, who are the principal representatives of the Āryan race in Southern India. The Brāhmans and higher classes of this race are often fine intelligent men, and sometimes great Pandits, but withal proud and bigoted. Their women are kept less secluded, and are far more independent than the women in Northern India, where Muhammadan influences are much stronger. It is common to see Marātha ladies walking about in the streets of large towns and showing themselves in public without any scruple.

The rest of Southern India, not including the Āryan portion of Orissa, is peopled first by the great Drāvidian races (so called from Drāviḍa, the name given by the Sanskrit speakers to the Southern, or Tamil, part of the Peninsula), whose immigrations into India in successive waves from some part of Central Asia immediately preceded those of the Āryans. These Drāvidians are of course quite distinct from the Āryans; their skin is generally much darker, and the languages they speak belong to what is sometimes called the South Turanian (agglutinative) family. They may be separated into four distinct peoples, according to their four principal languages — Telugu, Kanarese, Tamil, and Malayālam (see p. 151).

Secondly, Southern India is peopled by the wild primitive races, some of them Negröid in complexion, and others Negrito, of a type similar to the savages of Australia. They are now usually called Kolarians[1]. Their irruptions preceded the advent of the Drāvidians, and they are still

---

[1] See p. 149. I believe the convenient designation Kolarian (formed from the word *Kol*, the name of a particular race) is due to Sir George Campbell, who first used it.

CHARACTER OF THE PEOPLE. 189

found in the hills and other outlying localities. Of the Drāvidians the Telugu and Tamil speakers are by far the majority, each numbering fifteen or sixteen millions. The Tamil race, who occupy the extreme south from Madras to Cape Comorin, are active, hard-working, industrious, and independent. Their difficult and highly accentuated language reflects their character and possesses quite a distinct literature of its own. The Telugu people, inhabiting the Northern Circars and the Nizām's territory, are also remarkable for their industry; and their soft language, abounding in vowels, is the Italian of the East. The Kanarese of Mysor resemble the Telugu race in language and character, just as the Malayālams of the Malabar coast resemble the Tamils. I noticed that the seafaring Tamils of the Southern coast near Rāmnād, Rāmeśvaram, and Tuticorin are much more able-bodied and athletic than ordinary Hindūs. Numbers of them migrate to Ceylon, and at least half a million form a permanent part of the population of that island. They are to be found in all the coffee plantations, and work much harder than the Sinhalese.

Indeed, all the races of South India seem to me to show readiness and aptitude for any work they are required to do, as well as patience, endurance, and perseverance in the discharge of the most irksome duties. The lower classes may be seen everywhere earning their bread by the veritable sweat of their brow and submitting without a murmur to a life of drudgery and privation. But they are not, as a rule, physically strong, and their moral character, like their bodily constitution, exhibits little stamina. They have, so to speak, little solidity of backbone, either to keep them upright when they are brought into collision with stronger races, or to enable them to rise to the high standard of European morality. It must be borne in mind, too, that Europeans are sometimes strong in vices as well as in virtues; and that, as the Hindū rarely has the power of assimilating himself to our best qualities, he is apt to copy our worst. Even our Administrative Government, with all its moral purity, has introduced temptations which are to him a stone of stumbling. Yet I have been told by officers of long experience, who have witnessed the growth of much of our Indian Empire, that on the acquisition of newly-acquired territories, the inhabitants have never shown any immediate disposition towards deceit, litigiousness, subtlety, and avarice, or any of the faults they have afterwards displayed so conspicuously in our Courts of Justice, and in their dealings with us as rulers. The plain fact is, that the people of India are simply human beings with very human infirmities; and that, if the professing Christian finds it difficult to bear up against the tide of human care, crime, and trial which ever follows in the track of advancing civilization, much more does the non-Christian Hindū. I doubt, however, whether the worst Indians are ever so offensive in their vices as the worst type of low, unprincipled Europeans. At any rate, their vices are more secret and subtle. As servants, they are faithful, honest, and devoted, and will attach themselves with far greater affection than English servants to those who treat them well. They show greater respect for animal life than Europeans. They have more natural courtesy of manner, more filial dutifulness, more veneration for rank, age, and learning, and they are certainly more temperate in eating and drinking. I once asked a Peninsular and Oriental captain whether he preferred a crew of ordinary Indian or ordinary English sailors, and he unhesitatingly gave the preference to Indians, 'because,' said he, 'they are more docile, more obedient, less brutish in their habits, and can be trusted not to get drunk.'

Another point to be noted in comparing Indians with Europeans is that the rich among them are never ashamed of their poor relations, and, what is still more noticeable, neither rich nor poor are ever ashamed of their religion.

Religions of Southern India.

Religion is even more closely interwoven with every affair of daily life, and is even more showily demonstrative in the South of India than in the North. Unhappily, it is not of a kind to strengthen the character or fortify it against temptation. Yet its action on social, domestic, and political life is so potent, that to make clear the condition of the people, I must briefly explain the nature of their creeds.

A distinction has already been pointed out between Brāhmanism and Hindūism[1]. Brāhmanism is the purely pantheistic and not necessarily idolatrous creed evolved by the Brāhmans out of the religion of the Veda. Hindūism is that complicated system of polytheistic doctrine, idolatrous superstitions, and caste usages which has been developed out of Brāhmanism after its contact with Buddhism and its admixture with the non-Āryan creeds of the Drāvidians and Aborigines of Southern India. Brāhmanism and Hindūism, though infinitely remote from each other, are integral parts of the same system. One is the germ or root, the other is the rank and diseased outgrowth. It is on this account that they everywhere coexist in the same localities throughout the whole of India. Nevertheless, the most complete examples of both creeds are now to be looked for in Southern India, because the North has been always more exposed to Muhammadan influences. In fact, it was the South which produced the great religious revivalists, Kumārila, Sankara, Madhva, Rāmānuja, and Vallabha.

The followers of Śankara (who lived about the seventh or eighth century of our era, and whose successors reside at Śringeri, on the Mysor Ghāts) are usually strict Brāhmans. They call themselves Smārtas, as observers of Smṛiti or traditional doctrines and ceremonies, and their creed is

---

[1] I was the first to suggest this distinction in the use of the terms Brāhmanism and Hindūism, and am alone responsible for it.

generally pure Brāhmanism. In other words, they are pure Pantheists. They accept the Vedas, Itihāsas, Manu, and Purāṇas, and maintain the doctrine of one universal Spirit, manifesting himself equally in Brahmā, Vishṇu, and Śiva, and developing himself in every other form of divine, semi-divine, human and demoniacal personality.

The adherents of Madhva, on the other hand, call themselves Vaishṇavas—as worshippers of the god Vishṇu alone, whom they regard as the one Supreme Being, admitting that he has assumed various incarnations for the preservation of his creatures. They also differ from the Smārta followers of Sankara in maintaining an eternal distinction between the human and Supreme Soul. This is a form of Hindūism which has more common ground with Christianity than any other. I have met with many excellent and intelligent Brāhmans and others in the South of India who profess it.

But the great majority of South Indian Vaishṇavas are followers of Rāmānuja, who led the Vaishṇava revival in the twelfth century. These illustrate the operation of a law which appears essential to the vitality of every religious and political system. They have separated into two grand antagonistic parties—the Tengalais, or followers of the Southern doctrine, who maintain the doctrine of absolute faith in Vishṇu, which they illustrate by a kitten's passive dependence on the hold of the mother-cat ; and the Vadagalais, or followers of the Northern, who uphold the doctrine of man's co-operation with Vishṇu, illustrated by the young monkey's effort to grasp the mother-monkey when she moves from one branch to another. Their opposition is very similar to that which prevails in Europe between Calvinists and Arminians, and not unlike that between Protestants and Roman Catholics. Their quarrels in the present day relate more to the external mark of their sect than to differences in fundamental doctrine, the one party contending that this mark—made with a kind of white paint on the forehead—should represent both Vishṇu's feet and should extend half-way down the nose, while the other maintains that the mark should only represent one foot of Vishṇu and that the nasal organ is not entitled to be honoured with any paint at all. The proper marking of the idols in their temples is a special subject of contention and sometimes of litigation.

The Tengalai frontal mark, which has some resemblance to a trident, is represented below.

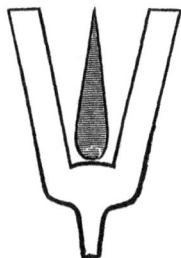

It is, however, no trident, if by that is meant a spear. The two outer lines which resemble prongs really stand for the two soles of Vishṇu's feet, while the line which extends down the nose is held to represent a kind of lotus throne on which the feet are supposed to rest, as in the annexed diagram.

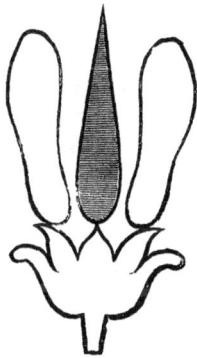

On the other hand the Vadagalai mark, as drawn on the next page, is said to stand for only one of Vishṇu's feet.

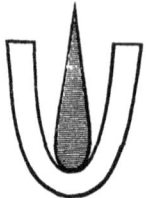

The Vadagalais contend that since the Ganges sprang from the sole of Vishṇu's right foot, his right foot should be held in special veneration, and its sign impressed on the forehead.

Both parties agree in employing a central mark to symbolize Vishṇu's wife Lakshmī. But, it ought to be stated that educated Vaishṇavas repudiate the idea of Vishṇu's being really married. Vishṇu, they say, is merely a name for the Supreme Being or in other words for the Infinite Spirit of the Universe, who cannot have an actual wife. The goddess Lakshmī, according to their view, is no real deity, but simply an ideal personification of the mercy of God. For the religion of the Vaishṇavas is, at least theoretically, one of love, tenderness, and compassion, while that of the Śaivas is inclined to take a sterner and more austere view of God's nature.

Besides these three principal sects there is another, called Lingavats (vulgarly Lingaits), who are the followers of a leader Basava (= Vṛishabha). They are worshippers of Śiva (symbolized by the lingam worn round their necks); but abjure all respect for caste distinctions and observance of Brāhmanical rites and usages. A great part of the Kanarese population below Kolapore and in Mysor is Lingait.

In short, Vaishṇavism and Śaivism (or the worship of Vishṇu and Śiva as personal Supreme Beings) constitute the very heart and soul of Southern Hindūism. As to Brahmā—the third member of the Hindū Triad, and original creator of the world—he is not worshipped at all except in the person of his alleged offspring, the Brāhmans. Moreover, Vaishṇavism and Śaivism are nowhere so pronounced and imposing as in Southern India. The temples of Kanjīvaram (Kāndīpuram), Tanjore, Trichinopoly, Madura, Tinnevelly, and Rāmesvaram are as superior in magnitude to those of Benares as Westminster Abbey and St. Paul's are to the other churches of London.

Furthermore, it must not be forgotten that, although a belief in devils, and homage to *bhūtas* or spirits of all kinds, is common all over India, yet what is called 'devil worship' is far more systematically practised in the South of India and in Ceylon than in the North. And the reason may be that as Drāvidians and Āryans advanced towards Southern India, they found it peopled by wild aboriginal savages, whose behaviour and aspect appeared to them to resemble that of devils. The Āryan and Drāvidian mind, therefore, naturally pictured to itself the regions of the South as the chief resort and stronghold of the demon race, and the dread of demoniacal agency became more rooted in Southern India than in the North. Curiously enough, too, it is commonly believed in Southern India that every wicked man contributes by his death to swell the ever-increasing ranks of devil legions. His evil passions do not die with him. They are intensified, concentrated, and perpetuated in the form of a malignant and mischievous spirit. Moreover, the god Śiva is constantly connected with demoniacal agencies, either as superintending and controlling them, or as himself possessing (especially in the person of his wife Kālī) all the fierceness and malignity usually attributed to demons.

Such demons though worshipped, or rather propitiated, have never any imposing temple-like structure dedicated to them. Often a mere heap of earth piled up in pyramidal shape, or a similar erection formed with bricks and painted with streaks of white constitutes the only devil-shrine, while another heap in front with a flat top does duty for the demon's altar. There is rarely any image, and probably a tree above, or near at hand, is the devil's supposed dwelling-place.

In fact, in the South of India, even more than in the North, all evils, especially drought, blight, and diseases, are attributed to devils. When my fellow-travellers and myself were nearly dashed to pieces over a precipice by some restive horses on a ghāt near Poona, we were told that the road at this particular point was haunted by devils, who often caused similar accidents, and we were given to understand that we should have done well to conciliate Gaṇeśa, son of the god Śiva, and all his troops of evil spirits, before starting. Of all gods Gaṇeśa is, perhaps, the most commonly conciliated, not, in my opinion, because he is said to bestow wisdom, but simply because he is believed to prevent the obstacles and diseases caused by devils. Homage, indeed, may be rendered to the good God, or Supreme Spirit pervading the universe, but he is too absolutely perfect to be the author of harm to any one, and does not need to be appeased. Devils alone require propitiation. Often the propitiating process is performed by offerings of food or other articles supposed to be peculiarly acceptable to disembodied beings. For example, when a certain European, who was a terror to the district in which he lived, died in the South of India, the natives were in the constant habit of depositing brandy and cigars on his tomb to propitiate his spirit, which was believed to roam about the neighbourhood in a restless manner and with evil proclivities. The very same was done to secure the good offices of the philanthropic spirit of a great European sportsman, who, when he was alive, delivered his district from the ravages of tigers.

Indeed, it ought to be mentioned that all evil spirits are thought to be opposed by good ones, who, if duly propitiated, make it their business to guard the inhabitants of particular places from demoniacal intruders. Each district, and even every village, has its guardian genius, often called its mother. If smallpox or blight appear, some mother (especially the one called Mārī Amman) is thought to be angry, and must be appeased by votive offerings. There are no less than 140 of these mothers in Gujarāt.

There is also one very popular male god in Southern India called Ayenār (*Harihara-putra*), son of Śiva and Vishṇu, to whom shrines in the fields are constantly erected. A remarkable point is that these guardian spirits —especially Ayenār—are supposed to delight in riding about the country on horses. Hence the traveller just arrived from Europe is startled and puzzled by apparitions of roughly-formed terra-cotta horses, often as large as life, placed by the peasantry round rude shrines in the middle of fields as acceptable propitiatory offerings, or in the fulfilment of vows during periods of sickness.

Another remarkable circumstance connected with the dread of demoniacal agencies is the existence in the South of India and Ceylon of professional exorcisers and devil-dancers. Exorcising is performed over persons supposed to be possessed by demons in the form of diseases. The exorciser assumes a particular dress, goes through various antics, mutters spells, and repeats incantations. Devil-dancing is performed by persons who paint their faces, or put on hideous masks, dress up in demoniacal costumes, and work themselves up into a veritable frenzy by wild dances, cries, and gesticulations. They are then thought to be actually possessed by the spirits and to become, like spiritualist mediums, gifted with clairvoyance and a power of delivering oracular and prophetic utterances on any matter about which they may be questioned. There seems to be also an idea that when smallpox, cholera, or similar pestilences are exceptionally rife, exceptional measures must be taken to draw off the malignant spirits, the supposed authors of the plague, by tempting them to pass into these wild dancers and so become dissipated.

I myself witnessed in Ceylon an extraordinary devil dance performed by three men who were supposed to personate or represent three different forms of typhus fever; and when I was at Tanjor, the learned Sanskritist Dr.

Burnell, who is Judge of that district, gave me some interesting information in regard to the demon-festivals which recur periodically in the district of Mangalor where he held office for some time.

One of the most popular of these festivals called Illeć-chida Nema is celebrated every fifteen or twenty years. At another called Kallyāta a wild dance is performed every 60th year before a particular rock or stone which is supposed to tremble and shake periodically.

Sometimes the performance takes place in a large shed in the middle of which burns a common lamp under a canopy. Around are images of the Bhūtas. At the distance of about a foot in front of the lamp is placed a common wooden tripod-stand, two or three feet high, on which is constructed a square frame of cocoa-nut leaves. Inside this frame a quantity of rice and turmeric is piled into a pyramid into which a three-branched iron lamp is inserted. Around are arranged offerings consisting of fruits and living victims such as fowls and goats. The latter are adorned with garlands, and both fowls and goats are afterwards decapitated, the warm blood being either poured out on the ground or on the altar, or else drunk by the officiating priest. The idea is that the demon thirsts for blood, and becomes irritated if his cravings are not satisfied. The sole object of sacrificing animals is to assuage his thirst and appease his anger.

All this is preliminary to the principal performance which takes place in an open space in front of the slaughtered victims. The priest, or some other devotee who has undergone a long preparatory fasting, comes forward to personate a particular demon. He is dressed up in a fantastic costume, often covered with grotesque dangling ornaments and jingling bells. Sometimes he wears a hideous mask; sometimes his face is daubed with paint of different colours. In one hand he holds a sword, trident, or other implement, and perhaps a bell in the other. He then commences dancing or pacing up and down in an excited manner, amid beating of tom toms, blowing of horns, and all kinds of noisy music, while an attendant sings songs or recites rude poems descriptive of the deeds of the demons. Meanwhile spirituous liquor is distributed, the performer becomes violently excited, and the demon

takes complete possession of him. Finally he succumbs in an hysterical fit, and gives out oracular responses to any inquiries addressed to him. Most of the bystanders consult him as to their several wants and destinies, or the welfare of absent relatives, but are not allowed to do so without first presenting offerings.

200   MODERN INDIA.

The figure on the preceding page represents a performer dressed up as a particular demon called Panjurli, whose worship is connected with some of the deeds of the god Śiva.

Another mischievous female demon called Kallurti, believed to be addicted to the unpleasant habit of throwing stones and setting fire to people's houses, is represented below with a torch in her hand.

This Kallurti is worshipped and conciliated by similar performances.

With regard to Buddhism, although its importation into Ceylon must have been effected to a great extent from Southern India, where its images still occasionally do duty as Hindū gods, yet it no longer exists there. In Ceylon it is a cold, negative, undemonstrative, sleepy religion, contrasting very remarkably with the showy, positive, and noisy form of Hindūism prevalent on the other side of the Straits. Its only worship consists in presenting flowers before images and relic shrines of the extinct Buddha, and in meditating on his virtues and on the advantages of doing nothing beyond aiming at similar extinction.

In times of sickness and calamity, the Sinhalese, having no Divine protector to appeal to, betake themselves, like the Hindūs, to the appeasing of devils or to the worship of idols borrowed from the Hindū Pantheon, whose temples often stand near their relic-dagobas. I myself saw several such temples near the celebrated dagoba erected over Buddha's eye-tooth at Kandy.

As to the South Indian Muhammadans, they are, of course, worshippers of one God, but I believe that even more than in the North they have made additions to the simplicity of Islām by the adoration of Pīrs, or saints, by the veneration of relics, and by conforming to Hindū customs and superstitions. In the Nizām's territory alone homage is paid to hundreds of Pīrs. The great Aurangzīb is buried near the tomb of a celebrated saint at Rozah, and crowds of pilgrims annually throng the shrine of a popular Pīr at Galbarga. In times of sickness I have seen the lower orders of Muhammadans resort to Hindū deities, especially to the goddess of smallpox. By far the majority are like the Turks, Sunnīs (not Shī'as), but from conversation I had with several learned men, I feel convinced that they have no idea of acknowledging the Sultan of Constantinople as their spiritual head, and that the existence of sympathy between India and Turkey (except perhaps in towns like Bombay) is a figment of political agitators.

The question now arises how far these creeds have tended to degrade the character and condition of the people of India. And here we must guard against confusing cause and effect. In my opinion, the present low intellectual and moral condition of the masses of the Hindū people is as much the result of their social usages as it is the cause of their own superstitious creeds. It is very true that these social usages, enforced by what are called caste-rules, are now part and parcel of their religious creeds, but they do not properly belong to the original pure form of the Hindū religion. They are merely one portion of its diseased outgrowth, and they are the true cause of that feeble condition of mind in which the later superstitions have naturally taken root and luxuriated.

Not that the rules of caste have been an unmixed evil. On the contrary, they have done much good service to India. Each caste has been a kind of police to itself, keeping its own members in check and saving them from lawlessness. But the advantage thus gained has been far outweighed by the irreparable harm done to the physical, mental, and moral constitution of the Hindū people by the operation of caste in three principal particulars—first. in making early marriage a religious duty; secondly, in enforcing endogamy—that is to say, in obliging castes, and even subdivisions of castes, to marry within themselves; thirdly, in surrounding family and home life with a wall of secrecy. The evils of early marriage are too manifest to need pointing out. I have sometimes examined the upper classes of Indian high schools in which half the boys have been fathers. In fact, the chief solicitude in the minds of parents is, not the education of their children, but their early marriage. When girls of twelve are mothers, and boys of sixteen fathers, it is surely too much to expect vigour of mind or body, and strength of character, either in parents or offspring. The children of mere children will probably remain children all their lives. They may have precocity and intelligence, but are very unlikely to develope manly qualities. Moreover, the universality of early marriages tends to increase population in a way which adds greatly to our difficulties in times of drought and famine.

As to the evils of endogamy they are too well known to need pointing out. I believe that physiologists are agreed that when first cousins and other blood relations marry, the resulting offspring is generally of a feeble type. In the India of the present day polygamy is scarcely known, but endogamy is beginning to be common, and I firmly believe that with increasing subdivisions of caste into mere groups of families, and inhibition of marriages out of these families, serious deterioration of brain-tissues is likely to take place among certain classes.

The weakness entailed by the two pernicious caste rules I have mentioned might, perhaps, be partially overcome or counterbalanced, if it were not for the third pernicious rule —namely, the seclusion of women and the surrounding of family life with an impenetrable wall of secrecy. All nations are but a collection of families, and as are the homes so will be the condition of the people. In truth, the welfare of a country radiates from its homes—one might almost say from its nurseries. But no one knows what is going on in an Indian home, much less can any one, except a member of the family, enter there. It is so shut in by the close shutters of caste that healthy ventilation is impossible. The fresh air of heaven and the light of God's day have no free entrance. Weakly children are brought up by ignorant, superstitious, narrow-minded mothers in a vitiated atmosphere. Hence, in my opinion, the present deteriorated character and condition of a large majority of the people of India.

What, then, is the chief hope for the future? It seems to me to lie in a complete reorganization of the social fabric, in a new ideal of womanhood, and an entire renovation of family life. Before the people of India can be much elevated by their connexion with England they must learn from us to abolish caste regulations about early marriage; Indian fathers must keep their daughters under education as long as we do, and members of different castes must intermarry, as peer and commoner do in Great Britain. This, it will be said, amounts to an upheaving of the whole social fabric. Yet it is not, in my opinion, a work of such hopeless magnitude as some would make it out to be. Symptoms of impatience under caste-restrictions are already observable among the wealthier, better educated, and more Europeanized classes of natives, and social reform is openly advocated in some quarters. A great advance may be expected when the increasing contact of Indians with English social institutions in England itself, becomes still more common; when the visits of influential men to our shores are oftener repeated, and when the Baniyahs, or wealthy traders of the old Vaiśya class (some of whom, nevertheless, are the incarnate curses of India by the facilities they offer for borrowing money), succeed, as they appear likely eventually to do, in interposing a strong middle class and a firm barrier of public opinion between the Brāhmans and the lower grades of society.

All honour, too, to those noble-hearted missionaries who, like Bishop Sargent and Mrs. Sargent at Tinnevelly, are seeking, by the establishment of female schools, to supply India with its most pressing need—good wives and mothers; or, like Mr. and Mrs. Lash, are training girls to act as high-class schoolmistresses, and sending them forth to form new centres of female education in various parts of Southern India.

But let our missionaries bear in mind that something more than mere preaching, than mere education, than the alteration of marriage rules, is needed for the regeneration of India. The missionary bands must carry their ark persistently round the Indian home, till its walls are made to fall, and its inner life exposed to the fresh air of God's day, and all its surroundings moulded after the pattern of a pure, healthy, well-ordered Christian household, whose influences leaven the life of the family and the nation from the cradle to the grave. My belief is that until a way is opened for the free intercourse of the educated mothers and women of Europe, trained to speak and understand the Indian vernaculars, with the mothers and women of India, in their own homes, Christianity itself, or at least its purer forms, will make little progress either among Hindūs or Muhammadans.

For Christianity is a religion which, before it can dominate over the human heart, requires a clear apprehension of certain great facts, and a manly assent of the reason to the doctrines and practice they involve. Although we Christians are required to be children in guilelessness, we are told to be men in understanding. That, indeed, is not true Christianity which does not make a kind of religion of manliness of character, healthiness of body and mind, and soundness of judgment. Now, it is certain that although exceptional cases of men of vigorous intellect exist in India, and its races differ considerably in physique, yet the ordinary Indian has hitherto inherited such a feeble condition of brain, such a diseased appetite for mental stimulants, such unhealthy biasses and habits of mind from his ancestors, that he is almost incapable of grasping plain facts, much less of incorporating them, like plain food, into the texture of his moral constitution. Nor is he generally at all capable of appreciating the importance of their bearing on daily life and practice. Hence the absence of all history in India, and hence the difficulty of obtaining any accurate, unexaggerated, or undistorted narrative of common occurrences. Here, too, in my opinion, lies the principal difficulty of convincing a Hindū of the superiority of the plain story of the Gospel to the wild exaggerations of the Rāmāyana. The chief successes of Christianity in India have been hitherto achieved by Roman Catholics, who offer to the Hindū mind a kind of Hindūized Christianity, or, at any rate, present him with the images, symbols, processions, decorations, miraculous stories, marvellous histories of saints, and imposing ritual of which his present mental condition appears to stand in need.

British Administration.

I am confirmed in the opinion I expressed after my travels in Northern India that the points we have most to guard against in the administration of our Indian Empire are, first, a desire to advance too rapidly and too uniformly; secondly, a tendency towards the over-centralization of authority.

It is common to say that India is a poor country. In real truth India is a rich country with a poor population, saddled with a costly Government. Naturally, therefore, we who form that Government are sensitively anxious to do work that shall really be worth the money we cost. Hence we are ever striving to benefit the people by fresh legislative measures, for which the country is not always prepared, and which we are inclined to apply too uniformly. Yet England's worst enemies cannot shut their eyes to the good our administration has effected. Indeed, my travels have convinced me that the Natives of India have no cause whatever to complain of our excluding them from their equitable share in the administration of their own country. Our Government is ever zealous for their interests, and ever on the watch to find competent Indians to fill responsible posts. For all the lower grades of executive offices they are now selected before equally competent Europeans.

In law courts, in police courts, at railway stations, post and telegraph offices, and in every department of the public service one meets with Indian functionaries doing the work which was formerly done by Europeans. English barristers and attorneys are now driven out of the field by Indian Wakeels. The same applies to the Educational Department. Headmasterships of High Schools, which were once reserved for Englishmen, and even filled by Oxford and Cambridge graduates, are now assigned to the ablest Native teachers. Even the highest judicial offices are now being filled by Natives who have gained admission to the Civil Service through the competitive examinations. The Judge of Ahmedabad, Mr. Satyendranāth Tagore, whose guest I was for a few days, is an Indian of a well-known family at Calcutta. He has been elevated to a higher position in the Service than competition-wallahs of his own year, and of at least equal ability. Another Indian gentleman, Mr. Gopāl-rāo Hari Deshmukh, whom I met frequently at Bombay—a man of great energy and ability, and a well-known social reformer—has lately been appointed joint Judge at Nāsik, with the personal title of Rāo Bahādur. The title was conferred the other day at a public meeting, and Judge Gopāl-rāo, in acknowledging the honour, is reported in the *Times of India* (September 4, 1877) to have said :—

'This Sanad is given to me for loyalty and services. I am sure that every sensible and well-informed man in this country is loyal. This country for many past centuries had no Government deserving the name. There was neither internal peace nor security from foreign invasion. There was no power in India which could put a stop to the evil practices of satī, infanticide, religious suicide, and human sacrifices. The whole nation presented a scene of stagnation and ignorance; but the case is now different. Under the auspices of a beneficent, civilized, and strong Government we have become progressive. Light and knowledge are pouring in upon the country. Old prejudices and errors are vanishing. We therefore count it a great privilege to be loyal subjects of the Empress of India. There is now security of life and property, as perfect as human institutions can make it. Those who are old enough are aware of the plundering excursions of Pindārīs, who, descending from the ghauts, spread terror in the Concan. These professional robbers have been extirpated by the British Government. We enjoy liberty of speech, petition, and press. We enjoy the blessings of education, useful public works, internal peace, and freedom from foreign invasions.'

Possibly, we are inclined to go beyond our duty in our appreciation of Native merit. It is certain that much bitterness of feeling is being excited among Anglo-Indians by the present laudable desire to do justice to Native ability. Everywhere I heard Englishmen complaining that their interests are set aside and their claims overlooked in favour of Natives. Language like the following is commonly used by members of the Civil Service :—' In thirty years,' say they, ' we English Judges and Collectors will be swept out of India. The Natives we have educated are gradually "crowding us out" of the country. Even our own Government is inclined to make light of our merits. We have harder work than ever laid on our shoulders; but we get neither thanks nor additional pay. If we were Hindūs we should be flattered and honoured, but, being Englishmen, we are snubbed and reprimanded.' Such language, though obviously too strong, may have elements of truth which call for careful consideration.

In the matter of over-centralization it seems to be now generally admitted that it results from an undue passion for what may be called administrative symmetry in an Empire far too vast, varied, and composite in its races, customs, religions, and climates, to admit of uniformity of treatment by means of telegraphic messages radiating from a central secretariat. Lord Lytton, who is supposed from his seat in the Viceregal council chamber of Calcutta and Simla to command the manipulation of the whole telegraphic system, was reported not long ago by one of *The Times*' Correspondents to be in favour of more decentralization in regard to taxation. I heard intelligent Natives in Madras complain that, although their ryotwary land tenure and their system of cultivation and irrigation bring in a larger revenue than the systems prevailing elsewhere, yet no benefit accrues to any particular districts in their Presidency, because their surplus goes to make up the deficit in other Provinces.

Nevertheless, it must be confessed that, if decentralization is carried too far, it will remove some salutary restraints on the eccentricities of inexperienced Provincial governors. If the strings of Government are pulled a little too strongly from the India Office and from the secretariats at Calcutta and Simla, they are also handled a little too freely by the array of secretaries at other central stations. In short, the India of the present period is becoming a little too secretariat-ridden. High functionaries, recently imported from England, are obliged, in their blank inexperience, to trust to their secretaries, and these, again, being often new to their work, have to trust to their under-secretaries, while these, again, are a good deal dependent on their head clerks. Thus the Government of a great Empire has a tendency to place too much power in the hands of a few clever under-secretaries' clerks, and to become, if I may be allowed to coin a new phrase, too much of a clericocracy. Half the time of a Collector is now occupied in replying to the inquiries of inquisitive under-secretaries. Every post brings piles of official documents and demands for reports and written statistics on every conceivable subject, while, in return, piles of foolscap find their way from the Collector's cutchery into the pigeon-holes of the Under-Secretary's office. There these precious bundles of foolscap are forthwith entombed, and from these graves there is seldom any resurrection to the light of day.

It is said that a Collector in the North-West Provinces was required, not long ago, to write a report on the habits of the Gangetic porpoise. Certainly it is not uncommon to hear language like the following from Collectors and Commissioners of long standing :—' It is impossible for me to get through my work as I did formerly. For instance, I cannot ride off 30 miles to the other end of my district to see that order is kept at a large religious fair now going on. I am no longer master of my own movements. I have to serve a dozen masters. I am compelled to furnish returns to the head of the Public Works Department, to Sanitary and Revenue Commissioners, to superintendents of police, to directors of public instruction, and to archæological and scientific surveyors. Then I have lately been politely requested to compile a complete Gazetteer of my own district, with an exhaustive account of its fauna and flora. In short, I am buried in piles of paper from morning till night.' There is certainly exaggeration in such language. Without doubt the writing of reports and compiling of gazetteers by some able civilians has already produced most valuable results, but the exaggerated language is an indication that in some directions we are attempting too much. At any rate, we are laying too great a burden on shoulders already overcharged.

In other directions we might do more. For example, we might carry on a more systematic defensive warfare against drought and famine by the storage of water in tanks, and its distribution by irrigation. India is blessed with abundant rivers. Why are not more anicuts, reservoirs, and canals made? Why should the water of any manageable river be allowed to lose itself in the sea? More might also be done in forest-management, in encouraging emigration, in developing the agricultural and mineral resources of the country; though judgment is here needed, especially in regard to agricultural improvements. For India, though potentially rich, has a poor population, not sufficiently advanced for the introduction of steam-ploughs, expensive machinery, and chemical manures. In some localities the land is so subdivided that its cultivation amounts to mere spade husbandry.

One thing requires instant attention. The connexion between agriculture, meteorology, and astronomy is now admitted on all hands, and no country in the world would be benefited more than India by systematic meteorological and astronomical observations carried on under Government direction. Much is already being done in this way. Yet I could only find one effective astronomical observatory, and that not adequately supported by Government, though I travelled from Kaśmīr to Cape Comorin. It is not generally known that from his observations of the present condition of the disk of the sun, in connexion with various atmospherical phenomena, the Madras astronomer, Mr. Pogson, prophesied in 1876 a recurrence of the drought and famine in 1877.

Again, more efforts might be made to promote the development of those industrial arts in which the natives are already skilled, and to teach them new trades and industries, such as printing, paper-making, book-binding, sugar-refining, and tobacco-curing.

One crying evil requires immediate redress. A limit should be put by law to the increase of native pleaders. If Indian money-lenders are metaphorically called incarnate curses, Indian Wakeels are rapidly earning a title to the same flattering appellation. I have heard natives complain of what they call the oppression of our Law Courts, with their elaborate machinery of expensive processes and appeals. What they mean is not that injustice is done, but that justice is overdone. They might, with more reason, complain of the oppression of their own Wakeels, who live by promoting quarrels, prey upon litigants, and drain the very life-blood out of their own fellow-countrymen.

The Native States of Southern India.

Under this head let me merely say that I visited three most prosperous and well-managed States of Southern India—Travankor, Cochin, and Hyderabad. Travankor and the little State of Cochin are both on the Malabar Coast. The former has a wise and enlightened Mahārāja, and his Prime Minister is a sensible high-minded man of large acquirements and great administrative ability. I sailed along the coast of Travankor from Cape Comorin to

Cochin, and was much struck by the constant succession of thriving villages clustering under beautiful groves of palm trees close to the water's edge. Nearly all were overlooked by the lofty façades of substantially-built Roman Catholic churches, which are conspicuous objects everywhere on the Malabar coast, testifying to the almost superhuman energy and devotedness of the great missionary Xavier. The interior of these churches presents an appearance very like a Hindū Temple. They all contain images of the Virgin Mary, dressed up and decorated much in the same way as the idols of the Indian goddess Bhavānī. In every direction Roman Catholic churches force themselves on one's notice. On saints' days they are brilliantly illuminated, while displays of fireworks and Bengal lights, with explosions of crackers and guns, are made in front of the churches, much to the delectation of the native converts. I was told, too, that their priests endear themselves to their flocks by living among them very much like Indian Gurus, and by attending to their bodily as well as spiritual needs. Those who come from Europe set our Protestant missionaries a good example in at least two particulars. They are satisfied with wonderfully small salaries, and never think of going home.

There are also two very singular colonies of Jews at Cochin. The one set are quite white in complexion, and the other quite black. I was present at the service in a synagogue, and saw the richly-decorated rolls of the Books of Moses carried round in procession and kissed by the congregation, after the law had been read by the Rabbis from a central reading-desk.

My visit to Sir Richard Meade, our able Resident at Hyderabad, enabled me to judge of the condition of the Nizām's territory, which occupies the central plateau of the Deccan, and has a population of 10,000,000 or 11,000,000. It owes its present prosperity, as most people know, to the excellent administration of Sir Sālār Jung, who delivered it from a condition of chronic mismanagement. Our large military station at Secunderabad, six miles from the capital, contains 40,000 inhabitants, and is under our own jurisdiction. We also hold Berār (commonly called the Berārs) in trust for the payment of the Nizām's contingent. It was taken by us from the Marāṭhas, and we have administered it since 1853. It has thriven wonderfully under our management; but as we gave it to the Nizām in 1803, the surplus revenue goes to his treasury. We restored to him the Raichor Doāb, between the Kṛishṇa and Tungabhadra rivers, in 1860. Whether Berār ought to be so restored is another matter. Some authorities think we did wrong to give up our claim to Mysor, and that we might with as good reason give up Berār. Probably Berār would not suffer much by being given back, so long as the continuance of so able a Minister as Sir Sālār Jung at the helm could be secured. But India is not likely to produce two such men as Sir Sālār Jung and Sir T. Mādhava Rāo more than once in two or three centuries. I conversed with both these great Ministers not long since in their own houses (one at Hyderabad, and the other at Baroda) and found them capable of talking on all subjects in as good English as my own.

Sir Sālār Jung (whose person is familiar to many of us from his recent visit to England) showed me his everyday working-room—a room not so large as an Oxford graduate's study, plainly furnished with a few book-cases filled with modern books of reference, chiefly English. He has an extensive library in an adjoining gallery, with a window commanding a courtyard, where those who have to transact business with him assemble every day. I may mention as an evidence of his enlightened ideas that on hearing that a deserving young Indian at Oxford was in need of assistance, he at once assigned an annual allowance for his support, stipulating that he should be trained for the Nizām's educational service. He has other young Indians under training in London, similarly supported.

I was told that I should see numbers of armed ruffians

and rowdies in the city of Hyderabad, and that I could not possibly traverse the streets unless lifted above all chances of insult on the back of an elephant. Yet I can certify that I saw very few armed men and no signs of disorder or lawlessness anywhere in the city, and that I dismounted from my elephant and walked about in the throng of people without suffering the slightest inconvenience, molestation, or rudeness. Of course, a town of 400,000 inhabitants is liable to disturbances, and it is certain that during my stay an Arab, whose father died suddenly, made a savage attack with his dagger in a fit of frenzy on the doctor who attended him. Nevertheless I am satisfied that the stories about murderous brawls in the streets are much exaggerated. Without doubt it must be admitted that the 7,000 armed Arab mercenaries, who form part of an army of 50,000 men, and the numerous armed retainers of the nobles, all of whom are allowed to roam about without much discipline, are generally ripe for turbulence and mischief. It is, moreover, a significant fact that about three-fourths of the wealth of Hyderabad is concentrated within the limits of the Residency, held to be British territory. These limits are carefully marked off from the rest of the city by walls and lines of streets; and here a population of 20,000 persons, including the chief rich bankers and merchants of the Nizām's dominions, cluster under the ægis of British jurisdiction and authority.

Education in Southern India.

South India is not behind the North in its zeal for education. Indeed, if advance of education is to be measured by its promoting among natives of all ranks the power of speaking English with fluency, the palm will have to be given to the Colleges and Schools of Madras. And here, as in other parts of India, missionary schools are, in my opinion, doing the best work. The education they impart is openly and professedly founded on a Christian basis.

They teach the Bible without enforcing ecclesiastical dogmas on their pupils. Indeed, my second tour has impressed me more than ever with the benefits which India derives from the active efforts of missionaries of all denominations, however apparently barren in visible results those efforts may be. Moreover, I think that the part that they have hitherto played is as nothing compared with the *rôle* they are destined to fill in the future of our Eastern Empire. The European missionary is daily becoming a more important link between the Government and the people. He is confided in by natives of all ranks, and is often able to do what the Government with its necessary profession of neutrality cannot effect. Missionary schools attract the children of parents of all creeds, though they openly aim at permeating their minds with a spirit hostile to those creeds. It may be very true that their bible-teaching tends to destroy without reconstructing, but it is gradually and insensibly infusing principles incompatible with the pantheistic ideas with which the Indian mind is generally saturated. If it does not always build up the true creed in place of the false, yet it lays the foundation of a future belief in a personal God. It substitutes for the slippery sands of Pantheism a basis of living rock, which may be afterwards thankfully occupied by evangelizing missionaries as a common standpoint, when the Gospel is confronted in argument with the Veda and Kurān.

My conviction is that the vast work of Christianizing India will not be accomplished entirely through missionary instrumentality, but rather through the co-operation of divine and human agencies, working in a great variety of ways. Yet I am equally convinced that it will be principally effected, and far more slowly, gradually, and insensibly than is commonly expected, through impressions made on the minds of children by a process of education like that which our missionaries are carrying out in their schools.

Of all such schools visited by me, in Southern India, there were two, the merits and effectiveness of which struck me very forcibly. They were those of the Free Church of Scotland at Madras, under Mr. Miller and Mr. Rae, where about 1,000 pupils are under education; and the Church Missionary schools, under Bishop Sargent, at Tinnevelly, in which latter district there are about 60,000 converts to Protestant Christianity. I regret I was unable to visit Bishop Caldwell's excellent schools at Edeyengoody. I could name a hundred others if space and time were at my disposal. Those founded by a native named Pacheappah at Madras and Conjevaram are rendering good service to the community. The Basle Mission schools at Mangalor are also most efficient and useful, and its members most devoted and self-sacrificing. Their example deserves to be followed in their plan of teaching trades and industries, and of instructing their converts how to be independent and support themselves. The schools of the Pārsīs at Bombay are also conspicuously good. And let it not be supposed that the work done by our Government schools and colleges is insignificant. Its importance can scarcely be overrated. Nevertheless, it is generally admitted that our whole educational system needs revision and amendment. The great complaint that one hears on all sides while travelling in India is that we are over-educating. We cannot, however, be accused of over-educating if our education is of the right kind. Quality, not quantity, is what is wanted for India. Excellence of quality can scarcely be over-done.

Probably there are three principal points that call for amendment in our present system. 1. We want more real education. 2. We want more suitable education. 3. We want more primary education.

As to the first point :—To secure more real education we have to make our native teachers understand that the human skull, which is their field of operations, is not in childhood a mere rigid case, or empty cavity, to be packed like a portmanteau with a given amount of knowledge in a given time, but rather an assemblage of organs and capacities to be gradually and carefully shaped, moulded, and expanded. We in England sometimes require to be reminded that the duty of an educator ought to be in accordance with the etymology of the word—that it should consist in gently drawing out rather than in roughly hammering in. Indian educators of Indian children are still more forgetful of this truth. Nor do they sufficiently bear in mind that the most valuable knowledge is that which is self-acquired when the faculties are matured, and that teachers are doing their business most effectively when they are teaching their pupils to be their own future self-teachers. I am afraid our Indian colleges and schools are turning out more well-informed than well-formed men, more free thinkers than wise thinkers, more silly sceptics than honest inquirers, more glib talkers than accurate writers, more political agitators than useful citizens. I do not mean to imply that our European principals and professors and directors of public instruction, generally chosen with care from our English Universities, are not perfectly aware of the defects in our system. On the contrary, I believe they are doing their best to make Indian education a reality. I have met, too, with native schoolmasters who are really able educators. What I mean is that a larger number of good normal schools and a better system of teaching how to teach are urgently needed in India, and some security is required that the applicants for masterships have really received adequate training. It is certain that assistant masters and subordinate teachers are too often found in positions for which they are not thoroughly qualified. Even in England the heads of our great public schools are beset with similar difficulties. Every one admits that national schoolmasters must be certificated as teachers, but no one dares to cast a suspicion on University first-class men, who would feel themselves humiliated at the bare suggestion that first-class scholarship and first-class teaching are two very different matters.

The next point is that we want more suitable education. The sons of persons of low social status ought not (except, of course, in special cases when they show evident signs of unusual ability) to receive an education above the rank of their fathers. Let their training be the best of its kind, but let it be suited to their position and prospects. Furthermore, greater efforts should be made to co-ordinate the education of daughters with that of sons. In brief, we ought to aim at educating children in their fathers' stations, rather than above them—at making the son of a potter a better potter, the son of a carpenter a better carpenter. To this end I submit that we should immediately raise our school and college fees for high-class education. Not that I would place obstacles in the way of the lower castes elevating themselves, but I would at once correct the mistake of putting too low a price on the highest form of education. No parent of inferior rank will then be ambitious of a University degree for his son unless he is likely to repay with interest the outlay necessary to secure it. When I was at Poona, I found on inquiry, that a student at the great central Deccan College there could obtain a first-class education by paying rather less than 1s. 6d. per month for his room-rent, 10s. per month for his tuition, and 18s. or 20s. per month for his board. Of course Indian students are much more simple in their habits than Oxford undergraduates. They are satisfied with one chair, one table, and a mattress on the ground. They make free use of the College library, and they eat little except rice, with perhaps once a day a modicum of curry-powder. But even for Indians, the present charge for room-rent, board, and tuition at a first-class college is ridiculously small.

Further, I submit that in all our Indian colleges and schools we pay too much attention to the linguistic and literary element in education, and too little to the practical and scientific. A great improvement, however, is observable in this respect in some parts of India.

EDUCATION. VERNACULAR LANGUAGES.

With regard to languages I cannot help thinking that a great mistake is committed—a mistake which calls for the immediate consideration of the directors of public instruction. We do not sufficiently encourage the vernaculars. The classical languages receive due respect and attention, but the vernacular dialects of India, which ought to be stimulated to draw fresh vitality and energy from Sanskrit, are everywhere showing signs of serious deterioration. Be it observed, however, that they are by no means dying out. It would be simple folly to suppose that we can impose English on 240 millions of people. But by enforcing English as a *sine quâ non* at our matriculation examinations, and by making a knowledge of it the only road to employment in the public service, we are dealing a fatal blow at the purity of the vernacular languages. My conviction is that unless more is done to encourage their cultivation, some of them will soon lapse into vulgar hybrid dialects. A highly-educated Marāṭha gentleman told me that he scarcely knew a man among his own fellow-countrymen who could write good Marāṭhī. Even the right spelling of the words derived from the Sanskrit, which ought to be carefully preserved, is becoming hopelessly corrupted. A vicious style of verbose and inflated composition, copied from Dr. Johnson's 'Rambler,' is becoming common, and English words are ostentatiously imported into it, when far more suitable expressions might be drawn from a Sanskrit source. Such great native poets as Tukarām and Morapant are becoming neglected; and intelligent men, who might do much to develope and improve their own languages, waste their time in concocting, and even printing and publishing, wretched English verses which no Englishman can read without a smile. The result of such a mistaken system is that India is flooded with conceited and half-educated persons who despise and neglect their own languages, and their own religious and political systems, without becoming good English scholars, good Christians, or good subjects of the Queen. And hence we are confronted with a difficulty which, even if it does not endanger our rule in India, is becoming more embarrassing every day—the difficulty of providing suitable employment for the thousands of young men we have educated badly and unsuitably. For excessive and misdirected education cannot be carried on with the same impunity in India as in England, where we have the safeguard of our Colonies and an outlet in India itself.

The third point is that we do not everywhere pay sufficient attention to Primary Education. It is superfluous to remark that no system of education can be satisfactory which does not begin at the right end, and rise from the lower to the upper strata of the community. In the villages and the indigenous rural schools a good system of teaching the vernacular dialects, with reading, writing, and arithmetic, is needed. And here is another reason for encouraging by every possible means the cultivation of the vernaculars, and their development and improvement by means of Sanskrit. I have seen a few excellent village schools, conducted in the open air under trees, where the children are taught to write on palm leaves, and can repeat the multiplication table up to a hundred times a hundred, and even multiply fractions together in their heads. The difficulty is to secure good village teachers. Sir George Campbell, and Sir Richard Temple, following his predecessor's lead, did admirable service in this way and started an excellent plan of primary instruction by trained teachers in Bengal. Much has been effected in the same direction all over India. In 1873 there were 30,477 primary schools, with 963,000 pupils. These seem sufficiently large figures, but remembering the increasing density of the population we have to deal with, we ought not to be satisfied till our system of primary instruction has really penetrated to the remotest corner of the lowest stratum of Indian society.

Disposition and Attitude of the Natives towards us and our rule.

I confess that in travelling through Southern India it seemed to me that there is even less social fusion between the rulers and the ruled in Madras than in Bombay and Calcutta. Doubtless there are faults on both sides. The longer we continue to hold the country, the more its condition before we took it in hand is forgotten. In those parts of the Madras Presidency which have been longest under our rule, the people having had no personal experience of the evils from which their fathers were delivered through our intervention, are unable to cherish a due sense of gratitude towards us. I fear that Englishmen, unless they are plainly and sensibly benefactors, are not otherwise liked for their personal qualities. They are thought to be proud, cold, and reserved. Very much the same, however, might be justly said by us of the natives of India. The Hindūs, we might fairly allege, are even more exclusive than we are. They have little sympathy with any one outside their own caste. The impenetrable barrier with which they surround their homes and their refusal to sit at meat with Europeans are fatal to mutual friendliness and sociability. On the other hand, Englishmen, by reason of a concurrence of changed conditions, are certainly living in India more like strangers and pilgrims who have no abiding resting-place there. Increased facilities of communication between Europe and Asia, which ought to have drawn the two races closer together, have only tended to widen the separation between them. In former days it was not uncommon for a civilian or military officer to remain a quarter of a century in India without going home. He had then time and opportunity to identify himself with the people, and interest himself in their interests—to form friendships among them and win their affection. Now, if he has only three months' leave, he rushes to England, *viâ* Brindisi, in three weeks, and undergoes inordinate fatigue, that he may spend six weeks in the old country, and then rush as quickly back to the land of his exile.

The competitive system, too, has had a bad effect in severing some of the ties which once bound the two races together. It has deprived India of the successive generations of Outrams, Prinseps, Macnaghtens, and other old families who were drawn towards it by a long train of inherited associations, who were inspired with goodwill towards its people by the examples of their forefathers, and who imbibed Indian tastes, ideas, and predilections with their earliest education.

Let no one, however, from this time forward, accuse us of want of sympathy with our Indian fellow-subjects in their hour of trial and affliction. There may be increasing race-antagonism, less social blending, and more frequent misunderstandings between the governing and the governed in India, but the best practical proof has now been given of our disinterested desire for the well-being of the great country committed to our charge. The voluntary subscription of more than half a million pounds sterling in a few months for the relief of the famine-stricken districts, and the self-sacrificing courage, zeal, and energy displayed by every one of the Queen's officers, from the Viceroy downwards, in their efforts to alleviate the sufferings of the people, have for ever wiped away the reproach that the attitude of Great Britain towards its Eastern Dependency is cold and unsympathetic. I believe there have been no less than four Indian famines during the past ten years, and these have finally culminated in a period of distress the like of which has not afflicted the land since 1833. Yet this last famine, however deplorable in the present suffering it is causing, will have effected a great benefit, if it opens our eyes to India's needs and to our own shortcomings; if it convinces our Indian subjects of England's devotion to their welfare; if it evokes feelings of gratitude in return for the active sympathy displayed; if it helps to

CAUSES OF DISCONTENT. 223

draw the rulers and the ruled closer together by bonds of mutual kindliness, confidence, and cordiality.

Let me, in conclusion, point out one or two causes of discontent which, so soon as the remembrance of our present efforts for the relief of the country has passed away, will most surely bring our rule into increasing disfavour with certain classes of the population. One cause is the constant necessity we are under of revising the land assessment. On the acquirement of any new territory, we have been obliged, of course, to settle the land revenue, and the first settlement has always been, very judiciously, a mild one. At the end of thirty years a new assessment has generally been made, and the necessary increase in the rate of payment has been demanded from the cultivators. Very naturally, this has always caused an outbreak of great discontent. Of late years a still more microscopic and, perhaps, occasionally vexatious revision of the assessment has led to still further irritation. The cultivators cannot be made to understand that with an increase in the value of land a higher rate of tax is justly due, and they will not be convinced that the Government is not breaking faith with them. There can be no doubt that Lord Cornwallis's permanent settlement of the Government demand in Bengal, Behar, and Orissa, though it has proved a lamentable loss to the Indian revenue, has had its advantages, and nothing would tend to conciliate the whole population of India more than the application of a similar principle everywhere. This, however, in present circumstances, is, I fear, almost an impossibility.

Another source of dissatisfaction is now looming in the horizon. The maximum age for competing for the Indian Civil Service will be fixed in 1878 at nineteen, and the minimum at seventeen. Many Indians have complained to me that this lowering of the age will practically exclude natives from the competition. 'How can we send mere boys,' say they, 'on a long voyage at a great expense to a place like London to prepare for an examination of such difficulty? The risks will be too great. A certain number of appointments ought to be set aside for India—say six every year—and the printed questions might then be sent out under seal to the local Governments, who would appoint examining committees.' There is, doubtless, much justice in this proposal, and I hope it will receive due consideration. If it is eventually adopted, all selected native candidates ought to be positively compelled to go to England for two years' probation. I fervently hope, too, that the Government scholarships which were formerly founded to enable deserving young Indians to complete their education in England, but which were for some inscrutable reason abolished before they were fully tried, will be re-established. In this regard our Government ought to follow the example so wisely set by Sir Sālār Jung. Let the residence of Indians among us be encouraged by all means, and let them return to India—not, indeed, denationalized—but imbued with some of our most refining and purifying home influences, elevated by intercourse with some of our best men and women, and penetrated with an earnest desire to aid in the regeneration of their country by assimilating, as far as possible, its social institutions to those of England.

INDIAN AND EUROPEAN CIVILIZATION IN THEIR RELATION TO EACH OTHER AND IN THEIR EFFECT ON THE PROGRESS OF CHRISTIANITY.

THE kind of civilization to which I shall first advert is not that which we Englishmen have introduced into India, but that which has existed in India for at least three thousand years.

Of course very different ideas may be attached to the word civilization, and some may doubt whether, if religion is an ingredient of civilization, the Hindūs have ever possessed any true civilization at all. But when a people have a refined language, an extensive literature, an organized social system, fixed forms of government, with elaborate religious and philosophical systems, however false such systems may be, and have, moreover, made some progress in the arts and sciences, they may surely be called civilized, though their civilization may be very different in kind from that of other ancient peoples, or from that of modern Europe.

Doubtless every civilized nation is inclined to pride itself on its own institutions and to despise other countries. The Chinese, for example, look down with contempt on Europeans, and distinguish Englishmen in particular by epithets equivalent to foreign devils and uncivilized barbarians. Similarly, the Greeks called all other nations barbarians, and in the same way the Indians call us *Mleććhas*. This was originally a contemptuous term applied by the Indo-Āryans to those who could not pronounce their sacred Sanskrit. It is now commonly applied by learned Hindūs to Europeans. But this term by no means represents the amount of disrespect in which the rulers of India are held by Brāhmans of the old school. I have met with bigoted Pandits, whose contempt for us and our boasted civilization, notwithstanding they travel by our railways, use our telegraphs, and live in security under our rule, and albeit they take pains to conceal their real estimate of our character, is, I am convinced, quite as great as the contempt of their forefathers for any non-Āryan savages, whether styled Dasyus or Nishādas.

I may mention, in illustration, that I often wondered, when in India, why certain great Pandits preferred calling on me very early in the morning, till I found out accidentally that, by coming before bathing, they were able afterwards to purify themselves by religious ablutions from the contamination incurred by shaking hands and talking with me.

Nor have the Muhammadans, as a rule, any greater respect for us, for our social institutions, or for our religion. When they are less scornful than usual they confine themselves to calling us *Kāfirs*, unbelievers. But in India this epithet scarcely represents the amount of contempt with which we are commonly regarded by bigoted Muslims. Many of them have been seen to spit on the ground on leaving the houses of eminent civilians, after interviews in which the most courteous expressions had been interchanged.

The point, then, which I wish to bring out strongly on the present occasion is, that the chief hindrance to the progress of Christianity among the people of India is their intense pride in their own supposed moral, religious, and even intellectual superiority. What says a member of the Brahma Samāj, in a letter written about a year ago to the editor of the *Times* newspaper—

'I am convinced,' he says, 'that the state of the poor

in the Christian countries of Italy, France, and England (all of which countries I have visited), especially in the large towns, is infinitely more wretched, godless, degrading, and barbarous than it is in heathen India.'

The fact is that the Hindūs believe that their whole national life and civilization, far from being heathenish, have been favoured above all countries with the special superintendence of the Supreme Being. Divine interposition commences with their very alphabet.

We in England think our A, B, C, a very human invention, which we owe to the Phœnicians, whereas to a Hindū every stroke of his complicated characters is thought to be due to direct supernatural inspiration. His Deva-nāgarī alphabet, as its name implies, came directly from the gods.

In the same way all the other elementary processes which lay the foundations of knowledge are divinely superintended. The whole of a Hindū's education is regulated directly by his god's guidance. We are accustomed to regard our European grammars as very human, and mostly very imperfect productions, whereas to a Hindū the great grammar of Pāṇini—the source of all other grammars—is not only the perfection of linguistic analysis, but Pāṇini himself is an inspired sage, who did not compose his own grammar with the painful thought with which such works are commonly elaborated, but *saw* it supernaturally, the opening rules having been directly revealed to him by the god Śiva.

Then, when we pass on to language and literature, we in England take a pride in the gradual welding together of our native tongue into one compact whole by Saxon, Dane, and Norman, but a Hindū prides himself on the alleged fact that the divine Sanskṛit came ready-made from the goddess Sarasvatī.

Moreover, in matters of literature our ideas are far behind those of a pious Hindū. We admit a human element even in our most sacred Scriptures, whereas to a Hindū, not only is the Ṛig-veda believed to have issued like breath from the Self-Existent, but every one of a hundred other works, constituting what may be called the canon of Hindū revelation, is either attributed directly to his god, or is thought to be more or less written under special Divine superintendence.

For example, the moral and political code propounded by Manu was revealed to that inspired sage by Brahmā himself.

Then, as to social institutions, it is difficult for us Europeans, notwithstanding our own peculiar caste feelings, to understand how the pride of caste, as a Divine ordinance, interpenetrates the whole being of a Hindū. He believes that his god created men different in caste, as he created different kinds of animals. Nay more, in the Ṛig-veda the Brāhman is declared to be the *actual mouth* of Brahmā, soldiers are his *actual arms*, husbandmen his *actual thighs*, while Sūdras or servants issued from his feet. No wonder, then, that a Hindū looks upon his caste as his veritable god ; and those very caste-rules which we believe to be a hindrance to his adoption of the true religion are to him the very essence of all religion, for they influence his whole life and conduct. And the lower the caste, the more do its members appear to regard the observance of its rules as an essential part of all religion and morality. To violate the laws of caste is the greatest of all sins.

For example, marriage is a Divine institution closely connected with caste. It is declared to be a *Sanskāra*, or sacramental purificatory rite. Every man, as soon as he is old enough, is under absolute religious obligation to have his own wife, and every woman her own husband. For a man not to marry, or to marry out of his caste, is, with rare exceptions, a positive sin, fraught with awful consequences in a future state. Husband and wife are sacramentally united. The wife is half her husband's body. They ought not to be parted, even by death.

Furthermore, all the caste-rules about food, its preparation, and the persons in whose company it may be eaten, are strictly a matter of religion. A Hindū abhors, as the most impious of beings, any one who allows himself unrestrained liberty in eating and drinking. Not only purity of blood, but religious purity also depends on purity of nutriment, and the distinction between lawful and unlawful food is even more observed as a Divine ordinance than it was with the Jews. No high caste will eat with a lower caste, and not even a low caste will eat with Christians.

Then, finally, in regard to the dead, funeral ceremonies among the Hindūs are of course solemn acts of religion, as in all other countries. But far more than this—the bodies of deceased Hindūs must be burnt by certain near relatives according to carefully prescribed rites, on pain of bringing misery on the disembodied spirits; and such rites must be repeated periodically. To maintain the perpetual memory of the dead, to make periodical offerings to the spirits of fathers, grandfathers, and great-grandfathers, is a peremptory religious duty.

But what are a Hindū's ideas about the nature of that God who thus superintends every act, and directs every step of his existence from the cradle to the grave? It is here that his pride in his own superiority may be said to culminate. The very point in which we think the Hindūs most mistaken is the very point in which they pride themselves most of all. We admit that they might, with reason, be proud of the perfection of their alphabet, of the symmetry of their language, of the poetry in their literature, of the subtlety of their philosophy, of the acuteness of their logic, of their invention of the ten arithmetical figures, of their advance in mathematics and science when all Europe was wrapped in ignorance, and even of the elevated sentiments in their moral code; but we cannot understand their being proud of their false ideas of the Supreme Being. The Hindūs, we affirm, have no knowledge of the true God. They have not one God, but many. They degrade their deities to the level of sinful creatures by the acts, characters, and qualities they attribute to them.

Yet the Hindūs themselves maintain that they are not polytheists at all, but worshippers of one God, who manifests Himself variously, and that they have conceived sublimer notions of this Deity than any other people, ancient or modern. 'Our sacred books,' say they, 'insist on the unity of the Supreme Being, and abound in the grandest descriptions of His attributes.'

He is 'the most Holy of all holies; the most Blessed of the blessed; the God of all gods; the Everlasting Father of all creatures; omnipotent, omniscient, omnipresent; He is the Life in all; the Father, Mother, Husband, and Sustainer of the world; the Birth, the Death of all; the Incomprehensible; the Ancient Sage, without beginning or end; the Universe's Maker; the one God hidden in all beings, and dwelling as a witness within their hearts.'

And are not we Christians bound to accept and approve such sublime descriptions of the attributes of the Deity, though we well know that in the books from which they are taken, abundant false conceptions are mingled with the true, and that a Hindū's boasted theism is simple pantheism, behind which, as behind an impregnable fortress, he retires whenever his polytheism and idolatry are attacked?

There is, however, one point left in which we think educated Indians must at last acknowledge themselves inferior to Christian nations. 'Your religion,' we affirm, 'leads to the grossest idolatry. Everywhere in India idol-worship and superstition are hideously rampant!' How great, then, is our astonishment when we are assured in India by the educated Hindūs that they are not really idol-worshippers. 'Worship *before* images, not *to* images,' say they, 'is practised by us as a condescension to weak-minded persons. The highest form of worship is the *Mānasa-pūjā* and the *Nirākāra-pūjā*—heart-worship and formless worship.'

Hear what Mr. Pramadā-Dās Mitra, of Benares, in a recent address delivered at the Benares Institute, replied to one who accused his fellow-countrymen of the grossest idolatry: 'If by idolatry,' he said, 'is meant a system of worship which confines our ideas of the Divinity to a mere image of clay or stone, which prevents our hearts from being elevated with lofty notions of the attributes of God—if this is what is meant by idolatry, we disclaim idolatry, we abhor idolatry, and deplore the ignorance and uncharitableness of those that charge us with this grovelling system.' And he then goes on to point out that, so far from worshipping material images, the Hindūs are too spiritual to believe even in the existence of matter, the only really existing essence being (according to a dogma of their philosophy) the one universal spirit, of which the numerous gods, represented by images, are but manifestations.

Clearly, then, the chief impediment to Christianity among Indians is not only the pride they feel in their own religion, but the very nature of that religion. For pantheism is a most subtle, plausible, and all-embracing system, which may profess to include Christianity itself as one of the phenomena of the universe. An eminent Hindū is reported to have said, 'We Hindūs have no need of conversion; we are Christians and more than Christians already.'

In short, it is the old story. Pride and self-complacency are the chief obstacles to the entrance of truth into the human mind. We go to the Hindūs with a true revelation and the good news of God's love and good-will towards them in becoming incarnate for their sakes, and we find that they claim to have possessed a true revelation of their own, incarnations of their own, and a more excellent way of salvation suited to themselves, long before Europe had any revealed religion at all.

I could proceed to point out other great hindrances in the Hindūs themselves, such as their peculiar mental constitution, their incapability of appreciating historical facts, their appetite for wild legends and monstrous exaggerations, their natural dislike to the doctrine of sanctification as the only evidence of regeneration; but it is time for me to come nearer home, and to direct attention to the hindrances arising from *our own self-complacency, our own pride in our own boasted civilization.*

Let me begin with the pride of race. It is now well known that, notwithstanding the recent demonstration of the original oneness of the Indo-Āryan and English races, there is at present little or no social blending between the rulers and the ruled in India. Both Indians and Englishmen may be equally in fault, and each lays the blame upon the other; but the simple fact is, that Indians and Englishmen keep as distinct from each other as oil and water. Even Christianity does not overcome this race feeling. It is, indeed, generally acknowledged that if a highly-educated Brāhman becomes a Christian, and thereby consents to sit at table with Christians, he ought to be admitted into the best European society, but the pride of race is generally too strong for the sense of duty, and I fear that, as a matter of fact, few English homes, except those of the missionaries, are really opened to high-caste converts.

Thus it arises that well-bred men, who are quite our own equals in rank and education, are deterred from an open profession of Christianity through the want of any respectable circle of society to which they can be admitted in the adopted religion. If the force of conviction compels them to seek baptism at any sacrifice, they are instantly excommunicated by their own community, and then, if no missionary family be near, have no choice except to live alone or put up with the society of low-born native converts, with whom, perhaps, they have nothing in common but their adopted faith.

Then, there is the pride of knowledge. The English in India must, of course, be conscious of their superiority in civilization and scientific knowledge, but they bring discredit on Christianity and hinder the missionary cause when they take no pains to conceal their contempt for Hindūs and Muhammadans; and, forgetting that India was given to us to elevate rather than to humiliate, make them feel their own inferiority too keenly.

But perhaps the greatest hindrance arising from ourselves is the pride of religion. We cannot glory too much in our possession of the Gospel of Christ. God forbid that we should not glory in what we believe to be the only power of God unto salvation to Jew, Greek, Hindū, and Muhammadan! But if our love for our Gospel truth leads us to shut our eyes to the elements of truth that underlie all false religions, how are we even to approach those religions, much less bring any force of argument to bear upon them?

The missionary who goes to a believer in the Kurān or the Veda with the Holy Bible in his hand, has no choice but to search diligently for a common standpoint. 'Anything in your Bible,' the Musalmān will say, 'which agrees with my Kurān I will accept, otherwise I will not even listen to it.' The same language will be held by the Hindū with regard to the Veda. It may, indeed, shock Christians in this Christian country of ours to think of our missionaries placing the Bible on the same platform with the Kurān and the Veda; but there is really no alternative.

Young and enthusiastic missionaries must not be surprised, nor must we in England blame them, if they are forced to imitate St. Paul — to become Muslims to the Muslims, Hindūs to the Hindūs (without, however, giving up one iota of the truth which they themselves hold), in order that both Muslims and Hindūs may be won over to Christ.

And is there really no common ground for the Christian

missionary, the Muhammadan, and the Hindū to stand upon? Are there not certain root-ideas in all religions which bear testimony to the original truth communicated to mankind? Hindūism, at any rate, may be shown to be a system which, on a solid basis of pantheism, has brought together almost every idea in religion and philosophy that the world has ever known. Even some of the greatest truths of Christianity are there, though distorted, perverted, caricatured, and buried under superstition, error, and idolatry.

And is it not a proof of the Divine origin of Christianity, and its adaptation to humanity in every quarter of the globe, that some of its grandest and most essential dogmas, and, so to speak, its root-ideas, do indeed lie at the root of all religions, and explain the problems of life which sages and philosophers in all ages of the world have vainly attempted to solve? Is it not the fact that all the gropings after truth, all the religious instincts, faculties, cravings, and aspirations of the human race which struggle to express themselves in the false religions of the world, find their only true expression and fulfilment—their only complete satisfaction—in Christianity?

When I began the study of Hindūism, I imagined that certain elementary Christian conceptions — such as the Fatherhood of God, the Brotherhood of God, and the indwelling of God in the human heart—were not to be found there, but a closer examination has enabled me to detect not only these, but almost every other rudimentary idea of our holy religion. They are nearly all to be found in Hindūism, like portions of adamantine granite beneath piles of shifting sedimentary strata, and they ought to be eagerly searched for by the missionary as a basis for his own superstructure.

Hindūism, in fact, is a mere general expression, invented by Europeans for all the innumerable phases of pantheistic worship which exist in India. And, verily, I believe that much has yet to be done before all the shapes, and, so to speak, dissolving views of this Protean system are thoroughly comprehended.

At any rate, we students of India (including missionary students) have not as yet produced, though we are trying to do so—witness the series of books just published by the Christian Knowledge Society — any thoroughly exhaustive and trustworthy account of Hindūism. We have not sufficiently studied it in its own sacred Sanskṛit. We under-estimate its comprehensiveness, its receptivity, its subtle compromising spirit, its recuperative hydra-like vitality; and we are too much given to include the whole system under sweeping expressions, such as 'heathenism' or 'idolatry,' as if every idea it contains was to be eradicated root and branch.

Again, our religious pride will operate prejudicially to the missionary cause if it leads us to expect a complete and universal adoption of our own form of English Christianity. We cannot indeed glory too much in our loved Church of England, in her organization and her Book of Common Prayer; but is our zeal altogether according to knowledge if we attempt to force the Act of Uniformity with too iron a hand on all our Indian fellow-subjects? Depend upon it, that when the fulness of time arrives, and the natives of India everywhere openly accept Christianity, they will construct for it a setting of their own. And bearing in mind that our religion originated in the East, and that the Bible itself is a thoroughly Eastern book, we shall not only expect, but joyfully acquiesce in an Indian framework for Indian Christianity.

I will merely allude to two other obvious hindrances which beset the missionary cause in India,—I mean our own divisions and our own inconsistencies. As to the first, after travelling from Kaśmīr to Cape Comorin, I am able to certify that I have found, as a general rule, Christians of all denominations working together harmoniously, and forgetting in their conflict with a common foe their own conflicts of opinion in unessential matters.

Still, grave differences have recently arisen in some localities; and I venture to submit that it may be well not to forget that in the first struggles of Christianity with the paganism of the Roman Empire, the one mark by which all Christians were singled out from the rest of the world was their love for each other. 'See how these Christians love one another.'

As to our inconsistencies, let me quote the same member of the Brahma Samāj. 'Why,' he says, 'do you not make more Christians among the respectable classes of society? Because there is little to recommend itself in your Christianity. Does it make your merchants honest men? Are their goods pure and unadulterated? Does it make your soldiers polite and moral?'

It is satisfactory, however, to note, as I have lately done, that although some professing Christians may still walk as if they were the enemies of the Cross of Christ, no glaring scandals are now common in India. Nor can it be said of us by the natives, as it was to Mr. Terry (the first English clergyman, I believe, who ever visited India) in 1616, 'Christian religion devil religion; Christian much drunk, Christian much do wrong, Christian much beat, Christian much abuse others.'

And surely there is comfort in the thought that our hindrances in India under our own friendly rule are not greater than the obstacles in Europe under the hostile Roman Empire; nor are they greater anywhere than they always have been everywhere and may be expected to continue. And is it not the case that a steadily advancing cause thrives best under impediments, and that success is only the last step in a series of failures, difficulties, and discouragements?

At any rate, it is certain that men may hinder and men may impede, but the living waters of the river of God's truth will flow on for ever. Nay more, it is certain that though barrier and embankment may obstruct their course, the heaped-up waters will only gather strength and volume, till, with accumulated force, they spread themselves irresistibly over every region of the habitable globe[1].

[1] The above was delivered as an address at a Missionary Congress held in Oxford on May 2, 1877.

INDIAN MUHAMMADANISM IN ITS RELATION TO CHRISTIANITY, AND THE PROSPECTS OF MISSIONARY ENTERPRISE TOWARDS IT[1].

IN my travels through India, I repeatedly passed from Hindū to Musalmān places of worship, and my spirit, troubled by the hideous idolatry witnessed in the temples of Vishṇu and Śiva, was instantly tranquillized by the severe anti-symbolism conspicuous in all the surroundings of Muhammadan mosques.

It is true that the transition was a little too abrupt. The atmosphere and aspect of the mosque seemed to strike me with a sudden chill; I appeared to have jumped from tropical glare to Arctic ice. But when I beheld the earnest bearing of Muslims prostrating themselves in adoration on the cold stone, and apparently worshipping God in spirit, if not in truth, I felt that there was nothing in the outward appearance of either building or worshippers incompatible with the spirit of Christian prayer. Nay more—I felt as I watched the devout Muslims, that I also might have prayed in the same place in my own way, and even learnt from them to pray with more solemnity and reverence of manner than I had ever before practised.

On such occasions I frequently asked myself the question—How is it that the attitude of Islām towards Christianity is far more hopelessly hostile than that of the other two great false systems of the world, Brāhmanism

[1] Speech at the Croydon Church Congress, October 1877.

and Buddhism? Have we not read of hundreds and thousands of Hindūs and Buddhists converted by Christian Missionaries? but where are the Muslims? Why is it that so few Muhammadans are found to give glory to God in the knowledge of Christ? We are verily guilty concerning forty-one millions of our Indian brethren, and we are bound to search and try our ways, and see where our fault lies.

In the first place, how do we meet the present intolerant bearing of Islām towards other religions? Our Government is wisely neutral, but in our Missionary efforts are we not inclined to fight Islām with its own weapon? do we not sometimes oppose intolerance by intolerance?

There is, I admit, a false and true tolerance. But do we bear with all that we can, and denounce as little as we can in a system whose founder, however fiercely intolerant of idolaters, never denounced the Founder of our own religion?

In an excellent work by a faithful Missionary, recently published [1], I find it advocated that the attitude of Christianity towards the religions of India ought to be one of true intolerance. And what is his reason? 'Because,' he says, 'there is none other name under heaven but one, given among men, whereby we must be saved.'

But need we give up one iota of this precious truth, because we welcome everything good in Muhammad's system, and because we hold that we can best overcome the uncompromising intolerance of modern Muslims by confronting it with the charity and forbearance of our Lord Himself, and the first Missionaries, His Apostles?

Let us never forget that however bitter the feelings of hostility now displayed by the followers of Muhammad towards the followers of Christ, the attitude of Muhammad himself towards Christ Himself and the Gospel, as exhibited in the Kurān, was not only tolerant, but friendly

---

[1] Robson's 'Hindūism, and its relation to Christianity,' p. 297.

and reverential[1]. Indeed, the more I have reflected on the present want of success in winning Musalmāns to our own most holy faith, the more surprise have I felt that we do not oftener advance to meet them on the common ground which belongs to the Bible and the Kurān—that we do not oftener remind them that the Kurān itself exalts Christ above humanity and teaches a manifold connexion between Islām and the Gospel.

We ought to bear in mind that the people we call Muhammadans call themselves Muslims, that is, persons who were taught by Muhammad to believe that salvation consists in holding as cardinal doctrines the Unity of God, and resignation to His Will. Muhammad himself never claimed to be the originator of these doctrines, and never allowed them to be called by his name. He was, in his own view of his own mission, the latest of four prophets (the others being Moses, Elias, and Christ), who were all followers of Abraham, the true founder of the doctrine of Islām[2], and were all Muslims, because all preached the Unity of God and submission to His Will.

O for more of the wisdom and courage of the great Apostle of the Gentiles! Were he at this moment unfolding before Muslims the unsearchable riches of Christ,

---

[1] Sir William Muir (p. 157 of his excellent work, 'The Life of Mahomet') shows that no expression regarding either the Jewish or Christian Scriptures ever escaped the lips of Muhammad other than that of implicit reverence. Both Jews and Christians, however, are repeatedly accused of having falsified certain texts (see Kurān, Sūra II. 39, 134).

Islām was really an illegitimate child of Judaism, and Muhammad owed much of the sternness of his monotheism to the teaching of the Jews. Christians as well as Jews are styled in the Kurān 'people of the Book.' The Pentateuch, and sometimes the whole Old Testament, is called Taurāt, and the New Testament Injīl. All three—the Law, the Gospel, and Kurān—are spoken of as the Word of God, and belief in them is enjoined on pain of hell, but the Kurān, according to Muhammad, was the latest revelation. See Kurān, Sūra III. 2; V. 52. The miraculous birth of Christ is asserted in Sūra III. 40-42.

[2] Muhammad always called Abraham the first of Muslims. Islām and Muslim are from the same Arabic root *salama*, signifying 'to submit to God's Will,' 'to trust in God.'

would he not begin by saying, 'I also, like Abraham, am a Muslim. I believe as strongly as you do in the Unity of God. I resign myself as submissively as you do to the Will of God. Whatsoever things are good, are true, are lovely, are of good report in your system, I think on them, I accept them, I welcome them, nay more, I call on you to hold them fast'?

And ought not every Missionary to begin by meeting the Muslim on the ground of his own Kurān, for the very reason that he may more effectually combat its soul-destroying errors.

I fear that the present position of the Church Militant on earth is making cowards of us all. We shrink from Unitarian Islām as if we dreaded the infection of a disease easily communicated. We are living in the midst of malarious influences — some outside, some inside our camp. Every man suspects the soundness of his neighbour's religious opinions. What excites especial alarm in our Indian Mission-fields is the spread of theistic and pantheistic ideas among educated natives. Even the religious atmosphere of Europe is believed to be largely impregnated with the subtle germs of many forms of deistic and materialistic philosophy. In our dread of wandering unguardedly into the neighbourhood of these contagious errors we are doubtless rightly careful to take our stand firmly on the sure foundation of the divinity of God the Son. But ought we on that account to insist less forcibly on the doctrines of God's Fatherhood and of Christ's humanity which equally lie at the very foundation of sound Christianity?

I trust I shall not be misunderstood if I venture as a layman deferentially to inquire why it is that nearly every sermon I have heard for many years, whether in India or England, has been eloquent of God the Son— few sermons of God the Father, and God the Holy Spirit? Why is Christ so constantly held up to believers and unbelievers as the one God—so rarely as the Man Mediator leading us by one Spirit unto the Father?

We cannot, indeed, wonder that deeply religious Christians should concentrate their affections on the Saviour of the world. Nor can they render to the world's Redeemer more love than is His due. Yet it seems to me that in combating Unitarianism in our Indian brethren we may possibly ourselves be fairly charged with lapsing into a subtle form of Unitarianism, if we habitually place the One Mediator in the position of the One God.

Let me not be mistaken. I trust no one believes more firmly than I do in the necessity for insisting on Christ's Divine nature. But I am persuaded that if we would achieve more success in our Missionary dealings with Muhammadans, our first care should be to convince them that Christianity alone satisfies the yearnings of the human heart for mediation and atonement, because Christianity alone presents us with the One perfect Mediator between God and men, the Man Christ Jesus.

For if Muslims admit that their own prophet believed himself to be an imperfect man who needed every day to pray for the pardon of his own sins[1], they are on that very account more likely to be impressed with the contrast, when we set before them Christ as the One perfect Representative of our race,—the One divine Mediator whose atonement was efficient, because He was in all points tempted like as we are, yet without sin.

Depend upon it that in seeking to win Muslims to the true faith, we require to cultivate more of the wisdom of the serpent. We require to creep into their hearts by a frank admission of the Unity of the Godhead, and of the excellence of Muhammad's teaching in regard to this and other doctrines. We may then perhaps induce them to meet us half-way—to relax a little of their stern monotheism—to concede that sinful man's necessity may have

---

[1] See Kurān, Sūra XLVIII. 2.

acted, like a prism on light, to exhibit a triple manifestation of the One God; and so may cautiously, tenderly, gradually, lead them on to a full sense of the complex existence of the Almighty Being Who created us in His own Image, and to an unqualified acceptance of the great central dogma of our Church. But even when we have brought the need of an everliving Mediator and eternal Paraclete home to their hearts, we may wisely hesitate to force upon them, before they are able to bear it, the acceptance of merely ecclesiastical terms not found in our Bible.

I know that we members of the Church of England are rightly jealous for the term Trinity. I know that half the Sundays of the ecclesiastical year remind us of our Trinitarian creed. I know, too, that we rightly fence round our great central doctrine with every possible ecclesiastical safeguard. But in our first efforts for the conversion of Muslims, we shall be equally right to bear in mind that the language of the Bible preceded the Book of Common Prayer, that Christ Himself declared the first of the commandments to be, 'The Lord our God is One Lord,' that in the first Article of our Church, and in all our Creeds, the Unity of the Godhead is asserted before the triple Personality.

Before I conclude let me express a doubt whether we Christians, who claim divine inspiration for the Bible, believed by us to be the only true Word of God, delivered through the minds of men, are quite as fair as we ought to be towards the book believed by Muhammadans to be a record of the actual words of the Almighty.

In travelling from Kaśmīr to Cape Comorin, I scarcely met a single Missionary who professed himself conversant with the language in which the Kurān is written. His chief knowledge of the book, held to be the direct word of God by forty-one millions of our Indian fellow-subjects, is derived from translations made by Christians who utterly disbelieve even its partial inspiration.

Moreover, although innumerable commentaries on the Kurān have been written in Arabic by pious Muslims, not a single one is generally studied by our Missionaries, nor has a single one ever been translated into English [1], nor do our Missionaries think of accepting any other interpretations of difficult passages than those given by unbelieving Christians.

I ask then what should we think of Indian Musalmāns if, after organizing a mission to convert England to Islām, they were to send us Missionaries who judged of our Bible not from their own knowledge of the original text, or even of our own English translation, but from translations into Indian languages made by unbelieving Muslims?

Or again, if Musalmān controversialists were to interpret all the difficulties of our sacred Scriptures, not from the point of view of such Christian writers as Butler, Pearson, or Hooker, but from that of hostile Muslim commentators?

One reflection more before I conclude. If only the self-deluded but fervent-spirited Muhammad, whose whole soul was stirred within him when he saw his fellow-townsmen wholly given to idolatry, had been brought into association with the purer forms of Christianity—if he had ever listened to the true ring of the Gospel—if, from the examples which crossed his path he had formed a correct ideal of the religion of Christ, he might have died a martyr for the truth, Asia might have numbered her millions of Christians, and the name of a Saint Muhammad might have been recorded in the calendar of our Book of Common Prayer.

As it was, alas! the only Christianity presented to the Arab enthusiast, thirsting for the well of living water, was

[1] The two Arabic Commentaries of highest repute, and indispensable for a right understanding of the Kurān, are those of Zamakhsharī and Baidhāwī, the latter especially valuable for grammatical and historical explanations. There are excellent editions of these Commentaries by Lees and Fleischer, but no English translation. Two other well known Commentaries are by the two Jalālu'd-dīns.

that adulteration of the truth prevalent in the seventh century, which he believed it his mission to supplant by a purer system. It has somewhere been affirmed that the religion of Jesus, and the precepts of the Gospel, may be found scattered piecemeal through the pages of the Kurān. What should rather be alleged is that the religion of a spurious Jesus, and the precepts of a spurious Gospel, may be extracted from such parts of Muhammad's pretended revelations as were communicated to him by the followers of a debased form of Christian doctrine.

Think, then, of the difference in the present condition of the Asiatic world, if the fire of Muhammad's eloquence had been kindled, and the force of his personal influence exerted on the side of veritable Christianity.

Ought not this thought to intensify the sense of responsibility in those of us who are living among Muhammadans? What examples are Christians setting in Muhammadan countries? What ideal of Christianity are they presenting to millions of Muslims in our own Indian territories?

It is I fear too true that the pages of the Kurān are ever presenting to the pious Musalmān yearning like ourselves for a perfect Mediator, the image of a counterfeit Christ and a counterfeit Gospel; yet the spuriousness of the copy will not be so clearly manifested by argument and controversy as by the exhibition of a true reflection of the Divine Original in the lives, acts, and words of Christian men.

THE THREE RELIGIONS OF INDIA COMPARED WITH EACH OTHER AND WITH CHRISTIANITY.

LET me begin by declaring my conviction that the time is approaching, if not already arrived, when all thoughtful Christians will have to reconsider their position, and, so to speak, readjust themselves to their altered environments.

Be it observed, I do not say readjust their most holy faith—not the doctrines once for all delivered to the saints, which cannot change one iota with changing circumstances—but readjust themselves and their own personal views. All the inhabitants of the globe are being rapidly drawn together by facilities of communication, and St. Paul's grand saying, that God has made all nations of the earth of one blood, is being brought home to us more forcibly every day.

Steam-presses, railroads, electric telegraphs, telephones, are producing effects quite without a parallel in the records of the past, and imposing on us Englishmen, the principal colonizers of the world, new duties and responsibilities.

A mighty stir and upheaving of thought is shaking the foundations of ancient creeds to their very centre; and those not reared on the living Rock are tottering and ready to fall. Thinkers, speakers, and writers, Christian and anti-Christian, throughout Europe, America, and Asia, are eagerly interchanging ideas on all the unsolved problems that have for ages baffled the powers of the human mind.

Christians, whether they will or no, are forced to regard the most sacred questions as admitting of other points of view besides their own. Christianity itself is tested like everything else—its time-honoured records placed (so to speak) in the crucible; its cherished dogmas submitted to that potent solvent, Reason.

Muslims, Brāhmans, Pārsīs, and even Buddhists and Confucianists, no longer ignore our Bible, presented to them in their own languages. Intelligent and educated adherents of these creeds are found to look upon Christianity with respect, though they regard it from their own respective stand-points, and examine it by the light of their own hereditary knowledge and traditional doctrines.

In fact, a conviction is everywhere deepening in men's minds, that it is becoming more and more the duty of all the nations of the world to study each other; to inquire into and compare each other's systems of belief; to avoid expressions of contempt in speaking of the sincere and earnest believers in any creed; and to search diligently whether the principles and doctrines which guide their own faith and practice rest on the true foundation or not.

And thus we have arrived at an important epoch in the history of the human race. Thoughtful men in the East and West are fairly trying to understand each other's opinions, and impartially weighing all that can be said in favour of every religion opposed to their own.

And we Christians are taking the lead, and setting the example. We are labouring to translate our own Holy Scriptures into all the languages of the world. We are sparing no expense in printing and distributing them lavishly. We are saying to unbelievers everywhere: 'Read, mark, learn,' judge for yourselves.

But this is not all. We are doing for the adherents of other religious systems what they are slow to do for themselves. We are printing, editing, translating, and publishing the ancient books which claim to be the inspired repositories of their several creeds. And thus to us

Christians is mainly due that now, for the first time, it is possible for the adherents of the four chief antagonistic systems prevalent in the world—Christianity, Brāhmanism, Buddhism, and Islām—to study each other's dogmas in the books held sacred by each.

Here, then, we have before us four sets of books. First, and in the forefront, our own Holy Bible. All honour to our Bible Society! this sacred book, which we hope may one day be carried into every corner of the globe, has already been translated into 210 languages; and if we include the labours of other societies, 296 different versions of it exist. Secondly, the Veda, a word meaning *knowledge*, on which Brāhmanism rests. There are four Vedas (namely, Rig, Yajur, Sāma, and Atharva, written in an ancient form of Sanskrit), each containing three divisions —Mantra, Brāhmana, and Upanishad—nearly all of which have been edited and nearly all translated. Besides the four Vedas, there are the eighteen Purānas which constitute the bible of popular Hindūism. Thirdly, we have the Tri-pitaka, or three baskets, that is, the three collections of writings on which Buddhism rests (written in an ancient language of the Sanskrit family, called Pāli). Three important portions of these collections have been edited by European scholars, and recently translated into English. They are called the *Dhamma-pada*, 'Precepts of Law;' *Sutta-nipāta*, 'occasional discourses;' *Jātaka*, 'previous births of the Buddha.' Fourthly, we have the Kurān, in Arabic, a word meaning '*the book to be read by all*,' on which, as every one knows, Islām rests, and of which Sale's excellent English translation has been long available.

I now give specimens of select passages from the Veda and Purānas, from the Tri-pitaka, and from the Kurān.

From the Atharva-Veda (IV. 16).

The mighty Varuna, who rules above, looks down
Upon these worlds, his kingdom, as if close at hand.
When men imagine they do ought by stealth, he knows it.

No one can stand, or walk, or softly glide along,
Or hide in dark recess, or lurk in secret cell;
The God detects him, and his conduct spies.
Two persons may devise some plot, together sitting
In private and alone, but *he*, the king, is there—
A third—and sees it all. This boundless earth is his,
His the vast sky, whose depth no mortal e'er can fathom.
Both oceans find a place within his body, yet
In that small pool he lies contained. Whoe'er should flee
Far, far beyond the sky, would not escape his grasp,
His messengers descend, for ever traversing
This world and scanning with a thousand eyes its inmates.
Whate'er exists within this earth, and all within the sky,
Yea, all that is beyond, the mighty king perceives.

From the Kaṭha Upanishad (Vallī 2).

The good, the pleasant, these are separate ends.
The one or other all mankind pursue,
But those who seek the good, alone are blest.
The careless youth, by lust of gain deceived,
Knows but one world, one life; to him the Now
Alone exists, the Future is a dream.
The highest aim of knowledge is the soul;
This is a miracle, beyond the ken
Of common mortals, thought of though it be,
And variously explained by skilful teachers.
Who gains this knowledge is a marvel too;
He lives above the cares—the griefs and joys
Of time and sense—seeking to penetrate
The fathomless unborn eternal essence.
The slayer thinks he slays, the slain
Believes himself destroyed, the thoughts of both
Are false, the soul survives, nor kills, nor dies;
'Tis subtler than the subtlest, greater than
The greatest, infinitely small, yet vast,
Asleep, yet restless, moving everywhere
Among the bodies—ever bodiless—
Think not to grasp it by the reasoning mind;
The wicked ne'er can know it: soul alone
Knows soul, to none but soul is soul revealed.

From the Vishṇu-purāṇa (V. 23).

Lord of the Universe, the only refuge
Of living beings, the alleviator
Of pain, the benefactor of mankind,

Show me thy favour and deliver me
From evil; O creator of the world,
Maker of all that has been and will be,
Of all that moves and is immovable,
Worthy of praise, I come to thee, my refuge,
Renouncing all attachment to the world,
Longing for fulness of felicity—
Extinction of myself, absorption into thee.

From the Tri-piṭaka (*Dhamma-pada*).

Conquer a man who never gives, by gifts;
Subdue untruthful men by truthfulness;
Vanquish an angry man by gentleness;
And overcome the evil man by goodness.

The following is a prophecy from the Lalita-vistara of what the Buddha was to do for the world (translated by Dr. John Muir).

The world of men and gods to bless,
  The way of rest and peace to teach,
  A holy law thy son shall preach—
A law of stainless righteousness.

By him shall suffering men be freed
  From weakness, sickness, pain, and grief,
  From all the ills shall find relief
Which hatred, love, illusion, breed.

His hand shall loose the chains of all
  Who groan in fleshly bonds confined;
  With healing touch the wounds shall bind
Of those whom pain's sharp arrows gall.

His potent words shall put to flight
  The dull array of leaden clouds
  Which helpless mortals' vision shrouds,
And clear their intellectual sight.

By him shall men who, now untaught,
  In devious paths of error stray,
  Be led to find a perfect way—
To final calm at last be brought.

From the Tri-piṭaka (*Sutta-nipāta*).

How can a man who has fallen into a river, having bottomless water and a swift-flowing current, being himself carried away, and following the current, cause others to cross it?

COMPARISON OF THE RELIGIONS OF INDIA. 251

As one, skilful, attentive, and acquainted with the mode of steering, going on board a strong ship provided with oars and rudders, causes by means of it many others to cross the ocean; even so he who has attained the knowledge of religious paths, being devoted to meditation, very learned, and of an unmoved nature, can teach others who listen with attentive ears to his preaching.

Drinking of the water of a life of seclusion and of the water of subjugating the passions, drinking also of the pleasant beverage called the perception of truth, one becomes freed from emotion and sin.

Thou art the Buddha, thou art the Teacher, thou art the Vanquisher of the evil one (*Māra*), thou art the Sage; having cut off all thoughts, and crossed the sea of repeated births, thou hast taken over these beings to the other shore.

From the Kurān (Chapters II, VIII).

To God belongeth the east, and the west; therefore, whithersoever ye turn to pray, there is the face of God; for God is omnipresent, and omniscient. And when he decreeth a thing, he only saith unto it, 'Be,' and it is.

The Jews say, the Christians are grounded on nothing, and the Christians say, The Jews are grounded on nothing; yet they both read the scriptures. But God shall judge between them on the day of the resurrection concerning that about which they now disagree.

Verily the true believers are those whose hearts fear when God is mentioned, and whose faith increaseth when his signs are rehearsed unto them, and who trust in their Lord; who observe the stated times of prayer, and give alms out of that which we have bestowed on them. These are really believers. They shall have superior degrees of felicity with their Lord, and forgiveness, and an honourable position.

O true believers! answer God and his apostle, when he inviteth you unto that which giveth you life; and know that God goeth between a man and his heart, and that before him ye shall be assembled.

O true believers! deceive not God and his apostle, neither violate your faith, against your own knowledge. And know that your wealth and your children are a temptation unto you, and that with God there is a great reward.

Having, then, these books before us, it is clear that we ought not to despise documents held sacred by our fellow-creatures, as if they were too contemptible even to be glanced at from the elevated position on which we stand. Rather are we bound to follow the example of the great Apostle of the Gentiles—who, speaking to Gentiles, did not denounce them as atheists or idolaters, but appealed to them as Δεισιδαιμονεστέρους, very God-fearing; and even quoted one of their own poets in support of a Christian truth—and who, writing to Christians, enjoined them not to shut their eyes to anything true, honest, just, pure, lovely, and of good report, wherever it was to be found; but that if there was any virtue anywhere, or any praise anywhere, they were to think on these things.

And have not we Englishmen, in particular, to whose rule India has been committed, special opportunities and responsibilities, brought as we are there into immediate contact with these three principal religious systems—Brāhmanism, Buddhism, and Islām?

Let us look for a moment at any modern map of India. The first glance shows us that it is not one country but many. Nor has it one race, language, and religion, but many races, languages, and religions. Mr. R. N. Cust, late a distinguished member of the Bengal Civil Service, and a member of the Legislative Council at Calcutta, has recently published a map of India (including all the territories subject to British imperial authority) in which the boundaries of all the languages are marked out. It is accompanied by a table which classifies the languages under eight heads. These are as follow:—(1) Āryan, 20; (2) Drāviḍian, 12; (3) Kolarian, 7; (4) Tibeto-Burman, 56; (5) Khasi, 1; (6) Tai, 5; (7) Mon-Anam, 5; (8) Malayan, 33; in all, 139 distinct languages. At least 100 dialects are not included in the above classification. We may safely affirm, therefore, that the languages and dialects of India amount to at least 200.

Its population, according to the recent census, now exceeds 240,000,000.

Of these, about 185,000,000 are Hindūs, nominal adherents of Brāhmanism.

Then, secondly, nearly 41,000,000 are Muhammadans, adherents of Islām—so that England is by far the greatest Muhammadan power in the world, and the Queen reigns

COMPARISON OF THE RELIGIONS OF INDIA. 253

over about double as many Muslims as the representative of the Khalifs himself.

Then, thirdly, there are about 3,000,000 Buddhists, including the Jains (whose peculiar tenets and sacred scriptures are described at p. 159). This will appear a small number to those who are aware that there are nearly 500,000,000 nominal Buddhists now in the world, the numbers of nominal Christians being far less—only about 360,000,000.

Nevertheless, the original home of Buddhism was India, which it did not finally leave till about the eighth or ninth century of our era. It is now found in the Chinese empire, Ceylon, Burmah, Nepāl, Assam, and scattered here and there throughout India in the form of its near relative, Jainism.

For what purpose, then, has this enormous territory been committed to England? Not to be the 'corpus vile' of political, social, or military experiments; not for the benefit of our commerce, or the increase of our wealth—but that every man, woman, and child, from Cape Comorin to the Himālaya mountains, may be elevated, enlightened, Christianized.

Let us now, therefore, briefly inquire what are the leading ideas which characterize these chief religions of the world, as represented in India; and in doing so let us rise from the false to the true.

1. To begin with Brāhmanism.

This has two sides—two aspects—and a vast chasm separates the two. One is esoteric, the other exoteric; one is philosophical, the other popular; one is for the few, the other for the many.

What, then, is the highest or philosophical form of Brāhmanism? Its creed, which rests on the Upanishad portion of the Veda, has the merit of extreme simplicity. It may be described in two words: Spiritual Pantheism; or, in the original Sanskrit, Ekam eva advitīyam, *One only Being, no second*—that is, nothing really exists but the one self-existent Spirit, called Brahma (neuter); all else is Māyā, or *illusion*. In other words, nothing exists but God, and everything existing is God. You, he, and I are God. We do not know that we are God, because God wills for a time to ignore Himself. When this self-imposed ignorance ceases, all distinction of personality vanishes, and complete oneness of being is restored. This is true philosophical Brāhmanism—*the unity of all being*.

An enormous gulf separates this pure pantheism from the popular side of Brāhmanism, which may be called Hindūism, and which rests on the Purāṇas, and is practically polytheism. But the gulf is bridged over by the word emanation. In the philosophical creed, everything is identified with Brahma; in the popular, everything emanates from Brahma. Stones, plants, animals, men, superior and inferior gods, good and bad demons, and every conceivable object, issue from the one self-existent universal soul, Brahma, as drops from the ocean, as sparks from fire. Men emanate in fixed classes. They cannot alter their social status in each separate existence. Born Brāhmans, they must remain Brāhmans; born soldiers, they must remain soldiers; born tillers of the ground, they must remain tillers of the ground; born menials, they must remain menials.

But what of stones, plants, animals? The spirit of men may pass into any of these, if their actions condemn them to fall in the scale of being; or, on the other hand, it may rise to gods.

And what of gods? There have been direct emanations from the Supreme Being in the form of personal gods: and it is noteworthy that these divine personalities are generally grouped in threes or multiples of three. In the Veda we have sometimes three principal gods, sometimes thirty-three gods named. The Vedic triad consists of—1. *Indra*, or the atmosphere personified; 2. *Agni*, Fire; 3. *Sūrya*, the Sun. The latter and better known triad consists of—1. *Brahmā* (masculine), the Creator; 2. *Vishṇu*, the Preserver; 3. *Rudra-Siva*, the Dissolver of the world, and its reproducer.

This leads to the doctrine of Incarnation. The god Vishṇu, as Pervader and Preserver, passes into men to deliver the world from the power of evil demons.

His most popular and best known incarnations are those of Krishṇa and Rāma. The history of Rāma is told in the great epic poem called Rāmāyaṇa.

Again, many stories of miracles worked by Krishṇa— the other principal incarnation of the god Vishṇu—are told in the second great epic, called Mahā-bhārata. He is there represented as fighting with and destroying many evil demons, notably one in the form of a serpent (Kāliya), on whose head he is sometimes depicted as trampling.

What, then, is the end of Brāhmanism? Men, animals, plants, stones, pass through innumerable existences, and may even rise to gods. But gods, men, animals, plants, and every conceivable emanation from the supreme Soul, aim at, and must end by, re-absorption into their source, Brahma. This is Brāhmanism.

2. Turn we now to *Buddhism*.

Buddha was the son of a king who reigned in Kapila-vastu, a district to the east of Oudh and south of Nepāl. He was, therefore, of the royal caste. The name Buddha is merely a title meaning *the Enlightened*. His othei names are Gautama, Śākya, Siddhārtha. He lived about 500 years B.C.; that is, about contemporaneously with Pythagoras, Zoroaster, and Confucius—all wonderful men. He was a great reformer of Hindūism; but it is a mistake to suppose that he aimed at an entire abolition of Brāhmanism, with the philosophical side of which his system had really much in common. His mission was to abolish caste, to resist sacerdotal tyranny, to preach universal charity and love, and to enjoin self-mortification and self-suppression through perhaps millions of existences, as the only means of getting rid of the evils of life and self-consciousness by an extinction of all being.

He was himself the model of a perfect ascetic. He never claimed to be a god, but only the ideal of that perfection of knowledge and self-subjugation to which every man might attain.

The Buddha had himself passed through millions of births, and was about to become extinct; but before his own attainment of Nirvāṇa, or annihilation, he was enabled, by perfect knowledge of the truth, to reveal to the world the method of obtaining it. He died, and exists no more. He cannot, therefore, be worshipped. His memory only is revered. Temples are erected over his relics, such as a hair or a tooth. The Dathāvanśa, a history of one of his teeth, has recently been translated from the Pāli. In the same manner every man must pass through innumerable existences, rising or falling in the scale, according to his conduct, until he also attains Nirvāṇa, and becomes extinct. The Buddha once pointed to a broom in a corner, which he said had, in a former birth, been a novice who had neglected to be diligent in sweeping out the Assembly Hall.

In Buddhism, then, there can be no God; and if no God, then no prayer, no clergy, no priests. By 'no God' I mean no real God. Yet action is a kind of God. Action is omnipotent. Action is all-powerful in its effects on future states of being. 'An evil act follows a man through a hundred thousand transmigrations, so does a good act.' By 'no prayer' I mean no real prayer. Yet there are two forms of words (meaning, when translated, 'reverence to the jewel in the lotus,' 'honour to the incomparable Buddha,') which repeated or turned in a wheel either once or millions of times, must produce inevitable corresponding results in future existences by the mere mechanical law of cause and effect. By 'no clergy,' I mean no real clergy. Yet there are monks and ascetics by thousands and thousands, banded together in monasteries, for the better suppression of passion and attainment of extinction. Many of these are religious teachers but not priests.

COMPARISON OF THE RELIGIONS OF INDIA. 257

Has Buddhism, then, no morality? Yes—a lofty system of universal charity and benevolence. Yet extinction is its ultimate aim. In this respect it is no improvement upon Brāhmanism. The more the depths of these two systems are explored, the more clearly do they exhibit themselves in their true light as little better than dreary schemes excogitated by visionary philosophers, in the vain hope of delivering themselves from the evils and troubles of life—from all activity, self-consciousness, and personal existence.

3. We now pass to *Islām*, sometimes called Muhammadanism, but not so called by Muhammad himself, who never claimed to be the founder of a religion. Its creed is nearly as simple as that of esoteric Brāhmanism. The one is stern pantheism; the other stern monotheism. The one says everything is God; the other says God is one, but adds an important article of belief—'Muhammad is the prophet of God.' In short, the mission of Muhammad, according to himself, was to proclaim the unity of God (*tawhīd*) and absolute submission to His will (*islām*). What is its end?

The Kurān promises to its disciples a material paradise (*jannat*) or paradises (for there are seven), with shaded gardens, fresh water—two great desiderata in Arabia—black-eyed Hūrīs, and exquisite corporeal enjoyments. It also declares the existence of seven hells. The seventh and worst is for hypocrites; the sixth for idolaters; the third for Christians; the second for Jews.

Islām is plainly a corruption of Judaism and Christianity, and in point of fact began by admitting the truth of both.

The end or aim then of Brāhmanism is absorption into the one Soul of the universe; of Buddhism is extinction; of Islām is admission to a material paradise.

4. So much, then, for the three great religious systems confronting Christianity. Now for Christianity itself, which, creeping onwards little by little, is gradually sur-

rounding them on all sides—sometimes advancing on them by indirect approaches, sometimes pressing on them by direct attack. And here I desire to speak reverentially, deferentially, and with deep humility. But I have the highest authority for what I am about to state. Christianity is a religion which offers to the entire human race access to God the Father through Christ by one Spirit.

The end and aim, therefore, of Christianity is emphatically union with God the Father, but such a union—mark here the important point—such a union as shall secure the permanence of man's personality, energy, and individuality; nay, even shall intensify these.

Let us now, the better to compare the four systems, inquire by what means the end of each is effected. And here let us change the order, and begin with the religion which we believe to be the only true religion in the world.

Christianity, then, asserts that it effects its aim through nothing short of an entire change of the whole man, and a complete renovation of his nature.

The direct means by which its end is accomplished may be described as a kind of mutual transfer, leading to an interchange and co-operation between God and man's nature, acting on each other.

Man—the Bible says—was created in the image of God. But the first representative man fell, and transmitted a taint to his descendants which could only be removed by suffering and death. Hence the second representative man, Christ, Whose nature was divine and taintless, voluntarily underwent a sinner's suffering and death, that the taint, transferred from the tainted to the Taintless One, might be removed.

This is not all. The grand central truth of our religion is not so much that Christ died as that He now lives and lives for ever. It is Christ that died—yea rather, Who is risen again—that He may bestow, first, life for death: secondly, a participation in His own divine nature for the tainted nature He has removed.

COMPARISON OF THE RELIGIONS OF INDIA. 259

This is the mutual exchange that marks Christianity—an exchange between the personal man descended from a corrupt parent, and the Personal God made man and becoming our Second Parent. We are separated from a rotten root and grafted into a living root. We part with a corrupt nature and draw re-creative force—a new nature—from the ever-living Divine stem of the Second Adam, to which by a simple act of faith we are united.

Other religions have their doctrines, their precepts of morality, which, detached from much that is worthless, may even vie with those of Christianity.

But Christianity has what other religions have not—a Personal God, ever living to supply the regenerating Spirit and Life by which man, being re-created and again made God-like, and again becoming 'pure in heart'—yet still preserving his own personality—obtains access to God the Father, and fitness to dwell in His presence for ever.

Secondly, *Islām*. What are its means of effecting its end? Muhammad was the prophet of God, says the Kurān, but nothing more. He claimed no combination of Divinity with humanity. Even his human nature was not asserted to be immaculate. He made no pretensions to mediatorial or vicarious functions. He died like any other man, and certainly did not rise that his followers might find in him eternal springs of divine life and power. Even Muslims do not regard him as the source of any re-creative force, capable of changing their whole nature. Muhammad sets forth faith in Islām and in his own mission, repentance, the performance of prayer, fasting, alms, pilgrimages, and the constant repetition of certain words (especially parts of the Kurān), as infallible means of obtaining Paradise. In one place, patience, perseverance, walking in the fear of God, and attachment to Him, are insisted on. Yet it must be admitted that the Kurān elsewhere maintains that good works have no real meritorious efficacy in procuring Paradise, and that the righteous obtain entrance there through God's mercy alone. Indeed, every action in Islām is done 'in the name of God, the merciful, the compassionate' (*b'ismillāh ar-rahmān ar-rahīm*). But it should be borne in mind that the Kurān is by no means systematic or consistent. It was delivered in detached portions according to the exigencies of the moment, and, being often confused and contradictory, had to be explained and developed by traditional teaching. It has some noble passages.

In one thing the Muslim sets the Christian an example —submission to the will of God. But can the submission enjoined in the Kurān bear comparison with the sublime example of the Redeemer in the Garden of Gethsemane? Is it the submission of a slave to the will of a master, or the dependence of a child on a loving Father for life and breath and all things?

Thirdly, *Brāhmanism*. What are its means of attaining its ends? In fairness we must allow that the lines of Brāhmanical and Hindū thought often intersect those of Christianity.

In the later Hindū system the end of union with a Supreme Spirit is effected by faith in an apparently personal God. But this seeming personality melts on scrutiny into a vague impersonal essence.

True, God becomes man, and interposes for the good of men. There is a seeming combination of the human and divine—an apparent interchange of action. Most remarkable language, too, is applied to Krishṇa (in the Bhagavad-gītā) as the source of all life and energy. But how can there be any permanent interaction and co-operation between divine and human personalities when both must ultimately merge in the Oneness of the Infinite?

Fourthly and lastly, *Buddhism*. What are its means of accomplishing its end? Extinction of being is effected by self-mortification, by profound contemplation, and by abstinence from action. The Buddha himself is extinct. He cannot therefore, of course, be the source of eternal life. Nor can indeed eternal life ever be desired by those whose highest aim is to be blown out like a candle.

It is refreshing to turn from such unsatisfying systems —however interspersed with sublime sentiments and lofty morality—to the living, energizing Christianity of European nations, however fallen from its true standard, however disgraced by the inconsistencies of its nominal adherents.

One more observation before I conclude.

Brāhmanism is not a missionary religion, and from its very nature never has been nor can be. Trades may be associated in castes, and such associations are even now admitted into the modern caste-system of Hindūism; but trade combinations are no part of its true creed. Brāhmanism cannot make a Brāhman, even if it would; and so far from distributing in other countries the texts or translations of its own sacred Vedas on which its creed rests, prohibits the general reading and repeating of them by its own people, indiscriminately. As to printing and editing these books, even for philological purposes, orthodox Brāhmans regard them as too sacred to be defiled by printers' ink. Had it not been for the labours of Christian scholars, their contents would have remained for ever a 'terra incognita' to the majority of the Hindūs themselves. Brāhmanism, therefore, must die out. In point of fact, false ideas on the most ordinary scientific subjects are so mixed up with its doctrines that the commonest education—the simplest lessons in geography—without the aid of Christianity, must inevitably in the end sap its foundations.

Buddhism, on the contrary, when it first arose in India, was pre-eminently a proselyting system. Hence its rapid progress. Hence it spread as no other false system has ever spread before or since. But its missionary zeal has now departed, its philosophy has lapsed into superstition, and of real religion it has none, nor ever claimed to have. Hence its fate in India, and hence the fate that awaits it everywhere. Buddhism does not seem to have been driven forcibly out of India; it simply pined away and died out. It could not maintain its hold upon the Hindūs, who are essentially a religious people, and must have a religion of some kind. Take away Brāhmanism, and they cannot again become Buddhists. They must become Christians, Muslims, or Theists.

Young Calcutta, Madras, and Bombay, educated and Europeanized without being Christianized, may glory in Positivism; but these are not the real population of India. The masses will never be satisfied with mere European knowledge, or with systems of philosophy and oppositions of science falsely so called. Christianity has many more points of contact with their ancient faith than Islām has, and when the walls of the mighty fortress of Brāhmanism are encircled, undermined, and finally stormed by the soldiers of the Cross, the victory of Christianity must be signal and complete.

And how does the case stand with Islām? Here we have a system which is still actively proselyting, and therefore still spreading. Indeed, if Christians do not collect and concentrate their energies so as to stem the tide of its progress in Africa, the advancing wave of the Muslim faith—a faith attractive to uncultured minds from its simplicity—will rapidly flood that whole continent.

But of no other religion can it be affirmed so emphatically as of Christianity that the missionary spirit is of its innermost essence; for Christ, Who is the Life and Soul of Christianity, was Himself a missionary—the first and greatest of all missionaries. And if He had not ordained the Apostles to be His missionary successors, and if they had not ordained other missionaries, there would be no Christianity among us here, no Christianity anywhere in the world.

PROGRESS OF OUR INDIAN EMPIRE.[1]

Part I.

MACAULAY, in his essay on Lord Clive, asserts that every English schoolboy 'knows who imprisoned Montezuma, and who strangled Atahualpa,' but doubts 'whether one in ten, even among English gentlemen of highly cultivated minds, can tell who won the battle of Buxar, who perpetrated the massacre of Patna, whether Sujah Dowlah ruled in Oude or in Travancore, or whether Holkar was a Hindū or a Musalmān.' Macaulay's review was written nearly forty years ago.

Whether the Tom Browns and Julian Holmes of the present day are equally well 'posted up' in Mexican history, and whether, when turned out into the world as educated men, they are equally ignorant of Indian history, admits of question. Probably the main facts of the material development of British India are better known than they were when Macaulay wrote his essays in the *Edinburgh*. Yet at a time when great statesmen speak of our Eastern Empire as 'founded on criminal ambition,' and when other politicians accuse Russia of a desire to extend her territorial possessions in a manner equally unscrupulous, it may not be unprofitable to recall attention to the irresistible current of circumstances which has landed us in our present position

[1] This and the following Essay appeared first in the *Contemporary Review*.

in India, and made British Indian interests and British Indian duties important elements of the momentous Eastern problem which the recent war has not yet finally solved.

The history of European enterprise in the East begins with the maritime supremacy of the Portuguese. The journeys of the Venetian traveller, Marco Polo, in Central and Eastern Asia, between 1291 and the close of the thirteenth century, and the narrative of his visit to the coast of India, excited much interest in Europe, and stimulated travellers and navigators to feel their way eastward.

Our fellow-countryman, Sir John Mandeville, left England in 1327, and, after wandering for thirty-three years through Europe and Asia, returned home and wrote his well-known narrative, which was printed in 1499. The marvels ' of Inde ' which he described probably contributed to stimulate the prosecution of maritime discovery, though it is doubtful whether he was ever in India at all. Nicolo Conti, a noble Venetian, is said to have travelled in India between 1419 and 1444; Athanasius Nikitin, a Russian, between 1468 and 1474; Hieronimo di Santo Stefano, a Genoese, between 1494 and 1499; Ludovico di Varthema between 1503 and 1508 [1]. The Portuguese navigator, Bartholomew Diaz, succeeded in rounding the southern promontory of Africa, called by him the Cape of Storms, and was the first real pioneer of the ocean route to India, about the year 1487. Ten years later his countyman, Vasco da Gama—whose tomb or cenotaph I saw in a large Protestant church at Cochin—sailed round the Cape and reached Calicut on the 11th May, 1498. The Portuguese found India torn asunder by internal dissensions, and were the first to take advantage of its condition of chronic disunion and so gain a footing on the western coast. But the Portuguese were not mere traders as we originally were—mere commercial speculators

---

[1] Dr. George Birdwood is my authority here. I had not had the advantage of reading his valuable Report on the Miscellaneous Old Records of the India Office when I wrote this and the succeeding paper for the *Contemporary Review.*

who went to India to make money, and to return home with it when made. They aimed from the first at settling in the country, at establishing themselves there as a conquering nation, and achieving political dominion.

Their first Indian viceroy was Almeyda. The second, Albuquerque, landed in 1508, took Goa from the kingdom of Bījāpur, and made it the capital of the Portuguese possessions. The Portuguese, however, never possessed any considerable territory in India beyond the limits of their factories. Their progress was too rapid and their career too adventuresome to be lasting. In less than a century their power began to decline, and by 1640 nearly all their ports and forts were wrested from them. Bassein was taken from them by the Marāṭhas in 1765, and only Goa, Diū, and Damān, on the western coast, now remain. Yet the Portuguese have left their mark on India—a more abiding mark, in the opinion of some persons, than the impression we should leave if our rule were to cease tomorrow.

The Dutch succeeded the Portuguese in the maritime supremacy of the Eastern seas. Their chief settlement was in Bengal, at Chinsurah, near Hūglī, which remained in their hands till 1824, when it was ceded to the English in exchange for our possessions in Sumātra. All their other settlements have gradually been made over to us.

The Danes never possessed more than two settlements in India—to wit, Tranquebar and Serampur (Sri-rāmapur), on the Hūglī, which our Government bought in 1845.

The English soon became rivals of the Dutch. The first Englishman known to have reached India viā the Cape of Good Hope was a man named Thomas Stevens, or Stephens (also called Stephen de Buston, or Bubston, in Dodd's Church History, ii. 133). He belonged to the diocese of Salisbury, and, having given proof of ability, was sent as a student to Rome, where he became a Jesuit. It is stated that he was once a member of New College, Oxford, but no such name is on the books [1]. His superiors despatched him as a missionary to the East Indies in one of five ships which left Lisbon on April 4th, 1579, and reached Goa in the following October. Thence he wrote a letter to his father, which is preserved in Hakluyt's collection of voyages (1st edition, p. 160). He resided at Goa about forty years, during five of which he was rector of a Jesuit college there. The inhabitants respected him as a kind of apostle. His familiarity with the dialects of the country is proved by his having published three works—a Konkanī Grammar, an Account of Christian Doctrine, and a History of Christ, which he called a Purāṇa. I have seen an edition of his Grammar in the India Office library, but have never met with his other two works.

In 1583, a merchant of London, named Ralph Fitch, 'being desirous to see the countries of the East Indies, shipped himself in a ship of London, called the *Tygre*, for Tripolis, in Syria.' He was accompanied by another English merchant, 'Mr. John Newberie,' who was the bearer of a letter of recommendation from Queen Elizabeth to ' Echebar (Akbar), King of Cambay ' (Hakluyt's Voyages, ii. 245). Messrs. Fitch and Newbury journeyed through Syria and by the Euphrates to Basora, whence they took ship to Goa. There the Portuguese authorities, jealous of the intrusion of two rich English merchants, found some pretext for throwing them into prison. Happily, the English Jesuit, Father Stevens, was already a man of influence, and procured their release. They fled from Goa to Bisapor (Bījāpur), where they saw ' idols standing in the woods, some like a cow, some like a monkey, some like buffaloes, some like peacocks, and some like the devil, with four arms and four hands.' The account they published of their travels (preserved by Hakluyt) would well repay republication in a modern form, especially if illustrated and annotated like Colonel Yule's ' Marco Polo.'

[1] I find that one Thomas Stevyns took his degree at St. John's College, Oxford, in June, 1577.

On the 31st December, 1600, little more than two hundred and seventy-nine years ago, the East India Company was incorporated by Queen Elizabeth. Though a second company was formed in 1698, it was amalgamated with the first in 1702.

As Queen Elizabeth gave Mr. Newbury a letter to Akbar, so James I sent Captain Hawkins to Sūrat, in 1608, with a letter to the Emperor Jahāngīr, who permitted the English to establish four factories in his dominions. Our first settlement was at Sūrat (improperly called Surāt), near the mouth of the River Taptī, in 1611, and here the Portuguese, the Dutch, and subsequently the French,—who made their first expedition to India about 1604,—erected factories near to ours. As early as 1608 Sūrat is described as 'one of the most eminent cities for trade in all India.' It had been conquered by Akbar in 1573, and was then called a first-class port. I have twice visited this place—the first focal point of all our operations in the East, and the centre of all our commercial dealings with the people of India. Every part of the town is suggestive of interesting reminiscences. The boundaries of the Portuguese, Dutch, English, and French factories may still be traced, and the fort built by the French is kept by us in good repair.

The first name of the town is said to have been Sūraj (Sanskrit, Sūrya), 'City of the Sun.' A Muhammadan ruler, wishing to change its Hindū name into one more significant of Muslim domination, converted Sūraj into Sūrat, 'a chapter in the Kurān.' Another name given to it was Bāb ul Makka, 'gate of Mecca,' and one part of the town is to this day called the Mecca quarter, because the Muhammadans of India made this western port their starting-point for the *hajj* or pilgrimage to Mecca.

It is greatly to be regretted that the River Taptī, once deep and navigable, has been allowed to accumulate silt till large vessels can no longer enter.

In 1615 James I sent Sir Thomas Roe as his ambassador to the Moghul Court. It is not surprising that a man so distinguished for diplomatic ability and conciliatory manners should have secured the concession of many advantages to the British merchants. But he recommended the Company to be satisfied with quiet trade, and warned them against using force to promote their commercial objects. 'If the Emperor,' he wrote, 'were to offer me ten forts, I would not accept of one.'

It is more remarkable that the extension of our commercial privileges on the western coast and in Bengal should have been due to the professional skill of an English doctor who lived at Sūrat. A certain Dr. Broughton cured the Emperor Shāh Jahān's daughter in 1636, and rendered similar services to his Viceroy in Bengal. This good man must have been a model of unselfish patriotism, for he might have enriched himself, but preferred to secure commercial benefits for his country. Another generous doctor, named Hamilton, procured similar privileges for the Company in the same way in 1716.

And here a point, too often forgotten, ought to be brought out conspicuously. The position of the English in India was at first merely that of a Company of commercial speculators, who had invested a large amount of hard cash in their speculation and wanted a good dividend. For a long period after their first settlement in Sūrat, they were simply a body of keen traders. They had no other thought than the improvement of their commerce, no other aim than the realization of good interest for their capital, no other policy than peaceful negotiation. They were willing to undergo toil, hardship, suffering, perils by land and sea, if money was to be had. But they were not fighting men. It was only when absolutely compelled to take up arms for the defence of their property, that they built forts and factories side by side. Rather than threaten force they were willing to stoop to the employment of language which nothing but long familiarity with Eastern servility could justify.

Even so lately as 1712, the President of the Bengal

settlements, Mr. Russell, is reported to have petitioned the Emperor of Delhi to the following effect:—

'The supplication of John Russell, whose forehead is the top of the footstool of the absolute monarch and prop of the Universe. We Englishmen having traded hitherto in Bengal, Orissa, and Behar, custom-free, are your Majesty's most obedient slaves. We have readily observed your most sacred orders, and have found favour. We crave to have your Majesty's permission in the above-mentioned places as before, and to follow our business without molestation.'

The first spark of England's military glory in India was kindled when the peace-loving, money-loving Company of British traders nobly defended Sūrat in 1664 against the founder of the Marāṭha power, Sivajī, who attempted to wrest it from the Moghul Empire. Our gallant defence of the town when deserted by the other European traders was rewarded by the concession of further commercial privileges.

It was then that military organization became a condition of our very existence in India. To the Sūrat merchants belongs the honour of having quickened the first germ of our now gigantic Eastern Empire. Naturally, therefore, the right of presiding over British Indian interests first devolved on these Sūrat traders. The Presidency of Sūrat was the first Indian Presidency, and with Sūrat the privilege of presiding over every other English factory remained till Bombay was given to Charles II by the Portuguese as part of the dowry of his Queen Catharine of Braganza in 1661. Bombay was delivered up in 1665 and made over to the East India Company in 1668. Its commanding position, and its magnificent natural harbour, gave it the superiority. It was then that the Presidency over British Indian commerce naturally passed from one town to the other, and Bombay became the chief centre of British trade on the western coast of India.

But even then no dream of empire disturbed the purely mercantile spirit of our fellow-countrymen. Money was their motive, money was their guiding principle, money was their end, intrigue and negotiation their *modus operandi*. In a paper of instructions issued by the Directors of the Company in 1689 occurs the first hint that territorial jurisdiction might become necessary for the security of their property.

Turning now to the Bengal side of India, we find that the first factory was established on the Hūglī, in 1640-42. The first fortress was erected in 1656. It is noteworthy that the Company had to encounter far more opposition from the natives in this part of India than they had experienced on the western coast.

The site of Madras was obtained by Francis Day, then president of the mercantile community on the eastern coast, as a grant from the Hindū King of Vijayanagar, and a factory was founded there about the same year as the Hūglī factory (1639). Only a few fishermen's huts were then to be seen on the spot. Soon afterwards Charles I built Fort St. George, round which clustered the nucleus of the future Madras. At the same time he conferred on the fort the privilege of presiding over the factories of the Coromandel coast, the term 'presidency' merely denoting, as before, superintendence over the other trading communities in that part of India.

It was not till about 1700 that the germ of the future Calcutta (*Kālī-kataka*, village of *Kālī*) was planted, not far from Hūglī, and the celebrated temple of the goddess Kālī. Here a collection of villages, originally obtained by the English settlers as a grant in return for a present to a son of the Emperor Aurangzīb, was converted by the Company's principal agent in Bengal, Mr. Charnock, into the nucleus of the great metropolis, whose population (794,645 according to the last census) now outnumbers that of every other city in the British Empire, London only excepted. A fort was commenced, but the 'Marāṭha ditch,' now almost obliterated, was not excavated till about 1742. Its object was to protect the Calcutta settlements from the attacks of the omnipresent Marāṭha armies which then overran the whole of India, demanding tribute (significantly called *chauth*, 'a fourth'). Fort William was completed soon afterwards.

The idea of founding an empire in India originated, not with the English, but with the French. The man on whose mind the conception first flashed was the French Governor, Dupleix. A French East India Company had been formed, under Louis XIV, in 1664, and a factory established near that of the English at Sūrat. Ten years afterwards Martin, to whom the French owe the foundation of the power they afterwards acquired in India, obtained Pondicherry from the King of Bijāpur, and fourteen years later Chandarnagar (Chandernagore), on the Hūglī, was received from Aurangzīb. It was not till 1741 that Dupleix was appointed Governor-General of the French Indian possessions. His aspiring genius not only conceived the idea of conquering India, but devised the expedient of making use of the Indians themselves to aid in subjugating their own territory. He was the first to discover any soldier-like qualities latent beneath the mild, apathetic exterior of the Indian character. He beheld around him men, if not equal in muscular power to Europeans, yet naturally careless of life, temperate, faithful, docile, and submissive. Drilled and disciplined they might be turned into an effective army. This was the brilliant conception which, emanating from French intelligence, was developed and improved upon by English administrative energy. It was evident that the ability of Dupleix was equal to the task of carrying his bold design of founding a French Eastern Empire into execution. But no sooner had he developed his plan of acquiring territorial dominion, than the English perceived that they would have to fight or abandon their property to French cupidity. Instantly our troops of merchants were transformed from peaceful traders into resolute soldiers, determined on disputing every inch of ground with their European rivals.

The history of India was now, for at least ten years, the history of the struggle between the French and English for political ascendency and territorial dominion. The Carnatic—a strip of country on the south-eastern coast from the river Kistna, north of Madras, to Cape Comorin—was the theatre of the conflict. For some time successes and reverses balanced each other on either side. At one period it appeared as if the French were about to gain the upper hand. The days of the English in the Carnatic seemed to be numbered. But this was never really so, although once (on September 21st, 1746) the English governor, Morse, was compelled to surrender Madras to La Bourdonnais, the colleague, and, happily for us, the rival of Dupleix. Defeat to an Englishman is almost a necessity of victory; not indeed to the traditional John Bull, surly, corpulent, and combative, but rather to the more worthy representative of English energy, the typical Tom Brown, trained at our public schools, reared in an atmosphere of discipline, taught to subdue self and sacrifice ease to duty. Our fellow-countrymen gathered strength from opposition, disappointment, and repulse. They were wholly disinclined to unsheathe their swords; but when their martial spirit was once roused, they were only beaten back to advance with more tenacity of purpose. Their blunders were their best teachers; their failures were the steps by which they mounted to ultimate success. The determination of the French to reign supreme and expel us from India was the principal factor among the various causes which resulted in the foundation of our Indian Empire. But many other circumstances combined at this time to force territorial dominion upon either the French or English.

The vigour of the Moghul conquerors of India was wonderfully shortlived. It commenced with Akbar's conquests in 1570, and endured barely as long as the career of the British conquerors of the Moghul conquerors has already lasted. It reached its culminating point under Aurangzīb, and began to decay at his death, in 1707. The constituent elements of the empire rapidly disintegrated during the first half of the eighteenth century. It was as if the imperial crown, studded with the jewels of Golconda, had suddenly fallen to the ground, and a scramble had taken place for the scattered gems. Those who took part in the struggle were first the emperor's own Muhammadan deputies, and secondly his own Hindū subjects. Among the former were the Nawāb of Oudh, the Nawāb of Bengal, the Nizām ul Mulk, or administrator of the Dekhan, and the Nawāb of the Carnatic, nominally subject to the Nizām. Among the latter were the Marāṭhas, a powerful tribe of marauding freebooters, who first acquired power in the west of India under Sivajī, about 1650, establishing themselves on isolated hills whose basaltic summits formed natural forts, and fixing the seat of their dominion at different central localities, first at Satāra, then at Poona (under the Brāhman Peshwa, or Prime Minister [1]), and finally at Nāgpur, Gwalior, Indore, and Baroda.

Each of these principal dependents of the Moghul Empire engaged in the struggle for dominion, and the more ambitious not only converted their own territories into independent sovereignties, but aimed at conquering the possessions of their neighbours. The French took advantage of the general disorder. They were not, like the English traders, averse from military operations. Contending chiefs sought their aid and solicited their alliance. Nothing could be more natural than that our French rivals, while intriguing with chiefs and ministers, and increasing by intervention the chaos of conflicting parties, should have thought more of constructing an empire of their own than of helping to build up that of any native potentate.

In the middle of the eighteenth century (about the year 1750), the power of the French reached its climax, and Dupleix erected a column, with an inscription in four languages, to commemorate his victories. It was then that a French army under Bussy utterly defeated our ally, Muhammad Alī, Nawāb of the Carnatic. The fortunes of

[1] The first of these ministers was Bālājī, and the second, his son Bājī Rāo I.

the English in India seemed hopelessly ruined. At this critical juncture, Clive's indomitable courage and extraordinary ability came to the rescue. A mere youth changed the whole aspect of affairs. With only 200 Europeans and 300 sepoys, he seized Arcot (in the year 1751), defended it for seven weeks against overwhelming numbers, and added victory to victory till the power of the French was completely broken. The final blow was given at the battle of Vandivash (Vandvās), in December, 1759, when Colonel Eyre Coote (Clive having been called to Calcutta to avenge the Black-Hole atrocity) completely routed the French armies under Lally and Bussy.

The idea of a European Empire in India then, as it were, changed minds. It was abandoned by the French, to be taken up by the English. Not that any such conception had as yet really taken hold of the East India Company at home, whose sole aim continued to be money, and not war or political supremacy. Nor did the idea at once enter the minds of their daring representatives in India—Clive and Warren Hastings. It was forced upon them by the exigencies of the situation in which they found themselves. More than once they endeavoured to return to their stools and their desks; but the irresistible course of events hurried them away. The East India Company made them clerks and book-keepers. Necessity transformed them into conquerors and rulers. What, in fact, was the state of affairs at this momentous period of Indian history? Two of the competitors in the general scramble for the scattered jewels of the crumbling crown of Delhi were obliged for a time to retire from the field—the French disabled by Clive and Coote, the Marāṭhas paralyzed by their defeat at Panipat. There remained the Nawābs of Bengal, of Oudh, and of the Carnatic, the powerful Nizām of Hyderabad in the Dekhan, the Muhammadan usurpers of Mysor—Hyder Ali and his son Tippū. Each of these aimed at expelling the English from India, hoping to clear the field for their own ambitious designs. The English had again to accept the alternative of defending themselves by sheer hard fighting from the bitter hostility of the various competitors for empire, or abandoning the country altogether. They could not retire like cowards from the sphere of activity in which circumstances had placed them. They were drawn into the *mêlée*. A peaceful policy was possible among the Directors of the trading company at home—impossible among the English on Indian soil.

For example, what happened in Bengal, where the Nawāb Alīvardi Khān had been succeeded by the atrocious Sūraj-ud-Dowla? This man seized the English factory near Murshidābād, taking the officers prisoners (Warren Hastings among the number), and marched on Calcutta. There the garrison capitulated, and the Black-Hole tragedy was enacted. Colonel Clive, then at Madras, came again to the rescue of the British arms. With a handful of Europeans and 2,100 sepoys he defeated Sūraj-ud-Dowla on the celebrated field of Plassey (so called because planted with groves of the Palāsa tree), on the 23rd June, 1757. It was then that the Zamīndārī of the twenty-four Pargannahs round Calcutta was made over to the English, and the germ of our vast Indian Empire was first thrust upon us. What was to be done? Were we to decline the gift, and hand it over to monsters of the Sūraj-ud-Dowla type—to any of those unprincipled and unscrupulous adventurers who swarmed everywhere, eager for political power and intent on enriching themselves at the expense of the natives? True, we found ourselves strong enough to annihilate the Black-Hole miscreant, but the country gained nothing by the substitution of our creature, his successor, Mīr Jāfir.

Mīr Jāfir's administration of Bengal was corruption worse corrupted. We dethroned him in 1760, and set up his son-in-law, Mīr Kāsim Alī. This man began well, but turned out as great a monster as Sūraj-ud-Dowla; for when we attacked him at Patna in 1763, with the intention of reinstating Mīr Jāfir, he had 148 English prisoners massacred by a German serving in his army, under the name of

Sumru (the native equivalent of Sombre)[1]. No one else would undertake the bloody task. Mīr Kāsim took refuge with Shuja-ud-Dowla, the powerful Nawāb of Oudh, with whom was the then less powerful Shāh Ālam, emperor of Delhi. The three combined against us, but our victory, under Munro's generalship, at Buxar, in October, 1764, made us virtually masters of the whole country from Calcutta to Delhi.

We were compelled, however, to clear Hindūstān of certain troublesome Afghān tribes in the Rohilla war of 1775. Then other wars were forced upon us; for as we had either to fight the Nawābs of Bengal and Oudh, or basely abandon that part of India to their tender mercies, precisely so had we to fight the other unprincipled competitors for empire—the usurpers, Hyder Ali and Tippū of Mysor, and the Marāthas. From the breaking-up of the Hindū kingdom of Vijaya-nagar a line of Hindū kings had reigned in Mysor till 1761, when Hyder Ali, a Muhammadan officer in the Hindū army, usurped the throne. The four Mysor wars followed, viz. those of 1767-9, 1780-4, 1790-2, and 1798-9. Finally we stormed Seringapatam, conquered Tippū, and brought part of his territory under our own jurisdiction in 1799.

As to the Marāthas, although their power had been broken at Panipat (7th January, 1761) by the Afghān chief, Ahmad Shāh Abdāli, or Durrānī, on his third invasion of India, yet in their case also four wars[2] had to be undertaken by us before they were subjugated. The treaty of Bassein, by which the Peshwa (Bājī Rāo II) engaged to receive a British subsidiary force, and to pay for its maintenance, ended the first war, and broke up the Marātha confederacy. The chiefs were then disunited. Sindia and Bhonsle would not accept the treaty, and prepared for the

---

[1] His real name was Reinhard. He was a native of Salzburg, and first served under the French, who nicknamed him Sombre, from his melancholy cast of countenance. The well-known Dyce Sombre was his grandson.

[2] These were the wars of 1780-82, 1803, 1804-5, and 1817-19.

second war, during which Wellington defeated the Marāṭha army on the renowned field of Assai (September 23, 1803). Two other wars followed. The Marāṭha chiefs did not venture on open hostility, but excited the Pindārīs—wild, predatory tribes, the Bashi Bazouks of the Marāṭha armies —to attack us. All these marauding powers were put down during the administration of Lord Hastings. The last Marāṭha hill-fort was taken in 1819.

In the case of Hyderabad, we made a treaty with the then Nizām, in 1798, by which he was bound (and is still bound) to support a contingent of 6,000 troops, and dismiss all French or other European officers from his territory. In the case of Oudh, we made the then Nawāb an independent king in 1818; but his country fell into such utter disorder that it had to be annexed under Lord Dalhousie's administration.

Clive was appointed Governor of Bengal a second time in 1765, and on the 12th of August in the same year the Emperor of Delhi, Shāh Ālam, conferred on the East India Company the Dīwānī, or right of collecting the revenue— equivalent to the whole sovereignty—of Bengal, Behār, and Orissa. Warren Hastings was our first Governor-General, from 1774 to 1785. With all his faults he was perhaps the greatest of our great Indian rulers. He was the parent of our whole civil administration. In England the mistake was made of judging him by European standards of political morality. In spite of occasional acts of injustice, oppression, and extortion—the excusable result of bewildering difficulties and brain-disturbing complications—his conduct on the whole was marked by a high-minded integrity redounding greatly to his honour. He made all the servants of the Company sign a covenant not to accept presents or engage in any kind of private traffic. Thenceforward they were no longer merchants and traders, but administrators. At that time our possessions in India were (1) Bengal, Behār, Orissa, and Benares, (2) a jāgīr of land round Madras, and the strip of country on the eastern coast, called Northern

Circars, (3) the island of Bombay. A few subsequent acquisitions may be here enumerated; for instance, the Carnatic in 1801; the upper Doab in 1803; Assam in 1826; Sindh in 1843; the Jullunder Doab in 1845; the Panjāb and Satāra in 1849; Pegu in 1852; Nāgpur and Jhansi in 1853-54; Oudh in 1856. Ceylon was taken from the Dutch in 1795-96. It was first annexed to Madras, but was made a Crown colony in 1803.

We see then that by a concatenation of circumstances unparalleled in the world's history, the whole of India from Kaśmīr to Cape Comorin, from Karāchī to Assam and Burmah, has gradually fallen under our rule.

Let us next inquire what statistics exist which will enable us to institute a comparison between the state of the country when its administration was first made over to us and its condition in our own time. Every good Government is sensible of the duty of making statistical investigations—of collecting, classifying, registering, tabulating, and comparing the facts of the every-day existence of the people committed to its rule. The Ayīn-i-Akbarī remains a monument of the great Emperor Akbar's efforts in this direction. He was far in advance of his age, and his successors were not equal to the task of carrying on his investigations. The East India Company, however, was never unmindful of its duties in this respect. Returns have occasionally been called for by the House of Commons. In every district a vast mass of knowledge on every conceivable subject relating to the condition of the country and its inhabitants has been collected, digested, and committed to writing; and from time to time the information thus gained has been carefully arranged and formulated. The first effort of this kind in Bengal dates from 1769, four years after that province began to be administered by the East India Company. In 1807, Dr. Buchanan-Hamilton was formally appointed to carry out a statistical survey of the Bengal Presidency. This survey, which only embraced the northern districts, including Behār, extended over seven years, but was never completed, though twenty-one thick volumes of manuscript were produced.

In fact, great difficulties have always impeded the progress of statistical investigation. Even to this day the natives of India are not sufficiently enlightened to understand our real motive. They have been so long accustomed to exactions, that, to their minds, government is only another name for oppression. They persist in expecting our little finger to be thicker than the loins of our predecessors. They are haunted by suspicions that every unusual inquiry is the precursor of a fresh assessment. During the taking of the census in 1871-72, a man detected in the act of hiding his babies gave as his excuse that they were too young to be taxed. Besides, designing agitators are always at hand to thwart the good intentions of our Government by exciting the superstitious fears of a credulous peasantry. In Murshidābād, the surplus population, according to popular report, was to be blown away from guns; in other places it was to be drafted to the hills, where coolies were wanted.

Sir William Muir, in his Report on Indigenous Schools, mentions that at the beginning of the inquiry a rumour spread among the natives of the North-West Provinces that four Christian missionaries, whom the Oriental imagination of the inhabitants converted into magicians, had come from Benares. One of them, it was alleged, was about to visit their houses in the garb of a mendicant; he would stretch a magic wand over the heads of their children, compel them to follow him, and turn them into Christians by witchcraft.

Notwithstanding these difficulties, the collection and registering of accurate information has proceeded with a certain degree of continuity, though in an unsystematic manner. The energy and wisdom of Mr. Thomason, who was appointed Lieutenant-Governor of the North-West Provinces in 1843, devised the first organised scheme. Every magistrate and collector was required to throw together and arrange all the information—historical, geographical, economical, educational—he could obtain regarding his own jurisdiction. These compilations were to serve as guides and companions for every district. One of them, by A. Shakespear, published in 1848, gives the result of a first census of the whole province, and the most minute information as to the area of revenues of each pargannah. A second census was made under Mr. Thomason's instructions on the night of December 31st, 1852. The results were published, and no such valuable returns were ever before obtained.

The year 1847 saw the first formation of a regular statistical department at the India-house, and the merit of constantly stimulating its activity belongs to one of the old Company's directors, the late Colonel Sykes. In 1853 this statistical office published the first series of statistical papers relating to India, illustrated by useful maps. A great deal of fairly accurate information was given under various heads, in sixty-seven folio pages. The latest orders of the Court of Directors on the subject of statistics were issued in 1855, three years before the government of India passed from the Company to the Crown. In 1867 the Governor-General in Council, in obedience to orders received from Her Majesty's Secretary of State, directed the preparation of a statistical account of each of the twelve great provinces of India.

In 1871 a department of revenue, agriculture, and commerce was established at Calcutta, having under its charge various statistical surveys — geological, ethnological, linguistic, archæological, industrial, and literary. Dr. W. W. Hunter was appointed Director-General of Statistics in India. He became the central guiding authority to all the local collectors of information; and great praise is due to him for the effective plan of operations he inaugurated.

In 1873 there issued from the India Office the first of a new series of statistical statements. It exhibited the moral and material progress and condition of India from 1871–

72. This was a great advance on all previous Blue-books. A volume for 1872-73 followed. This was a revised and improved edition of that for the previous year. Since then supplementary statements have been published annually; but that for 1872-73—by Mr. Clements R. Markham—is incomparably the best work of the kind that the Home Government of India has ever produced. Its pages, though by no means free from inaccuracies and inconsistencies, are full of valuable information on every subject connected with our Eastern Empire—even including missionary progress — and the carefully-drawn maps with which it is illustrated are a highly instructive study in themselves. Its purely literary excellence is not the least of its merits. Every decennial period will, I believe, be marked by the publication of a similar volume.

Perhaps still greater praise, in respect of scientific completeness and accuracy, is due to Sir George Campbell's exhaustive report on his own administration of Bengal during 1872-73. This forms a thick octavo volume of about nine hundred pages. It is a perfect mine of valuable information.

Dr. Hunter's Statistical Account of Bengal in twenty volumes[1] is the crowning production. Considering the difficulties with which the editor has had to contend, and, notwithstanding a few errors, omissions, inconsistencies, and repetitions, unavoidable in statistical returns comprising a record of the condition of countries and populations more numerous and varied in character than those of Great Britain, Norway, Holland, Switzerland, and Italy put together, we must pronounce this work to be a monument of scientific skill and patient elaboration. It shows the extent to which a desire for correct information has been diffused through all grades of the executive service. It represents the first effective advance towards a complete knowledge of the country. When Dr. Hunter commenced his labours, no

[1] A Statistical Account of Bengal. By W. W. Hunter, B.A., LL.D. London: Trübner & Co. 1877.

regular census of the population had been taken; and the enumeration of 1872-73, which gave the enormous result of 240 millions for the whole of India, inclusive of the native States, disclosed that the official estimates had been wrong as regards Lower Bengal alone, by more than 25 millions of souls. The estimate had stood at 40 millions for that province, whereas the total by the census amounted to $66\frac{3}{4}$ millions. The population of British India alone was about 190 millions, and the whole of India contained twice as many Muhammadans as the whole Turkish Empire. The result revolutionized our ideas in regard to the amount of the population, its distribution in different districts, its classification according to races, occupations, and religions. It quite altered our calculations in respect to the incidence of taxation, the consumption of salt, and many other matters.

When it is borne in mind that Dr. Hunter's twenty volumes represent the statistical account of the Province of Bengal alone, and that the materials for an Imperial Gazetteer of the whole of India, whose population exceeds that of all Europe exclusive of Russia, have already been collected, it must be admitted that our Government is doing its duty to the full in endeavouring to acquire a correct knowledge of the vast country committed to its rule.

But now comes the question: Are we availing ourselves of that knowledge for the benefit of the people? Having made ourselves thoroughly acquainted with what India was and is, do we make it our first endeavour to improve her own ancient institutions, to stimulate her own inherent energies, to utilize and develop her own existing resources, to direct and extend her own inherited civilization, to guide, mould, and expand her own deep-seated religious instincts, feelings, and convictions? Do the statistics we have collected furnish sufficient data on which to ground a fair opinion as to whether our government is advancing, stationary, or retrograde? Do they bear witness to the justice, the disinterestedness, the wisdom of our rule ? Do they tell of order, organization, and progress in every department of our administration ?

For example, do we find in India a thoroughly efficient system of education ascending from the lowest strata of society, pervading every corner of the social fabric, and supported by the State, the municipalities, the landholders, and the parents of the children ? Is the education imparted something more than mere information ? Does it have regard to forming the character as well as informing the mind ? Is there adequate machinery for training qualified teachers, for supplying good class-books, and for testing the value of all instruction given ? Are there good schools of science and art, equipped with effective laboratories, libraries, and museums ? Is the press free ? Are the native newspapers, for the most part, loyal in tone, and generally engines of good rather than of evil ? Is there entire toleration by the State, and by the people, of every form of public worship, so long as such worship does not offend against police regulations and public morals ? Is the welfare and contentment of the people secured by a wise adjustment of the sources and incidence of taxation ? Is the State assessment on land fairly and judiciously fixed, either in perpetuity or for the average lifetime of a generation? Is the revenue collected by honest and efficient officers ? Does the collection cause sales, ejectments, or imprisonments ? Are there courts of civil and criminal justice presided over by independent and properly qualified officers, not afraid to decree against the powerful, using the vernaculars of the people, and guided by laws of procedure fixed and published ? Are all men equal before the law ? Is any class precluded from giving testimony, from conducting suits, or demanding justice, on account of religion or civil status ? Is there any form of disguised or open slavery, helotry, serfage, unlawful apprenticing, &c. ? Is there unlimited license of petition from the poorest to the highest official ? Are

State officers bound to receive and dispose of all petitions and record an order upon each several petition, a copy of which can be claimed by the petitioner with a grant of appeal to the officer of higher grade? Are the civil and executive officers constantly moving about in suitable weather from village to village, and living unarmed among the people? Are odious and abominable practices, such as female infanticide, burying alive, burning widows, human sacrifices, self-immolation, sitting in Dharnā, hook-swinging, allowed or winked at, in any class from rāja to peasant? Are capital executions rare? When they take place, are they conducted with decency? Are the gaols strictly supervised? Is it possible to imprison without a legal warrant? Is the formation of good roads, bridges, canals, irrigation-works, railways, telegraphs, postal communication, sedulously promoted in every province? Is travelling safe by night and by day? Are all bands of robbers, Thugs, and poisoners extirpated? Are measures taken to prevent or alleviate famines? Are sanitary arrangements promoted everywhere? In time of pestilence and scarcity are the sick and starving properly cared for? Are there abundant hospitals and dispensaries? Is there any military conscription? Have the military authorities any power whatever beyond the limits of the cantonments? Do the people show confidence in the honour and integrity of the State? Do they avail themselves of the post-office, the money-order offices, the savings banks, the State loans? Are the public officials paid regularly by a fixed salary, and rendered absolutely incapable of all corrupt practices, bribery, malversation, and oppression?

It is not too much to say that the most cursory examination of the India Office Statistical Returns must convince even a hostile critic that a favourable reply may be given to nearly all of these questions. Tried by these tests in 1879, the Government of India may hold up its head, and look its enemies in the face. Tried by some of these tests fifty years ago the Government of India must have sunk humiliated to the dust, with almost as much ignominy as the Turkish Government does now. In proof of this assertion let me next give a more particular account of the progress of India under two or three principal heads, commencing with education.

No one now disputes the proposition that one of the most sacred duties of every government is to promote and superintend the education of its subjects. We rulers of India are at length fully sensible of the obligation under which we lie to deliver the masses from the ignorance and superstition which have for centuries enslaved them. We are at length bestirring ourselves to bring the blessings of sound and useful European instruction within reach of the poorest and most insignificant member of the Indian body politic.

Yet fifty or sixty years ago the very reverse was the case. Our rule was believed to be accepted by the people as a boon after the oppression of their own masters. They longed for rest, and our supremacy secured it. They needed tranquillity, and our government enforced it. They had no desire for knowledge, and we had no desire to impart it. *Quieta non movere* was thought to be a maxim even more suited to Asiatics than to Europeans. To educate the masses was to sow the seeds of disquietude. To give them knowledge was to give them power, or at least to puff them up with a conceit of their own ability to govern themselves. Our security in India was believed to be bound up with the continuance of a blissful condition of crass ignorance in two hundred millions of living souls. Hence, when at the renewal of the Company's Charter in 1813, an agitation was set on foot (chiefly I believe at the instance of a party inspired by William Wilberforce) for the promotion of education among our Indian subjects, very little effect was produced. Yet the House of Commons resolved at that time that a sum of £10,000 a year was to be set apart out of the Indian revenue for 'the encouragement of the learned natives of India, and for the introduction of a knowledge of European sciences among the people.' It is noteworthy that two distinct objects—the revival of Eastern learning and the introduction of European science—were clearly set forth in that resolution. It was not forgotten, in fact, that all Hindūs of the Āryan stock were already literary people. At a time when our ancestors were clothed in skins, and could neither read nor write, the Hindūs had made great advances in science and art. They were the first cultivators of the science of language. They fashioned for themselves one of the most complete alphabets, they constructed for themselves one of the most perfect grammatical systems, they elaborated for themselves by a process of analysis (*vyākaraṇa*) and synthesis (*sanskaraṇa*) one of the most finished languages that the world has ever seen. They were the original inventors of the ten arithmetical figures and invaluable decimal notation, which have done such good service in Europe. They devised their own processes of arithmetic and algebra. They calculated eclipses and made many shrewd astronomical guesses centuries before the existence of Copernicus and Kepler. They investigated for themselves the laws of thought, and contrived a logical method, which, if not equal to that of Aristotle, has peculiar merits of its own. They excogitated for themselves six most subtle systems of philosophy, of which all European systems are mere repetitions and reproductions. They wrote learned treatises on theology, long before any European thinker had bestowed a thought on the nature of God, or the relationship of spirit to matter. They cultivated the imaginative faculties more diligently, if not more successfully, than European nations, and composed long epic poems very little inferior, and in some respects—for instance, in the portrayal of domestic life — superior, to those of Greece and Rome.

It was thought that a people so acute in intellect, so remarkable for erudition, so successful in industrial arts, and the actual possessors of vast literary treasures, ought first to be encouraged to develop their own resources, to make use of the immense literary capital inherited from their ancestors, and then to make good their own deficiencies and extend their own acquirements by cultivating the more fruitful fields of European lore, and drawing fresh life from the fountain of European scientific truth.

But three main hindrances have always impeded the advance of education among the people of India. The first has arisen from the pride and selfishness of those who in ancient times secured the monopoly of all learning. The Brāhmans, having obtained possession of the temple of knowledge, resolved to keep the key in their own hands. They soon discovered that the maintenance of their intellectual supremacy, no less than the promotion of their material interests, depended on their excluding the *profanum vulgus* from access to the interior shrine. They never, it is true, discouraged the communication of mere rudimentary instruction to the people in the vulgar tongue, but instruction in their sacred Sanskrit—the repository of their literature, religion, science, and law—has ever been reserved for their own sacred order.

A second hindrance has arisen from the utter narrow-mindedness of Indian Pandits. They have believed the whole circle of human knowledge to be contained in Sanskrit writings. To this very day, the most bigoted are fully persuaded that to learn anything beyond the Śāstras is quite useless.

A third hindrance has arisen from the peculiar organization of Indian society. The Hindūs have always been great believers in division of labour as a divine institution. Learning, with them, has ever been regarded as the province of learned men. Pandits, writers, and accountants have formed, like agriculturists, soldiers, and merchants, separate divisions of the community. Each has belonged to a distinct caste, and each caste has been expected to confine itself to its own business. A fourth hindrance, to which I propose recurring hereafter, has been caused by the difficulty of teaching the complicated Indian alphabets.

Under such circumstances it was not surprising that the promulgation of the House of Commons' resolution of 1813 was received in India with apathy and indifference. The rulers feared the evil consequences of education for the ruled, and the ruled anticipated no good results for themselves. It was not till the 17th July, 1823, that action of any kind was taken by either one side or the other. This date marks the commencement of what may be called the first educational epoch in India. On that day it was resolved by the Governor-General in Council that a General Committee of Public Instruction should be constituted for the purpose of ascertaining the state of public education, for the introduction of useful knowledge, and for the encouragement of native literature. Of this committee Sir Charles Trevelyan, who, when a member of the Bengal Civil Service, published a valuable little volume on Indian Education, was one of the most active members.

Two institutions were already in existence for the encouragement of Oriental learning—the Madrassa or Arabic College established by Warren Hastings at Calcutta in 1781; the Sanskrit College founded by Mr. Jonathan Duncan at Benares in 1791, 'with a view to endear our Government to the Hindūs by exceeding, in our attention to them and their systems, the care ever shown by their own native princes.'

A third college was founded in 1816 by the voluntary contributions of the natives themselves. This latter seminary was called the Hindū Mahā-vidyālaya, 'great Hindū seat of learning,' but its principal aim was to instruct young Indians in English literature and the sciences of Europe. It owed its origin to the exertions of Sir E. H. East, Mr. David Hare, and Rāja Rām Mohun Roy, but was taken in hand and improved by the new committee of public instruction.

The committee also opened a Sanskrit College at Calcutta, in 1824, and another College at Delhi in 1825, for instruction in the three classical languages of India, acting no doubt under the inspiration of the then celebrated Orientalist, and future Boden Professor, H. H. Wilson. There were also a few schools, and notably those founded at Chinsurah in 1814 by a worthy dissenting minister, Mr. May.

Here, then, we have the two distinct educational lines indicated in the House of Commons' resolution of 1813, definitely laid down. The one line led to the desired goal through the classical languages of India—Sanskrit, Arabic, and Persian; the other through English. Both were recognized as media for the communication of European knowledge. Nevertheless, for the greater part of what I call the first or Orientalizing educational epoch, Oriental learning was in the ascendant. In the committee there was internecine war. Orientalists and Anglicists were irreconcilable. Each party contended for the exclusive application of its own instrument of education. Neither was tolerant of the other. In 1833 the committee consisted of only ten members. Five were for educating by means of Oriental learning. These were Messrs. Thoby Prinsep, James Prinsep, H. Shakespear, Macnaghten, and Sutherland. Five were Anglicists, viz. Messrs. C. E. Trevelyan, J. R. Colvin, Bird, Saunders, and Bushby. The latter were not only for imparting an European education through the medium of English; they were for cutting down the sum annually lavished on the support of Oriental students, and on the printing of Sanskrit and Arabic translations. The fundamental difference of opinion between the two halves of the committee ended in a dead lock. No movement either forward or backward could be effected, because of the perfect balance between the two parties.

At this juncture (about the close of 1834) Macaulay arrived in India. The conflicting opinions of Orientalists and Anglicists were laid before him in his capacity of legislative member of the Supreme Council, and called forth his celebrated Minute of February 2nd, 1835. 'All parties,' he wrote in that Minute, 'seem to be agreed on one point, that the dialects commonly spoken among the natives of this part of India contain neither literary nor scientific information, and are, moreover, so poor and rude that, until they are enriched from some other quarter, it will not be easy to translate any valuable work into them. It seems to be admitted on all sides, that the intellectual improvement of those classes of the people who have the means of pursuing higher studies can at present be effected only by means of some language not vernacular amongst them.' He then decides in favour of English, and goes on to say :—

> 'The question before us is simply whether, when it is in our power to teach English, we shall teach languages in which, by universal confession, there are no books on any subject which deserve to be compared to our own; whether, when we can teach European science, we shall teach systems, which, by universal confession, whenever they differ from those of Europe, differ for the worse; and whether, when we can patronize sound Philosophy and true History, we shall countenance, at the public expense, medical doctrines, which would disgrace an English farrier,—astronomy, which would move laughter in girls at an English boarding school,—history, abounding with kings thirty feet high, and reigns thirty thousand years long,—and geography, made up of seas of treacle and seas of butter.'

This Minute—all the more misleading because penned by the most effective writer of his time—was followed by Lord W. Bentinck's equally celebrated Resolution of the 7th March, 1835, in the second clause of which his Lordship in Council expresses his opinion, 'that the great object of the British Government ought to be the promotion of European literature and science amongst the natives of India.' The concluding paragraph directs that 'all the funds at the disposal of the committee be henceforth employed in imparting to the native population a knowledge of English literature and science, through the medium of the English language.' The date of this Resolution marks the commencement of what I venture to call the second or Anglicizing educational epoch.

Of course the Governor-General's decision was final. The Anglicists were triumphant, and, to clinch the whole matter, Macaulay was made President of the Committee. Then followed the establishment of twelve new Seminaries, and a series of corresponding measures for the promotion of English studies. Dr. Duff sided with the Anglicists. A sudden passion for European literature, and its cultivation through the acquisition of English, sprung up among the higher classes of Bengālīs. English became an object of ambition, as the only avenue to good appointments, and to an improved position in society. Nor need it excite surprise that our Government should have encouraged the upper classes in their desire to become good English scholars. What strikes one as extraordinary is, that such a man as Macaulay should have set himself against vernacular education. To force English on the unlettered millions of India was, of course, impossible. Though we English-speakers in Great Britain are by far the majority, we have not yet succeeded, after more than a thousand years of close contact with the Welsh people, in inducing them to adopt our own language. Is it likely that in a vast and remote country, a few thousand Englishmen, who, although conquerors and rulers, are every year less disposed to treat India as their home, will ever succeed in imposing English on two hundred and forty-one millions of Asiatics, who possess about two hundred different dialects of their own, and whose organs of articulation and habits of thought, framed under opposite climatic and social conditions, are generally incapable of adapting themselves to European peculiarities of utterance, idiom, and syntax?

In Henry VIII's time there was scarcely anything to read for an Englishman who could not read Latin. So in India, in Lord Macaulay's time, there was scarcely anything worth reading for a native of Bengal who could not read Sanskrit. Indeed, Sanskrit was to all India more than what Latin was to all Europe. And what happened in England? The vernacular of the people, instead of decaying, drew vitality and vigour from the very language whose influence for a long time kept it in abasement. Strengthened and enriched by Latin, and recruited from other sources, English has grown into the most sturdy, copious, and effective of all languages. It has produced a literature more valuable than that of Rome or Greece.

Lord Macaulay did not seem to see that the same process had been going on in India. The vernaculars of India were quite as capable of being invigorated by Sanskrit and Arabic as European vernaculars were by Latin and Greek. In point of fact, this had been partially effected long before Macaulay's time. A *lingua franca*, like French in Europe, had existed in India since the invasion of Timūr, A.D. 1400. Hindūstānī, a language formed by engrafting the Persian and Arabic of the Musalmān conquerors on a Sanskrit-Hindī stock, had already been generally adopted by the natives of India as a common medium of communication. It was a thoroughly composite and eclectic language, which, like English, had a peculiar power of extracting from other languages the materials for its own expansion and development. It had naturalized Turkish and Portuguese words, and was assimilating English. It was a living and a growing language—so instinct, indeed, with life and growth, that the Hindūstānī of the early part of this century, as represented by the Bāgh o Bāhar, may be said to be already obsolescent. What Lord Macaulay and the Committee ought to have aimed at was first the improvement and enrichment of Hindūstānī by the introduction and assimilation of more words and expressions from Sanskrit, Arabic, Persian, English, and other modern European languages, and secondly the composition of good Hindūstānī class-books, and the formation of a pure modern Hindūstānī literature. And if the natives of Bengal and of other parts of India were incapable of being instructed in European science through the medium of Hindūstānī class-books, their own vernaculars, Hindī, Bengālī, Marāṭhī, Tamil, and Telugu were capable of being amplified, improved, and made the vehicle of scientific truth. And here it is to be observed, that although the Orientalists on the one side, and the Governor-General's Resolution of March 7th, 1835, on the other, very unaccountably omitted all mention of the vernaculars, a majority of the Education Committee seem in the end to have come to the conclusion that the exclusive encouragement of English could only be a temporary expedient, and 'that the formation of a vernacular literature was the ultimate object to which all their efforts ought to be directed.' Even Mr. (now Sir Charles) Trevelyan, the most enthusiastic and energetic of all the Anglicists, to whose educational labours India is deeply indebted, was of the same opinion. He looked through a vista of English to a time when Hindūstānī and Bengālī would become well fitted for every purpose of literature and science.

Lord William Bentinck, too, was far too wise, clear-sighted, and sagacious, not to have discerned the only possible method of reaching the mass of the people. A great impulse was given to the cultivation and development of the spoken dialects under his administration. Act XXIX of December 1st, 1837, abolished Persian and substituted the vernaculars as the language of all revenue and judicial proceedings in our Courts. 'The extraordinary ease,' wrote Mr. Trevelyan, 'with which this change was effected proves that it took place in the fulness of time. In Bengal the Persian language had disappeared from the Collectors' offices at the end of a month. It melted away like snow.'

Perhaps a still more important step had been taken previously. It was thought that before the Government did anything for the country, steps should be taken to ascertain what the country had done and was doing for itself. In a

Minute, written as far back as January 20th, 1835, Lord W. Bentinck pointed out that at a time when the establishment of education upon the largest basis had become an object of solicitude, it was essential to ascertain the number of indigenous village-schools already existing in India, the nature and amount of instruction imparted in them, with all the particulars of their foundation and support. And he expressed his belief that the 'important end might be attainable, of making these institutions subsidiary and conducive to any improved general system which it might be hereafter thought proper to establish.' Accordingly an experienced, painstaking missionary, Mr. W. Adam, versed in the spoken dialects, was appointed to conduct an educational survey of Bengal. The investigation extended over three years, and a report was published containing valuable statistics and important information in regard to the intellectual condition of the peasantry. What that condition must have been in 1835 may be inferred from the fact that in 1873 (according to Sir George Campbell's statistics) only $2\frac{1}{2}$ per cent. of the population of Bengal could read and write. The proportion for all India was only 1 in 400, while in England it was 1 in $7\frac{3}{4}$.

Nevertheless, it is remarkable that the number of Hindū indigenous schools, and of Maktabs or Muhammadan schools attached to mosques, was found to exceed all expectations. They were ascertained to be most numerous in secluded parts of the country remote from European influence, and from the disturbing effects of wars and invasions.

The Hindū indigenous schools are of two kinds—schools of Sanskrit learning, called in Bengal Tols, and vernacular schools for instruction in reading, writing, and arithmetic, conducted by village schoolmasters, and called Pāṭha-śālās. These two kinds of schools have no interconnection. Pupils never pass from one to the other.

I made a point of visiting the well-known Sanskrit Tols at Nuddea, and found them frequented by students from all parts of India, some learning grammar, which may occupy from seven to twelve years; some law, which may require a ten years' course; and a large number studying the Nyāya system of logic, which may necessitate from thirteen to twenty-two years' curriculum. Both teachers and students in these schools of learning are of course Brāhmans.

The Pandits, so far from receiving money from their pupils, not unfrequently contribute towards their support, being themselves supported by rich patrons. When the students have finished their course of instruction they receive from their masters an honorary title, which they retain for life. I also visited schools of native learning in other parts of India, and arrived at the conclusion that the old type of Pandit, trained to repeat whole departments of Sanskrit literature by heart, is dying out. On the other hand, it seemed to me that Sanskrit learning, as encouraged by us and learnt on principles of European philology, is decidedly on the increase.

Again, in traversing the country I often came across village vernacular schools, conducted in the open air or under trees. And here I may remark that no people in the world have been so long accustomed to self-government as the inhabitants of India. The whole country is studded with little independent republics. Every village has its headman, its council of five (*Panchāyat*), its regularly organized society, its complete assortment of servants, functionaries, and officials necessary to the corporate existence and well-being of the whole community. Among them is a schoolmaster (*guru*), from whom the children of the leading villagers receive a rude kind of education. We have elsewhere noticed a proverb current among the natives—*Panch men paramesvarah*, 'the voice of God is in the council of five;' and the village school, no less than the village council, is in its way regarded as a kind of divine institution. Wars, revolutions, rebellions have desolated the land; famines and pestilences have decimated the population; but the school system has survived all convulsions—not, however, everywhere equally, and not always in its entirety. In some parts of the country vernacular schools have been swept away, while Sanskrit schools have survived. In other districts rural schools abound, while schools of learning are unknown.

Of course, nothing is learnt in the village vernacular schools but the merest elements of reading, writing, and arithmetic. No books are employed. The children are taught to read and write on the sand or on palm-leaves. What struck me as a remarkable feature of the teaching was the skill attained in multiplication. The multiplicand generally ascends to forty and often higher. The whole class of, perhaps, a hundred children repeat their tables together as if with one voice, the accumulated force of which rises to a deafening scream. They can all multiply by fractions, particularly by $\frac{3}{4}$, $1\frac{1}{4}$, $1\frac{1}{2}$, and $2\frac{1}{2}$, and they can multiply $2\frac{1}{2}$, $3\frac{1}{2}$, and $4\frac{1}{2}$, by the fraction $\frac{1}{2}$.

Many of the punishments employed would probably be considered peculiar from a European schoolmaster's point of view. For instance: A boy is condemned to stand for half-an-hour or an hour on one foot. A boy is made to sit on the floor with one leg turned up behind his neck. A boy is made to hang for a few minutes with his head downwards, from the branch of a neighbouring tree. A boy is put up in a sack along with nettles, or a cat, or a noisome creature of some kind, and then rolled along the ground. A boy is made to measure so many cubits on the ground, by marking it with the tip of his nose. A boy is made to pull his own ears, and dilate them to a given point on pain of worse chastisement. Two naughty boys are made to knock their heads several times against each other. Some of these punishments are now discontinued.

The suggestion for basing all schemes of Indian education on existing indigenous institutions seems to have originated with Mr. W. Adam, in 1835. The idea was taken up, as we have seen, by Lord William Bentinck, but the merit of first carrying it into execution belongs to Mr. Thomason, who, ten years later, when he was Lieutenant-

Governor of the North-west Provinces, organized a plan for utilizing the existing village schools, and training the native schoolmasters. He was the first to start what is called the Halka-bandī system, about the year 1845. A number of villages were linked together in a Halka or circle, and a central school under a trained native teacher was established within reach of each village, the expense being met by a local cess of 1 per cent. on the land-revenue, nominally voluntary. Unhappily, the efforts made to train the village Gurus did not always succeed, and the whole indigenous system had to be rehabilitated. But one great merit of Mr. Thomason's scheme of popular education was that it contained in itself great aptitude for internal development and improvement. His method was adopted as a model by other Governments, and led in the end to the celebrated educational Despatch from the Court of Directors to the Governor-General of India (Lord Dalhousie), dated July 19th, 1854.

This remarkable document—on which the whole system of education at present in force throughout India is founded—was really written by Sir Charles Wood (Lord Halifax), when President of the Board of Control, assisted by the late Viceroy, Lord Northbrook, when acting as his secretary. It commenced what I venture to call the third or Anglo-vernacular educational epoch.

As the main principle of the first educational epoch (commencing in 1823) was the prominence given to the learned languages of India, and of the second (commencing in 1839) the stress laid on English as an exclusive medium of education, so the special characteristic of the third was the importance assigned to the vernaculars. In fact, the first object of the great Despatch of 1854 was to insist on the communication of correct European knowledge to the mass of the people through the medium of their own spoken dialects. The second object was to lay down a complete scheme of higher education in which, without neglecting the vernaculars, English and the Indian classical languages, but especially English, were to be made the principal instruments of education.

And here it may be observed that as there is really as yet no considerable middle class in India, so there can be really only two principal kinds of education, higher and lower. It is true that what are called middle-class (Zillah) schools have been established, but the distinguishing feature of these seems to be that they combine the superior lower with the inferior higher kind of education.

With regard to the higher, the Despatch declared that the time had arrived for the founding of universities at Calcutta, Bombay, and Madras, not as places of education, but to test the value of the knowledge received in colleges and schools, and to confer degrees.

All the principal colleges, collegiate institutions, and schools already existing throughout the country, whether founded or aided by Government or independent, and conducted by persons of every variety of religious persuasion, Christians, Hindūs, Muhammadans, Pārsīs, Sikhs, Buddhists, and Jains, were to be affiliated to the universities, and to lead up to them. The indigenous schools were to be improved by Government aid and superintendence, and were to supply suitable education to the villages and rural population. The so-called middle-class Zillah schools (answering to the Tashīlī schools of the North-west Provinces), established at the chief towns of each district, were to educate the townspeople and prepare them for the high schools. The high schools, established at the larger towns and attached to every college, were to educate the higher classes up to the university matriculation examination, English being in that case the medium of instruction. The colleges were to admit matriculated students, and educate them up to examination for Bachelor degrees. The whole system was to be tied together by means of scholarships, which were to lead selected pupils from the Zillah to the high schools, and from the high schools to the colleges. The first university examination after matriculation was to be called First Arts (F.A.) examination, and to take place after a two years' course at the colleges, and the examination for the Bachelor's degree was to follow after a further interval of two years. The final university examination was to be for the Master of Arts degree, which was to be a real distinction, only attainable by a select few who could give proof of high intellectual culture.

All these provisions and arrangements were gradually carried into execution. The three Universities of Calcutta, Bombay, and Madras were incorporated in 1857. They were quietly founded during the worst troubles and most appalling terrors of the Sepoy insurrection. A great stimulus was given to education everywhere. New colleges were founded and old ones improved. The Calcutta and Madras Presidency Colleges, the Bombay Elphinstone College, the Poona Deccan College, the Thomason Engineering College at Roorkee, and a large number of other colleges and schools were quickened into vigorous vitality. In short, a vast moral and intellectual revolution was inaugurated, and that, too, at a time when the downfall of our power was confidently predicted, and the very foundations of the Indian social system appeared likely to be upheaved. The undisturbed progress of Sir Charles Wood's great scheme of education is a valuable evidence that the agitation caused by the Sepoy revolt never spread among the masses of the people. And what are the results?

At the commencement of 1823 only two Government colleges existed in India, the pupils in which might possibly have numbered 300. In 1824, soon after the establishment of several new seminaries by the Committee of Public Instruction, the number of pupils in Government institutions rose to rather more than 3,000. In 1854 there were about 12,000 pupils. In 1859 educational institutions of different kinds had increased to such an extent that the pupils amounted to more than 180,000. The latest statistical returns from all India in 1875 showed that the number of pupils in colleges and schools of all kinds—Government, missionary, aided, and unaided—amounted to 1,689,138.

Yet we have hitherto made little or no impression on the countless millions reachable only through the vernaculars. The chief end aimed at by Sir Charles Wood's Despatch of 1854 has as yet been very imperfectly attained. Too much importance is assigned to English, and too little encouragement given to the native dialects. English is made a *sine quâ non* at the matriculation examinations. I saw 1,263 candidates being examined for matriculation at Bombay in 1875, and among them some young native princes. But not more than 12, or at most 15 per cent. of those who matriculate proceed to prepare for the degree examination. The great object is to gain a knowledge of English, and through that knowledge employment under Government.

Lord Lytton, in an eloquent address delivered the other day before the pupils of the Martiniere College, Calcutta, very significantly reminded his youthful audience that the object of education was not the improvement of their positions, but the improvement of their characters. I fear we too often wean boys from the plough, the chisel, and the loom, to make them ambitious of Government appointments, which they cannot all obtain.

PROGRESS OF OUR INDIAN EMPIRE.

Part II.

It is related of the Moghul Emperor Baber, that when the idea of conquering India first took possession of his mind, he resolved not to embark on so vast an enterprise till he had made himself thoroughly acquainted with the country and its people. The better to effect this object, he is said to have disguised himself as a religious mendicant, and to have traversed the Panjāb and Hindūstān, noting the best approaches, marking the strongest positions, collecting the most minute information, and planning the whole scheme of his future military operations.

The result of his circumspection and forethought is well known. It cannot be said of our great generals that they were equally wise in their generation. They conquered by dint of dash and daring, combined, it may be, with occasional master-strokes of strategic skill and astute policy. They were aided by a strong tide of concurrent and cooperating circumstances. But they were innocent of long antecedent explorations of the enemy's ground. They were guiltless of deep-laid plots and tedious predeliberations.

Yet the present Empress of India is more securely seated on the throne of Delhi, than the most successful of the Mogul invaders. English pluck and prowess have effected more than Baber's forethought and energy, Akbar's wisdom and vigilance, Aurangzīb's cleverness and cunning. We have surpassed all other conquerors in the completeness of our material conquest. No power disputes our supremacy over a range of territory extending 2,000 miles from the Himālaya mountains to Adam's Peak. Are we inclined to be puffed up with the conceit of what we have effected? Let the knowledge of what remains to be done dissipate every thought of self-complacency. Let the sense of our failures neutralize all tendency to pride in our successes.

True, we are entitled to some credit. We are able, with a mere handful of our fellow-countrymen, to control two hundred and forty-one millions of Asiatics, to make laws, to administer justice, to preserve the peace. We have changed the whole face of the country by our railways, roads, canals, telegraphs, and public buildings. We have done more than any other Rāj to promote the physical prosperity and welfare of the people. We have even laboured successfully to stimulate the intellects and instruct the minds of the upper classes. We have founded Universities, established colleges, built schools, trained teachers, appointed directors of public instruction, and spent large sums on educational institutions, old and new.

All this we have done. Yet infinitely more has been left undone. We have yet to take in hand the poor benighted ryots; to elevate, to enlighten the myriads upon myriads of those who till the ground in the veritable sweat of their brow; to deliver the masses of the population from the tyranny of caste, custom, ignorance, and superstition. The moral conquest of India remains to be achieved. And to effect this second conquest we are wisely discarding all the dash and daring by which our first conquest was secured. We are advancing with careful predeliberation. We are even perhaps a little too tardy in our preliminary investigations. We have only recently instituted a thoroughly organised system of statistical inquiry, of which Dr. Hunter's twenty volumes of Bengal statistics are the first-fruits.

I closed my last paper with a summary of the present educational status in India, and I pointed out that Sir Charles Wood's despatch of 1854 is the basis on which the whole system rests. Excellent and carefully worded as the whole tenor of that despatch undoubtedly is, it makes one cardinal mistake. It encourages the false idea that instruction is a co-extensive term with education. The despatch had, as we have seen, two main objects. One was to promote the instruction of the higher classes in European science through the medium of English. The other was to provide proper teaching for the lower classes by means of the vernaculars. Its words are: 'We look to the English language and to the vernacular languages of India together as the media for the diffusion of European knowledge.'

And if our whole educational responsibility is bounded by the instruction of the upper classes of the people in European knowledge, we may perhaps take credit to ourselves for a fairly respectable fulfilment of our obligations.

But if our mission be to educate as well as instruct, to draw out as well as put in, to form the mind as well as inform it, to teach our pupils how to become their future self-teachers, to develop symmetrically their physical as well as mental, moral, and religious faculties, then I fear we have left undone much that we ought to have done, and acquitted ourselves imperfectly of the duties our position in India imposes upon us. Let me first glance at our so-called higher education.

In traversing India from north to south, from east to west, I visited many High Schools, examined many classes, conversed with many young Indians under education at our colleges, and was brought into contact with a large number who had passed the University matriculation examination, as well as with a few who had taken their degrees, and earned distinction for high proficiency. I certainly met some really well-educated men—like Rao Bahādur Gopal Hari Deshmukh, lately appointed a joint-judge— who, by their character and acquirements, were fitted to fill any office or shine in any society. But in plain truth, I was not always favourably impressed with the general results of our higher educational efforts. I came across a few well-informed men, many half-informed men, and a great many ill-informed and ill-formed men—men, I mean, without true strength of character, and with ill-balanced minds. Such men may have read a good deal, but if they think at all, think loosely. Many are great talkers. They may be said to suffer from attacks of verbal diarrhœa, and generally talk plausibly, but write inaccurately. They are not given to much sustained exertion. Or if such men act at all, they act as if guided by no settled principles, and as if wholly irresponsible for their spoken and written words. They know nothing of the motive power, restraining force, or comforting efficacy of steadfast faith in any religious system whatever, whether false or true. They neglect their own languages, disregard their own literatures, abjure their own religions, despise their own philosophies, break their own caste-rules, and deride their own time-honoured customs, without becoming good English scholars, honest sceptics, wise thinkers, earnest Christians, or loyal subjects of the British Empire.

Yet it cannot be said that we make higher education consist in the mere imparting of information, and nothing more. We really effect a mighty transformation in the character of our pupils. We teach a native to believe in himself. We deprecate his not desiring to be better than his fathers. We bid him beware of merging his personality in his caste. We imbue him with an intense consciousness of individual existence. We puff him up with an overweening opinion of his own sufficiency. We inflate him with a sublime sense of his own importance as a distinct unit in the body politic. We reveal to him the meaning of 'I am,' 'I can,' 'I will,' 'I shall,' and 'I know,' without inculcating any lesson of ' I ought,' and 'I ought not,' without implanting any sense of responsibility to and dependence on an Eternal, Almighty, and All-wise Being for life, for strength, and for knowledge—without, in short, imparting real self-knowledge, or teaching true self-mastery, or instilling high principles and high motives. Such a system carries with it its own nemesis. After much labour we rulers of India turn out what we call an educated native. Whereupon he turns round upon us, and, instead of thanking us for the trouble we have taken in his behalf, revenges himself upon us for the injury we have inflicted on his character by applying the imperfect education he has received to the injury of his teachers.

The spitefully seditious writing which our Government has lately found it necessary to repress by summary measures is due to this cause.

And how have we discharged the debt we owe to the lower classes? Let the truth here also be told with all plainness. In their case we have not yet matured any effective scheme—not even for the proper informing of their minds, much less for the proper forming of their characters.

Mr. Thomason, as we have seen, started a system of careful statistical inquiry. He ascertained the generally benighted condition of the masses within the area of his own administration. He was also the first to conceive the idea of stimulating the people to co-operate in educating themselves. It occurred to him that the necessity for registering land under the revenue settlement of the North-western Provinces might be turned to good account. He determined to use it as an incentive to the acquisition of so much knowledge of reading, writing, arithmetic, and measurement as would qualify each man to look after his own rights. Thereupon he organized a scheme of primary education based on the utilization of indigenous village schools. His method was held up as a model to other local governments. It was wisely followed and improved upon by other administrators, and notably by Sir George Campbell in Bengal. A good beginning has been made in some parts of India. But I fear we have as yet barely stirred the outer surface of the vast inert mass of popular ignorance and superstition.

Where, then, lies our fault? Are we carrying into execution the admirable views expressed in Sir Charles Wood's despatch? Are we doing our best to encourage the improvement and enrichment of those vulgar dialects through which alone the masses can be instructed? I think not. What says the despatch?

'It has hitherto been necessary, owing to the want of translations or adaptations of European works in the vernacular languages of India, and to the very imperfect shape in which European knowledge is to be found in any works in the learned languages of the East, for those who desired to obtain a liberal education, to begin by the mastery of the English language as a key to the literature of Europe; and a knowledge of English will always be essential to those natives of India who aspire to a high order of education. But it is neither our aim nor desire to substitute the English language for the vernacular dialects of the country. And any acquaintance with improved European knowledge which is to be communicated to the great mass of the people,—whose circumstances prevent them from acquiring a high order of education, and who cannot be expected to overcome the difficulties of a foreign language,—can only be conveyed to them through one or other of these vernacular languages.'

If, then, the Government of India were true to its own principles it would give more encouragement to the cultivation of the vernacular dialects. It would not expose them to the danger of degenerating into jargons—of becoming unfit to be converted into vehicles of European knowledge. It would not appoint any one to superintend educational work as a Director of public instruction, or as a principal or head master, without requiring him to give evidence of complete familiarity with at least two spoken languages—Hindūstānī and one other. It would not make proficiency in English an indispensable condition of matriculation examinations. It would be satisfied with proficiency in general knowledge displayed through the medium of any one or two of the principal vernaculars, Hindūstānī, Hindī, Bengālī, Telugu, and Tamil—especially through Hindūstānī, which should be encouraged to become the common medium of communication for the lower classes throughout all India, just as Sanskṛit is for the learned.

And here I must advert to a point which, in my opinion, has an important bearing on the spread of European knowledge among the masses of our Indian subjects, I mean the application of the plain and practical Roman alphabet to the Indian vernaculars, especially to Hindūstānī.

I have elsewhere striven to show that the Indo-Āryans probably derived their alphabets from foreign sources. The first Indian idea of grammar was not that of a collection of written rules ($\gamma\rho\acute{a}\mu\mu a$). It consisted simply in the analysis (*vyākaraṇa*) of language and the solution of etymological problems by means of brief memorial aphorisms so contrived as to be transmitted orally. In time, however, a growing literature defied even the prodigious memories of indefatigable Brāhman Pandits. Suitable graphic symbols had to be employed, and in all probability particular symbols were introduced into India by those trading nations whose commercial necessities led to the invention of writing. The first notion of representing ideas and language by pictorial signs seems to have originated in Egypt. Thence it passed into Phœnicia where a syllabic system was developed. This led to the phonetic alphabet afterwards adopted by the Greeks, and subsequently improved upon by the Romans. Doubtless some forms of writing found their way into India, but, like the acute Greeks, the subtle-minded Hindūs felt the imperfection of the consonantal systems current among Semitic peoples. If they received some symbols from foreign sources, they altered their forms and developed them in their own way. Moreover they invented for themselves their own system of vocalization, just as they worked out their own theory of grammar.

Nor did any ordinary standard of completeness satisfy the requirements of Indian scholars. With their usual love of elaboration they excogitated a philosophically exact system. But they overloaded it with symbols. They overdid the true theory of the necessary vocalization of consonants. They declared it impossible for any single consonant to stand alone without its inherent or associated vowel. Hence, we have an immense assortment of simple and conjunct letters, necessitating the employment of five hundred distinct types in the printing of the most ordinary Sanskrit book. Such an overstraining of alphabetical precision was to the learned Hindūs a great recommendation. The perfection of its structure made the Deva-nāgarī alphabet a fit medium for the visible embodiment of their divine Sanskrit. Even the very letters themselves came to be regarded as divine.

Now this superstitious adoration and quasi-deification of an intricate alphabet as the medium for the expression of a sacred language like Sanskrit, was perhaps natural and excusable. But when it led to the employment of complicated symbols for the ordinary work-day spoken dialects, it placed a serious obstruction in the path of advancing education. And what is the actual fact at present in India? The process of learning to read is surrounded by a kind of thorn fence, bristling with a dense array of crooked strokes and tortuous lines. Difficulties unknown to an English child have to be surmounted at the very outset, and make every step painful. I am only now speaking of the Indian printed alphabets. What shall be said of the written characters? The worst English handwritings are no measure of their illegibility. The difficulty of deciphering them increases in a kind of compound ratio. Who, except grey-bearded scholars, can penetrate the mysteries of the inscrutable Shikasta? Who but veteran experts can unravel the intricacies of the Kaithī, or Hindī running-hand employed by the writer caste? of the Modī, or written scratches in use among the Marāṭhas? of the hopelessly illegible Mārwārī and equally indecipherable handwriting prevalent in Sindh? of the twists, twirls, and convolutions current in Southern India? If any one thinks I am here exaggerating, let him turn to a volume of specimens of different written characters which daily pass through the Indian Post Office, published by the Post Office authorities.

For this reason many eminent Indian administrators and scholars—at the head of whom must be placed Sir Charles E. Trevelyan, a true friend to Indian educational progress —have long felt that the application of the simple Roman alphabet to the Indian vernaculars would greatly facilitate the diffusion of knowledge among the unlettered millions of our Indian Empire. The recent formation of ' *The Roman-Urdū Society*' by educated Indians at Lahore, and the publication of an able Journal by that Society in support of the Romanizing movement, is a significant fact. I may mention, too, that successful employment of what may be termed an Indo-Romanic alphabet—that is, the Roman letters adapted to Indian requirements by the use of dots and accents—in the printing of Sanskrit books, is an evidence of its applicability to the Āryan languages of India with as much suitability as to the Āryan languages of Europe. But inveterate custom, early association, and inherited bias, are forces too strong to be easily overcome by the most beneficent and energetic of reformers. Changes, however manifestly advantageous, have no hope of general acceptance. Here in England we continue to resist the introduction of a decimal system; we adhere with obstinacy to all our worst spelling-anomalies, and we ridicule such convenient astronomical expressions as thirteen or fourteen o'clock, which correctly mark the rotation of our earth, and which, if adopted, would be an invaluable boon to the students of Bradshaw. In the same manner, without doubt, many generations must pass away before the superstitious veneration for existing alphabetical symbols is abandoned in India, and the simple Roman alphabet adopted for the expression of the more ancient Āryan vernaculars, Hindī, Marāṭhī, and Bengālī. With regard to the more modern Hindūstānī, which ought to be taught as a *lingua franca* in every school of India, the case is different. It has really no alphabet of its own, and the

Directors of Public Instruction might reasonably, in my opinion, insist on its being expressed by the Indo-Romanic letters.

I come now to a subject which is perhaps the most momentous of all, in its relation to the progress of India and the promotion of Indian civilization. In England it has been said that the working people are our masters, and that we must educate our masters. There is another saying—equally true in India and England—that

'She who rocks the cradle sways the world.'

In plainer language, it may be said, that if the working men rule the world, the women rule, or at least influence the working men, and so become the world's mistresses. Clearly, then, it is important that the world should take the most direct and decided interest in the education of its own mistresses.

And here I must recall attention to a point to which I have before adverted, that, in all our schemes for educating and elevating the teeming millions of our Eastern Empire, we have to deal with a people who were among the earliest civilized nations of the earth, who in the best periods of their history were active promoters of social and intellectual progress, who have a literature abounding with lofty moral and religious maxims, who still preserve a profound veneration for learning, and who still maintain two lines of educational institutions, suited to the upper and lower classes of the male population, and distinct from the systems introduced by us. Manifestly, therefore, before propounding any scheme of our own for the education of the women of India, we have to ask the question, Is India herself doing anything, or has she ever done anything herself, for the promotion of female education? To answer this question properly, it will be necessary to glance first at the condition of women in ancient times, as depicted in early Indian literature; and, secondly, at their present condition, as shown by the statistics prepared under Government authority.

In regard to the first point, no one can read the Vedic hymns without coming to the conclusion that, when the songs of the Rishis were current in Northern India (fourteen or fifteen centuries B.C.), women enjoyed considerable independence. Monogamy was probably the rule, though polygamy existed and even polyandry was not unknown. In Rig-veda i. 62. 11, it is said, 'Our hymns touch thee, O strong god, as loving wives a loving husband.' The Aśvins had only one wife between them (i. 119. 5). Women were allowed to marry a second time (Atharva-veda ix. 5. 27). Widows might marry their deceased husband's brother (Rig-veda x. 40. 2). There were even allusions to a woman's choosing her own husband (*svayamvara*), which was a common practice among the daughters of Kshatriyas in the heroic period. One hymn reveals a low estimate of feminine capacity, declaring that women have minds incapable of instruction (*aśāsya*) and fickle tempers (viii. 33. 17).

The condition of women, as represented in the laws of Manu several centuries later (perhaps about 500 B.C.), was one of less liberty. But the contradictions in the code show that no settled social organization unfavourable to women prevailed at that epoch. True, a woman is said to owe her condition of inferiority to sins committed in former births. She is declared to be unfit for independence. She belongs to her father first, who gives her away in childhood to a husband, to whom she belongs for ever. Marriage is the final cause of her existence—to bear children the sum of her duty and the great end of her being. Women, says Manu (ix. 96), were created to be mothers. As a mother, he declares, a woman is entitled to more respect than a thousand fathers (ii. 145). And, to this day, marriage and the hope of giving birth to a family of sons form the sole object of ambition—the one all-absorbing subject which engrosses every Indian woman's mind. On the other hand, in one place Manu alludes to circumstances under which a maiden might be allowed to choose her own husband, although he visits her with penalties for doing so (ix. 92). He makes no mention of Satī (*suttee*), and permits—as the Mosaic law did (Deut. xxv. 5, St. Matt. xxii. 24)—a widow, under certain circumstances, to marry a deceased husband's brother.

As time went on, the jealousy of the opposite sex imposed various restraints, restrictions, and prohibitions. A more settled conviction as to some inherent inferiority and weakness in the constitution of women took possession of men's minds. Yet through the whole heroic period of Indian history, and up to the commencement of the Christian era, women had many rights and immunities from which they were subsequently debarred. It cannot, indeed, be said that any Eastern nation has ever been free from a tendency to treat women as inferiors. Even the Greeks and Romans were wanting in that reverence for the female sex which marked the Teutonic races, and was the result of their believing 'inesse feminis sanctum aliquid.' Nevertheless, in India, mothers have always been treated with the greatest reverence. We may note, too, that something of the spirit of chivalry was displayed in the tournaments of Indian warriors, who contended for the possession of the heroine of the Svayamvara. Women were certainly not yet incarcerated. They were not yet shut out from the light of heaven behind the Pardah or within the four walls of the Zanāna. It is even clear from the dramas that the better classes had received some sort of education, or could at least read and write; and it is noteworthy, that although they spoke the provincial dialects, they understood the learned language, Sanskrit. They often appeared unveiled in public. They were not confined to intercourse with their own families. Sītā showed herself to the army. Sakuntalā appeared in the court of King Dushyanta. Damayantī travelled about by herself. The mother of Rāma came to the hermitage of Vālmīki. Rāma says in reference to his wife, 'Neither houses, nor vestments, nor enclosing walls are the screen of a woman. Her own virtue alone protects her.' All these characters may be more mythical and ideal than historical, but they are true reflections of social and domestic life in the heroic age of India. Nothing can be more beautiful than the pictures of the devoted wife in the two great Indian epics. Sītā's noble pleadings (in the Rāmāyaṇa) to be allowed to accompany her husband into banishment are well known. Addressing him, she says :—

'Thou art my king, my guide, my only refuge, my divinity.
It is my fixed resolve to follow thee. If thou must wander forth
Through thorny trackless forests, I will go before thee, treading down
The prickly brambles to make smooth thy path. Walking before thee, I
Shall feel no weariness: the forest thorns will seem like silken robes;
The bed of leaves, a couch of down. To me the shelter of thy presence
Is better far than stately palaces, and paradise itself.
Protected by thy arm, gods, demons, men shall have no power to harm me.
Roaming with thee in desert wastes, a thousand years will be a day;
Dwelling with thee, e'en hell itself would be to me a heaven of bliss.'

Many other examples of noble language expressive of conjugal fidelity might be adduced from Indian literature, and notably that of Sāvitrī, whose story is told in the other great epic (the Mahā-bhārata). When the god of death appears to summon her husband Satyavān, who was doomed to die a year after his marriage, she pleads passionately for a reprieve: 'Let my husband live! Without him, I desire not happiness, not even heaven itself.'

Yet obviously such sublime devotion to a husband as to a god, was incompatible with independence of character. It is evident that any such useful domestic institution as a sternly critical wife was very unlikely to be common in a nation which made Sītā its paragon of female excellence.

Nor is there any evidence that the women of the heroic period had received much systematic education. They were certainly not thought capable of as high a form of religion as men, and seclusion must have been more or less practised by the upper classes, as indicated by

Pāṇini's epithet for a king's wife, *asūryam-paśyā*, one who never sees the sun. Marriages were generally arranged without reference to the wishes of either bridegroom or bride. Polygamy prevailed among the richer classes, and polyandry, though a non-Āryan custom, to a certain extent counterbalanced it. Daśaratha had three wives. One of Pāṇḍu's wives became a Satī. Draupadī married five brothers together.

All this shows that woman's downward course of degradation commenced in the earliest times. Step by step the decline went on, and every century added to her debasement. The introduction of Muhammadan customs after the first Muslim invasion of India (about A.D. 1000) greatly hastened the deteriorating process.

And what has been the condition of women under our own rule?

In Warren Hastings' time a number of the best Pandits were invited to Calcutta from all parts of India. They were directed to draw up an authoritative summary of Hindū law as laid down in their sacred works. A compilation was carefully made by these learned men from the code of Manu, and from all the best legal authorities of later date. A certain Mr. Halhed was directed to translate it for Government. The introduction is curiously characteristic of Hindū toleration.

'The truly intelligent well know that the differences of created things are a ray of the glorious essence of the Supreme Being. He appointed to each race its own faith, and to every sect its own religion; and having introduced a multiplicity of different customs, he views in each place the mode of worship respectively appointed to it. Sometimes he is with the attendants upon the mosque; sometimes he is in the temple at the adoration of idols— the intimate of the Musalmān, the friend of the Hindū, the companion of the Christian, the confidant of the Jew.'

Here are some specimens from the chapter on women:

'A man both night and day must keep his wife so much in subjection that she by no means be mistress of her own actions. If the wife have her own free will, she will behave amiss. A woman must never go out of the house without the consent of her husband. She must never hold converse with a strange man. She must not stand at the door. She must never look out at the window. She must not eat till she has served her husband and his guests with food. She may, however, take physic before they eat. It is proper for a woman after her husband's death to burn herself in the fire with his corpse.'

Warren Hastings wrote a letter to the Court of Directors in 1775, commending this compilation to their attention. We must bear in mind that law, according to Hindū ideas, is part and parcel of divine revelation. It is promulgated by human lawgivers; but they are divinely inspired. Smṛiti rests on Śruti. These ideas had acquired the greatest intensity when Warren Hastings was laying the foundation of our Empire. All the utterances of Manu and the later lawyers were accepted as echoes of the voice of God. They were held to be infallible guides. They represented women as created inferior to men; as born with evil dispositions; as incapable of education; as made worse by knowledge. Wives were divinely ordained to be the servants of their husbands. Their natures were too weak to stand upright, unsupported by the strongest safeguards. There was no security for their virtue but the absence of temptation. They were the absolute property of their husbands in death as well as life. Hence for a long time our Government felt that it would be dangerous to prohibit the practice of Satī. The Hindūs believed it to be enjoined by inspired authority. Nor was it discovered till quite recently that modern Hindū lawyers, to obtain the highest sanction for their deliverances, had fraudulently substituted the word *agneh*, 'of fire,' for *agre*, 'first,' at the end of a well-known Rig-veda text (x. 18. 7. See p. 72). In one year the number of widows burnt in Bengal alone was 839. In other years the average was 500. This after all is no very large number when considered in relation to the density of the population. It proves, at any rate, that the custom was not universal.

And what is the present position of women in India?

A little study of the India Office Statistics reveals a condition of prostration which even the most sanguine might pronounce hopelessly irremediable. One hundred millions of women, supposed to be actual subjects of the British Empire, are, with few exceptions, sunk in absolute ignorance. They are unable to read a syllable of their mother-tongue, they are never taught the rules of life and health, the laws of God, or the most rudimentary truths of science. In fact a feeling exists in most Hindū families that a girl who has learnt to read and write, has committed a sin which is sure to bring down a judgment upon herself and her husband. She will probably have to atone for her crime by early widowhood. And to be a young widow is believed to be the greatest misfortune that can possibly befall her.

Not indeed that an Indian woman's married life can be described as a blissful elysium. The women of India are victims of the worst form of social tyranny. They are allowed no voice in the selection of their own husbands. According to Dr. Hunter's Statistics (i. 56), infants are sometimes betrothed when but two or three months old.

'As soon as a daughter (of a particular tribe of Brāhmans) is born, the father immediately looks out for a male child belonging to a family equal in rank with himself. When he has succeeded in his search, and obtained the consent of its parents, he returns to his house, summons his relatives and neighbours to a feast, and solemnly affirms before them that his daughter is betrothed to such and such a man's babe. Nothing will induce him to break the oath which he thus takes.'

This is exceptional. As a rule, girls are betrothed at three or four (a barber being sometimes the match-maker) and married at six or seven to boys of whom they know nothing. They are taken to their boy-husbands' homes at the age of ten or eleven. From that moment they lose their freedom and even their personality. They merge their individuality in the persons of their husbands. They may be loved, and they are rarely ill-used, as they too frequently are in Christian countries, but they are ignored as separate units in society. They never pronounce their husbands' names, and they are never directly alluded to by their husbands in conversation. For another person to mention their names or inquire after their health would be a gross breach of etiquette. They never appear unveiled before their husbands in the presence of a third person. They often become mothers at eleven or twelve. Their life is then spent in petty household duties, in cooking for their families, in gossiping with female friends, in arranging the marriages of their children, in domestic jealousies and envyings, in a thousand foolish frivolities, in a wearisome round of burdensome religious ceremonies imposed by exacting priests. Add to this that the upper classes are cooped up behind Pardahs or in the stagnant atmosphere of Zanānas. There they are prisoners in apartments set apart for their exclusive occupation. They have no opportunity of listening to the intellectual conversation of educated men. They are shut out from every wholesome influence, and debarred from every healthy occupation likely to conduce to the improvement of their physical condition, or to their social, moral, and intellectual elevation. They become enfeebled in mind and worn out in body at a period of life when European women have barely reached their prime. They are neither fit for independence, nor have they any desire for it.

And what of the young widows? If a young wife has no individuality apart from her husband, a young widow has practically no existence. It is true that our law has prohibited a widow from being burnt with her dead husband. It is true, too, that an old widow is cared for by her children if she has remained a wife long enough to have a large family. She is even more than cared for. Every mother in India is an object of veneration to her offspring. As a wife she may be nothing. But as a mother, even though a widow, she is all in all to her children. It is only a young widow or a childless widow who is regarded as worse than dead. But nearly every household possesses a widow of this kind. Such a widow belongs for ever to her dead husband. A widower may marry again, but a widow never. She is made a household drudge. She is expected to get up at four a.m. before the servants of the family. No one will supply her with water. She must go to the well and fetch water for herself. It is unlucky to meet her. She is supposed to be in eternal mourning for her deceased lord, though she may never have seen him except at her child-wedding. She must practise a perpetual fast, and only eat one meal a day. If her young husband had acquired property of his own before his death and the household is still undivided, all such property is taken by her brothers-in-law. She retains nothing but her ornaments, which she must on no account wear. She is told that she cannot have food given to her till she has 'eaten her jewels.' In other words, she is expected to sell her ornaments to prevent herself from starving. In short, she suffers a living death, and would often cheerfully give herself up to be burnt, if the law would allow her.

Of course, there are exceptions to all this. In some parts of India—as for instance in the Marāṭha country—women of all classes are more independent, and assert themselves with more boldness.

There is also a bright side to the picture of female life and character. Hindū women must be allowed full credit for their strict discharge of household duties, for their personal cleanliness, thrift, activity, and practical fidelity to the doctrines and precepts of their religion. They are generally loved by their husbands, and are never brutally treated. A wife-beating drunkard is unknown in India. In return, Indian wives and mothers are devoted to their families. I have often seen wives in the act of circumambulating the sacred Tulsī plant 108 times, with the sole object of bringing down a blessing on their husband and children. In no other country in the world are family affection and reverence for parents so conspicuously operative as in India. In many households the first morning duty of a child on rising from sleep is to lay his head on his mother's feet in token of filial obedience.

Nor could there be a greater mistake than to suppose that Indian women are without influence. If there is any one thing that would lead a thoughtful person to despair of the regeneration of India, it is that female influence is as strong there as in other countries. For it must not be forgotten that the word family in India means much more than in England. An Indian family does not merely consist of husband, wife, and children. The universal prevalence of early marriages leads to an indefinite enlargement of the family circle. It is said that a Hindū family sometimes consists of a hundred members, including great-grandfather and great-grandchildren. Anarchy is prevented and harmony maintained by vesting supreme authority in the hands of the oldest member, whether male or female. A father often has no voice in the management of his own children. A grandmother or great-grandmother may be omnipotent. Unhappily her influence is generally exerted on the side of ignorance and error. Even in small families the women are powerful for harm. They mould the character of the younger children. They are often adepts in artifice and stratagem. They know how to hide their power over husbands and brothers under the guise of a simulated submission. To them is mainly due the maintenance of superstition and idolatry. The men would willingly emancipate themselves from the tyranny of caste, from the despotism of Brāhman priests, and from the bondage of senseless religious forms and absurd religious creeds, but they are prevented by female influence. Many an educated Indian is as bold as Luther in his public character, but sinks to the condition of a timid, priest-ridden, caste-ridden, wife-ridden imbecile in private life. He is a lion out of doors, but a lamb at home. He is cowed and crestfallen in the presence of the women of his family.

In some Native States women secretly pull all the wires

of Government with consummate craftiness and ability. Great Britain itself is scarcely so opposed to a Salique *régime* as some Indian Principalities. Women not only reign, they are the real rulers and administrators. Even comparatively young widows have often great authority, if, at least, they have gained much previous influence as mothers. In the same manner ordinary families are often practically subject to feminine jurisdiction. A single old widow will sometimes keep order among a number of sons and daughters-in-law all living together under one roof. Her household is like a magazine filled with the most inflammable materials; yet she knows how to allay outbreaks of jealousy, keep down rivalries, and calm down explosions of temper.

Nor must it be supposed that the women of India are generally unhappy; that they regard themselves as slaves; that they long for independence; that they protest against seclusion; that they hanker after knowledge. They are too feeble-minded and apathetic to be conscious of degradation, too wedded to ancient customs to repine under absence of freedom or want of education. They esteem it an honour to wait on their husbands. The necessity for privacy, and the undesirability of a woman's learning letters, are ideas so intermingled with their earliest feelings—so interwoven with the whole texture of their moral being—that they have become cherished customs with the women themselves. They are more than customs: they are sacred religious obligations. So far from submitting to these restrictions from compulsion, no respectable woman would, as a rule, show herself freely in public, or allow herself to be taught reading and writing or any feminine accomplishment, even if permission were accorded to her. She has no conception of any benefit to be derived from a knowledge of letters, except for the promotion of female intrigue; and she would prefer to be accused of murder than of learning to dance, sing, or play on any musical instrument. She loves ornaments, but she regards ignorance as her truest decoration. She considers herself disgraced by sterility of body, but glories in sterility of mind. Education, music, and dancing are supposed to go together, and are to her badges of a life of infamy. When a sister is observed imitating a brother's first childish attempts at penmanship, she is peremptorily ordered to desist, and that too by the women of the household.

Is there, then, no remedy for this great social evil? Are we Englishmen, who are responsible for the welfare of our Indian Empire, and who derive so much of our own welfare from the purifying and elevating influence of our own home-life, chargeable with indifference to the condition of the women of India? We have made, and are still making, strenuous efforts to bring some sort of education within reach of certain classes of the male population. What are we doing, and what have we already done, to supply India with its greatest need—good wives, good mothers, and well-ordered homes?

All that can be affirmed is that we have been engaged for more than half a century in feeling our way towards the desired end.

In the case of male education the natives themselves have always, as we have seen, been ready to co-operate with us. Nay, they have eagerly seconded our efforts. Their own indigenous institutions have furnished a common standpoint for concerted action. The ground has been prepared and the way smoothed for the introduction of European knowledge. The same men who would have wasted their powers in elaborating ingenious word-puzzles in Sanskrit verse, or in trying to comprehend the incomprehensible abstractions of Sanskrit philosophy, have devoted themselves to the acquisition of scientific truth, through the medium of English. But in the case of female education all the conditions have been reversed. No basis of common action has been found, no ground has been cleared, no open door has invited us to enter. Every avenue of approach has been barred and barricaded. The natives have been more than content to leave their women engulphed in the depths of profound ignorance. They have opposed every attempt at raising or enlightening them as an offence against religion and morality. Without doubt, any scheme of direct Government interference for the education of Indian women would have threatened the people with vast social changes. It would have contravened the sacred usages of the most obstinately conservative nation in the world.

Wisely, then, has our Government proceeded in this matter with caution and circumspection. Something, indeed, has been effected by private efforts, by missionary operations, and even by indirect Government assistance. The first attempt to teach native girls in a regular school was made, I believe, by the worthy Dissenting missionary, Mr. May. He was the pioneer of lower female education, as he had already been of male. He opened a girls' school at Chinsurah, shortly before his own death in 1818, but it had so little success that its continuance was discountenanced by our Government. In April, 1819, other Baptist missionaries, wishing to commence an organized scheme of female education, circulated an appeal for help, in which it was stated that 'in the province of Bengal alone, at least ten thousand widows were annually sacrificed; and thirty times a day a deed was repeated, which ought to call forth our tenderest pity.' Such an exaggeration was rather inexcusable, but it had the effect of rousing the sympathies of a number of English ladies, who thereupon founded the Calcutta Female Juvenile Society, for the education of native females. At the end of the first year the number of its scholars amounted to only eight. At the end of five years it reckoned a hundred and sixty pupils in six schools.

In 1818, an institution called the 'School Society' was founded at Calcutta. Its object was male education. But in the course of its preliminary inquiries into the educational status of the people generally, it ascertained that out of forty millions of Hindū females, not four hundred could read or write. When the appalling fact was known in England, the British and Foreign School Society selected Miss Cooke, afterwards Mrs. Wilson, and sent her to Calcutta in 1821 to prepare herself for the delicate task of opening a girls' school. She commenced operations under the auspices of the Church Missionary Society in 1822, and on the 28th of January in that year, seven pupils assembled round her in one of the rooms of the School Society. In 1825, the number of scholars in various little day schools had increased to four hundred. But to bring the girls together it was necessary to employ a female messenger, who received a small gratuity from the Society for each child, and a breakfast of rice had to be given to each pupil, which the mother accepted as an equivalent for the loss of her child's services. In 1826, a wealthy Bābū (Rāja Baidanāth Roy) came forward and gave £2,000 to promote female education by the erection of a central school in the heart of the native city, with a residence for the European female superintendent. Mrs. Wilson took possession of this building in 1828, and here all her subsequent labours were concentrated. She was a noble-hearted, energetic woman, and her exertions were rewarded for a time with considerable success.

Similar efforts were attended with partial success in other parts of India, notably in the Bombay Presidency, and in Bombay itself, where the Pārsīs, who number about fifty thousand, were among the first to set an example of promoting female education. Their schools are to this day a model of good management, and are attended by nearly as many girls as boys, seven hundred and seventy girls being at this moment under instruction in three schools in the town of Bombay.

As a rule, however, female education has not hitherto extended beyond the lowest of the population, while male education has not extended beyond the higher classes. None of the female children of respectable or high-caste natives are permitted to leave their houses. It has not hitherto been possible to reach the Zanānas, or female apartments, of the better classes, except by a system of house to house visitation. This plan has been tried with some success in Bengal, and has been carried on here and there in the Bombay Presidency, and in other parts of India. But competent lady visitors are greatly needed. No lady is fit to undertake the arduous and delicate task, who is not thoroughly conversant, not only with the vernaculars, but with female manners, female habits of thought, female phraseology, and even female 'slang' (zanāna-bolī).

Something, too, has been done in the way of training native school-mistresses, especially under the auspices of the Church Missionary Society at the Sarah Tucker Institution, Palamcottah. I visited this institution in the beginning of 1877, and can testify to the reality of the work effected by its managers, Mr. and Mrs. Lash. They have successfully trained a large number of native female teachers, and established them at various centres in the Tinnevelly district. They have even succeeded in attracting high-caste girls to some of their best schools.

It is clear, then, that a few energetic missionaries and a few philanthropic private individuals have been the pioneers of female education in India. It is clear, too, that the British Government for a long time purposely abstained from acting towards its female subjects as it acted towards the male. It refrained from any systematic establishment of girls' schools. It doubted the wisdom of direct interference with long-cherished social usages, and deep-seated religious prejudices.

Lord Dalhousie was the first to commit the Government to a more active interest in the instruction of Indian women. In 1849 he ventured to announce that the British Government would encourage female education by its 'frank and cordial support.' And he was not a man of mere words. This great ruler boldly aided existing girls' schools by considerable grants of money from the revenues of India, and took care to bestow honours on all founders of such schools. It was during his administration that the Bethune schools were established for the education of the daughters of the respectable citizens of Calcutta, and when the founder died, Lord Dalhousie himself defrayed the cost of supporting them out of his own pocket.

Sir Charles Wood's great Education Despatch of 1854 only devoted one paragraph out of one hundred to the important subject of female education; but it expressed concurrence in Lord Dalhousie's declaration. Paragraph 83 begins as follows:—

'The importance of female education in India cannot be over-rated, and we have observed with pleasure the evidence which is now afforded of an increased desire on the part of many of the natives of India to give a good education to their daughters. By this means a far greater proportional impulse is imparted to the educational and moral tone of the people than by the education of men. We have already observed that schools for females are included among those to which grants in aid may be given, and we cannot refrain from expressing our cordial sympathy with the efforts which are being made in this direction.'

Here there is a clear promise of sympathy and of indirect support, but no allusion to direct Government action or interposition.

Soon after the mutiny Lord Canning's Government declared that unless female schools were really supported by voluntary aid they had better not be established at all. In 1867 a circular was issued which practically admitted that Government had no desire to take the initiative in the case of girls' schools as it had done in that of boys, but was ready to encourage existing schools by grants in aid.

Nevertheless it cannot be denied that some direct action was taken. In 1870 out of £316,509 of public money spent on education in the whole Bengal Presidency a sum of £1,173 was assigned to Government girls' schools, and £4,462 to aided schools, chiefly in the North-west and

Panjāb. In Bombay out of £198,182 a sum of about £4,000 was allotted to Government female schools. In Madras not a single girls' school was directly maintained by our Government.

In the year 1872 out of about 1,100,000 children in Government and non-Government schools of all kinds, only fifty thousand were girls, and only twenty-two thousand in Government schools. In 1873 there were only one thousand six hundred and forty girls' schools of all kinds in British India; but an American lady had organized a system in Calcutta by which forty or fifty governesses taught native girls in their own homes. In 1875 there were about one thousand Government female schools, with about thirty-four thousand pupils, in all the eight Provinces under Governors, Lieutenant-Governors, and Commissioners.

In some places and in some years there appears to have been a falling off rather than an increase. Thus, in 1872 the Government female normal school at Calcutta was abandoned as a failure, and the Lieutenant-Governor was inclined to think it 'dangerous to give native women education and a certain freedom of action without the sanction of some religion.'

In short, there is clearly as yet no constantly-increasing demand for either female teachers or female pupils. What demand really exists is generally confined to the low-caste population. Even those girls who are placed at schools are only half instructed, because they are removed to become wives at the age of ten or eleven.

The great question then is: Ought our Government to make direct efforts for female education in the same way as for male? And is this a mere question of supply and demand? And if there is no demand among the people of India, ought its rulers to create a demand? Ought they to force into existence what does not exist voluntarily?

In my opinion the demand ought to be created. But

we ought to create it in the right way, and begin at the right end. We require to elevate and enlighten the men of India, before we can hope to elevate and enlighten the women. We require to raise up a whole generation—perhaps two or three generations—of really educated men—men, not only well instructed in scientific truth, but well imbued with moral and religious truth—with the spirit, if not with the letter of Christian teaching—and with European views on all social subjects. And to this end, we have not to denationalize the men of India: we have to strengthen and consolidate their own nationality. We have not to extinguish their own civilization: we have to refine and elevate it. We have not to sweep away their social institutions: we have to shape and mould them according to a higher pattern. We have not to erase every feature of their moral code: we have to expunge the bad and retain the good. We have not even to exterminate their religions: we have only to lay the axe to every root and fibre of error, and, after eradicating the false, to engraft the essential doctrines of Christianity on pre-existing germs of truth.

When we have thus elevated the condition of the men, the elevation of the women will follow as a matter of course. The men will themselves raise their own women. They will throw down the barriers which at present surround their homes. They will tear down their Pardahs, pull down the shutters of their Zanānas, throw open the doors of their inner apartments, invite us to enter in—entreat us to do for their wives and daughters what we have done for themselves.

But how is this previous process of elevating and Christianizing the men to be effected? We must begin with the schools. Our Government has wisely decided to be neutral in religious teaching. We have abstained from imitating the conquering Musalmān—from enforcing our religion by Government influence and authority. It would, indeed, be doubtful morality on our part to take money out of the pockets of native parents, and with it to pay teachers to teach the children of those parents a religion which they believe to be false. Nor under any circumstances could a sufficient number of Christian teachers be found. But our neutrality need not, and should not, imply indifference and inaction in regard to moral teaching; nor even in regard to instruction in certain fundamental truths common to all religions. The principles of true morality, be it remembered, are not confined to Christianity. They are to be found in Hindūism, in Buddhism, in Islām. Nay, I do not hesitate to affirm, that certain lines of rudimentary religion are discoverable in the texture of two of these false systems. I contend that a warp-like basis of truth is traceable in both Hindūism and Islām, though concealed by a thick woof of error and delusion. The fundamental threads of God's attributes and perfections, of His wisdom, goodness, omnipotence, and love for His creatures—of His indwelling as a guide and monitor in the human conscience—of man's duty towards Him as his Maker, and of man's duty towards his fellow-creatures—are all there, and ought to be carefully preserved. Even some essential threads of Christian doctrine (such as the Unity and separate personality of God, man's original corruption, the need of purity of heart, the uselessness of external forms) are there, and ought to be thankfully made use of, while every cross-thread of falsehood, superstition, and fatuous delusion is ruthlessly torn away. Nor are the sacred scriptures of India wholly destitute of true teaching in regard to the principles of domestic economy and social science.

My conviction is that we are bound to search for, and utilize educationally, every true idea in Hindūism, Buddhism, and Islām. And just as we have endeavoured to ground our system of literary instruction on inherent literary tendencies, and inherited literary knowledge already existing among Hindūs and Muslims, so we should ground our moral and religious teaching on their inherent moral and religions tendencies, and such inherited rudimentary truth as their own scriptures contain. We should collect their best moral, social, and religious precepts, separating them from everything false. We should teach them in conjunction with scientific truth in our Government schools. In this way we shall best prepare our Indian school-boys for a voluntary acceptance of Christian truth when their judgments are matured.

And more than this. We should strive to develop our youthful Indian physically as well as mentally, morally, and religiously. We should endeavour to introduce something of our public-school manliness of tone into Indian seminaries. We should aim at educating the whole man in his quadruple constitution of body, mind, soul, and spirit. In a word, we should convert our 'Directors of public instruction,' who are generally able and efficient officers, into 'Directors of public education.'

And when we have formed our real man, whether Hindū or Muhammadan, we should admit him to our homes. Having destroyed his caste-feelings, we should give up our own caste-feelings. We should receive our educated Hindū and Muhammadan on terms of social equality. In no other way, and by no other process, can we hope to reach the women of India.

The really educated and enlightened native who has been freely admitted to an English home, will return to his Indian home penetrated by the conviction that, if he would assist in raising his country, he must begin by raising his own household. He will accept the Christian truth that woman was created to be a help-meet for man. He will enter into the meaning of the Christian allegory that, when God formed woman, she was taken out of man's side to be his coadjutor; not out of his head, to be his intellectual rival; not out of his feet, to be trodden down and kept in subjection. He will educate his daughters, and keep them under education till they are eighteen years of age. He will on no account allow them to become wives and mothers till their bodily and mental powers are matured. He will aim at educating them up to the English poet's standard of an ideal wife—

> 'A perfect woman, nobly planned,
> To warn, to comfort, and command.'

He will permit them to choose their own husbands. He will open his house-doors to every refined and educated guest of whatever caste. He will expose the inner life of his own family to the fresh air of God's day. He will endeavour to mould his household after the fashion of a pure, healthy, well-ordered Christian home, whose influences leven the life of each of its members from the cradle to the grave.

I have left myself little space for two other tests of national progress to which I ought to advert, however briefly. One of these is the improvement in means of communication. I can bear testimony to the present excellence of the roads in various parts of India. I travelled over some which were as smooth and hard as a billiard-table, and unequalled by anything I have seen in Europe. On the other hand, my whole frame seems still to ache at the bare recollection of the joltings I endured in less frequented places. One of my contemporaries at Haileybury, Mr. Cust, has favoured me with a few notes of his journey from Calcutta to Delhi in 1843. He hired a palanquin in Calcutta, and set out in the cool of a January evening. Borne on the shoulders of coolies, and travelling all night and for a greater part of each day, he was five days in reaching Benares. The journey thence to Allahābād took another whole day. At Allahābād his palanquin was placed on a truck, and drawn by horses to Cawnpore. Thence to Agra and Delhi the palanquin was borne in the usual way by coolies. Travelling in this manner without a single day's rest, he was a month in reaching Delhi from Calcutta. The only line of carriage-road was between Allahābād and Cawnpore, and in no other part of the route were the streams bridged.

The year 1845 witnessed the introduction of what was called an equirotal carriage. A palanquin was fitted to four equal wheels, and pushed by coolies. This was a proof of a great advance in the metalling of roads. Then followed the comparative luxury of the Dāk ghārī. These carriages were drawn by relays of Government post-horses, on what became at last the great trunk road traversing the entire country between Calcutta and Delhi. The jaded and dust-smothered traveller emerged half-stupefied at the end of his journey with the rattle of a ten days' continuous roll concentrated in the orifice of his ears. The Dāk system of travelling was not perfected till about the year 1852.

The turning of the first sod of the first railway line in India took place in 1851. In that year the East India Railway was commenced, and in September, 1854, a distance of thirty-seven miles was opened for traffic. In February, 1855, the line was opened as far as Rānīganj, a distance of 121 miles, and about ten years later as far as Delhi. The line between Bombay and Madras was completed on the 1st of May, 1871. The total mileage open on all Indian railways in 1866 was 3,472, and the number of passengers carried in the year was nearly thirteen millions. Ten years later, in 1875, the mileage open was 6,352, and the number of passengers carried nearly twenty-seven millions.

The late Lord Lawrence once told me that when he first went out to India he was allowed six months to find his way from Calcutta to Delhi. The journey may now be performed in forty-four hours. One of the most remarkable sights in India is afforded by the throng of natives of all castes, and conditions at the principal railway stations. The popularity of this mode of travelling, with people who are supposed to dread indiscriminate contact with each other, is astonishing. About thirty years ago, when the expediency of introducing railroads into India was first talked about, a great authority, Professor H. H. Wilson, expressed an opinion that they were quite unsuited to the habits of the natives, and that the rules of caste would prevent their being much used. What is the fact? To every solitary European lolling at full length amid rugs and cushions in a first-class compartment, hundreds of natives will be found jammed together in the third-class carriages. Crowds alight at every small town, and crowds are ready to take their place. No one can doubt that railways are among the greatest boons our rule has conferred on the country.

Next to railways come canals. But in India, as in Europe, the day of canals as effective lines of way and transit is over. No canals can ever be as effective as railways in conveying passengers or merchandise, or in transporting the surplus produce of a fertile province to remote districts whose crops are liable to fail in regularly recurring seasons. Besides, Indian canals have not sufficient water to serve for both navigation and irrigation. It is for purposes of irrigation that they are of incalculable importance. In times of severe drought, tanks and wells become dry, while canals are supplied with a perpetual stream of running water from mountain springs. Wherever it is physically and geographically possible to construct canals without ruinous outlay, and with some prospect of a return for the capital expended, there, without doubt, no amount of public money is likely to be thrown away in their construction. Nor has our Government been as unmindful of its duty in this matter as some critics have lately alleged. The Ganges canal—the greatest irrigation work ever constructed—is entirely the creation of British engineers. It was commenced in 1846, and opened by Lord Dalhousie in 1854. I heard natives complain that this canal has brought fever to previously healthy localities; and I believe that whenever a canal is constructed, drainage should be carried on simultaneously, to prevent the adjacent soil from becoming swampy and waterlogged.

Other gigantic works have been undertaken in the basin

of the Ganges, as well as in that of the Indus, and in the portion of Orissa watered by the deltas of the Mahā-nadī, Brāhmaṇī, and Baitaraṇī rivers. While I was traversing the famine districts in 1876 and 1877, I witnessed a marvellous contrast in the regions fertilized by the grand system of irrigation which stretches between the Godāvarī, Kistna, and Kāverī rivers, and the vast tracts of arid wastes where no streams penetrate. Let no one doubt the good effected by the energetic and enthusiastic Sir Arthur Cotton.

No country in the world is so rich in running water as India. Any one who has observed with his own eyes what the country owes to its rivers, will not be surprised at their being deified by a people who connect every advantage they enjoy with direct divine agency. No wonder that the rain-god Indra—for ever battling with the demon of drought and darkness—is the chief god of the Ṛig-veda. No wonder that the Ganges is believed to have its source in the foot of Vishṇu; that its waters are believed to descend from heaven, cleansing from all sin; that its very sight is supposed to confer beatitude; and that every river of India is personified and worshipped by those who derive their wealth, their food, their health, their life from the beneficent influences of flowing streams.

No wonder, too, that the people of England are asking with some impatience: why is a single drop of this precious liquid allowed to find its way into the ocean? Without doubt, more might be done in storing up these fertilizing waters. Tanks and wells ought not to be suffered to fall into decay. It might even be possible, say some, by means of anicuts to intercept the onward flow of streams, and diffuse every particle of liquid by a network of small channels and feeders over every tract of arid country. But such admirable theorists forget that the dry regions of India are often on table-land, and that no engineer can make water flow up hill. Nor can even the most skilful cope with the vagaries of mighty unmanageable rivers, which at one season roll down millions of tons of water with ungovernable fury, at another shift their channels, and shrink to tiny rills at the bottom of immense beds of burning sands.

Happily, the prevention of famines does not depend on anicuts and canals alone. Railroads have already done much, and will hereafter do more. After all, perhaps, the best remedy lies in the improvement of the condition of the people.

One important result of improved means of communication is an increase in postal facilities. Letters are now delivered in every village of India. In 1866, sixty-one millions of letters, newspapers, and packets passed the various post-offices. In 1875 the number had risen to more than one hundred and sixteen millions.

With regard to steam communication between England and India, most middle-aged people can remember that Mr. Waghorn was the pioneer of what was called the Overland Route. He was employed in this capacity by the Bengal Steam Committee between 1827 and 1835. No man ever deserved more credit, and ever received less, for successfully battling with every kind of difficulty and discouragement. A steamer called the *Hugh Lindsay* was the first to accomplish the voyage between Bombay and Suez. Every arrangement connected with its equipment and navigation was organized by Mr. Waghorn. She succeeded in passing up and down the Red Sea six times between 1830 and 1835 without encountering any accident, notwithstanding numerous dangers from unknown rocks and reefs. Her shortest run between Bombay and Suez was in thirty-one days and a half. The next steamer, called the *Forbes*, took sixty-nine days in the voyage from Calcutta to Suez. This vessel broke down after her first voyage. The first P. and O. steamer to reach India was the *Hindūstān*. She sailed round the Cape towards the end of 1842, landed passengers at Calcutta, and thence proceeded to Suez, whence she returned to Calcutta at the beginning of 1843, taking about six weeks to accomplish the latter run. A mail service was also established between Suez and Bombay, but was worked for some time by steamers of the Indian navy. Since then, facilities of steam transit between England and India have steadily advanced every year, and the opening of the Suez Canal in 1869, has converted the dreaded voyage from Southampton to Bombay into a pleasurable trip of twenty-six and even sometimes twenty-five days, while that from London *viâ* Brindisi is often effected in nineteen days.

I cannot conclude my sketch of Indian progress without touching on the important subject of finance. Of course the crucial test of a well-managed State, as of a well-ordered household, is its financial condition. Do those who administer its affairs make both ends meet? Is the expense of governing the country covered by the revenue it can be made to yield? Is there any surplus capable of being laid out either in clearing off debt, or in diminishing the burdens of the people, or in public works of national utility? or is there a deficit making it constantly necessary to borrow money?

The capital expended by the East India Company in establishing itself in India was nominally six millions sterling, the interest for which (£650,000) had to be paid out of its Indian income. It was agreed that in consideration of the successful issue of a great commercial speculation, the shareholders were to have their principal reckoned as if doubled, making £12,000,000 of East India Stock. In addition to this, under Clive, the first conqueror of Indian territory, money had to be borrowed to the amount of about two millions. In the ten years from 1775 to 1785, we spent a great deal in extending our territory, and the debt increased to about eight millions sterling. Warren Hastings left a considerable revenue and surplus. For Bengal alone the income was nearly five and a-half millions; expenditure, nearly four and a-half millions; surplus, about one million sterling. Under Lords Cornwallis and Teignmouth the debt did not increase. Expensive wars were carried on by the Marquis Wellesley (1798–1805), and with great extension of territory in 1805, came an augmentation of the debt to about twenty-five and a-half millions.

Lord William Bentinck's administration (1828–35) was one of peace and prosperity. He conciliated the natives, abolished Satī, put down the Thugs, encouraged European education, and converted a deficit into a surplus of nearly one and a-half millions.

Then came the Afghān war under Lord Auckland, the conquest of Sindh under Lord Ellenborough, the two Sikh wars, and of course a consequent augmentation of the debt.

Lord Dalhousie's administration was marked by the greatest vigour and activity. He is said to have doubled the area of our Indian possessions. Besides conquering the Panjāb, and establishing our supremacy from Cape Comorin to the Himālayas, he undertook a second Burmese war, and annexed Pegu (British Burmah).

Then came the annexation of Nāgpur and the Central Provinces in 1853, and that of Oudh and Tanjor in 1856. Our progress was too rapid. Our debt nearly doubled itself and reached about fifty millions. A reaction became inevitable.

Lord Canning succeeded in 1856, and found much excitement prevailing among the native populations. Malicious agitators spread a rumour that all India was to be forcibly Anglicized. The English language was to be everywhere imposed on the country; religious prejudices were no longer to be respected; the Enfield cartridges were to be greased with the fat of cows and pigs; caste was to be summarily put down, and the Bengal army to be enlisted for general service. This agitation led to the mutiny of 1857, but the stability of our Empire was never really endangered. The mass of the people were unaffected by the Sepoy rebellion, and, when it was suppressed, the country settled down into immediate tranquillity, as if nothing had occurred. As a matter of course, however, our debt and obligations went on increasing rather alarmingly.

We have not space to follow out all the statistics. Let it suffice to note that repeated wars, annexations of territory, and famines, have caused repeated borrowings, and the return for 1875 gives no less a sum for our Indian debt than £130,493,284. The gross revenue for that year is returned at £50,570,171; the expenditure at £54,500,545; the deficit £3,930,374. Of that income £21,296,793 came from land, £6,227,301 from salt, and £8,556,629 from opium. Nearly eight and a half millions were produced by Excise, Customs, and Stamps. These are the six principal sources of Indian revenue. The income for the year ending on the 31st March, 1877, was £56,022,277; the expenditure £58,205,055; deficit £2,182,778. For the year which closed at the end of March, 1878, the revenue was expected to be £56,310,900. During the year 1876-77 about ten millions were spent on the moral and material improvement of the country—on education and public works of all kinds. No one can say that this sum, large as it is, was not well expended. Dr. Forbes Watson has shown that a gigantic trade has sprung up in articles formerly of small importance; for example, in grain, cotton, jute, wool, tea, and coffee. The exports of tea in 1857 were equal to 121,000 lbs., in 1877 to 2,607,000 lbs.

With these figures before us we may well ask ourselves the question: How is it that India—a country possessing unusual natural defences, vast internal resources, a perfect network of rivers, rich alluvial plains, a population easily governed because incapable of political combination, and, as a rule, singularly industrious, submissive, docile, peaceable, and law-abiding—is not able to pay the expense of its administration?

The Muhammadan Emperors were conquerors like ourselves, yet under them the Empire generally had a full treasury, spent a good deal on public works, and never contracted debts. How is this remarkable fact to be explained? It is obvious that imperial crowns, military pomp, princely palaces, gilded halls, a full treasury, and even good roads, railways, telegraphs, and canals, may all consist with abject penury, wretchedness, and degradation in the mass of the people.

The Emperor Akbar aimed at governing for the good of his subjects, but even under his administration the condition of the ryot was one of utter destitution. A yawning chasm separated the palace and the mud hovels of the cultivators. No intermediate links existed, by help of which the gulf might be bridged over. Under his successors the peasantry were ground down. The whole revenue system became corrupt. There was no idea of a reciprocity of duties between the governors and the governed. Nor did the Muhammadan Emperors permit, as we do, rich native states and principalities, possessing fertile tracts of soil, to enjoy the full revenue of their lands, and yet benefit by the general order and security maintained at the cost of the districts subject to imperial taxation.

Perhaps, some may contend that the condition of the peasantry under our rule is not one whit better. For my own part, after travelling over a great part of India I arrived at the conviction that there is more general comfort and happiness among the people than in any other country of the world. Certainly the peasantry are poor, but their condition under our administration has improved beyond all expectation during the last thirty years. It must, of course, be borne in mind that the wants of the natives of India are few. They never require more than two good meals a day. But not a single person (except in times of famine) ever has less. Nor is any one without a hut to shelter him at night. A labourer may not earn more than threepence a day, but he may purchase two pounds of nourishing grain for about a halfpenny. In Orissa the family of a husbandman, consisting of six persons, would be considered in good circumstances if able to spend sixteen shillings a month in food, and would consume every day ten pounds of rice valued at fourpence, vegetables, split peas, and fish, to the value of three farthings, oil and spice to the value of three farthings—in all fivepence halfpenny (Hunter's Statistics, xix. 93). With wants so easily satisfied it is difficult to make out cases of destitution when the seasons are propitious.

It is true that the cultivators of the soil, who constitute at least three-fourths of the whole population—instead of one-fourth as in Europe—are generally improvident. They live from hand to mouth. They have no reserve fund to fall back upon in times of scarcity, and, if able in any one year to save money, are prone to squander it in marriage-feasts, in caste entertainments, in jewelry, and personal decorations. It is true, too, that the financial condition of the country cannot at present be considered satisfactory. Famines are periodical. Deficits recur annually, and the public debt increases. What, then, is the remedy? Is more to be extracted out of a people already taxed to the utmost limit of their capabilities? Can more be wrung out of the three principal sources of revenue—land, salt, and opium? The slight turn of the screw to which the salt-tax has been recently subjected will weigh, like an additional incubus, on the poor, while the rich are left unaffected.

As to opium, a feeling in England seems to be gaining ground—not that it ought to yield more—but that this source of revenue ought to be wholly abolished. The Government is constantly reproached for sending poison to the Chinese. Let the finances of India be ruined, say these conscientious critics, rather than prop them up by an iniquitous traffic. Can it be right for our Government to degrade itself by dealing wholesale in a poisonous drug which it also produces and manufactures? On the other hand, the defenders of opium have plenty to say for themselves. Opium, in moderation, say they, is no more poisonous than spirituous liquor. In some parts of Assam, as well as in China, occasional doses are positively needed for the preservation of health. At any rate to abolish the distillation of spirits in Great Britain would be easier and involve a far less financial catastrophe. Besides, it is certain that, if our Government, yielding to the outcry, were to give up the opium monopoly, they would save their credit at the expense of both consumers and cultivators. The Chinese would certainly be more poisoned under a system of free trade, and the cultivators would probably be oppressed. At present we regulate both the strength and purity of the drug—we make advances to the ryots and treat them justly. I believe it is admitted on all hands that a system of excise in opium would be preferable to direct Government traffic. Excise has been already substituted in the case of salt. But how should we provide for the interval of transition ? The revenue would collapse during the period needed for private companies to take up a vast concern involving complicated arrangements and an enormous outlay of capital.

It is clear that the abolition of what is styled an iniquitous traffic is easier to talk about than to carry into execution.

It is equally clear, however, that our hungry Indian finance-ministers cannot expect to grow fatter on opium any more than on salt. There remains the *pièce de résistance*—land. One of the great questions of Indian administration is: Do the rulers of India own the land ? High authorities, like Lord Lawrence and Sir Fitzjames Stephen, deny that they do. What the Government claims, say they, is what all previous Governments have claimed—not any proprietary right in the soil, but the first charge on the crops. The people are the real owners of the soil. It was the object of Lord Cornwallis' permanent settlement to protect and create private property in land, and encourage the outlay of capital for its improvement by fixing the Government demand in perpetuity. That this policy was wise is as certain as that it was badly carried out in Bengal, where a number of persons called Zamīndārs or landholders, who were not the real landowners, were converted into proprietors and allowed to reap all the benefits of a far too liberal assessment. It is well known that the Zamīndārs show no pity to their tenants. The last anna is extorted from the impoverished ryot; the Government is deprived of about half its due, and the money so gained is squandered. No part of it is spent on improvements.

Unhappily the bad application of a good principle in Bengal has prevented its wise application elsewhere. On the annexation of new territories we have generally fixed the assessment for a term of thirty years, and as favourably as possible to the cultivators. At the end of the term the land has been revalued, and a fresh assessment made. At present (as I am told by Sir William Muir) the rule in the North-west is that, if the gross produce of a piece of land is worth, say, Rs. 104 or 105, four or five rupees are taken for what are called cesses—that is, extra charges on the land for road-making, police, education, &c.— and one-half of the remainder, or Rs. 50, for the Government demand. It is admitted that if a landholder by skill, industry, and the employment of capital, improves the productive qualities of his holding, the Government, which does not take part in the industry or improvements, has no right to share in the increased value of the produce. The tax can only be justly augmented on general considerations, such as an advance in the prosperity of a country caused by roads, railroads, canals, and new markets. As a matter of fact, however, the fear of fresh microscopic revaluations at the end of periods of thirty years paralyses the productive energies of the people. Wells are filled up, land is allowed to deteriorate, and various expedients for its depreciation are resorted to when a fresh assessment is impending.

In the opinion of those who know India best, a more moderate Government charge on the produce of the soil—not necessarily uniform, but adjusted to suit the circumstances of particular provinces—would in the end improve the financial condition of our Indian Empire. Our truest wisdom, it is thought, would be to encourage the outlay of capital on lands already under cultivation, and to attract capital towards those vast potential sources of revenue latent in lands not yet brought under culture, or not yet thoroughly cultivated. We can only effect this by securing fixity of tenure — by closing the account and fixing the assessment permanently when a district has been cultivated to the fullest extent. In this way we shall create a class of well-to-do contented landed proprietors, whose increased wants will help to fill the State treasury, and whose interest in the soil will be the best guarantee for the maintenance of our rule. Nothing will tend more to conciliate the people, to consolidate our empire, and make our revenue balance our expenditure. The extraordinary progress of the country during the last thirty years proves that India, with all her supposed immobility, is capable of rapid expansion, and responds instantaneously to the efforts of those who strive to develop her resources. Her potential income is beyond all calculation. If we educate the cultivators of the soil to be self-reliant and provident, to keep out of the clutches of the money-lender, to invest their savings wisely, and accumulate a reserve against times of scarcity, part of their growing wealth will as surely find its way into the coffers of the State, as running water flows into the sea. This is the true remedy for our present financial difficulties. Nevertheless, in the application of this, as of all other Indian remedies, there is need of cautious progress, slow haste, and a wise consideration of varying conditions, circumstances, and interests.

PROMOTION OF GOODWILL AND SYMPATHY BETWEEN ENGLAND AND INDIA.

ANY remarks on the best method of promoting goodwill between England and India may appear at the present moment[1] somewhat ill-timed. Two nations in the East of Europe have been locked together for the last few months in a deadly embrace. Their struggle has been marked by worse incidents of savagery than ever disgraced the world's first periods of primeval barbarism. Raging passions have been let loose. A portion of this fair Europe of ours—the boasted home of true Christianity—has been converted into a scene of deplorable atrocities. We Englishmen, who have happily played no part in the dreadful tragedy, have nevertheless watched with a kind of fascination the ebb and flow of the blood-stained tide of war. We have allowed our minds to be engrossed with graphic narratives of military evolutions;—our thoughts to run on fortresses and sieges;—our curiosity to be directed towards the effectiveness of terrible instruments of destruction, Krupp guns, breech-loaders and torpedoes;—our imaginations to be excited by the horrors of the battle-field, by images of dead and dying soldiers, mangled bodies and stiffened corpses;—our hearts to be torn by tales of inhuman cruelty, borne with superhuman resignation.

[1] This was delivered as an address at a Meeting of the National Indian Association, held, December 12th, 1877, at the Langham Hall, London, the Earl of Northbrook in the Chair. Peace had not then been concluded between Russia and Turkey.

At such a time, I may be told, it would be more appropriate to discuss the best means of restoring peace and promoting goodwill between the two nations engaged in mortal strife. Or supposing it to be admitted that the exciting tragedy of the present war ought not to engross our attention to the exclusion of other interests, still I may be confronted, at the outset of my remarks, with a very natural enquiry;—Is this a suitable moment to plead for the display of more sympathy between the people of England and the people of India?

England has just given a conspicuous proof of her profound sympathy with her Indian brethren. She has voluntarily subscribed more than half a million sterling in a few months for the relief of the famine-stricken population, and in India itself every member of our Government—from the Viceroy downwards—has displayed the most self-sacrificing zeal and energy in efforts to prevent death and alleviate suffering. All this is of course true. And yet, I am persuaded, there is no one in this room with any experience derived from actual residence in India, who will regard an address on the subject which constitutes the very *raison d'être* of the National Indian Association, as either out of place or out of time at a season like this. The sympathy of the English people has indeed been evoked by a terrible calamity. And deep down in the lowest depths of the great British heart there is always a spring of true sympathy ready to gush forth and flow at the cry of suffering, whether towards wounded Turks, mutilated Russians, or famine-driven, fever-stricken Indians. If it is a sad reflection that war and famine are never likely to cease out of the land, there is at least some comfort in the thought that the battle-fields of Europe and the famine-desolated fields of India are never likely to be cut off from the healing, quickening influences of the perennial stream of English sympathy and English charity.

Let me, however, remind my hearers that there is yet

another field, which, though it gives forth no hurtling sound of shot or shell, no piercing cry of wounded soldiers or famished peasantry, is not the less a field of conflict, of suffering, of loss and gain, of defeat and victory. I mean the battle-ground of daily life and daily work—with its fightings within and its fears without, its grapplings with duties, its wrestlings with temptations, its struggles with opposing forces, wills and interests. It is on this arena that the people of England and the people of India are brought together, not as enemies fighting for the victory over each other, but as fellow-soldiers striving together for the mastery over every form of evil; as fellow-subjects yielding allegiance to the same sovereign; as fellow-men and brethren, members of the great human family, owing love and sympathy and tender consideration towards each other.

And is not mutual sympathy needed by all who meet together as fellow-labourers on this common working-ground of daily duties and monotonous occupations—needed all the more because too frequently believed to be uncalled for and superfluous? Is it not needed by members of the same household, however nearly drawn together by bonds of family relationship? Is it not needed by people of the same country, however closely bound together by ties of social union and interest? Much more then is it needed by two peoples of two widely different countries, thrown by the force of circumstances into intimate political association, though separated from each other as far as the East is from the West by diversities of language, religion, customs, habits of thought, and social institutions.

What then are the best means of promoting this much-to-be-desired goodwill and sympathy between the people of England and the people of India? This is the question I have set myself to answer in the present lecture, and the answer is not difficult. I have nothing new to suggest, no special nostrum, no wonder-working panacea of my own to proclaim, no startling discovery to announce. I can only insist on principles well known to every one around me; I can add nothing to the trite truisms already familiar to all of us. How are goodwill and sympathy promoted between any collection of individuals of widely different characters who have to live in daily intercourse with each other? They must learn mutual forbearance, they must consider one another to provoke unto little acts of kindness—little abstinences and wise reticences—they must be charitable in judging of each other, in making allowance for each other's infirmities, in thinking no evil of each other, in bearing, believing, hoping and enduring all things. In a word, they must cultivate mutual charity.

Are, then, the people of England and the people of India wanting in this most excellent gift of mutual charity? Let Indians look into their own hearts, and examine their own consciences. My business as an Englishman is to enquire particularly into our own shortcomings. The question is one which cannot be lightly set aside. For if we are wanting in common charity,—including, of course, in that term the exercise of kindly feelings towards the people committed to our rule,—then it is clear that all our doings in India are nothing worth. We may make laws, administer justice, preach the Gospel, educate the people, lay down railroads, telegraphs, and telephones, develope the resources of the country, tame and control the forces of Nature for the public weal,—nay, more, we may bestow all our goods to feed the famine-stricken poor,—but our rule will not be rooted in the hearts of the people, our legislation will be as hollow as sounding brass, our preaching and teaching as unmeaning as the tinkling of a cymbal, our Empire as insecure as a tower built on sand, which some great storm will suddenly sweep away.

Now I am not here to look at the black side of anything, not even of my own character as an Englishman.

I believe there is no nation in the world so abounding in true charity as the great British nation. I appeal to obstinate facts. I appeal to stubborn statistics. Nevertheless, without agreeing with those who consider it their privilege as Englishmen to be ever finding fault with themselves, I desire to face the plain truth. I am ready for my own part to confess that we are not all of us as charitable as we ought to be in our everyday ordinary relations with our Indian brethren,—not as fair as we ought to be in our judgment of their character, our estimate of their capacities, our toleration of their idiosyncracies, our appreciation of what is excellent in their literature, customs, religions and philosophies. And I am persuaded that both our want of charity and our want of sympathy proceed from no innate incapacity for charitable and sympathetic feelings, which are always ready to show themselves on great occasions; nor from any real want of fairness, which is usually a conspicuous feature in our national character, but simply and solely from our insufficient knowledge of India, its people and its needs. To put the matter plainly, we are only unsympathetic and uncharitable when we are ignorant.

Certain Hindū philosophers assert that all the phenomena of the universe are caused by ignorance. We cannot, however, quite go with the Vedāntist to the length of affirming that this beautiful world, this wonderful city of London, this fine Hall and everything good in it owe their origin to ignorance. But thus much, I think, we may allow, that all sin and misery, all war and enmity, all evils great or small that mar the fairness of God's earth—doubtings, difficulties, jealousies, misunderstandings, envyings, wrath, seditions, heresies,—all these are rooted in ignorance, and in ignorance alone. And is it not the case that we Englishmen often go to India with minds more ignorant than they ought to be of India's condition and India's needs? Sometimes, I fear, we do not even know enough to know that we do not know, and when we commence work on Indian soil, the pressure of necessary duties makes the task of acquiring any thorough knowledge of the country and its people very difficult of accomplishment.

Let me not be misunderstood. I am quite aware that many of the Queen's Indian officers, in spite of insufficient early training, become able Indian statesmen, and accomplished Indologists. What I am speaking of is the general ignorance of India—of its moral, religious, and intellectual history and condition—which prevails among younger men on their first arrival, who nevertheless become in the end quite conversant with the affairs of their own districts. As to the ignorance of India and its wants, which is nearly universal in this country, and even conspicuous in some of our most distinguished University men,—our first-class men and wranglers, our professors and writers, our magistrates and legislators (happily, however, not in all),—I cannot do better than quote the words of a citizen of Bombay who came to England as an agent of one of the native States, and in a letter to the *Times* wrote as follows (December 21, 1874):—' In my own experience among Englishmen, I have found no general indifference to India, but rather an eager desire for information. But I have found a Cimmerian darkness about the manners and habits of my countrymen, an almost poetical description of our customs, and a conception no less wild and startling than the vagaries of Mandeville or Marco Polo concerning our religion.'

I come, therefore, to what may be called the keynote of all I have to say in this lecture, namely, that if we wish to promote goodwill and sympathy between the people of England and the people of India, we must labour to promote *mutual knowledge*—that is—a correct knowledge of England in India, of India in England. And here, I may observe, that if want of sympathy is rooted in want of knowledge, it must not be assumed that the absence of knowledge is all on one side. The people of India are even more wanting in correct knowledge of England than we are in correct knowledge of India. Let Indians look to their own deficiencies. My present concern is to look at home and ask the questions :—What are *our own* shortcomings ? What are *our own* needs ?

Many they are, and of various kinds and in various degrees. Even our ablest Indian statesmen have to confess ignorance about many things. Such men would be the first to tell us that if we wish to promote a better knowledge of India among ourselves we ought to begin at the right end. We ought to introduce Indian studies as an element of education at our Schools and Universities.

I deeply regret that the study of Indian and Oriental subjects generally is practically under a ban at my own University, because Eastern acquirements are at present no avenue to a degree, but rather a hindrance. Any undergraduate who devotes himself to Oriental studies is likely to imperil his place in the class-list, and if he remains in England, his future prospects in life. That we Englishmen, with our enormous Indian and Colonial Empire, our vast Eastern commerce, our increasing interest in Egypt, Turkey, Mesopotamia, Burmah, Tibet, and China should show such indifference to studies which other nations, with little interest in the East, regard as important branches of education, seems, indeed, wholly unaccountable. For the most superficial observer must be convinced that the political interdependence, and, so to speak, solidarity of England and India, are becoming every day more complete, the affairs and interests, the loss and gain, the honour and dishonour, of the two countries more and more interwoven. Witness the increasing space accorded to news from India in our leading journals. Witness the vacation speeches of our leading legislators. Witness the debates on India and the Eastern question in both our Houses of Parliament. In fact, the improvements in telegraphy are constantly causing increased centralization of authority, and India is at present more governed by mandates and influences emanating from the central terminus of Queen, Lords and Commons, than by orders and enactments issuing from the Council Chambers of Calcutta, Madras and Bombay.

Surely, then, we are bound to ponder our heightened duties, our deepening responsibilities. We are bound seriously to lay to heart the undoubted fact that our rule over two hundred and forty-one millions of the human race depends more than it has ever done before—not only for its excellence but for its very continuance—on the promotion of a better knowledge of the history and condition of India among the few hundred individuals constituting our two legislative assemblies, most of whom have been educated at our public schools and Universities. It may be very true that the old ignorance and apathy of Parliament have passed away, and that the commencement of an Indian debate no longer acts like a dinner-bell on hungry members. Yet, I venture to assert, that no little indifference and a good deal of sciolism still prevail, and that urgent need exists for securing by early training a more solid foundation of correct knowledge on all Eastern subjects among all classes of the community: in other words,—that the neglect of Oriental knowledge, as a department of education, calls for immediate attention at the hands of our educators.

Let me substantiate my assertion by a few instances, beginning with the simple subject of Geography. An educated European may perhaps be pardoned for betraying ignorance of the exact position of Quetta, but is it not somewhat startling to be asked by men of rank and education in this country whether Lahore is near Benares, and whether Calcutta lies south of Bombay? Even in India itself I have met with many able civilians who have confessed to me their inability to pass an examination in the geography of India outside their own Presidency.

Much the same may be said of physical geography. India is blessed with numerous magnificent rivers, yet, even among Anglo-Indians, how many of those long resident in particular districts would be able to give an accurate account of India's marvellous network of running water, or the best method of utilizing it? Then how little is generally known of the Zoology and Botany of India! Doubtless there are scientific men to whom the fauna and flora of certain districts are familiar, but few Englishmen have an adequate conception of the marvellous wealth of India's animal and plant life. Sportsmen indeed abound everywhere by hundreds, but how many care for animals except to kill or eat them? It may be very true that some forms of life are a little too exuberant. Yet what country affords such beautiful specimens of the insect world? And how is it that Indian Zoologists and Entomologists may be counted on the fingers?

Then as to the vegetable kingdom. Nowhere in the world are there such opportunities for the study of botany, and nowhere is a knowledge of botany less common. Even well-informed persons have to confess their ignorance of India's vast and varied agricultural capabilities. For example, much has yet to be learnt about India's capacity for developing the cultivation of cotton. Again, quite within living memory the remarkable discovery has been made that the tea-plant is indigenous on Indian soil. Much ignorance, too, remains to be dissipated about the culture and preparation of coffee, cinchona, ipecacuanha, and above all of tobacco. Who can tell how far the latter may one day supply the eight or nine millions of revenue which must be sought for somewhere, should the conscience of Great Britain become too sensitive to permit her Indian Government to continue its dealings in opium? Who can tell, too, how far drought and famine may be averted when more is known about irrigation, the storing of water and the conservation of woods and forests? As to geology and mineralogy, it is difficult to estimate how much has yet to be ascertained about India's mineral resources—the exploration of coal-fields, the production of salt and iron, the exploitation of gold, silver, copper, and lead.

Archæology, again, presents an unbounded field, not yet adequately investigated. We are scarcely yet alive to the duty of searching out and preserving India's valuable antiquities, and of copying important historical inscriptions, all traces of which the climate is rapidly obliterating. I will not enter on the boundless subject of ethnology, except to remark that some of the oldest amongst us can remember the time when the near relationship of Englishmen to Brāhmans and Rājputs was barely suspected. I may mention, too, that no one in India could give me any clue to the ethnical classification of the Bhīls, and that the existence of Negrito and Negroïd races on the hills is a mystery.

Perhaps I should scarcely be believed if I were to relate with richness of detail the story of an intelligent young person, supposed to be fully educated, who was present the other day at a lecture on Zanāna work, and was heard to inquire with much *naïveté* whether the Zanānas were not a tribe of Afghāns. As to Indian history, all that can be said, I fear, is that the minds of most men are a perfect blank—a complete *tabula rasa*.

In regard to the languages and dialects of India, cultivated and uncultivated, how many persons are aware that their number amounts to at least two hundred? To know even two of these well is, of course, as much as can be expected of our administrators, and I willingly admit that they are generally well versed in at least one language. But I may be pardoned for bemoaning the almost universal ignorance of the classical languages of India,—Sanskrit, Arabic and Persian, with their respective literatures. I have often been asked by learned Europeans—Has Sanskrit any literature? The fact is that since the abolition of Haileybury in 1858 the study of Sanskrit has remained voluntary. It is much to be regretted that few Indian probationers address themselves to this important language, and that those who begin learning it, rapidly drop all the knowledge they have gained in this country as soon as they commence their official duties.

Still more to be regretted is the neglect of Sanskṛit by missionaries. Happily there are signs of a better appreciation of its value in the future, and I even look forward to its eventual adoption in England as an element of linguistic training. Let us not forget that Sanskṛit is as closely allied as Greek to our mother-tongue, that its symmetrical grammar is the key to all other grammars, that its system of synthesis is as useful to the mind as the study of geometry, and that its literature contains models of true poetry and some of the most remarkable treatises on philosophy, science and ethics that the world has ever produced.

Above all, let those who are preparing for an Indian career bear in mind that Sanskṛit is the only source of life, health and vigour to all the spoken languages of the Hindūs, the only repository of Hindū religious creeds, customs and observances. 'The popular prejudices of the Hindūs,' said my illustrious predecessor at Oxford, 'their daily observances, their occupations, their amusements, their domestic and social relations, their local legends, their traditions, their fables, their religious worship, all spring from and are perpetuated by the Sanskṛit language.' Yes—to know a country, its people, its needs, and necessities, its mistakes and errors, all these things must be known and understood. Without such knowledge no respect can be felt for all that is good and true, no successful attempt made for the eradication of all that is evil, false and hurtful.

Indeed, I am deeply convinced that the more we learn about the ideas, feelings, drift of thought, religious and intellectual development, eccentricities, and even errors of the people of India, the less ready shall we be to judge them by our own conventional European standards—the less disposed to regard ourselves as the sole depositories of all the true knowledge, learning, virtue and refinements of civilized life—the less prone to despise as an ignorant and inferior race the men who compiled the laws of Manu, one of the most remarkable literary productions of the world—who composed systems of ethics worthy of Christianity—who imagined the Rāmāyaṇa and Mahā-bhārata, poems in some respects outrivalling the Iliad and the Odyssey—who invented for themselves the science of grammar, arithmetic, astronomy, logic, and six most subtle systems of philosophy. Above all, the less inclined shall we be to stigmatize as benighted heathen the authors of two religions, however false, which are at this moment professed by about half the human race.

And this leads me to express my sense of our remissness, whether as laymen or missionaries, in neglecting to study the sacred works on which the various religions of India rest. We cannot, of course, sympathize with all that is false in the several creeds of Hindūs, Buddhists, Jains, Pārsīs, Sikhs and Muslims. But we can consent to examine them from their own point of view, we can study their sacred books in their own languages, Sanskṛit, Pāli, Prākṛit, Zand, Gurumukhī and Arabic, rather than in imperfect translations of our own. We can pay as much deference to the interpretations of their own commentators as we expect to be accorded to our own interpretation of the difficulties of our own sacred Scriptures. We can avoid denouncing in strong language what we have never sufficiently investigated, and do not thoroughly understand.

Yes, I must speak out. It seems to me that the general ignorance of our fellow-countrymen in regard to the religions of India is really worse than a blank. A man, learned in European lore, asked me the other day whether the Hindūs were not all Buddhists. Of course ignorance is associated with indifference. I stayed in India with an eminent Indian civilian who had lived for years quite unconsciously within a few hundred yards of a celebrated shrine, endeared to the Hindūs by the religious memories of centuries. Another had never heard of a perfectly unique temple not two miles from the gate of his own compound. Ignorance, too, is often associated with an attitude of unmitigated contempt. Another distinguished civilian, who observed that I was diligent in prosecuting my researches into the true nature of Hindūism, expressed surprise that I could waste my time in 'grubbing into such dirt.' The simple truth, I fear, is that we are all more or less ignorant. We are none of us as yet quite able to answer the question:—'What is Hindūism?' We have none of us as yet sufficiently studied it under all its aspects, in its own vast sacred literature stretching over a period of more than two thousand years. We under-estimate its comprehensiveness, its super-subtlety, its recuperative hydra-like vitality; and we are too much given to include the whole system under sweeping expressions such as 'heathenism' or 'idolatry,' as if every idea it contains was to be eradicated root and branch.

Again I must speak out. I deeply regret that we are in the habit of using opprobrious terms to designate the religious tenets of our Indian brethren, however erroneous we believe those tenets to be. Unfortunately it is difficult to find any substitute for the convenient expression 'heathen,' but we ought to consider that the translators of our Bible only adopted this word as an equivalent for Gentile nations, and that the term is now frequently applied to wicked, godless people. I have constantly heard it so applied by our clergy when speaking of the most degraded section of the population of our large cities,—atheists, thieves, lawless people and criminals of all kinds, such as, in former times, congregated on wild *heaths*, remote from civilized towns. We are surely untrue to our own principles when we associate all unbelievers in Christianity with such people, by the use of a common term for both. Does not our own religion teach us that in every nation he that feareth God and worketh righteousness is accepted with Him?

I deplore, too, the ignorance displayed in regard to Indian religious usages. A recent book on India by an eminent Member of Parliament describes the mark on the forehead of the Southern Rāmānujas as the trident of Śiva, whereas it really represents the footprints of Vishnu. Errors of this kind swarm even in the works of missionaries, and are generally caused by ignorance of Sanskṛit. As to caste, its working is very imperfectly understood, and few are aware that the Hindūs regard it as an imperfect condition of life, and hold that to attain supreme happiness caste must be abandoned. Again, we are apt to indulge in a wholesale condemnation of caste and to advocate its total abolition, forgetful that as a social institution it often operates most beneficially. Doubtless caste-rules are generally a great hindrance to progress, but their very connection with religious faith and practice may often furnish a salutary check where the mere belief in Vishnu and Śiva is powerless to exercise any restraint at all.

Then, how often do we offend caste prejudices simply from ignorance of their strength and of their connection with venerated religious usage and deep religious feeling!

I, for my part, can believe that an earnest-minded Englishman might well hesitate to eat the flesh of oxen, while resident in certain districts of India where Hindū religious prejudices continue strongest, and where cow-killing is regarded as nothing short of impious sacrilege, remembering the words of a high Christian authority, 'if meat make my brother to offend, I will eat no flesh while the world standeth.' The Deputy-Commissioner at Rohtak was murdered the other day by a fanatical Hindū, who never spoke afterwards till the moment of his execution, except to whisper that he had a call from heaven to destroy cow-killers.

When I was at Jammu, one of the Mahārāja's Ministers told me that the punishment in Kaśmīr for killing oxen was imprisonment for life, and that he himself had such a horror of eating the flesh of oxen that, if the alternative were submitted to him of tasting beef or being beheaded, he would unhesitatingly choose decapitation.

It is said that a holy Brāhman who lived near Saugor determined to wrestle with the Deity till he should reveal to him the real cause of the general scarcity under which the land was groaning. After three days and nights of fasting and prayer, he saw a vision of some celestial being, who stood before him in a white mantle, and told him that all the calamities of the season arose from the slaughter of oxen by Englishmen and Muhammadans. Colonel Sleeman asserts that this actually occurred, and that it created a great sensation in the neighbourhood. At any rate, we may learn from such stories how deep-seated are the religious convictions on which the sacredness of the cow is based, and can understand how our practice of eating beef may generate bitter feelings of ill-will towards us. Let us suppose for a moment an imaginary case. Let us ask ourselves what our own feelings would be if a number of Chinese were to settle down in this country, and insist on constantly eating boiled rats with chop-sticks before our eyes. Yet our disgust would be as nothing compared with the revulsion in the mind of a pious Hindū caused by our devouring with avidity the flesh of animals which from his infancy he is taught to believe permeated with the essence of divinity.

Of course, I am not advocating a general abandonment of beef-eating throughout India. I am aware that many consider it a duty to show openly their disapproval of what they consider the absurd prejudices of a weak-minded people, and I admit that when religious customs are degrading and do violence to nature and humanity, like the rite of Satī, they ought to be put down. All I maintain is, that the time-honoured usages of particular districts, when intimately bound up with religious feelings, ought, as far as possible, to be respected. Ought we not, too, without making any concessions to what we believe utterly false in the religions of India, to be more diligent in searching for some common religious ground on which Europeans and Asiatics may take their stand together? Is it not the case that, among ourselves, people of the most opposite opinions find their religious differences softened down and their sympathies evoked by meeting face to face on the common platform of Conference and Congress Hall? Has England advanced with such gigantic strides beyond Eastern nations that no points of agreement in ideas, customs, usages, and religion can be found with an ancient people who had a polished language, an extensive literature, and a developed civilization when our forefathers were clothed in skins and could neither read nor write? Is so great a gulf now fixed between two races who once occupied the same home in Central Asia that no community of thought, no interchange of ideas, no reciprocity of feeling is any longer possible between them? I verily believe that an unfairly low estimate of the moral, social and religious condition of the people of India, and of their intellectual capacity, is really the principal obstacle to the promotion of sympathy between the two races.

The great historian Mill, whose History of India is still a standard work, has done infinite harm by his unjustifiable blackening of the Indian national character. He has declared (I quote various statements scattered through his work) that 'the superior castes in India are generally depraved, and capable of every fraud and villany; that they more than despise their inferiors, whom they kill with less scruple than we do a fowl; that the inferior castes are profligate, guilty on the slightest occasion of the greatest crimes, and degraded infinitely below the brutes; that the Hindūs in general are devoid of every moral and religious principle; cunning and deceitful, addicted to adulation, dissimulation, deception, dishonesty, falsehood and perjury; disposed to hatred, revenge, and cruelty; indulging in furious and malignant passions, fostered by the gloomy and malignant principles of their religion; perpetrating villany with cool reflection; indolent to the point of thinking death and extinction the happiest of all states; avaricious, litigious, insensible to the sufferings of others, inhospitable, cowardly; contemptuous and harsh to their women, whom they treat as slaves; eminently devoid of filial, parental, and conjugal affection.'

No wonder that young Englishmen, just imported from the ruling country, and fresh from the study of Mill's History, sometimes affect a supercilious air of superiority when first brought into contact with their Indian fellow-subjects. No wonder that Mr. Nowrozjee Furdoonjee should have delivered a lecture three or four years ago before this Association and attempted to prove that the natives of India are often treated by Europeans 'with incivility, harshness, and even contempt and personal violence—that they are frequently stigmatized as Niggers, a nation of liars, perjurers, forgers, devoid of gratitude, trust, good-nature, and every other virtue, as rude barbarians and inhuman savages.'

Of course, we know that this Indian gentleman has overstated his case, and that his description applies to a condition of things which may have partially existed thirty years ago, but which has to a great extent passed away. Still, it cannot be questioned that, conscious of our own superiority in religion, science, morality, and general culture, we are too apt to under-estimate the character and acquirements of our Indian brethren. We may regret that they are not Christians, that they have not the moral stamina of Englishmen, that their social institutions are a source of weakness and an obstacle to all fusion between European and Asiatic races, their caste-rules a bar to progress, and the low condition of their women fatal to their elevation. We may tell them plainly that we aim at raising them—men and women—socially, morally, intellectually, to our own standard. But we must bear in mind, all the while, that they are human beings like ourselves, with feelings and infirmities like our own. We must give them credit for whatever is good, true, and lovely in their own national character; we must even be ready to admit that in some points—such as patient perseverance in common duties, courtesy, temperance, filial obedience, reverent demeanour towards their elders and betters, dutiful submission to governors, teachers, spiritual pastors and masters, faithfulness in service, tenderness towards animal life, toleration of religious diversities in foreigners and each other — they may possibly be our equals, if not our superiors.

Contrast with Mr. Mill's estimate of the Hindū character the opinion of the great Abūl Fazl (well called 'the father of excellence'), Akbar's celebrated Minister, who, though a Muhammadan, wrote in his Ayīn-i-Akbarī —'The Hindūs are religious, affable, courteous to strangers, prone to inflict austerities on themselves, lovers of justice, given to retirement, able in business, grateful, admirers of truth, and of unbounded fidelity. Their character shines brightest in adversity. Their soldiers know not what it is to fly from the field of battle. When the success of the combat becomes doubtful they dismount from their horses and throw away their lives in payment of the debt of valour. They have great respect for their tutors; and make no account of their lives when they can devote them to the service of their God. They believe in the unity of the Godhead, and although they hold images in high veneration, yet they are by no means idolaters, as the ignorant suppose.'

I must admit that in another place he says that the Hindūs differ widely in different places, and that some have the disposition of angels, others of demons.

If I may be allowed to speak of my own experiences, I confess that to me the Indian character has seemed neither angelic nor demoniacal. But if the best Christian found a law in his members bringing him into captivity to the law of sin, so that when he 'would do good, evil was present with him,' how much more must this be true of the best Hindū! Surely, then, on the common ground of conflict with evil, both Christian and Hindū, though equipped for the fight with armour of very different temper, may meet and sympathize with each other. And if his own religion is to the one a power and to the other a weakness, surely the strong man armed may have some strength to spare for the encouragement and support of his more feeble brother.

I will not enter into the question of how far the social gulf which is now separating the two races is capable of being bridged over. When I was at Calcutta I found all the highest State functionaries — Lord Northbrook himself, our noble Chairman here, — the late high-minded Bishop Milman, and many others I could name, vying with each other in their efforts to conciliate the natives, and bring about more social fusion between the rulers and the ruled. I found, too, many of our devoted fellow-countrywomen doing their best to work their way lovingly and tenderly into the interior of many an Indian family. The present Viceroy, Lord Lytton, is not a whit behind his predecessors in endeavouring to counteract, by his personal example, the estrangement caused by race-antipathies. But I fear that little success will be achieved till the impenetrable barrier which now surrounds the homes of India is thrown down, till Hindūs and Muhammedans consent to eat and drink with Europeans, and till Indian wives, mothers, and daughters are elevated to their proper position in the family circle.

Nor will I now discuss the question of the duty of redressing so-called Indian grievances, because this is acknowledged on all hands. Traversing India as I have recently done from Kaśmir to Cape Comorin, I have found all intelligent natives generally satisfied with our rule. It is useless, however, to conceal from ourselves the existence of much discontent, chiefly among the men we have educated above their stations. When I have inquired of such men: What are your grievances? What does India want which India has not got? 'We want,' they have replied, 'complete social and political equality; we want admission to the highest executive offices; we want a more economical Government; we want a more permanent and moderate settlement of the land-tax; we want less tedious and costly litigation; we want power of sending a few representatives to the House of Commons; we want a certain number of covenanted civil appointments to be competed for in this country.' These are a few specimens of alleged wants. If any of them are *real* wants which it is possible and proper to meet, the Government seems to me to be inclined to go even beyond its duty in endeavouring to meet them. Our Indian Government, too, is now doing its best (just as the Emperor Akbar did more than 300 years ago) to organize in India systematic efforts for the acquisition and dissemination of accurate information on all the points I have mentioned in this address, and indeed on every minute particular bearing on the condition of the people committed to its rule.

The best evidence of this is afforded by the statistical account of Bengal, in twenty volumes, just completed by Dr. W. W. Hunter, Director-General of Statistics, and published in London by Messrs. Trübner and Co.

Yet in the preface of this great national work—a monument of exemplary industry as well as of literary ability—Dr. Hunter owns that it represents the first organized advance towards a better knowledge of India. 'When I commenced,' he says, 'the survey, no regular census had been taken of India, and the enumeration of 1872 disclosed that the official estimates had been wrong as regards Lower Bengal alone by more than twenty-five million of souls. No book existed to which either the public or the administrative body could refer for the most essential facts concerning the rural population. Districts lying within half-a-day's journey of the capital were spoken of in the Calcutta Review as "unexplored."'

PROMOTION OF GOODWILL.

What I plead for, then, is a similar systematic organization and concentration of effort in this country for instilling a better knowledge of India into the rising generation. Unless we bestir ourselves, England will rapidly lose its position as the proper centre and focus of Eastern learning in Europe. Germany, France, and Russia are doing their best to take our place. Even Holland and Italy are rivalling us. All these countries have established chairs of most of the Indian languages, especially of Sanskrit, Arabic, and Persian. Even now we often have to go to Germany for our Indian Professors, Librarians, Secretaries, and Cataloguers of manuscripts [1].

What are our requirements, then, with a view to more systematic organization for the promotion of Indian studies? In my opinion principally four, namely :—1. Formal University recognition by the establishment of an Indian School for obtaining degrees. 2. The appointment of Professors and Teachers of Indian subjects at Colleges and Schools. 3. The encouragement of Indian students by the foundation of Indian scholarships and fellowships. 4. Local centralization by the founding of Indian Institutes, containing libraries, museums, and lecture-rooms, at great educational centres—for example, here in London (according to the plan long advocated by my friend, Dr. Forbes Watson), and especially at Oxford. But why, it may be asked, especially at Oxford? I reply for two reasons :—1st. It can be proved by statistics that a large proportion of our members of Parliament—the real rulers of India—are Oxford men. I believe the majority over Cambridge is at present represented by 136 over 100, and there are now eight Oxford first-class men in the Cabinet, including the Secretary of State for India himself. 2ndly. Our Oxford system,

---

[1] I am told that there is not in England a single person who knows Tibetan, although teachers of this language are to be found in Germany, France, and Russia, and although it is spoken by numbers of our own subjects and by millions inhabiting neighbouring countries.

which lays great stress on languages, history, law, and political economy, affords the best training for every kind of Indian career.

At last, therefore, I come to the goal to which my remarks have been converging—the need of founding at Oxford an institution which shall be a centre of union, intercourse, inquiry and instruction for all engaged in Indian studies. The Indian Institute will, I hope, be equipped in the most effective possible manner—both materially and personally. It will have Lecture-rooms, Museum, Library, and Reading-room, all aiding and illustrating each other, and closely connected with it an ample staff of University Professors and teachers, many of whom will have resided in India and have an intimate knowledge of the country. It will I trust, adapt itself to the needs of young Indians, who often go astray in this vast metropolis from the want of proper supervision; and who, as soon as our Oxford Indian School and Indian Institute are established, will probably frequent our University more than they have hitherto done. Oriental Fellowships, Indian Travelling Fellowships, Scholarships for Indians pursuing their studies at Oxford, Scholarships for Englishmen pursuing Indian studies, will, I trust, in time be connected with the Institute. It will, I hope, give prizes for essays on Indian subjects, and will invite able natives to deliver lectures in its lecture-rooms, where meetings and conferences on various topics relating to the welfare of our Indian fellow-subjects will occasionally be held. In brief, *its one aim* will be to concentrate and diffuse accurate information on every subject connected with the condition of our Indian Empire; *its one work* will be to draw England and India closer together, by promoting mutual knowledge, by furthering interchange of ideas, by encouraging reciprocity of feeling, by fostering goodwill and sympathy between the two countries.

This great aim—this great work, cannot and must not rest with the University of Oxford alone. Every society, every individual interested in the well-being of our Eastern Empire, will, I trust, lend a helping hand. The National Indian Association, with whose operations both in England and India I have cherished the warmest sympathy ever since the late lamented Miss Carpenter and myself met together for the promotion of similar aims in various parts of India, will, I am sure, co-operate with the Oxford Indian Institute, and both will direct their best endeavours towards the same high objects.

And need I add how much I believe the maintenance of goodwill and sympathy between England and India depends on the attitude and bearing of those who are highest in authority? It is said that what distinguished the great Emperor Akbar from all previous rulers was his personal attention to all the minutiæ of government, and his deference to the opinions of his subjects, however conflicting or opposed to his own. It would be impertinent in me to speak in praise of our noble Chairman on this occasion, but it seems to me that the success of Lord Northbrook's administration was not more due to his conversancy with every detail of State affairs than to his tact in preserving harmony between the discordant elements of which the Queen's Indian Empire must always consist, and his unvarying kindness and courtesy of manner towards every individual, whether Englishman, Hindū, or Muhammadan, with whom, as the Queen's representative, he was brought into contact.

The problem before us, then, has been—How can more cordial and sympathetic feeling be promoted between the people of England and the people of India? The solution of this problem may have been demonstrated by words, but the desired end will not be effected till the people of both countries join heart and hand in united efforts for the conciliation of each other's goodwill, and for the verification of the sublime doctrine—for the establishment of the eternal truth—that 'God has made all nations of men of one blood.'

INDEX[1].

Abûbakr, 165.
Abûl Fazl, 360.
Abyla, 4.
Adam, W., 294.
Aden, 23.
Âdil Shâh, 134.
Âdîśvara, 133.
Administration, 120, 121, 168, 206.
Afghânistân, 135, 136, 138.
Afghânistân, British, 129.
Afghâns, 136, 276.
Âgamas, 159.
Agglutinative languages, 153.
Âghâ Khân, 25.
Aghrib, 20.
Agriculturalists, 39.
Âg-wâlâs, 9.
Ahmad-nagar, 134.
Ahmad Shâh Abdâli, 276.
Ahriman, 93.
Âjmîr, 137.
Akbar, 136, 278, 301, 338, 362, 365.
Akbar and Elizabeth, 266.
Albuquerque, 265.
Ali Masjid, 139.
Alîvardi Khân, 275.
Allahabad, 131.
Almeyda, 265.

Alphabet, 227, 286, *307*, *308*.
Al-Sirat. *See* 91.
Amangala, 104.
Ambâ, 53.
Amita, 112.
Ancestor-worship, 162.
Ândhra, 130, 134.
Angas, 159.
Angushtha-mâtra, 104.
Anhalwâra, 132.
Animalli, 182.
Animals, 30, 32, 34, 35, 184.
Anna, 341.
Annexations, 278, 336.
Antyeshti, 104.
Appearance of natives, 60.
Âra, 141.
Ârâvali, 140.
Arcot, 274.
Ardha-Gangâ, 143.
Areca, 186.
Ariano-Pâli, 129.
Aristocracy, 42.
Art, 56, 57.
Aśâsya, 311.
Aśoka, 128.
Asambhu, 182.
Assai, 277.
Assâm, 140.
Astronomy, 146.
— and the weather, 211.

Asûryam-paśyâ, 314.
Athornan, 89.
Athravan, 89.
Attâka, 20.
Attitude of the natives, 176, 221.
Auckland, Lord, 336.
Aurangzîb, 136, 201, 301.
Authority, evil of. *See* Revelation.
Âvali, 141.
Avanti, 131.
Awadhî, 150.
Ayah, 2.
Ayenâr, 197.
Ayîn-i-Akbarî, 278, 360.
Ayodhyâ, 131.

Bâbar, 136, 301.
Bâbû, 323.
Bâb ul Makka, 267.
Bâbu'l mandib, 22.
Baghdad, 135.
Bâgh o Bâhar, 292.
Bahâdur Shâh, 136.
Bahâdur, Sir Jung, 78.
Bahmanî, 134.
Baidanâth Roy, 323.
Baidhâwî, 244.
Baitaranî, 143, 333.
Bajî Râo I, 273.
Bakhshish, 27.
Bâlâjî, 273.

[1] In this Index—kindly compiled by Mr. Albert J. Edmunds, now Librarian at Philadelphia—the long vowels are marked thus, â instead of ā; and the dots belonging to some of the letters are omitted.

B b

INDEX.

Ballâla, 134.
Bandela, 141.
Bandelkhand, 140.
Bangalor, 182.
Banijas, 147.
Baniyahs, 25, 49, 147, 160, 204.
Banyan, 186.
Bâolî, 37.
Baptism, 95, 99.
Barbers, 44.
Barîd Shâh, 134.
Baroda, 143, 273.
Basava, 194.
Basil, 110.
Basle Mission. 216.
Basora, 266.
Bassein, 265, 276.
Baths, 30.
Bazaar, 57.
Beames, Mr., 150.
Bedding, 30.
Behadîn, 89.
Bengal, 133.
Bentinck, Lord W., 72, 290, 293, 336.
Berâr, 134, 213.
Bethune schools, 325.
Bettiah, 130.
Bhât-band, 162.
Bhangî, 46, 49, 50.
Bhavânî, 212.
Bhâwalpur, 139.
Bhîls, 152, 352.
Bhîmapâl, 133.
Bhîstî, 27.
Bhojpurî, 150.
Bhonsle, 276.
Bhopâl, 139.
Bhore Ghât, 182.
Bhrigu-kacha, 142.
Bhrigu-pâta, 71.
Bhûpâl, 139.
Bhûtân, 153.
Bhûtas, 195.
Bible, 248.

Bid, 141.
Bîdar, 134.
Bigotry, 287.
Bihishti, 45.
Bîja-nagar, 134.
Bîjâpur, 134, 266.
Bilûchistân, 141.
Bind, 141.
Bird, Mr., 289.
Birds, 32.
Birdwood, Dr. G., 264.
Bishanpad, 103.
B'ismillâh arrahmân arrahîm, 260.
Bleeck, 91.
Bodh-Gayâ, 102.
Bolan, 139.
Bolî, 324.
Bombay, 27, 183, 188, *269*.
Bo-tree, 102.
Brahmâ and the Brâhmans, 194.
Brâhmanî, 143, 333.
Brâhmans, 37, 44, 50, 59, 60, 101, 103, 106, 111, 123, 287, 357.
Brahma-putra, 142, 143.
Brahma Samâj, 226, 236.
Braj, 150.
Brih, 155.
Broach, 30, 142.
Broughton, Dr., 268.
Buchanan-Hamilton, Dr., 278.
Buddha, images of, 158.
Buddhism in Ceylon, 200.
Buddhist kings, 130.
Bukka, 135.
Burnell, Dr., 197, 198.
Bushby, Mr., 289.
Buxar, 276.

Calanus, 70.
Calcutta, 183, *270*.

Caldwell, Bishop, 216.
Calicut, 264.
Calpe, 4.
Calvinists and Arminians, 192.
Câma, Mr. *See* Cursetjee.
Campbell, Sir G., 18, 188, 220, 281, 305.
Camp life, 30.
Canals, 332.
Canning, Lord, 325, 336.
Carnatic, 272.
Carpenter, Miss, 365.
Caste, 10, 30, 123, 162, 202, 287, 331, 332, *356*.
Castes, 50, 148.
— low, 49.
Cavagnari, Major, 138.
Census, 279.
Ceuta, 4.
Ceylon, 132.
Chaitanya, 69.
Chakra, 44.
Châlukya, 133.
Chamâr, 46.
Chambal, 141, 142.
Chand, 132.
Chandana, 100.
Chandarnagar, 271.
Chandra-gupta, 127.
Character of the natives, 29, 33, 37, 45, 48, 49, *50, 54*, 60, 61, 66, 114, 118, 122, 154, 173, 177, 189, 190, 205, 212, 213, 220, 271, 286, 295, 303, 304, 314, 316, 318, 339, 341, 356, 358, *360*.
Charmers, 47.
Charnock, Mr., 270.
Chaukidâr, 45.
Chaura, 132.

INDEX.

Chauth, 271.
Chenâb, 173.
Chera, 133.
Children, 62.
Chinsurah, 265, 289, 322.
Chinvat-peretum, 91.
Chittûr, 141.
Chola, 133.
Cholera, 118, 124, 183.
Chota hâzirî, 36.
Chotâ Nâgpur, 149.
Christian lands and India, 226.
Christian Purâna, 266.
Christianity and Hindûism, 165–167, 192.
Cinchona, 187.
Circars, 182.
Cities, Indian, 52, 53, 56, 57.
Civilisation, Indian and European, 225.
Civil Service, 179, 223.
Clericocracy, 209.
Climate, 145, 180.
Clive, 274.
Cocoa-nut, 186.
Cochin, 212, 264.
Coffee, 186.
Colebrooke, 72.
Collectors, 33, 42.
— work of, 119.
Colleges, 299.
Colvin, J. R., 289.
Condition of the natives, 338.
Conjeveram, 133, 216.
Conjugal fidelity, 313.
Conjurers, 47.
Conti, Nicolo, 264.
Cooke, Miss, 323.
Coorg, 137.
Cornwallis, 335, 340.
Cossyra, 6.
Cotton, 351.
Cotton, Sir A., 143, 333.

Croydon speech, 238.
Cunningham, Col., 129.
Cursetjee Rustamjee Câma, 84, 89, 91.
Cust, R. N., 18, 129, 252, 330.
Custom, 60.

Dâk ghârî, 331.
Dakhin, 140.
Dakhmas, 81.
Dakkin, 182.
Dakshin, 182.
Dâl, 11.
Dalhousie, 297, 324, 325, 332, 336.
Damân, 265.
Damayantî, 312.
Danes, 265.
Dâr, 41.
Dârâ Gushtasp, 127.
Darbar, 119.
Darjîling, 112, 187.
Darzî, 45.
Daśama-śrâddha, 100.
Daśaratha, 131.
Dastûr, 89.
Dasyus, 226.
Date, 186.
Dathâvansa, 256.
Datura, 66.
Daulatâbâd, 134.
Day, Francis, 270.
De Buston, 265.
Deccan, 182.
Decimal notation, 286.
Δεισιδαιμονεστέρους, 252.
Dekhan, 140.
De Lesseps, 15, 16.
Delhi, ancient, 131.
Deogarh, 134.
Deśa, 141.
Deśâî, 41.
Deśmukh, 41.
Desert, Indian, 140.

Deshmukh, Mr., 207.
Deva-nâgarî, 129, 173, 308.
Devâ-śunî, 92.
Devils, 111, 195.
Dhamma-pada, 248.
Dharnâ, 77.
Dhaulî, 129.
Dhed, 2, 46.
Dher, 46, 49.
Dhobî, 45.
Diaz, B., 264.
Dîdan, 91.
Diet, 46, 52, 218, 338, 339.
Dig-ambaras, 159.
Dîpa-mâlâ, 58.
Disease, 56.
Distance in India, 181.
Diû, 265.
Divisions, modern, 137.
Dîwânî, 277.
Doâb, 213, 278.
Dodd's Church History, 265.
Dogra, 172.
Dogo, 91.
Dramas, 312.
Drâvidâh, 149.
Drâvidians, 188.
Dress, 28, 29, 60, 61.
Dualism, 194.
Duff, Dr., 291.
Duncan, J., 288.
Dupleix, 271, 273.
Durrânî, 276.
Dushyanta, 312.
Dutch, 265.
Divâra Samudra, 134.
Dyce Sombre, 276.
Dynasties, 130.

East India Company, 120, 335.
East, Sir E. H., 288.

B b

INDEX.

Eating, 123.
Echebar, 266.
Edeyengoody, 216.
Education, 174.
— and instruction, 303.
— beginning of, 288.
Educational Despatch, 297, 303, 306, 325.
Educational epochs, 297.
Egypt and England, 18.
Elephanta, 158.
Elichpur, 152.
Ellenborough, Lord, 336.
Elphinstone, 299.
Endogamy, 202, 203.
English language in India, 154.
English servility, 269.
Epics, 354.
Erwad, 89.

F. A., 299.
Fa-hian, 126.
Faith, 192.
Families, 319.
Famines, 116, 121.
Farrukh-Siyar, 136.
Fath-Allah, 134.
Felucca, 18.
Female education, 175, 322, *323*, 324.
Filial love, 318.
Finance, 335.
Firoz Shâh's Lât, 130.
Fitch, Ralph, 266.
Fo, 112.
French, 273.
French East India Company, 271.
Fuel, 52.
Funerals, 97.

Gâdi, 59.
Gaikwâr, 138, 139.
Gairsappa Falls, 182.

Gajapati, 134.
Galbargah, 134, 201.
Gandakî, 142.
Ganeśa, 53, 112.
Gangâ, 142.
Ganjam, 129.
Gapurgârî, 47.
Gardabha, 110.
Gâthâs, 86.
Gati, 105, 112.
Gauda, 133.
Gaur, 133.
Gayâ, 101.
Gâyatrî, 111, 166.
Gaywâl, 106.
Geography, 140.
— Purânic, 144.
Ghaenjo, 44.
Ghanchî, 47.
Ghâts, 182.
Ghatta, 182.
Ghî, 98.
Ghori, Muhammad, 132, 135.
Ghosts, 104.
Gibraltar, 3.
Girls, 63, 78.
Girnâr, 71, 129.
Goa, 266.
God, Hindû conception of, 166, 230.
Go-dâvarî, 143.
Gogra, 131.
Golkondah, 134.
Gomukhî, 111.
Gond, 152.
Gopâl-râo, 207.
Gor, 44.
Govardhan, 78.
Governors, 335, 336.
Govinda, 152.
Grâma, 40, 66.
Grammar, 227.
Grantha, 151.
Grievances, 178, 362.
Gujarâtî, 80.

Gulâb Singh, 172.
Gulâl, 98.
Gunî, 48.
Gupta, 132.
Guru, 46.
Gurus, 212.
Gurumukhî, 354.
Gwâlior, 139, 273.

Haidar, 134.
Haileybury, 352.
Hajj, 25.
Hajjâm, 44.
Hâjjîs, 6.
Hakluyt, 266.
Halâ, 141.
Halhed, Mr., 314.
Halifax, Lord, 297.
Halka-bandî, 297.
Halwâî, 47.
Hamada, 163.
Hamilton, Dr., 268.
Hanûman, 58.
Hare, D., 288.
Harihara-putra, 197.
Hastinâpur, 131.
Hastings, Lord, 185.
Hastings, W., 274, 277, 288, 314, 335.
Hawâ Khânâ, 36.
Hawkins, Capt., 267.
Haya, 110.
Heber, Bishop, 73.
Hemeleia vastatrix, 186.
Herbad, 89.
Himâlayas, *141*, 145, 182.
Hindûism, 355.
— pre-Âryan, 161.
Hindûstânî, 153, 292, 309.
Hiouen-Thsang, 126.
History, 126.
History of India for schools, 131.
Holkâr, 139.

INDEX. 371

Hos, 152.
Hûglî, 270.
Human sacrifices, 65.
Humâyûn, 136.
Hunter, Dr. W. W., 65, 68, 280, 281, 362.
Hyderâbâd, 134.
Hyder Ali, 274, 276.

Idolatry, 230.
Ignorance as a cause of things, 347.
Ignorance, native, 294, 320.
Ignorance of India, our, 348, 350, 352, 354, 363.
Ilichpur, 134.
Illećchida Nema, 198.
Imposture, 122.
— pious, 74.
Indian Institute, 364.
Individuality, eternal, 192.
Indore, 139, 273.
Indra-prastha, 131.
Infanticide, 67.
Injîl, 240.
Inscriptions, 129. *See also* Rock.
Insects, 146.
Irrigation, 116.
Iskander, 127.
Islâm, 162 etc., 238.
Ism-i'azîm, 115.

Jabalpore, 182.
Jabalu't târik, 4.
Jagan-nâth, 67.
Jâgîr, 277.
Jahândâr Shâh, 136.
Jahângîr, 136, 267.
Jainas, 159.
Jaipâl, 133.
Jalâlu'd-dîns, 244.

Jama-bandî, 43.
Jambu, 173.
Jammu, 172, 356.
Jamsetjee, Sir, 81, 88.
Jana, 41.
Janagurh, 129.
Janaka, 131.
Jangadha, 129.
Jangîz Khân, 136.
Jannat, 257.
Japa-mâlâ, 108.
Jâtaka, 248.
Jatâyus, 121.
Jesuits, 266.
Jewels, 61, 62.
Jews, 212.
Jhansi, 278.
Jibal Târik, 4.
Jodhpur, 139, 150.
John Bull, 272.
Joshî, 46.
Jûangs, 149.
Jullunder Doab, 278.
Jung, Sir Sâlâr, 213.

Ka'ba, 163.
Kachahrî, 31.
Kachâr, 187.
Kacherî, 31.
Kâfir, 226.
Kaira, 55.
Kaithî, 308.
Kâka-bali, 92.
Kâlahandî, 152.
Kâlâ pânî, 10.
Kaliân, 134.
Kâlî-kataka, 270.
Kâliya, 255.
Kalki, 49.
Kallurti, 200.
Kallyâta, 198.
Kanara, 152.
Kanauj, 131.
Kanaujî, 150.
Kânchîpuram, 133, 195.

Kandhs, 65.
Kandy, 201.
Kanjîvaram, 195.
Kantárá, 14.
Kanwa, 130.
Kanyâ-kubja, 131.
Kâuyakubja Brâhmans, 150.
Kapurda-garhi, 129.
Kaśmîr, 138.
— Mahârâja of, 172.
Kaśmîrî Pandits, 151.
Kasârî, 47.
Kâsim Alî, 275.
Kâsim, Muhammad, 135.
Katak, 129, 134.
Kataka, 270.
Kâthi, 140.
Kâthi-âwâd, 10.
Kâthiâwâr, 132.
Kâthiwâr, 10.
Kâverî, 143.
Kâverî, Falls of, 182.
Kâyastha, 133.
Kesari, 134.
Keshab Chandra Sen, 167.
Khairpur, 139.
Khalâsis, 10.
Khalsi, 129.
Khambâtâ, Mr., 91.
Khânâ, 34, 36.
'Khânâ lâo,' 34.
Khândhiâs, 86, 90.
Khârâ pânî, 10.
Khasi, 252.
Khaskhas, 100.
Khâtraj, 52.
Kheda, 55.
Khodiyâr, 53.
Khoja, 25.
Khond, 152.
Khuram, 139.
Khwâja, 25.
Kingdoms, 131.
Kistna, 143.

INDEX.

Kodâgu, 152.
'Ko-î hai?' 34
Kol, 149, 152, 188.
Kolapore, 194.
Kolî, 47.
Konkanî, 151.
Koorg, 152.
Kośala, 131.
Kota, 152.
Kumârila, 191.
Kumârin, 140.
Kumbhâr, 44.
Kumbî, 40.
Kurân, 248.
Kurnoul, 175.
Kuśa, 100.
Kustî, 95.
Kutb ud dîn, 136.
Kutb-ul-Mulk, 134.

Labour, division of, 278.
La Bourdonnais, 272.
Lahor, 132.
Lakshmî, 194.
Lambardâr, 41.
Land, 340.
Languages, 150, 252.
— classical, of India, 289.
Lash, Mr. and Mrs., 204, 324.
Laskars, 10.
Lât, 130.
Lauriya, 130.
Lavana, 143.
Law, Hindû, 315.
— of inheritance, Hindû and Muhammadan, 41.
Lawyers, 211.
Lawrence, Lord, 331, 340.
Learning, Hindû, 286.
Legislation, 169.
Lepers, 72, 78.
Lethbridge, E., 131.
Library, public, 59.

Lies, 213, 214.
Lingavats, 194.
Locusts, 30.
Lohâr, 45.
Lorû, 143.
Lota, 60.
Lunî, 143.
Lytton, Lord, 208, 300, 361.

M. A., 299.
Macaulay, 263, 289-292.
Macnaghten, 222, 289.
Madhvas, 192.
Madhya, 141.
Madhyawâr, 139.
Madras, 183, 270.
— Presidency, 134.
Madrassa, 288.
Madura, 133, 195.
Magadha, 128.
Maga-pati, 89.
Mahâkâla, 70.
Mahâ-nadî, 143.
Mahârâjâdhirâja, 130.
Mahârâshtra, 150.
Mâhâtmyas, 103.
Mahî, 143.
Mahmûd-âbâd, 55.
Mâhmûd of Ghaznî, 133, 135.
Mail steamer, 25.
Maiwâr, 139.
Mâjan, 55.
Majmûdâr, 43.
Maktabs, 294.
Malabar, 133.
Mâlava, 141.
Malik Ahmad, 134.
Malleson, Col., 139, 171.
Malta, 7.
Mâlwa, 131, 141.
Mânasa-pûjâ, 231.
Mandal, 41.
Mandeville, Sir J., 264.
Mangala, 104.

Mangalor, 216.
Mangoes, 186.
Mani-karnikâkund, 99.
Manipur, 137.
Manu, 40, 43, 111, 311, 354.
Marâthas, 61, 188, 270, 273, 276, 318.
Marâthî, 150.
Mârî Amman, 196.
Markham, C. R., 281.
Marriage, 63, 316.
— early, 202.
Martin, 271.
Mârwâr, 139.
Mârwârî-s, 49, 150, 160, 308.
Mâtâ, 53, 66.
Match-makers, 44
Matting, 122.
Maurya, 127, 130.
May, Mr., 289, 322.
Mâyâ, 254.
Meade, Sir R., 212.
Menials, 46.
Mercy, 194.
Methven, Capt., 13.
Mewâr, 132, 139.
Mewârî, 150.
Mhâr, 2, 46.
Middle class, absence of, 298.
Mill, James, 358.
Miller, Mr., 216.
Milman, Bishop, 361.
Mîr Jâfîr, 275.
Mîr Kâsim Alî, 275.
Missionaries, 279, 353, 356.
Mithilâ, 131.
Mithra, 91.
Mleććha, 37.
Mobed, 89.
Mochî, 45.
Modi, 84.
Modî, 308.

INDEX. 373

Moghuls, 272, 337, 338. See Mongol.
Mon-Anam, 252.
Mongols, 136.
Monotheism, 55, 58, 230.
Moor, Mr., 157.
Morality. See Character.
Morapant, 219.
Morse, 272.
Mothers, 317.
Muhammad, 163.
— story of, 19.
— Shâh, 136.
Muir, Dr. John, 250.
Muir, Sir W., 240, 279, 341.
Mukaddam, 41.
Mukti-kshetra, 99.
Mulliga tanir, 123.
Mundas, 152.
Munro, 276.
Murshidâbâd, 275.
Muslim conquest, 135.
Muslim influence on women, 314.
Muslim kingdoms, 134.
Muslims, 18, 19, 41, 149, 164, 201, 282, 294.
Mutiny, 336.
Mysor, 133, 134.
Mythology, 99, 103.

Nâdir Shâh, 136.
Nagar-sheth, 55.
Nâgpur, 152, 273.
Nâî, 44.
Nama, 112.
Names of Allah, 115.
Nâpit, 44.
Narbadâ, 142.
Narma-dâ, 142.
Naśus, 92.
Nasarwânjee Byramjee, 81.
Nasa-sâlârs, 86, 90.

Nâsik, 207.
Native benevolence, 118.
Native states, 170, 211.
Natives. See Appearance; Attitude; Character; Condition; Ignorance; Learning.
Nâvar, 89.
Nawâbs, 273.
Negrito, 352.
Nepâlî, 153.
Newberie, John, 266.
Nikitin, A., 264.
Nîlgiri, 182.
Nirâkâra-pûjâ, 231.
Nishâdas, 226.
Nizâm, 171.
Nizâm ul Mulk, 273.
Non-Âryan beliefs, 49.
Northbrook, Lord, 297, 361, 365.
Northcote, Sir S., 138.
Northern India, 125.
Nowrozjee Furdoonjee, 359.
Nuddea, 133, 294.
Nudity, 60.
Nyâya, 295.

Omar, 165.
Omito Fat, 112.
'Om mani padme hum!' 112, 256.
Ootacamund, 182.
Opium, 337, 339.
Orâon, 152.
Orientalists and Anglicists, 289.
Oriental studies abroad, 363.
Orissa, 134.
Ormazd, 93.
Ostâ, 89.
Othman, 165.
Oudh, 131.

Oujein, 131.
Outram, 222.
Overland Route, 334.
Ox, 57, 117, 356.
Oxford, 363.
— Oriental studies at, 349.

Pachcappah, 216.
Paharî, 45.
Pahlavî, 129.
Pakhâli, 45.
Pakhtu, 153.
Pâl, 133.
Palamcottah, 324.
Palâśa, 101, 275.
Pâlî, 129, 158.
Palladius, 108.
Palms, 186.
Palmyra, 186.
Pamîr, 148.
Panćâla, 131.
Panchâyat, 42, 53, 81.
Panda, 106.
Pandharpur, 59, 103.
Pandits, 287, 295.
Pandya, 133.
Pânî, 10.
Panis, 92.
Pânini, 227, 314.
Panipat, 274.
Panjurli, 200.
Pâns, 65.
Pantellaria, 6.
Pardah, 312.
Parganah, 40.
Parsîs, 93, 161, 216, 323.
Parthians, 132.
Pashtu, 153.
Pata, 41.
Patan, 132, 133.
Patel, 41, 42.
Pathân, 25.
Pâtha-śâlâs, 294.
Pâti-dâr, 41.

INDEX.

Patti-wâlâ, 33.
Patwârî, 43.
Payment, 42, 45, 46.
Payoshnî, 143.
Pâzand, 89.
Peaceable beginning of our Indian empire, 268, 269, 274.
Perim, 22.
Persian, 293.
Persians, 132, 136.
Peshin, 139.
Peshwa, 273, 276.
Phalgû, 101.
Phœnician, 129.
Phrenology, 216, 217.
Physical features, 181.
Piety, 54, 55, 109, 356, 357.
Pillars, 129.
Pinda, 98, 105.
Pindârîs, 207, 277.
Pîpal, 53, 58, 102, 185.
Pîrs, 165, 201.
Pisâcha, 104.
Pitri, 105.
Plantain, 186.
Plants, 184, 185.
Plassey, 275.
Pogson, Mr., 211.
Poisoning, 66.
Polo, Marco, 264.
Polygamy, 203, 311, 314.
Poona, 182, 273.
Population, 55.
Portuguese, 265.
Post-office, 334.
Potter and clay, 44.
Pradakshina, 54.
Prajâpati, 44.
Pramadâ - Das Mitra, 231.
Pratishthâna, 131.
Prayer, secret, 111, 112.
Praying-wheels, 112.
'Presidency,' 270.

Presidencies, 137.
Preta, 104.
Prinsep, T. and J., 222, 289.
Prithivî Râja, 132, 136.
Progress, 342.
— of British justice, 284, 285.
Proverb, 43.
Pûjâ, 99, 101, 105, 161.
Pulney, 182.
Punnâr, 143.
Purâna, Christian, 266.
Pûrbî, 150.
Pûrna-śubhakara, 99.
Purohita, 44.

Quetta, 139, 350.
Quietists, 114.
'Qui hai?' 34.
Quinine, 187.

Races, 147.
Rae, Mr., 216.
Râhtor, 132.
Raichor, 182.
Railways, 62, 331, 332.
Rainfall at Aden, 23.
Râjmahal, 152.
Râjputana, 132.
Râjputs, 147, 352.
Rakhewâd, 45.
Râma, 131, 312.
Râmânujas, 134, 356.
Râmâyana, 313.
Ramazân, 19.
Râmeśvaram, 189, 195.
Râm Mohun Roy, 288.
Râmnâd, 189.
Râmpur, 139.
Rânchî, 152.
Rangârî, 47.
Rânîganj, 331.
Râo Bahâdur, 207.
Râo Bahâdur Gopal Hari Deshmukh, 303.

Râo, Sir T. Mâdhara, 213.
Ratha-yâtrâ, 67.
Ratnâgar, 86.
Râvî, 173.
Reinhard, 276.
Religions, 155, 191, 246.
Revâ, 142.
Revelation, 227, 287, 315.
Revenue, sources of, 339.
Revivalists, 191.
Rewah, 142.
Rhinoceros-hide, 45.
Rig-Veda, corruption of, 71, 72, 315.
Ritualism, 107.
Rivers, 333.
Robson's 'Hindûism,' 239.
Rock-inscriptions, 129.
Roe, Sir Thos., 267.
Rohilla War, 276.
Rohtak, 356.
Roman Catholicism, 212.
Roman Catholics, 205.
Roman - Urdû Society, 309.
Roorkee, 299.
Rosaries, 108.
Rozah, 201.
Rudrâksha, 110.
Rudra-Śiva, 255.
Russell, Mr., 269.
Russia, 18, 138, 263.
Ryot, 41, 302, 338.
Ryotwary, 208.

Śakas, 131, 133.
Śakuntalâ, 312.
Śâkyas, 158.
Sâlâ, 58.
Sâlagrâm, 104.
Sâlivâhana, 133.
Sânti, 104.

INDEX. 375

S'aurasenî, 150.
S'ilâditya, 132.
S'iva, 53, 195.
S'ona, 142.
S'râddha, 104.
S'ringeri, 191.
S'vabhra, 143.
S'vetâmbaras, 159.

Sabaktagîn, 135.
Sâbharmatî, 143.
Sadara, 95.
Sâdhu, 59.
Sag-dîd, 91.
Sago, 186.
Sâgrîs, 81, 90.
Sâh, 132.
Salama, 240.
Sale, Geo., 248.
Salonkhyas, 132.
Salt, 337, 339.
Samâdhi, 72.
Samâj, 166.
Samaranî, 108.
Samudra-Gupta, 132.
Samvat, 131.
Sanad, 207.
Sanchî, 130.
Sandstorm, 21.
Sanga Râjas, 130.
Sanskâra, 228.
Sanskarana, 286.
Sanskrit, 37, 153, 287, 353.
Santâls, 149, 152.
Santo, 264.
Saramâ, 92.
Sarang, 11.
Sârasvata, 150.
Sârasvatî, 227.
Sarayu, 131.
Sargent, Bishop, 216.
Sargent, Bishop and Mrs., 204.
Sarhang, 11.
Sârî, 61.

Satâra, 273, 278.
Satî, 59, 71, 315.
Sâtpura, 70, 141, 152.
Satyavân, 313.
Satyendranâth Tagore, 207.
Saugor, 65, 357.
Saunders, Trelawny, 137.
Saunders, 289.
Saurâshtra, 140.
Sâvitrî, 313.
Sâyanâćarya, 135.
Schoolmasters, 44.
Schools, 62, 294, etc.
Scythians, 131, 133.
Secunderabad, 182.
Sehore, 132.
Self-government, 295.
Self-immolation, 67-73.
Self-reliance, 192.
Sena, 133.
Sepoys, 33.
Serampur, 265.
Seringapatam, 276.
Seton-Karr, Mr., 18.
Shâh Âlam, 136, 277.
Shâhjahân, 136, 268.
Shakespear, H., 280, 289.
Shamsa, 108.
Sheppard, Mr., 74.
Shî'as, 165.
Shikasta, 308.
Shîr Shâh Sûr, 136.
Shops, 57.
Shuja-ud-Dowla, 276.
Sibi, 139.
Sikandar, 127.
Sikkim, 187.
Simpî, 45.
Sindia, 138, 139, 171, 276.
Sinhalese, 153.
Sinhas, 132.
Sipî, 45.
Sîtâ, 131, 313.
Sîtalâ, 58.

Sivajî, 273.
Slang, 324.
Sleeman, Col., 29, 70. 73, 185, 357.
Smârtas, 191.
Somali, 24.
Sombre, 276.
Somnâth, 135.
Southern India, 180.
Spenta-mainyus, 93.
Spiritualism, 197.
Spirit-worship, 196.
Sportsmen, 351.
Srinagar, 172.
Sri-râmapur, 265.
Stanhope, Earl, 138.
Statistics, 278.
Stefano, H. di, 264.
Stephen, Sir Fitzjames, 340.
Stevens, Father Thomas, 265, 266.
Students, 294, 295.
Subanrekha, 143.
Sûchi, 45.
Suez, 18.
Suez Canal, 12.
Sûî, 45.
Suicide, 77.
Sulaimân, 141.
Sumbhulpur, 152.
Sumru, 276.
Sunnîs, 165.
Sun-power, 122.
Sun-worship, 54.
Sûra, 240, 267.
Sûraj, 267.
Sûraj-ud-Dowla, 275.
Sûras, 143, 267.
Suspicion, native, 279.
Sûtâr, 44.
Sutherland, 289.
Sûtras, 110.
Sutta-nipâta, 248.
Suvarna-rekha, 143.
Svâmi-Nârâyan, 111.

Svayamvara, 311, 312.
Swaheli, 25.
Sykes, Col., 280.

Tai, 252.
Tâj, 182.
Talati, 43.
Talipot, 186.
Tamarind, 186.
Tamâshâ, 29.
Tângâ, 31.
Tanjor, 133.
Tap, 142.
Tapantî, 142.
Tapatî, 142.
Taptî, 267.
Tartars, 135, 149.
Tasbîh, 108, 110.
Tashîlî, 298.
Tattoo, 2.
Taurât, 240.
Tavî, 173.
Tawhîd, 257.
Taxes, 279, 340, 341.
Tayaman Nâle, 133.
Tea, 187, 351.
Teignmouth, Lord, 335.
Telî, 46.
Temple, Sir R., 220.
Temples, Southern, 195.
Temples v. public-houses, 57.
Tengalais, 152.
Teutonic reverence for women, 312.
Thags, 66.
Thânesvar, 136.
Theists, 166.
Thomason, 279, 280, 296, 299, 305.
Tibetans, 149.
Tila, 100.
Times, Hindû's letter to, 226, 236.
Timsah, 15.
Tîmûr, 136.

Tindals, 11.
Tinnevelly, 195.
Tirhut, 131.
Tobacco, 187, 351.
Toda, 152.
Tol, 294.
Toleration, 98, 114, 314.
Tonk, 139.
Tooth-cleaning, 57.
Toramâna, 132.
Town-hall, 53.
Trades, 44.
Transition stage in Hindû minds, 304.
Travankor, Mahârâja of, 174.
Travellers, early, 264.
Travelling, 330.
Trees, 31.
Trevelyan, Sir C. E., 289, 293.
Tucker, Sarah, 324.
Tukarâm, 219.
Tulasî. *See* Tulsî.
Tulsî, 53, 58, 110.
Tungabhadra, 213.
Turkey and India, 201.
Turks, 135.
Tuticorin, 189.
Twice-born, 111.

Udaipur, 132, 139.
Ujjayinî, 131.
Universe, limit of, 144.
Universities, 298.
Unsectarian education, 327.
Upângas, 159.
Ûrdhva-bâhu, 77.
Ûrdû, 154.

Vadagalais, 192.
Vaid, 46.
Vaiga, 143.
Vaiśvadeva, 92.

Vaiśyas, 147, 148.
Vaishnavas, 68.
Vaitaranî, 143.
Vallabhî, 132.
Vâlmîki, 312.
Vandidâd, 83.
Vandvâs, 274.
Vâpî, 100.
Varasîo, 95.
Varthema, 264.
Vata, 143.
Vedântist, 347.
Vedas, 311.
Vedi, 100.
Vegetation, 33, 185.
Verbal diarrhœa, 304.
Vermilion, 58.
Vernaculars, 292, 293, 297, 300, 306.
Videha, 131.
Vidyâlaya, 288.
Vijaya-nagar, 134, 135, 276.
Vikramâditya, 131, 133.
Vindhya, 141.
Viśveśvara-nâth, 100.
Vishnu-pada, 101.
Vision of a Brâhman, 357.
Vithobâ, 59.
Vrishabha, 194.
Vyâkarana, 286.

Waghorn, Mr., 334.
Wakeels, 211.
Wâland, 44.
Wâlid I, 135.
Wârand, 44.
Warangal, 134.
Waterfalls, 182.
Water, holy, 100.
Watson, Dr. Forbes, 337, 363.
Wau, 37.
Widows, 78, 317.
Wilberforce, W., 285.

Williams, Lieut.-Colonel Monier, 50.
Wilson, Prof. H. H., 72, 289, 331.
Wilson, Mrs., 323.
Women, 54, 60, 175, 176, 188, 203-205, *311*.
Women, influence of, 319.
Wood, Sir C., 297, 299.

Worship, 161.
Writers, 133, 308.
Writing, 296.
Wynaad, 187.

Xavier, 212.

Yâdava, 134.
Yamunâ, 142.
Yaśna, 85.

Yava, 100.
Yule, Col., 266.

Zamakhshari, 244.
Zamíndâr, 42, 341.
Zanâna, 312.
Zanzibar, 25.
Zillah, 298.
Zoroaster, 87.

For Product Safety Concerns and Information please contact our EU representative GPSR@taylorandfrancis.com
Taylor & Francis Verlag GmbH, Kaufingerstraße 24, 80331 München, Germany

www.ingramcontent.com/pod-product-compliance
Lightning Source LLC
Chambersburg PA
CBHW051626230426
43669CB00013B/2190